FUNKY BOLLYWOOD:

The Wild World of 1970s Indian Action Cinema

A SELECTIVE GUIDE

The Wild World of 1970s Indian Action Cinema

A SELECTIVE GUIDE

BY TODD STADTMAN

FUNKY BOLLYWOOD
The Wild World of 1970s Indian Action Cinema, A Selective Guide

First edition published by FAB Press, March 2015

FAB Press Ltd., 2 Farleigh, Ramsden Road, Godalming, Surrey, GU7 1QE, England, UK

Acknowledgements are due to the following production and distribution companies:

21st Century Productions LTD, A.G. Films (P) Ltd., Associated Films & Finance Corporation, Bharati International, Bollywood Entertainment, Bombino Video Private Limited, BR Films, Choudhary Enterprises, Dynamo International, Eagle Films, Eastern Films, Eros International Ltd., Eros International Media LTD, Eros Multimedia PVT LTD, Eros Multimedia (Europe) Ltd., F.K. Films Pvt. Ltd., FK International, Gopi Enterprises, Hirawat Jain & Co, Indus Video Pvt. Ltd., Kapleswar Films Pvt. Ltd., Kapur Films, Laxmi Films, Laxmi Judson Productions, Mewar Films, M.I. Films Pvt. Ltd., M.K.D. Films, Moser Baer India Ltd., Movie Temple, Nariman Films, Nasir Hussain Films Pvt. Ltd., Nav Jeevan Films, Navaratna Films, Navketan Films, Navketan International Films Pvt. Ltd., N.N. Sippy Films, NP International, Parthiva Pictures, P.N.R. Pictures, Prakash Mehra Productions, Pramod Films, Prithvi Pictures, Pashupati Pictures Pvt. Ltd., Rajendra Kumar, Rajshri Productions (P) Ltd., Rose Movies, Sadanah Brothers, Sagar Art Enterprises, Sagar Arts, Sargam Pictures Private Limited, Sangam Enterprises, Seven Arts Pictures, Shankar Movies, Shanti Enterprises, Shemaroo Entertainment Pvt. Ltd., Shemaroo Video Pvt. Ltd., Shilpkar, Shiv Shakti Films, Sippy Films, Subodh Mukerjee Productions, Suresh Desai & Associates, Tahir Hussain Films, Trimurti Films Pvt. Ltd., Ultra Distributors Pvt. Ltd., United Producers, Vijaya and Suresh Combines, Vishal International Productions (P) Ltd., Vision Universal, Yash Raj International Ltd.

SIBLING VS. SIBLING: Gun designed by Erik Wagner from the thenounproject.com, Wrench (hand) designed by Mourad Mokrane from the thenounproject.com, DRUNKENNESS: Drunk designed by Dan McCall from thenounproject.com

Though most of the reviews herein are original to this book, some appeared previously, in edited form, on the websites Teleport City (teleport-city.com) and Die, Danger, Die, Die, Kill! (diedangerdiediekill.blogspot.com). All applicable permissions have been obtained.

Design: chairgiant.net

Production manager: Harvey Fenton @ FAB Press

Printed in China.

A CIP catalogue record for this book is available from the British Library.

ISBN 978-1-903254-77-6

Acknowledgements

As you might guess, a lot of suffering went into making *Funky Bollywood* and most of it wasn't mine. I'd first like to thank Keith Allison of Teleport City, not only for allowing me to write for his fine website, but also for being the man who, by example, inspired me to write about cult cinema in the first place. As a writer, Keith walks a narrow and necessary line, proving that you can write about such topics with humor and affection in a field rife with snark and pedantry. He is also an incredible source of knowledge, and I can't imagine doing what I'm doing right now without his support and generous assistance.

To the members of the Bollywood blogging community, who have provided me with an education in Indian cinema while frequently making me laugh my ass off, I offer my humblest appreciation. Foremost among this assortment of wags, wits and wise women is Greta Kaemmer of Memsaabstory (memsaabstory.com/), who lent her keen proofreader's eye to the project, along the way correcting my translations and clearing up the odd historical detail. If I can make any claim to this book being definitive, it is largely due to her contributions.

This, of course, is not to give short shrift to my frequent podcast partner Beth Watkins of Beth Loves Bollywood (bethlovesbollywood.blogspot.com/), Angela Ambroz of The Post-Punk Cinema Club (p-pcc.blogspot.com/), Rumnique Nannar of the sadly retired Roti Kapada aur Rum (rotikapadarum.blogspot.com/) and Amrita Rajan of the also sorely missed Indiequill (indiequill.wordpress.com/). Another erstwhile member of this group is Michael Barnum, who has been extremely generous in sharing with me both his expansive knowledge and the contents of his marvelous collection of Bollywood ephemera—in addition to being an overwhelmingly kind and positive spirit. I am also humbled by the generosity shown by Per-Christian of the fine blog Music from the Third Floor (mft3f.com), who allowed me to reproduce cover scans from his enviable collection of original Bollywood soundtrack LPs.

As for those who served as ad hoc editors, I must first pay tribute to Andrew Nahem, who has been such a constant and welcome presence in my life that he has long ago staked out a permanent editor's perch inside my head, correcting my grammar, spelling and syntax often without even knowing it. Family members have also been recruited to this task, and I would especially like to thank my sister Kristen Stadtman and brother-in-law George Pursley for their valuable feedback. David Wells, author of the wonderful Soft Film blog (softfilm.blogspot.com), has also made himself readily available to have ideas both crackpot and inspired bounced off his head over serial bowls of ramen.

I should also mention that the writing of *Funky Bollywood* coincided with a medical crisis on my part and I thank Doctors Millender, Efron, Peak and NP Mady Stovall for keeping me alive to finish it. And lastly, the person who makes me more glad to be alive than I'd previously thought possible, my beautiful wife Liza, who throughout this project has maintained an admirable balance between tolerance and enthusiasm. This is for your eyes first and foremost, honey. *Mera dil tumhara hai.*

CONTENTS

Funky Bollywood

INTRODUCTION

THESE DAYS PRETTY MUCH every westerner has some idea in their head of what a Bollywood movie looks like: The vibrant colors! The over-the-top acting! The constant singing! However, those ideas are more frequently derived from the countless parodies and pastiches of Bollywood that are floating around popular culture than they are from any exposure to the real thing.

In fact, in my own United States, there are no doubt many people who would tell you, with absolute conviction, that they had seen a Bollywood movie. This despite the fact that what they had actually seen was something along the lines of *Slumdog Millionaire* or *Bride and Prejudice*—both of them British productions, albeit with some ethnic Indians among their cast and crew, that pick and choose from Bollywood traditions as suits their creative ends, but which ultimately fall short of bearing all the hallmarks of that very particular branch of world cinema.

Of course, there are also those rare Westerners, cineastes and cultural tourists alike, who harbor a genuine curiosity about Bollywood. And for those folks there exists no shortage of published materials on the subject. In my experience, the books on Hindi cinema that are available in English tend to fall into one of two categories. On the one hand, there are scholarly tomes that will tell you all you want to know about the canonical classics of Indian popular cinema—films like, for instance, Mehboob Khan's *Mother India*, or the works of auteur director Guru Dutt—and discourse eloquently upon subjects such as the trauma of partition and how it evidences itself in the films of Bollywood's golden age. On the other, there are those lush coffee table books that celebrate the glamour of modern Bollywood—with all of its gorgeous stars, lavish production design and fabulous costumes—as a return to the irony-free glitz of old Hollywood.

But what if you are someone whose interest in Bollywood is neither academic nor motivated by a desire to worship at the altar of its current stars? What if you are, for instance, someone like me—a person who has left the world of high-brow film connoisseurship behind and dedicated himself to trolling the more disreputable regions of world popular cinema in search of, for lack of a better word, cheap thrills?

Perhaps, also like me, you've exhausted the highs that classic Asian action and grindhouse cinema once provided and have gone on to sample more exotic celluloid delicacies, things like Mexican lucha libre films and Turkish superhero mash-ups. And, even then, you've *still* found yourself wanting more. You're not interested in art or beauty, and least of all in subtlety. What you *are* looking for is all of the speed, violence and garish style that you've come to depend upon from more well-traveled avenues of pop cinema, but cloaked in a cultural context that makes it all seem somehow fresh and new again.

Well, if that's you, welcome to the world of 1970s Indian action cinema.

◇◇◇◇◇◇◇◇◇◇◇◇◇◇◇◇◇◇

The 1970s were a time of great cultural change in India, much as the 1960s were in many parts of the West, and the nation's commercial film industry could not help but be infected by the restive social spirit that prevailed. Disaffection on the part of the country's youth paved the way for the creation of a new cinematic archetype, the Angry Young Man, a brooding, morally ambiguous figure who marked a sharp departure from the pious, teetotaling mamas boys who had been the typical film protagonists during the 1960s.

While the creation of the Angry Young Man is widely credited to a pair of young screenwriters by the names of Javed Akhtar and Salim Khan, no one was to personify him as definitively as Amitabh Bachchan, a young actor who—thanks to the success of Salim-Javed penned films like *Zanjeer, Deewaar* and *Sholay*—went in short order from being a mere movie star to being the most widely recognized face in all of India. Not even a subsequent failed career in politics or a graceful transition into elder statesmanship could dim the iconic image of the young Bachchan as a righteous, denim clad street brawler, and it was that image that set the tone for many of the young stars who came in his stead—as well as for many older ones who sought to reinvent themselves in alignment with changing tastes.

Of course, the cinema-going habits of movie mad India have never been sustained by Bollywood product alone. Neither has the country's film industry been shy about borrowing from whichever filmic imports were currently holding sway over the public mind. As such, the emergence of the Angry Young Man dovetailed nicely with the increasing influence of the grittier, more action-oriented fare coming out of the "New" Hollywood of the early '70s. Bollywood's tendency toward glitz and flamboyant artifice didn't prevent it from co-opting the hardboiled, decidedly urban tenor of American hits like *The French Connection,* nor did it discourage attempts to remake such films—as was the case with *Khoon Khoon*, Mohammed Hussain's all-singing, all-dancing reimagining of Don Siegel's *Dirty Harry.*

Among the more conspicuous foreign influences upon Indian films during this era was that of the distinctly American subgenre known as Blaxploitation. Represented by international hits like *Black Caesar* and *Foxy Brown*, these films' emphasis on funky threads, even funkier music, and rough-edged action—coupled with tales of scrappy underdogs fighting their way up from the urban streets—made them ideal models for Amitabh Bachchan blockbusters like 1977's combustive *Don*. At the same time, Indian audiences were also falling under the spell of Hong Kong's prodigious output of martial arts films. It soon seemed no film was complete without its stars at some point trying to approximate the moves of Bruce Lee or Jimmy Wang Yu, albeit with varying degrees of clumsiness (and, of course, aided by the repeated use of that impossibly loud, car-door-slam sound effect that Indian cinema fans have come to affectionately refer to as "dishoom dishoom").

The prolific Italian film industry also found echoes in 1970s Bollywood, most vividly in "curry westerns" like Ramesh Sippy's astonishingly popular *Sholay*, which owed a not inconsiderable debt to the Spaghetti Western genre as a whole and Sergio Leone's *Once Upon A Time in the West* in particular.

Of course, while these outside influences can provide a familiar point of entry for those curious about 1970s Bollywood, it should also be mentioned that, in most cases, they come swathed in traditions of cinematic storytelling that are uniquely India's own. These include lengthy running times that often approach three hours; sprawling narrative structures that would make the average Western screenwriting instructor throw up his hands in despair; a seeming hostility to conventional notions of genre that can see a narrative

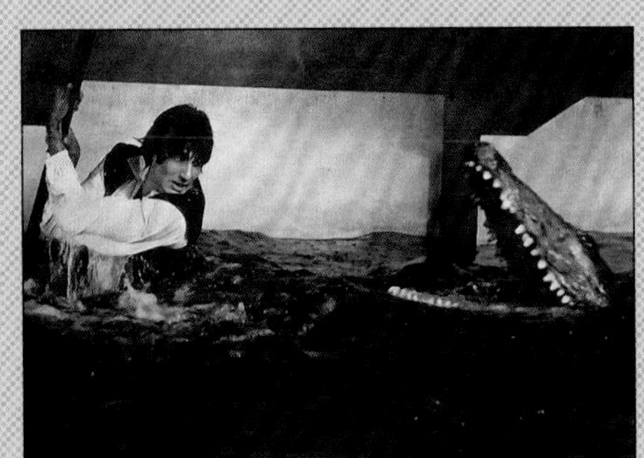

"Giallo" thrillers and low budget, continental Bond knockoffs—or "Eurospy" films—also made their way to the nation's cinema screens and in turn got churned into the stew of inspirations igniting Indian filmmakers at the time. Even French master criminal Fantomas, *au courant* once again thanks to a series of 1960s European hits directed by Andre Hunebelle, made his presence known, popping up as a guest villain in the 1975 Dharmendra vehicle *Saazish*.

lurching from crime thriller to romantic comedy to handwringing family melodrama with little transitional cushioning; and lastly, those famous song and dance numbers, which are included regardless of whether a film conforms to your personal idea of what a "musical" should be.

Beyond that, there is the requirement, laid down by both time honored Indian theater traditions and the country's stringent film censorship standards, that all distinctions between good and evil be made perfectly explicit. At the feet of such strictures can be laid much of the blame for the often mocked "over-the-top" quality so often seen in these films' performances—one that perhaps wouldn't be out of place in films of the silent era, but which can indeed seem strange in movies made during the era of Altman and Scorsese. Many actors made long careers out of their ability to personify the ideal Indian male in all his conspicuous virtue and righteous patriotism, as did others turn their mastery of the maniacal laugh, villainous leer and mustache twirl into steady gigs as screen bad guys. At the same time, no matter how much audiences may have thrilled to the rebellious antics of Amitabh's angry young man, you could rest assured that, if he didn't see the errors of his ways by the final reel, he was bound to be punished for his transgressions.

During the Seventies in particular, such proscribed moralism had an interesting way of clashing with the Indian film industry's more strictly commercial concerns. Bollywood was a dream factory, after all, and among its chief mandates was that of providing its audience, many of whom came from India's lower economic strata, with dazzling fantasies of escape. These fantasies often took the form of hallucinatory waking dreams of spectacular wealth and excess, typically realized through an exuberantly exaggerated approach to costume and set design. If you think of the already garish aspects of 1970s fashion and decor, especially as represented in Hollywood urban crime thrillers and blaxploitation pictures of the day, and then imagine them magnified through a giddy cartoon lens, you'll start to get some idea of what I mean.

As a result, shirt collars that were already large according to current fashion dictates became as enormous as gull wings, and were

as likely as not to be lined with fake leopard fur. Plaid, pleather and paisley became not aberrations but the norm, and were often accented with elephant flares, frilly pirate sleeves, and peek-a-boo cutaways designed to better display a bit of décolletage or a lushly upholstered man torso. Even a figure as authoritative as Bachchan couldn't escape the indignities of polka dot tuxedoes and hip-hugging matador outfits. This, Bollywood seemed to be saying, was the look of living large in the 1970s.

Yet at the same time, morality decreed that a price be paid for all of this excess. Thus nowhere was consumption more conspicuous than in the accoutrements of a film's villain. Indeed the greatest expression of this tendency was in the elaborate lairs that these master criminals typically called home. The obvious influence here was the James Bond series, which kitted its heavies out with ever more impressive high tech digs hidden within the recesses of hollowed out volcanoes and the like. Yet Bollywood set designers added an eye-rending level of nouveau-riche gaucheness—a sort of *Goldfinger*-meets-Graceland sensibility—to this already ostentatious concept. As such, a typical kingpin's hideout might come complete with such appointments as built-in bubble saunas and perpetual go-go girls grinding behind colored scrims—or, as in Sadhana's *Geetaa Mera Naam*, sliding floor panels through which underperforming minions could be dumped into pits of boiling wax, only to emerge later as human statuary in gleaming glass tubes.

1970s Bollywood's combination of the funky and the classical, the gritty and the gaudy, the traditional and the transgressive can certainly provide the uninitiated with a bumpy ride. But, to my mind, it's the many jaw unhinging sights and sounds that result from those colliding sensibilities that make acquiring the taste well worth the effort. After all, the spectacle of hirsute he-men in hip-hugging pleather flares engaging in preposterously loud, fake kung fu battles with mustache-twirling villains—more often than not taking place in ridiculously accessorized underground lairs to the accompaniment of brassy, wa-wa-fied Hindi-funk music—is one that can be found nowhere else in world cinema.

And bumpy or not, chances are good that, once you've taken that ride, you'll find yourself making a sharp turn down the road to addiction. Whether you find them good, bad, or simply too strange for categorization, these movies will show you things that you have never seen before, while what you have seen will be presented in ways you could not previously have imagined. For compulsive consumers of pop cinema like me, such is the dragon we endlessly chase—that raw-edged thrill of the unfamiliar, the unorthodox, and the new, whose deep, soul-satisfying tingle has launched a million lifelong habits. This is Funky Bollywood.

You're welcome.

How this book works

Following through on my addiction analogy above, my intention is for this book to be your "gateway drug" into the world of 1970s Indian action cinema. While a fool I may be, I am not one to the extent that I'd attempt a comprehensive accounting of what turned out to be one of the most popular genres during one of the world's most prolific film industry's most fruitful eras. Instead, I offer you a sampling that includes some of my favorites, hopefully most of the touchstones, and a few random stinkers just for balance. (These last also because I took the trouble to watch them and feel that you should at least humor me by taking the time to read about them, as much as you might ultimately regret it.) To further narrow the field, I focused almost exclusively on modern day urban crime thrillers, passing over the many period films and rural "Dacoit" (bandit) dramas that could fall under the action umbrella. I have, however, included a special section dealing with the curry westerns, a noteworthy subgenre that I felt couldn't go without mention. For those who want to explore further, there's good news to be had in the surprisingly large number of '70s Indian films currently available on DVD, most of which can be purchased easily and affordably from outfits like Induna.com. To make your search even easier, I've prefaced the reviews with a section spotlighting all of the personnel, both in front of and behind the camera, whose names will pop up most often as you read about the individual films. Basically I've done everything except watch the films for you, which, of course, I've also done. Nonetheless, I'm confident you'll quickly realize that they're something much better experienced firsthand.

—Todd

The Heroes

AMITABH BACHCHAN The son of a renowned Hindi poet, Amitabh Bachchan arrived in Bollywood armed with a letter of recommendation from none other than prime minister Indira Gandhi herself. His tony pedigree did not, however, prevent him from rising to fame as the screen personification of the scrappy, working class antihero—this in large part due to the success of gritty dramas like 1973's *Zanjeer* and the one-two punch, in 1975, of twin blockbusters *Deewaar* and *Sholay*. Tall, imposing and intense—and gifted with a booming baritone that would make even God jealous—Bachchan brought an undeniable gravitas to his performances, but also had the gift for comedic and romantic roles necessary in the "everything goes" Masala cinema of the 1970s. After derailing his career with an ill-advised detour into politics in the mid '80s, Bachchan made a major comeback in the 2000s thanks in part to his gig hosting the Indian version of *Who Wants to be A Millionaire*. He today enjoys revered elder statesman status, presiding over a white hot acting dynasty that consists of his superstar son Abhishek and daughter-in-law/world's-most-beautiful-woman Aishwarya Rai.

DHARMENDRA In light of his fame as a matinee idol during the '60s, Dharmendra's 1970s success was something of a career second act—spurred in part by his starring opposite rising star Amitabh Bachchan in the phenomenally successful *Sholay*. Like Bachchan, Dharmendra excelled on screen as a champion of the common people, and could often be seen standing astride a table, accusing glare aimed along a steadily pointing finger, as he boomed out one of his signature defiant oaths at the corrupt powers that be. At the same time, Dharmendra—full name Dharam Singh Deol—had a rakish good humor and beefy physicality that made him perfect for cartoonish swashbucklers like 1978's *Azaad* and the Manmohan Desai hit *Dharam Veer*. In recent years, his status as one of the great action stars of Indian cinema has buoyed the careers of two actor sons, Bobby and Sonny, both of whom are aspiring action heroes in their own right.

VINOD KHANNA Of course, as big as Amitabh Bachchan was during the '70s, it's not as if he didn't have to stay on his toes. Of the handful of challengers to his reign, perhaps the most formidable was the handsome Vinod Khanna, who made the transition to lead, or "hero," roles with 1971's *Memsaab*. Knowing a recipe for box office magic when they saw it, wily producers were soon pairing the two stars in a string of hits that included Manmohan Desai's back-to-back smashes *Amar Akbar Anthony* and *Parvarish*. Khanna would further prove himself as a reliable integer in the buddy equation with *Qurbani*, in which he matched his screen partner Feroz Khan macho for macho. At the same time, he was well capable of carrying films on his own sizable marquee value alone. Despite this, Khanna would turn his back on Bollywood at the height of his 1970s fame, quitting in 1979 to pursue a more spiritual path as a follower of Bhagwan Shree Rajneesh. However, his fame was such that he was able to return to the fold eight years later with his luster little diminished.

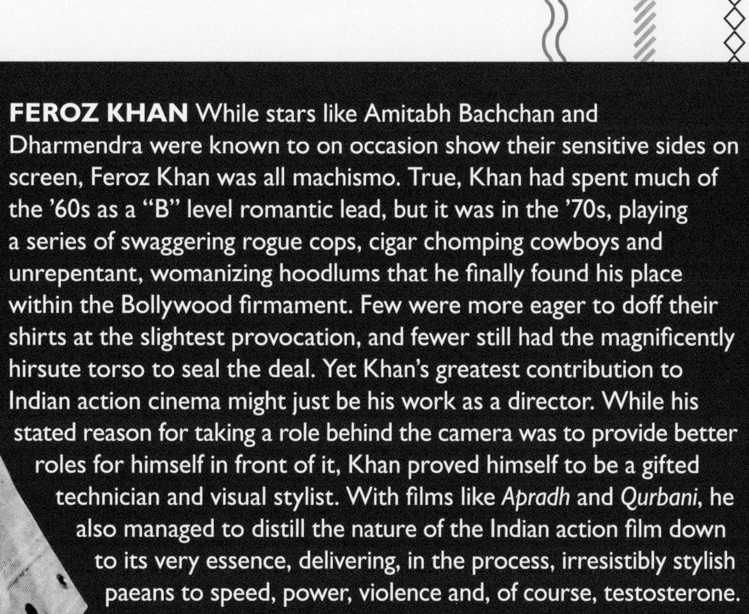

FEROZ KHAN While stars like Amitabh Bachchan and Dharmendra were known to on occasion show their sensitive sides on screen, Feroz Khan was all machismo. True, Khan had spent much of the '60s as a "B" level romantic lead, but it was in the '70s, playing a series of swaggering rogue cops, cigar chomping cowboys and unrepentant, womanizing hoodlums that he finally found his place within the Bollywood firmament. Few were more eager to doff their shirts at the slightest provocation, and fewer still had the magnificently hirsute torso to seal the deal. Yet Khan's greatest contribution to Indian action cinema might just be his work as a director. While his stated reason for taking a role behind the camera was to provide better roles for himself in front of it, Khan proved himself to be a gifted technician and visual stylist. With films like *Apradh* and *Qurbani*, he also managed to distill the nature of the Indian action film down to its very essence, delivering, in the process, irresistibly stylish paeans to speed, power, violence and, of course, testosterone.

The Heroes

SHASHI KAPOOR The scion of a formidable acting dynasty that included his revered elder brother Raj, Shashi Kapoor had the soulful eyes and delicate features ideally suited to the role of teen idol. Yet, while he certainly fostered his share of schoolgirl crushes, to focus on that aspect of his career alone would be to deny his contributions as an artist, be it via his work in the theater, in India's "alternative" cinema, or in English language productions such as James Ivory's *Shakespeare-Wallah*. If any of that makes you think that I'm going to get through this entry without somehow mentioning Amitabh Bachchan, however, you are sadly mistaken. You see, starting with his supporting role in *Deewaar*, for which he won a Filmfare award, Kapoor was cast opposite Bachchan in a string of 11 features—pyrotechnic, wannabe crowd pleasers like 1980's *Shaan* among them. In fact, of all the pairings of Bachchan with other male stars that took place over the course of the decade, it just might be those with Kapoor that were the most beloved by audiences. This did not, however, mean that Kapoor needed to be attached to Bachchan in order to explore his more rough and tumble side, as slam bang headlining outings like 1976's *Fakira* demonstrate.

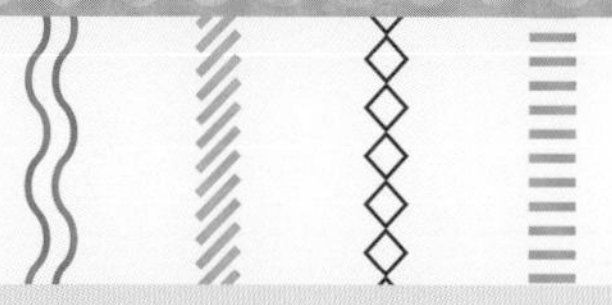

RAJESH KHANNA Rajesh Khanna entered the Indian film industry as the winner of a national talent competition sponsored by United Producers and Filmfare Magazine, and went on, over the course of the next several years, to achieve a then unprecedented level of success and adulation. In a record that has yet to be matched, he enjoyed an unbroken chain of consecutive box office hits with fifteen starring vehicles between 1969 and 1971. Accompanying this was a fan hysteria of the type that authorities deemed a threat to public safety on more than one occasion. While Khanna was known more for sober dramatic roles, the emergence of—you guessed it—Amitabh Bachchan in the mid '70s, and the accompanying shift in focus to more action oriented fare, pushed him increasingly toward pacey thrillers like 1977's *Chhaila Babu* with Zeenat Aman. A growing reputation as a prima donna and the scandal arising from his troubled marriage to teenaged starlet Dimple Kapadia contributed to a dip in Khanna's fortunes as the '70s progressed, though he continued to work steadily throughout the '80s and into the '90s. Nevertheless, when he passed away in 2012, Khanna left behind a collection of honors, awards and box office records that no change in public tastes or fashion could diminish.

MITHUN CHAKRABORTY During the '70s, Mithun Chakraborty was marketed as a kind of poor man's Amitabh Bachchan, though he truly came into his own during the '80s with the public embrace of Babbar Subhash's garish pop musical *Disco Dancer* (from whence came the M.I.A. covered hit "Jimmy Aaja"). Still, if for nothing else, his starring role as Gunmaster G-9, a singing and hip swiveling South Asian James Bond, in Ravikant Nagaich's hysterical *Surakksha* makes him worthy of inclusion here.

The Heroines

ZEENAT AMAN UCLA educated Zeenat Aman was 1970s Bollywood's first truly modern heroine, bringing to the screen a procession of sensual free spirits and bold women of action who contrasted starkly with the dutiful wives and mothers who had preceded them. Making her starring debut as Janice, the doomed pothead in Dev Anand's *Hare Rama Hare Krishna*, Aman, with her in-your-face sexuality and westernized, fashion-forward sense of style, also came to serve as a signifier of hipness, making her a key ingredient in films targeted at the youth market.

While her body baring outfits caused scandal throughout pious society, Aman also forged new paths for women in the realm of action cinema. With characters like Roma, the revenge seeking karate expert in Chandra Barot's *Don*, Aman helped bring the iconic figure of the high-kicking female badass—represented elsewhere by the likes of *The Avengers*' Emma Peel and Pam Grier's Foxy Brown—into the Bollywood mainstream. Alongside Amitabh Bachchan, she is one of the few Indian actors who could truly be said to personify the 1970s.

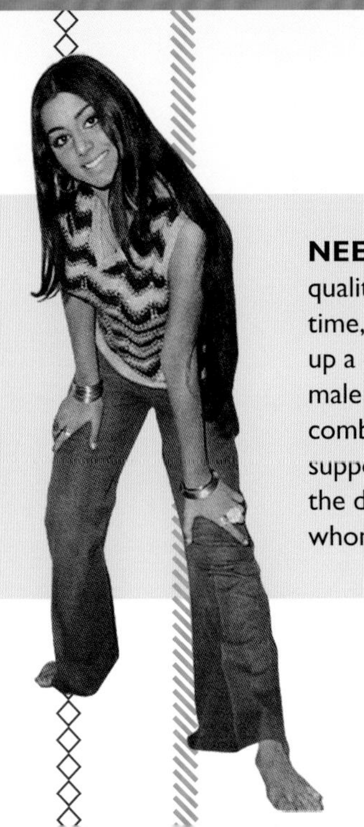

NEETU SINGH Former child star Neetu Singh had a tomboyish, kid sister quality that those inclined to use such language might call "spunky." At the same time, as demonstrated in *Yaadon Ki Baarat*, she had the ability to really steam up a room with her dance moves, in the process indelibly impressing upon the male moviegoers of India that she was, in fact, no longer a kid. This agreeable combination of attributes allowed her to play both actual kid sisters, in numerous supporting roles, and romantic leads opposite some of the biggest male stars of the day, including, on numerous occasions, Kapoor family scion Rishi Kapoor—whom she married in 1980, effectively ending her screen career.

HEMA MALINI A versatile actress, classic beauty and skilled dancer, Hema Malini so epitomized the ideal of the Bollywood dream girl that audiences, at the prompting of the industry's publicity apparatus, just took to calling her "Dream Girl" for short. Making her cinematic debut at the end of the '60s, she was already one of Bollywood's most popular actresses by the time she took on the iconic role of Basanti in *Sholay*, having enjoyed success in blockbusters like the 1972 hit *Seeta aur Geeta*, in which she played a dual role. It was while filming *Sholay* that she fell for her onscreen love interest and frequent costar Dharmendra, whom she subsequently married. Controversy arose around the fact that Dharmendra was already married to another woman—a technicality circumvented by the newlyweds' conversion to Islam—but public adoration for Malini was such that she was able to weather the attendant PR storm with little damage to her image. Like so many Indian film stars, Malini took to political life later in her career, taking a hiatus from acting during the '90s to pursue a successful run for parliament. In the ensuing years she has also proved herself as a talent to be reckoned with behind the camera, working as a director, producer and choreographer, in addition to continuing to work steadily as an actress.

PARVEEN BABI Like Zeenat Aman, Parveen Babi was a star very much of her time, lionized as both a sex symbol and style icon. At the same time, she exhibited a somewhat more traditional femininity that made her come across as a safer alternative to the smoldering Aman.

This is not in any way meant to suggest that Babi was a lightweight, however, as she held her own as a leading lady against most of the biggest stars of the day, including, on numerous occasions, the big "B," Amitabh Bachchan. Babi's conformity to a very Western standard of beauty (less charitable female bloggers of my acquaintance have called her "Parveen Barbie") even landed her on the cover of Time Magazine in 1976. Tragically, Babi's struggles with mental illness forced her to withdraw from the film industry at the peak of her fame in the early '80s, leaving behind only a decade's worth of films from which we can extrapolate what might have been.

REKHA The elegance and glamour that Rheka came to embody belie her hardscrabble beginnings in the Indian film industry. The product of a financially troubled household in the country's Tamil region, she began working in films as a young teenager to support her family, with little in the way of star ambition or expressed interest in acting for its own sake. She was nonetheless possessed of raw talent and a strong work ethic, yet still found herself blocked from advancement by Bollywood's Eurocentric standard of feminine beauty. With her dark skin and comparatively thickset South Indian features, Rheka—born Bhanurekha Ganesan—was not going to win heroine roles in Hindi pictures without undergoing a physical and cosmetic transformation (and this without mentioning her troubles with the Hindi language, of which she was not a native speaker). A strict program of diet and exercise—along with, perhaps, some alleged but unconfirmed sessions under the surgeon's knife—eventually got her the lithe body and sleek, feline looks that contributed to her unique screen presence. But to credit her appearance alone for her success would be to give short shrift to the range and intensity of her performances, which won her three Filmfare Awards and one National Film Award over the course of a career spanning almost two hundred features. Among her many crowd pleasing achievements was a successful pairing with Amitabh Bachchan, which saw the two superstars—and rumored lovers—cast opposite one another in nine hit movies between 1976 and 1981.

JYOTHI LAXMI Jyothi Laxmi was often employed within Southern India's Telegu language film industry as an "item girl," or featured dancer. But she also had a side career as a star of violent action films, playing a series of hard fighting cowgirls, lady bandits, and femme fatales in films like *Pistolwali* and *James Bond 777*. Glowering and imposingly big boned, Laxmi provided a stark contrast to the demure heroines of Hindi cinema, and must certainly have raised eyebrows on those occasions when she crossed over—as she did in Telegu director K.S.R. Doss's Hindi feature *Rani aur Jaani*. Furthermore, while Hindi starlets relied on either stunt doubles or wan stage fighting moves on those rare occasions when they were required to fight, Laxmi threw herself into her many stunt scenes with conspicuous gusto. Equally ardent was her approach to her often raunchy song and dance numbers, which made her an attraction many Indian men of a certain age remember fondly to this day.

The Heavies

AMJAD KHAN Amjad Khan was but a humble bit player when he accepted the role of villain Gabbar Singh in Ramesh Sippy's *Sholay*. Little could he have known at the time that, by the end of *Sholay*'s record shattering theatrical run, Gabbar Singh would be a household name, and, as a result, he would be doomed to playing similar roles in dozens of subsequent films. The thing is, though, that he was just so damn good at it. Certainly, Khan did his share of sipping Vat 69 in resplendent lairs, but, in contrast to the dissolute urbanity displayed by competing screen bad guys like Ajit or Madan Puri, his was a much more bestial, unhinged, and close-to-the-surface brand of evil. When the script called for a sweaty, wild eyed maniac prone to childlike explosions of volcanic anger, there was simply no one else for the job. Of course, less representative roles, like that of the wily police detective in Feroz Khan's *Qurbani*, demonstrated Khan's true range, but Indian audiences apparently preferred him in only one flavor. And who can blame them? Amjad Khan is like the Chunky Monkey of Bollywood villainy.

AMRISH PURI Amrish Puri's notoriety as a Bollywood heel reached its zenith in the '80s, with his iconic performance as the tyrannical Mogambo in Shekhar Kapur's *Mr. India*. Nonetheless it was in the '70s, following a distinguished stage career, that his cinematic mean streak began. Though he was reportedly the sweetest guy you could hope to know, it's hard to imagine Puri, with his severe features, rumbling voice, and imposing brow, playing anything other than a sadistic thakur or egomaniacal would-be dictator. Unless, of course, you picture him as the chrome-domed high priest of a maniacal Thugee cult. Yes, that's right; if you recognize Puri, it's likely for his one foray into Hollywood: playing the role of Mola Ram in *Indiana Jones and the Temple of Doom*.

MADAN PURI Certainly more visible during the decade was Amrish Puri's older brother, Madan, who competed head to head with Amjad Khan and Ajit to be the artist most likely seen trying to throw Amitabh Bachchan into a tiger pit. With his patrician bearing and leonine features, Puri specialized in heavies who practiced their evil from behind a veneer of legitimacy, like *Chor Machaye Shor*'s corrupt politician Jamanadas. Yet—as his role as Samant in the breakout hit *Deewaar* demonstrated—he also excelled at playing underworld dons, and even had the wit and versatility to pull off cartoonish mustache twirlers like *Saazish*'s Fu Manchu-like Mr. Wong. Alongside this staggering assortment of entertaining bad guy turns, perhaps what we should be most grateful to Puri for is that he used his clout to make a place for Amrish in the business, thus ensuring that Bollywood villainy would bear the Puri stamp for decades to come.

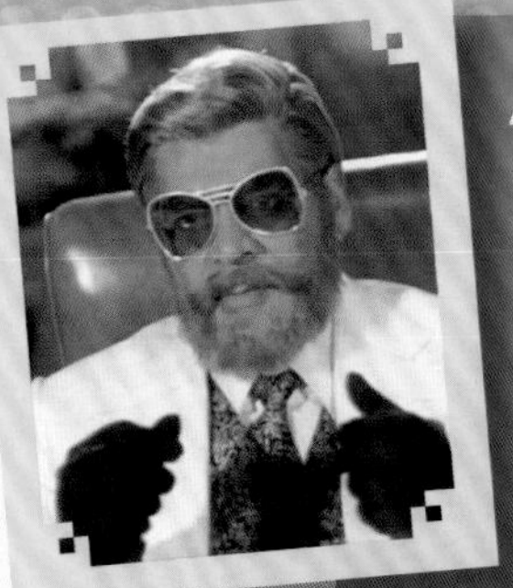

AJIT Ajit's long journey to screen villainy is an interesting one. Unlike career maniacs like Amjad Khan, he began life on screen as a hero, playing romantic leads in films throughout the '50s and into the '60s. He started to dabble in negative roles with H.S. Rawail's *Suraj*, but it was his role as Teja in the 1973 smash *Zanjeer*, opposite Amitabh Bachchan, that cemented his place within Bollywood's pantheon of infamy. Ajit—full name Ajit Khan—parlayed his cultivated suavity into a signature brand of sophisticated treachery. His typical villain was a dapper, sharply attired Mr. Big—the type who would lounge in his plushly upholstered lair, snifter in one hand and cigarette holder in the other, as the hero ran his paces through a course of cunningly laid death traps. This, of course, made Ajit an ideal foil for the righteous working man's heroes of the day. As the very personification of wealth's decadence and corruption, he was an ideal target for defiant finger pointing from the likes of Dharmendra and Amitabh.

PREM CHOPRA
As the career of Amjad Khan demonstrates, all it takes is one performance to forever typecast an actor in the role of a meany. In Prem Chopra's case that performance was in Nasir Hussain's 1966 smash *Teesri Manzil*, in which Chopra memorably played the villainous Ramesh. With his cherubic face and unique, soft voiced delivery, Chopra bridged the gap between Ajit's dissolute masterminds and Khan's infantile tyrants, making him an ideal choice to play either a cravenly amoral son of wealth or a dirty faced and wild eyed wannabe despot. Subsequent iconic bad guy portrayals, such as his eponymous turn in Raj Kapoor's 1973 classic *Bobby*, insured that—despite the considerable number of sympathetic portrayals and character roles found throughout his 300 plus films—Chopra is today remembered almost exclusively as one of Indian cinema's most reliable heels.

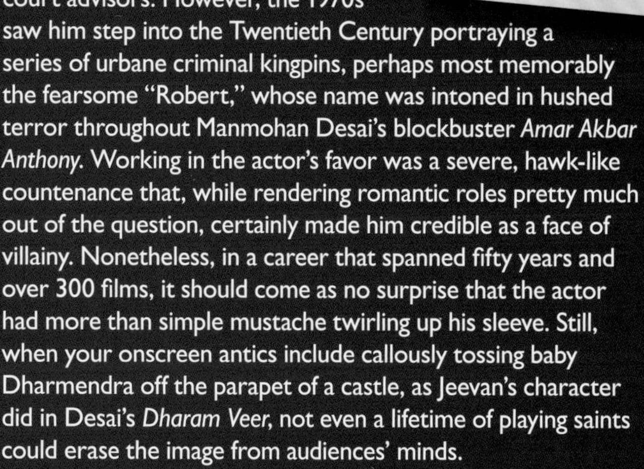

JEEVAN Jeevan can be found in a number of B grade Indian "sword and sandal" films from the 1960s, playing an assortment of evil, pointy bearded vazirs and cruelly self interested court advisors. However, the 1970s saw him step into the Twentieth Century portraying a series of urbane criminal kingpins, perhaps most memorably the fearsome "Robert," whose name was intoned in hushed terror throughout Manmohan Desai's blockbuster *Amar Akbar Anthony*. Working in the actor's favor was a severe, hawk-like countenance that, while rendering romantic roles pretty much out of the question, certainly made him credible as a face of villainy. Nonetheless, in a career that spanned fifty years and over 300 films, it should come as no surprise that the actor had more than simple mustache twirling up his sleeve. Still, when your onscreen antics include callously tossing baby Dharmendra off the parapet of a castle, as Jeevan's character did in Desai's *Dharam Veer*, not even a lifetime of playing saints could erase the image from audiences' minds.

STARCAST

The Supporting Players

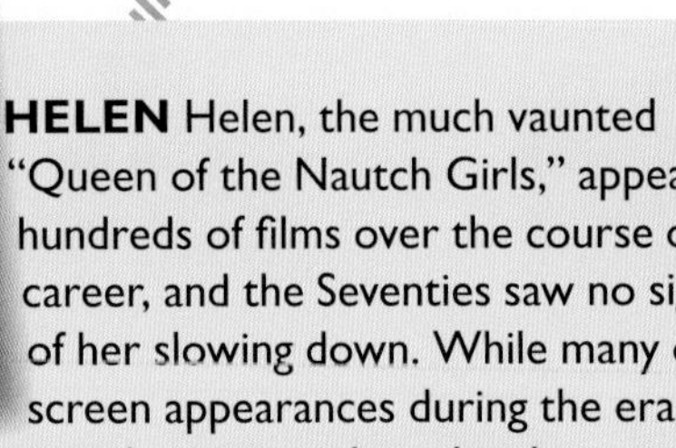

HELEN Helen, the much vaunted "Queen of the Nautch Girls," appeared in hundreds of films over the course of her career, and the Seventies saw no signs of her slowing down. While many of her screen appearances during the era were limited to a single song number, she also did her share of memorable supporting turns, playing an assortment of vamps, tramps and gun molls. In fact, so ubiquitous was Helen during the Seventies that, on the rare occasion when one comes across a film in which she does *not* appear, it's hard not to wonder why that one didn't make the cut.

ARUNA IRANI Early in her career, Aruna Irani was known primarily for her skills as a dancer, but, by the '70s, she had become another of Indian popular cinema's versatile MVPs. Whether as a steely eyed dragon lady in *Qurbani*, a rough and tumble action heroine in *Rani aur Jaani*, a good girl tragically led astray in *Charas*, or playing a succession of memorable vamps, Irani is always a sexy, magnetic presence. While it could be said that her many stellar supporting turns are our gain at the expense of Irani's leading lady dreams, it can't be said that her work has gone unrecognized or unsung. She's been the recipient of multiple nominations and awards over the course of her career, with the latest, at the time of this writing, being a Filmfare Lifetime Achievement Award in 2012.

DANNY DENZONGPA Danny Denzongpa's shooting schedule on Feroz Khan's *Dharmatma* prevented him from taking the role of Gabbar Singh in *Sholay*, a part that ultimately went to Amjad Khan. Judging by the typecasting trap that subsequently befell Khan, we can at least say that Denzongpa, in missing out on playing the most iconic villain in Indian screen history, was allowed to enjoy a more varied career as a result. Certainly his Sikkimese heritage made him the top choice to play a wide range of Asiatic "others"—from Arabian warlords to Feroz Khan's Tonto-like sidekick in *Kaala Sona*. But alongside those, there was a wide range of other roles, heroes and sympathetic supporting parts among them, in addition to the traditional mustache twirlers. On top of that, Denzongpa, an accomplished singer with a few hit records under his belt, has the rare distinction of being one of the few Indian stars who could actually provide his own vocals for one of those ubiquitous song and dance numbers if called upon.

PRAN I could have easily fit Pran in the "Heavies" category due to his roster of memorable negative portrayals. But the truth is that this actor's versatility made him something of an MVP in 1970s Bollywood. The dedicated Pran fan knows that loathing his character in one film doesn't preclude one from being beguiled by his warmth and affability in the next. And that doesn't even account for all of the oddball turns that populate the space between those two extremes: the noble samurai (don't ask) who masters birds of prey in *Dharam Veer*; the gimp legged, reformed crook turned tightrope walker in *Don*; the cartoonish hippy—a live action, South Asian version of *Scooby Doo*'s Shaggy, really—in *Jangal Mein Mangal*. Arriving in Bombay in 1947 after a fitful early career in regional cinema, Pran—full name Pran Krishan Sikand—soon thereafter made an impressive Bollywood debut as a villain in the hit *Ziddi* (which also launched the career of its hero, Dev Anand). Many more bad guy parts came his way afterward, but he was still able to venture successfully into heroic and comedic roles, establishing the eclectic range of performances that enabled him to slip primarily into character parts during the 1970s and beyond. This later era marked the peak of Pran's career, a period during which he was paid more than many of the young marquee names, like Amitabh Bachchan, whom he appeared opposite. Switching audience sympathies on and off like a light switch from picture to picture as he did, it's hard to argue he didn't earn it.

NIRUPA ROY It could be (and has been) said that the mothers in Indian cinema are stand-ins for Mother India herself. True or not, there's no denying that the mother is an important figure in these films—a fact which might lead to a disconnect for some Western viewers. In America, for instance, we're more accustomed to the archetype of the "loner" hero; a guy who seems to have sprung into the world of a piece—bad attitude, torn levis, awesome wheels and all—without the aid of traditional biology. For a character such as that to be seen kneeling with trembling lip at his old mother's knee, as we see so many Indian heroes do, would be an invitation to ridicule. But India's heroes... those boys sure do love their moms. And in the 1970s, that mom was more often than not played by Nirupa Roy. Of course, the bitter irony of all this is that Roy, having turned 40 in 1971, was only a decade older, if that, than some of the adult stars, like Amitabh Bachchan and Shashi Kapoor, whom she played parent to. Still, she played the part well, if not to a fault. You see, being the mother of a seething rakehell and man of action like Bachchan's Angry Young Man meant a life of worry and suffering, and Roy could tear her hair and rend her garments with the best of them. In short, if you don't call your own mom after seeing one of her performances, you clearly have no soul.

STARCAST

The Supporting Players

JAGDEEP For better or ill, the "something for everyone" formula of 1970s masala cinema necessitated that comedy always be part of the mix, with comedic performers often commanding entire subplots within films that were otherwise no laughing matter. Every era had its particular "go to guy" for such roles—Johnny Walker in the '50s and '60s, Johnny Lever in the '80s and onward—and, in the '70s, that guy was Jagdeep, born Syed Ishtiaq Ahmed Jaffry. Like so many comedy relief performers before and after him, Jagdeep was a master of being demonstratively afraid of things, throwing himself into an elaborate state of "feets do your stuff" style jibber jabbers whenever the script required. This put him in especially high demand in horror films, leading to appearances in a number of the Ramsay Brothers' supernatural thrillers, including *Veerana* and *Purana Mandir*. Still, as demonstrated by the over 250 films in which he appeared, Jagdeep showed a versatility that made him more than just a frightened face. As someone who tends to find comic relief shtick neither comical nor particularly relieving, the nicest thing I can say about him is that he doesn't always completely irritate me. The *Dirty Harry* remake *Khoon Khoon*, for instance—in which he played the hero cop's trusty, albeit buffoonish partner—showed me that Jagdeep was capable of providing amusement without derailing the tone of an otherwise serious film, which is about as much as we can ask in such circumstances.

RANJEET Ranjeet's typical character was someone on a lower tier of the ladder of villainy, either a lieutenant or foot soldier of the movie's Mr. Big. What qualifies him for mention over other actors who specialized in such parts—like Mac Mohan or Yusuf Khan—is Ranjeet's apparent role as a designated clothes horse for eye-rending 1970s sartorial what-the-fuckery. Be it a mesh shirt, peek-a-boo blouse, or blinding psychedelic print, no outfit was too impractical, cumbersome or attention getting for the violent men of action Ranjeet, born Gopal Bedi, portrayed. With a wife who designed costumes and a daughter who would go on to become a fashion designer, it's easy to assume that Ranjeet himself had an interest in the cloth trade. However, like many of India's screen villains, his modest, teetotaling ways off screen suggest that he perhaps didn't take quite as naturally to the dirty work required of him on it. "In audience lexicon," he bemoaned in one interview, "rape became synonymous with Ranjeet." Maybe so, but in our lexicon, Ranjeet is synonymous with "Oh my eyes! What have you done to my eyes!"

KESHTO MUKHERJEE Any scholar of the art of cinematic storytelling will tell you that it's sometimes impossible to convey the impact of an action without showing a wino doing a drunken double-take at it. In 1970s Bollywood, Keshto Mukherjee was the man for that job. Though reportedly not a drinker himself, Mukherjee found himself typecast in comical drunk roles starting with 1970's *Maa aur Mamta*. Though his drunks on occasion turned out to be substantial (if drunken) supporting characters, he was also frequently hauled out just to do a cross-eyed spit take during an isolated fight scene, or to see a booze addled vision of multiple dancing Parveen Babis in *Kalaa Sona*.

IFTEKHAR If ever there was a case study in Bollywood typecasting, it would be Iftekhar. Chances are, if you're watching a Hindi film from the '70s in which a distinguished looking law enforcement official—be he police chief, head of the CID, or an officer of Interpol—appears, Iftekhar is playing him, and playing him well. A testament to his acting range is the fact that, on those occasions when he did branch out, it was often in villain roles, such as his iconic turn as Davaar, opposite Amitabh Bachchan, in *Deewaar*, or as the noble, aging hood "The Professor" in *Gaddaar*. All of these contributed to a filmography that extended to over 400 films and included Western productions such as 1992's *City of Joy*. Give this veteran actor a stiff backed salute next time you see him enter a room; he's earned it.

SHETTY Among the unsmiling herd of henchmen and gunsels employed by Bollywood's various Mr. Bigs, it is Shetty—bald, hulking and with a bone chilling scowl—who is the most immediately recognizable. This was not his only claim to fame, however, as Shetty—who also went by the name M.B. Shetty—was also Bollywood's most employed fight coordinator throughout the '70s and '80s, earning the "Fights" credit in dozens of pictures. This not only makes him a multi-talent but also a very good sport, as much of his job involved him coaching much less imposing looking actors on how to convincingly beat him up on screen. Hell, he even let a dog get the best of him in *Raani aur Jaani*.

STARCAST

The Directors

MANMOHAN DESAI A dedicated entertainer and cinematic populist, Manmohan Desai more than anyone else defined the something-for-everyone "masala" aesthetic that dominated Indian cinema throughout the '70s and '80s. The typical Desai film was an event picture with a sprawling cast of A list stars, often with a ridiculously convoluted plot that made room for equal parts romance, overwrought family melodrama, slapstick comedy, and breathtaking action set pieces. Desai was also a serial perpetrator of the time tested "lost and found" plot device, in 1977 alone helming three hits that centered around families torn asunder by fate and later, also by fate, reunited. A number of his biggest hits of the decade featured Amitabh Bachchan as their lead, but other stars, including Dharmendra, would also benefit from his golden touch.

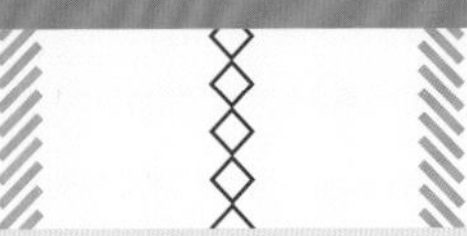

RAVIKANT NAGAICH A former cinematographer, Ravikant Nagaich had a fondness for oddball trick photography that lent his films an at times glaring artificiality, not to mention an air of unintentional surrealism. Starting out in Telegu films, he made his Hindi debut with *Farz*, an early James Bond knock-off. Spy films continued to be a touchstone throughout his career in both mainstream and low budget cinema, with perhaps his crowning achievement being the brain-busting *Gunmaster G-9* films starring Mithun Chakraborty. Along the way, he also created stylish thrillers (*The Train*), hallucinatory and somewhat troubling children's fantasies (*Rani aur Lalpari*), trippy westerns (*Kaala Sona*) and horror films (*Jadu Tona*). It says a lot about Nagaich that, in a cinema as prone to hyper-reality as India's, his films nonetheless stand out for their jaw dropping color schemes and bizarre simulacra.

RAMESH SIPPY Ramesh Sippy—part of a directing dynasty that started with his father, G.P. Sippy, and which continues today with his son Rohan Sippy—would deserve mention here even if 1975's *Sholay* were his sole directorial effort. Because *Sholay*, as you'll quickly tire of hearing me say, is THE MOST BELOVED INDIAN FILM OF ALL TIME!! Truthfully, Sippy's contributions to 1970s action cinema were rather sparse, due in no small part, I'm sure, to his exacting standards. His insistence on numerous reshoots contributed to *Sholay* taking a staggering two and a half years to complete, and it would be another five years before Sippy would follow it up with *Shaan*. Given the typically feverish pace of production at the time, such deliberate parsing out of product is noteworthy in itself. (To put things in perspective, Manmohan Desai released eleven films to Sippy's four between 1970 and 1980, and Ravikant Nagaich twelve.) Yet it's hard to argue with the man's approach upon viewing the final results. *Sholay* was a film of incredible impact and influence, shaping much in Indian cinema that followed it, while *Shaan* was… well, *Shaan* was a film that featured Amitabh Bachchan wrestling a crocodile, a black marketeer with a high tech island lair out of a James Bond movie, and a murder plot involving a blackmailed circus sharpshooter. For our purposes, movies like that are every bit as momentous as any hallowed classic.

K.S.R. DOSS K.S.R. Doss, who worked primarily within Southern India's Telegu language film industry (or "Tollywood," as it's often called), has laid claim to making India's first "100 percent action film" with his 1970 feature *Rowdy Rani*. While that's a difficult claim to verify, it's easy to see how Doss's rough edged style might have seemed novel to audiences at the time. Mainstream Bollywood films certainly had their share of fisticuffs and gunplay, but they could only come across as dainty and restrained compared to the go-for-broke approach Doss took to filming action, which often involved tumbling the camera end over end as if it was itself a participant in the carnage. Doss was also ahead of the pack in terms of featuring women in demanding physical roles—a call back to the "stunt" films of India's past and to swashbuckling female stars like Fearless Nadia in particular. Thanks to Doss remaking some of his Telegu hits for the Hindi market, as well as a few original films made within the Bollywood system, wider audiences were introduced to hard fighting Southern starlets like Jyothi Laxmi and Vijaya Lalitha. It's hard to imagine anyone being quite the same afterward.

PRAKASH MEHRA Among the great actor/director combos in cinema history—Scorsese and De Niro, Ford and Wayne, Kurosawa and Mifune—you've got to include Mehra and Bachchan. Amitabh Bachchan gained his first taste of superstardom with *Zanjeer*, a film both directed and produced by Prakash Mehra, a young former production controller who'd made his directing debut with *Haseena Maan Jayegi* five years earlier. Having with that film effectively established Bachchan's groundbreaking "Angry Young Man" persona, the director and star then went on to collaborate on six more major hits throughout the '70s and early '80s, including such '70s classics as *Hera Pheri*, *Muqaddar Ka Sikandar* and *Khoon Pasina*. (A seventh collaboration in 1989, *Jaadugar*, ended up being a disappointment at the box office.) Although the director worked with other stars throughout his career, it is his association with The Big B that is most cemented in the minds of the Indian public. Upon the occasion of his death in 2009, Bachchan, writing on his personal blog, praised Mehra for his intuitive, no nonsense approach to filmmaking: "A simple man who had the capacity to narrate great stories through the medium of cinema in the most simple manner. No fuss, no calisthenics. Just very ordinary camera placements and extraordinary content."

NASIR HUSSAIN Nasir Hussain was a Bollywood veteran by the time the '70s rolled around, having started his career as a writer in the late '40s and then turning his hand to directing in the following decade. After starting his own production company in the 1960s, he wrote and produced the colorful blockbuster *Teesri Manzil*, which cannily combined the mystery and romance of a Hitchcock thriller with all the youthful froth and pop driven hijinks of an Elvis musical. More hits followed, and by the dawn of the following decade, Hussain had proven himself as a reliable source of splashy, youth oriented crowd pleasers, more often than not driven by the rocking, boundary-pushing scores of R.D. Burman. Action was a key element in Hussain's hits during the '70s, as classics such as *Yaadon Ki Baaraat* and its rollicking follow up *Hum Kisise Kum Naheen* amply demonstrate.

The Music

R.D. BURMAN Composer Rahul Dev ("R.D.") Burman, more than any other musician, is credited with bringing the influence of Western pop and rock into Bollywood film music, paving the way for the electrified Bolly-funk that would become a staple of Indian action films during the '70s. Starting out as an assistant to his father, famed composer Sachin Dev ("S.D.") Burman, R.D. earned his first credits as a solo music director during the '60s. But it was not until the '70s, with youth oriented films like *Hare Rama Hare Krishna* and *Yaadon Ki Baaraat* (both starring Zeenat Aman), that he would truly come into his own. In addition to scoring countless films, R.D. is also known to have on occasion lent his own, very distinctive voice to his compositions. If you're hearing someone who sounds like a scat singing, Hindi version of Louis Armstrong, that's probably him.

KALYANJI-ANANDJI While it was R.D. Burman who opened the door, it was Kalyanji-Anandji who truly brought the funk to Bollywood—a fact loudly testified to by their classic scores to such action packed '70s hits as *Qurbani*, *Apradh* and *Don*. Pulsating wah-wah guitars, percolating synths, and slap bass were frequent guests at their musical table, testing even further the extent to which Western pop and R&B sounds could encroach upon Indian cinema's traditional musical formula. Getting their start in film in the early '60s, this sibling duo—comprised of brothers Kalyanji and Anandji Virji Shah—has in more recent years gained appreciation in the West through their prominent inclusion on a number of hipster-oriented Bollywood beats compilations, such as Dan The Automator's *Bombay the Hard Way*. This embrace by DJ culture culminated in samples from their songs being used in the Black Eyed Peas hit "Don't Phunk with My Heart." Don't hold that against them, though.

LAXMIKANT-PYARELAL

With over 600 film scores to their credit, Laxmikant-Pyarelal were the most prolifically employed of all Bollywood's great musical duos. Comprised of childhood friends Laxmikant Shantaram Kudalkar and Pyarelal Ramprasad, the team worked with both Kalyanji-Anandji and R.D. Burman in subordinate roles before striking out on their own as music directors in the early '60s. Building up their reputation gradually with a string of mid to low budget features in which, often times, their songs were the most memorable feature, K-P came to reign over 1970s Bollywood, along with Burman and Kalyanji-Anandji, as the figure-heads of a new musical generation. At the same time, their approach to composition was more conservative than that of their adventurous peers, relying more heavily on traditional instrumentation and arrangements derived from Indian classical music—a family friendly, middle-of-the-road approach that goes a long way toward explaining their broad appeal. Nevertheless, when called upon, the team showed that they could come up with a suitably thumping, contemporary sound, as they did in their hip shaking score to the great *Geetaa Mera Naam*.

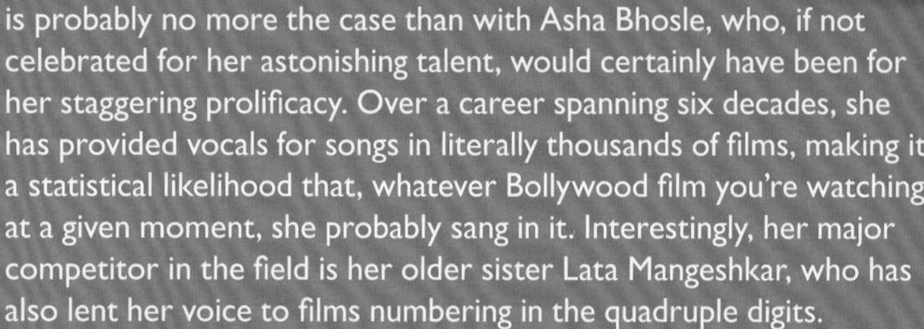

ASHA BHOSLE One very crucial thing to understand about the songs in Bollywood movies is that the stars don't actually sing them—and, more importantly, that everyone is okay with that. In fact, the "Playback Singers" who provide those vocals—which are then "picturized" upon the miming stars—often achieve a level of fame comparable to "that" of the "on camera" "talent."(Can you tell I hate shock quotes?) This is probably no more the case than with Asha Bhosle, who, if not celebrated for her astonishing talent, would certainly have been for her staggering prolificacy. Over a career spanning six decades, she has provided vocals for songs in literally thousands of films, making it a statistical likelihood that, whatever Bollywood film you're watching at a given moment, she probably sang in it. Interestingly, her major competitor in the field is her older sister Lata Mangeshkar, who has also lent her voice to films numbering in the quadruple digits.

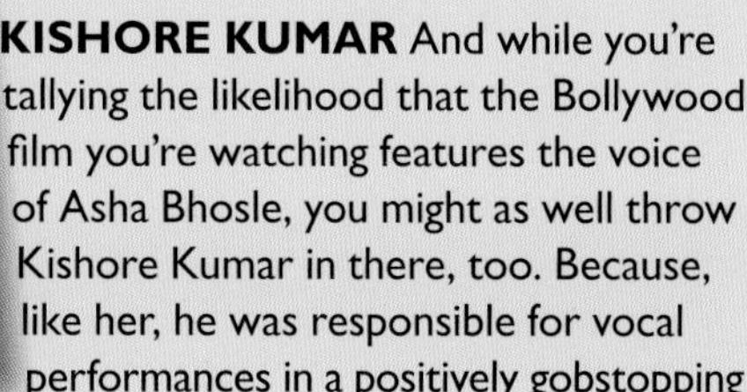

KISHORE KUMAR And while you're tallying the likelihood that the Bollywood film you're watching features the voice of Asha Bhosle, you might as well throw Kishore Kumar in there, too. Because, like her, he was responsible for vocal performances in a positively gobstopping number of features. Making that more impressive is the fact that he also managed to star in front of the camera in a considerable number of them and even, on occasion, composed their music. During the '70s, Kumar's distinctive voice made him a favorite of the heavy hitters among the industry's music directors, especially R.D. Burman, for whom he was the male vocalist of choice. This resulted in him being the most oft heard musical voice of many of the era's big action stars, including Bachchan, Dharmendra, Vinod Khanna and even Mithun Chakraborty.

The Screenwriters

SALIM-JAVED Judging by how seldom you hear Bollywood screenwriters singled out for their contributions, it's easy to assume that they don't carry a whole lot of weight. After all, in India, as most elsewhere, it's the stars who drive demand, with perhaps a small handful of name directors also feeding into a picture's box office "oomph." To this rule, then, Salim-Javed are a rare exception, at their peak commanding a status that saw their names prominently featured on the posters for their films. The legend surrounding the team—composed of friends Salim Khan and Javed Akhtar—takes as gospel that their rise to notoriety was inseparable from that of Amitabh Bachchan. But it should be noted that they'd tasted success prior to that association; notably with *Seeta aur Geeta*, a 1972 hit for Hema Malini, and Rajesh Khanna's "a man and his elephants" story *Haathi Mere Saathi*, among others. Still, one can't ignore that they were responsible for writing virtually all of Bachchan's defining hits during the '70s—including *Zanjeer, Deewaar, Sholay*, and *Don*—and as such were as much the authors of the star's distinctive screen persona as Bachchan himself. Young men themselves at the time, it was Salim-Javed on whose doorstep was commonly laid credit for creating the archetypal "Angry Young Man" of 1970s Hindi cinema. Given that figure's influence, I think it's safe to say they were as responsible as anyone for the tone that defined Funky Bollywood.

KEY

Like any national cinema, Bollywood has its share of unique tropes, themes and narrative touchstones that show up again and again in its films. Some of them, however, show up a lot more than others. In an effort to streamline your journey, I offer this handy key.

LOST AND FOUND: It's literally staggering how often the plot device of families being torn apart and later reunited comes up in Indian cinema—so often, in fact, that, by the late '70s, the term "lost and found" had become common parlance for describing it. Often such divisions are of the "separated at birth" variety, frequently ending in tragedy when siblings meet again at opposite sides of an uncrossable moral divide. It can also, however, be used as a testament to the preternatural strength of familial bonds, such as in those films in which a separated family's long, coincidence-dependent journey toward reunion is chronicled as something inevitable and smiled upon by the gods. Of course, if the film in question is an action film, the reunited family must then go about the business of exacting bloody vengeance against those responsible for separating them in the first place.

SIBLING VS. SIBLING: Of course, as most of us well know, family members need not be separated by fate and unaware of their blood relation in order to find themselves at each other's throats. Thus is the plot of siblings coming to face each other from opposite sides of the law right behind "lost and found" as one of the most oft told of all the oft told tales in Indian cinema. Probably the best example is *Deewaar*, one of the greatest Bollywood films of the '70s, in which Amitabh Bachchan plays the son of a broken home who grows up to be a criminal kingpin, while his brother, played by Shashi Kapoor, is the upright cop who must bring him to justice. Overwhelmingly these stories concern brothers, but there are distaff versions as well, most notably 1972's *Rani aur Jaani* in which Telegu temptress Jyothi Laxmi plays the kidnapped sister turned fearsome bandit and Aruna Irani the fearless policewoman tasked with catching her.

DOUBLES: Doubles—be they actual twins, or just one of those perfectly identical random strangers everyone encounters from time to time—are an absolute must have. How else is one to pull off all of those daring capers and comical masquerades that are so necessary to the navigation of everyday life? In addition, doubles act as a ticket out of screenwriters' jail for Bollywood scribes who've gotten too carried away with plot convolutions to resolve things without having someone be either in two places at once or both alive and dead at the same time. (This happens a lot.)

KEY

LAIRS: Bollywood has a tendency to define its bad guys through their lavish displays of consumption. After all, no villain is easier to hate than a rich villain. In the 1970s—thanks, no doubt, to the influence of the James Bond movies—this meant that no criminal mastermind was significantly *ee-vil* unless he came equipped with an elaborate, high-tech lair filled to the brim with sparkly loot and baubles. Interestingly, the girth and size of a crook's lair was not always commensurate with his place on the criminal food chain; *Shaan*'s Shakaal, for example, was a mere black marketer, yet still had a sprawling island compound worthy of Dr. No. Bootleg DVD sales must have been particularly good that year.

BROMANCE: Refreshingly, in Bollywood, the expression of affection between one platonic man pal and another means never having to say "no homo." Nevertheless, the practice may prove rankling for audience members accustomed to Western buddy movie conventions, even though it is much less a flaunting of those conventions than it is a laying bare of them. Who can doubt that some obvious tensions would have been immeasurably reduced had Danny Glover been able to lovingly cup Mel Gibson's face in his hands the way that Feroz Khan does to Vinod Khanna in *Qurbani*? Thankfully, Bollywood's celebration of man-man love seems to be at its most blatant the more it's surrounded by scenes of cars blowing up, so rest assured that you'll be seeing this symbol plenty over the next pages.

DRUNKENNESS: As much as the Hindu religion might frown upon the drinking of alcohol, it's impossible to deny the entertainment value of a person who's drunk too much of it. Thus add to the many varieties of song and dance numbers in Bollywood films the "drunk" number, in which an otherwise reticent individual cuts loose in an uninhibited musical manner thanks to having over indulged. This, of course, does nothing to explain why all of those other, apparently sober people are constantly bursting into song in these films, and in fact only deepens the mystery. Nevertheless, look to this symbol as a sign that the subject film warrants at least being fast forwarded through to witness just such a sloppy spectacle.

HELEN: As Bollywood's premier "item girl," Helen danced her way through hundreds of films, starting with 1957's *Howrah Ridge* at the rheumy old age of 17. This often entailed her appearing in no more than a single song and dance number within a given picture, but also extended to her essaying a number of meaty supporting roles—most of which, of course, also involved dancing. By the 1970s, so ubiquitous had she become that she was something of a legitimizing presence. Think of this symbol, then, as an indication that the subject film bears the hallowed "Helen Seal of Approval".

The Movies

Masala noun:
A popular form of Indian cinema that, in the interest of pleasing as wide an audience as possible, incorporates a variety of disparate genre elements—action, melodrama, comedy, song and dance, devotional—that to the outsider might seem incompatible. Especially popular during the 1970s.

DON

Released: 1978
Director: Chandra Barot
Stars: Amitabh Bachchan, Zeenat Aman, Pran, Iftekhar, Om Shivpuri, Satyendra Kapoor, P. Jairaj, Kamal Kapoor, Arpana Choudhary, Helen, Shetty, Mac Mohan, Azad, Yashraj, Devaraj, Jagdish Raj, Amar, Pinchoo Kapoor, Keshav Rana, Maruti, Ranvir Raj, Shakeel, Leena, Baby Bilkish, Alankar Joshi, M.A. Latif, S.U. Khan, Moolchand, Abhimanyu Sharma, Mama, Shah Agha, H.L. Pardesi, Bihari, Soul, Ramesh Shrimali, Vinay Randhawa, Gurjinder Virk, Kalwa, Mohiuddin, P.K. Chander, Sharad Kumar, Gulshan, Rajan Haksar, Yusuf Khan, Prem Sagar
Writers: Salim-Javed (Salim Khan & Javed Akhtar)
Music: Kalyanji-Anandji (Kalyanji Virji Shah & Anandji Virji Shah)
Lyrics: Anjaan (Lalji Pandey), Indeevar
Thrills: A. Mansoor

Ramesh (Sharad Kumar), a lieutenant of the fearsome and elusive crime lord Don (Amitabh Bachchan), is preparing, with the help of his sister Roma (Zeenat Aman), to flee Bombay and leave his life of crime behind. Unfortunately, word of his defection has leaked to Don, who sees to it personally that Ramesh doesn't live to betray him. Seeking revenge, Ramesh's fiancé Kamini (Helen) then attempts to lure Don into the arms of the police by posing as a seductive bar girl, only to also meet an untimely death at Don's hands. With this, the baton of vengeance is passed to Roma, who, after training rigorously in martial arts and adopting a butch new look, infiltrates Don's gang as its newest member.

Soon thereafter, Don is trapped in a police sting staged by D.S.P. D'Silva (Iftekhar), but escapes after being badly wounded. He later stows away in D'Silva's car, but promptly dies of his injuries with no one but D'Silva to witness his passing. D'Silva decides to keep this bit of information to himself, planning instead to substitute a double in Don's place in order to gain intelligence on his organization. The double he has in mind is Vijay (Bachchan again), a betel leaf chewing simpleton who earns spare rupees singing and dancing for the crowds on the waterfront. The kindly Vijay cares for two abandoned children, Deepu and Munni (Alankar Joshi and Baby Bilkish), and it is by appealing to Vijay's concern for them that D'Silva wins his cooperation, promising in return to generously provide for the kids' wellbeing.

Unknown to all of these parties, Deepu and Munni's real father has just been released from prison. This is J.J. (Pran), a reformed safe cracker turned circus high-wire artist who was shot and crippled by DSP D'Silva during a robbery planned by Narang, Don's right hand man (Kamal Kapoor). J.J. took part in the robbery in order to get cash for a life-saving operation for his wife, but, thanks to D'Silva's intervention, he now has neither a wife nor a properly functioning leg to show for it. Now back on the street, he's set his sights on getting payback against both Don and D'Silva for his loss, all the while desperate to be reunited with his two children.

After a crash course in all things Don, Vijay "returns" to the gang under the pretense that Don's injuries have left him with amnesia, necessitating that the gang tell Vijay everything about themselves and their operations in order to bring him up to speed. In the course of this, Don/Vijay and Roma strike up what is by all appearances a romance, much to the disdain of Don's steady girl Anita (Arpana Choudhary). Of course, behind the scenes, Roma is still planning to kill Don at the first opportunity, and that opportunity, when it arrives, forces D'Silva to step in and inform her of the truth. Thus are she and Vijay freed to pursue their courtship in earnest.

One of Vijay's biggest scores as an undercover op is a ledger containing the names of all the gang's cohorts and contacts. This he turns over to D'Silva, who places it in a safe along with a note explaining Vijay's role in the investigation. Unfortunately, D'Silva is shortly thereafter killed during a raid on Don's hideout and, as he is the only official who can support his story, Vijay is at pains to convince the arresting officers of his real identity. As he is now at risk of being thrown into a cell with the entire gang—who, thanks to Vijay's protestations, now know who he really is—it is imperative that he get his hands on the ledger and with it, D'Silva's note. This, however, will be harder than imagined, as J.J. has since broken into D'Silva's home and stolen the ledger, hoping to use it as blackmail material against Narang and the rest of the gang.

DON HAS BECOME SOMETHING of a Bollywood gateway drug for Western cult film fans. Perhaps this is because they've been seduced by that iconic still of Amitabh Bachchan—dapper, gun wielding, and bow tied—in which he looks like a South Asian version of Al Pacino's Tony Montana. Or maybe they've heard a selection from Kalyanji-Anandji's wild psych-funk score and were lured in by that music's suggestion of something half *Godfather* and half *Superfly*. In any case, it's a safe bet that, with *Don*, they ended up getting much more than they bargained for.

After all, who could prepare them for the fact that this movie called *Don* kills its Don at roughly the forty minute mark, burying with him the promise of a straightforward narrative and instead plunging into one that's almost hopelessly convoluted? Or the fact that what at first seems like a grim revenge tale finds room for a zany musical number in which a drunken Amitabh Bachchan extols the virtues of chewing betel leaf—or a madcap climactic fight involving the whole cast that's filled with goofy acrobatics and cartoon sound effects? Lastly, how to make them understand that the film's title character, who technically is *a* Don, is also apparently *named* Don?

All of which is not to say that those people will necessarily be disappointed by *Don*, as it is indeed one of the quintessential Bollywood action movies of the '70s. Director Chandra Barot and screenwriters Salim-Javed keep things fast paced and violent, doling out the thrills at reliable intervals, while at the same time honoring the expected patchwork of tones and genre elements. Generous homage is also paid, as in most great actioners of the era, to Hong Kong martial arts films (Amitabh even engages in a Gordon Liu-style pole fight at one point), as well as to the contemporary American organized crime films that were an obvious influence. And then there is the cast, populated

by most of the genre's great character actors, including a delightful murderer's row of henchmen—the bald pated Shetty, the shaggy Mac Mohan, and the douchey muscle farmer Yusuf Khan—that makes Don's gang the most fearsome ever assembled by Central Casting.

Don also comes with a surfeit of iconic moments: Pran's perilous and woefully rear projected tightrope walk to freedom with a child tucked under each arm; the beautiful Zeenat Aman as a dark, karate kicking avenger; and, of course, Helen's visualization of the Asha Bhosle sung "Yeh Mera Dil"—which, like many of her greatest item numbers, sees Helen doing a tightrope walk of her own, with Thanatos on one side and Eros on the other. "Khaike Paan Banaraswala," another of the film's musical highlights—that aforementioned ode to altered states, sung by Kishore Kumar—became quite a hit with the public at the time, helping to fuel the movie's success at the box office as a result.

Such song numbers are often used in Bollywood films to create a space within which the characters can step outside the narrative and reveal their true selves. This is a practice that's pushed to fascinating extremes in *Don*. Vijay and Roma, as we'll learn, are not the only ones in *Don* who are wearing a false face, and the film repeatedly courts tension by having them seemingly pull those masks off for all to see. In "Jiska Mujhe Tha Intezar," Roma sings openly and cheerily of her plan to murder Don ("I must either give you death or I must die") as Vijay/Don and his men happily nod along. Likewise, in the celebratory "I am Don" ("Main Hoon Don," sung again by Kishore Kumar), what Vijay is actually telling his men is that he is *not* Don, yet they, too, obliviously nod along. Both serve as perfect examples of how Indian film songs can be used, not only to drive a film's story forward, but also to create parallel and counter narratives within it.

Lastly, no discussion of *Don*'s many virtues could be complete without focusing upon its star. Put simply, if you don't "get" Amitabh Bachchan's appeal after watching this film, no amount of exposure or study will change that. The actor leans hard on his natural authority here—the imposing height, the booming voice, the penetrating gaze—while also imbuing Don with an alluring combination of menace and sensuality. At the same time, his Vijay is a creature of almost pitiable vulnerability, not to mention a literal clown. Bachchan at first ratchets back and forth between these two extremes, but eventually starts to show us a Vijay who, through his impersonation of Don, is gradually gaining in command and confidence. As the genre requires, it's a performance both broad and multifaceted, and, typical of these types of performances from Bachchan, more than a little exhausting to watch.

Of course, when evaluating Bachchan's work in *Don*, it might be more instructive to simply fall back upon the actor's undeniable "badass" factor. Granted, that's a lazy and overused term, but no more appropriate phrase comes to mind when confronted with the image of steely-eyed cool that Bachchan so effortlessly presents. This is clearly a star who's earned his place in the pantheon of a certain breed of '70s male movie idol, right alongside the likes of Steve McQueen and Clint Eastwood—neither of whom, I might add, could rock a bow tie with comparable panache.

GEETAA MERA NAAM
"Geetaa Is My Name"

Released: 1974
Director: Sadhana Shivdasani
Stars: Sadhana Shivdasani, Sunil Dutt, Feroz Khan, Ramesh Deo, Helen, Achala Sachdev, Jankidas, Manmohan, Keshto Mukherjee, Rajendra Nath, Murad, Mehmood Jr., Agha, Birbal, Rajendra Nath
Writers: R.K. Nayyar, Madan Joshi
Music: Laxmikant-Pyarelal (Laxmikant Shantaram Kudalkar & Pyarelal Ramprasad Sharma)
Lyrics: Rajendra Krishan
Fights: Mohammed Ali

Little Neeta and her siblings are separated when a gang of bandits storm a crowded marketplace. In the ensuing melee, Neeta's brother Suraj, still clinging to his favorite stuffed monkey, is carried off by one of the bandits. Twenty years later we see that all four have somehow never managed to find one another and, as a result, have all grown up separately with no knowledge of the others' whereabouts. Suraj (Sunil Dutt) is still clinging to his stuffed monkey, which is helpful for purposes of identification, as he is now the wildly unstable leader of an international smuggling operation and goes by the name Johnny. Neeta's other brother, Chandu (Ramesh Deo), is now a righteous, by-the-book police officer who, naturally, has bringing Johnny to justice as his top priority—although he's blissfully unaware of their blood relation. As for Neeta, she is now a virtuous schoolmarm with the pronounced problem of having just been sold by her sleazy adoptive parents to a lascivious underworld character named Mohan.

Fortunately for Neeta, Mohan happens to be on Johnny's bad side, and ends up being coincidentally murdered by him just as he's in the process of forcing himself upon her. Unfortunately, this leaves Neeta as the prime suspect in his death. She is thrown in jail, whereupon she encounters a familiar face. It's her long lost twin sister Geetaa! Geetaa (Sadhana again), is every bit as street wise as her sister is innocent, and vows, upon learning Neeta's predicament, to pin Johnny for the crime. This she does by insinuating her way into the gang, using her feminine charms upon Johnny's trusted right hand man Raja (Feroz Khan). This does not sit well with Raja's girlfriend Savitri (Helen), who schemes to soil the two would-be lovers in Johnny's eyes. Meanwhile, Geetaa's criminal exploits—including a daring train robbery by motorcycle—lead her deeper and deeper into Johnny's criminal milieu.

SADHANA SHIVDASANI—or simply "Sadhana," as she is often referred—rose to fame in the '60s as one of the decade's defining Bollywood glamour girls, the embodiment of an elegant beauty and sophisticated sense of style that encouraged comparisons to Audrey Hepburn. It seems, however, that, by the time of making *Geetaa Mera Naam*, she no longer wanted to encourage such comparisons. After spending

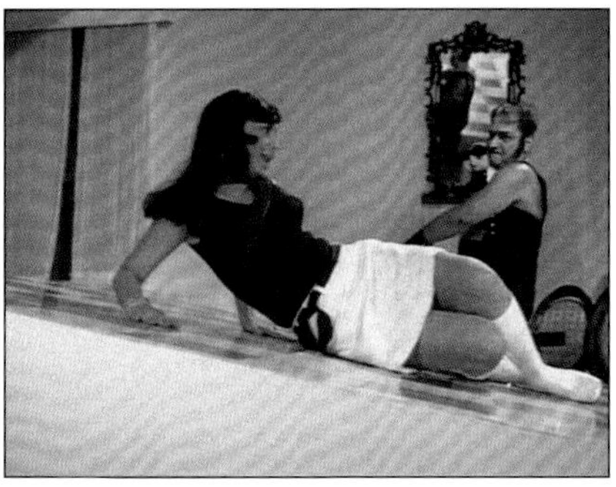

What amazes most about the sequence is that the mind-numbing level of kitsch on display fails to rob it of its power.

years battling a debilitating thyroid condition, she decided to leave the profession on a high note, hand picking *Geetaa* as both her acting swan song and directorial debut, with her director husband R.K. Nayyar acting as co-writer and producer.

Tellingly, *Geetaa* bears little resemblance to the slick thrillers and gauzy romances upon which Sadhana established herself. It instead shares more in common with rowdy, South Indian style actioners like K.S.R. Doss's similarly named *Rani Mera Naam*, which was released two years previous. Not that Sadhana commits to her many fight scenes with anywhere near the same level of reckless enthusiasm as *Rani*'s Vijaya Lalitha. In fact, she often conducts herself as if worried she's going to break a nail. But what she lacks as a credible action heroine, Sadhana makes up for as a director with a distinctly freaky sensibility, loading her film with kink and weirdness. S&M, self flagellation and foot worship all find their way into the mix, combining with the insanely convoluted and aggressively implausible plot to make *Geetaa Mera Naam* one of the most fevered creations of the era.

Evidence of there being a certain go-for-broke attitude behind *Geetaa* abounds, starting with the device of having a morose Sunil Dutt carry a grotesque monkey doll at all times as a signifier of his lost childhood. Johnny/Suraj's psyche is further laid bare, and with comparable subtlety, in a scene that sees him retire to a specially purposed room in his lair to be voluntarily flogged for his sins by a leather trussed strong man. Oh, and about that lair: Say what you want about its combination of twin-toned tiling, recessed track lighting, globular chandeliers, and stained glass, but I think what most people will take away from it is the novel method it provides for the disposal of Johnny's underperforming minions.

Said lair opens out onto a cavernous assembly hall lined on either side with chairs in which Johnny's numerous henchpersons sit. Each of these men, we soon see, is just one flick of the switch away from being dumped backward through a trapdoor into a vat of molten wax, from which he will later emerge as one of many pieces of human statuary that line the hall in gleaming glass tubes. As you'll see after watching a few of these movies, such mechanisms of goon removal are an important consideration in the construction of these villain haunts, ranging from acid baths to piranha pits to giant, flesh rending busy box gears. Johnny's, if nothing else, is easily the most "green" of these, as you don't just lose a goon, but also gain a nice piece of art in the process.

BREAKDOWN: **Waxworks Of Death!**

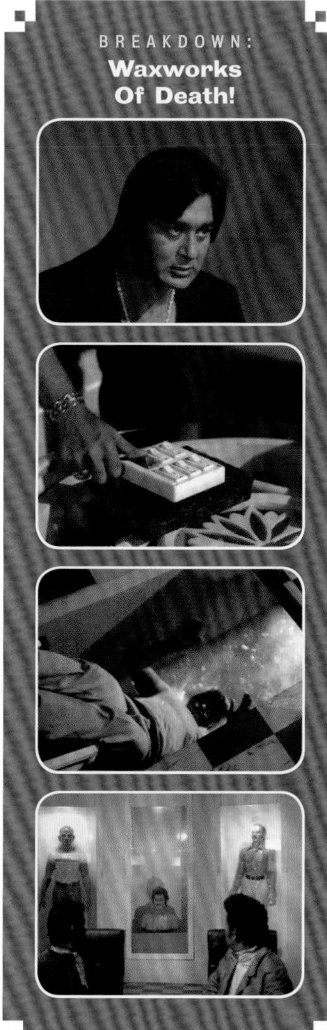

Johnny's lair also provides the setting for *Geetaa Mera Naam*'s most astonishing sequence, visualizing the song "Haan Mujhe Maar Daalo."The song is mimed by Sadhana, clad in white mini and go-go boots, as she's being lashed by Johnny's whip-wielding dungeon master, who stalks her mercilessly around the confines of the lair. At the opposite end of the hall, Helen, clad in a spangly chorus girl get-up, also mimes the song, albeit with a great deal more brio, and while dancing in a giant bubble sauna equipped with disco lights, mirrored walls and its own waterfall. In this she is accompanied by the serpentine writhings of a paunchy, pompadoured gentleman in a beige polyester bodysuit that looks like one of the uniforms from *Space: 1999.* "There is life in death, death in life," mime both women in turn. But in Sadhana's case the refrain is a mournful yet resigned acceptance of life's tragic nature, while in Helen's it's a dark celebration of eroticized violence. To drive this home, Helen's partner begins to pull her hair, slap her, and push her to the ground as the song reaches its crescendo, she all the while wearing an expression of pained ecstasy. In the end, what amazes most about the sequence is that the mind-numbing level of kitsch on display fails to rob it of its power.

Finally, *Geetaa Mera Naam* must be praised for providing an ideal showcase for the great Feroz Khan at his most breathtakingly manly. I can think of no moment more mythmaking than the picturization of the song "Mohabbat Hi Mohabbat," which Khan mimes while happily beating up a group of thugs who've interrupted his attempts to peacefully feed some monkeys in a grove—and this while simultaneously wooing both Sadhana and Helen. Here as elsewhere, the songwriting team of Laxmikant-Pyarelal really steps up to the plate, showing themselves capable of setting aside their traditionalist tendencies and delivering a score that is delightfully funky and thumping. All in all, it's emblematic of a film to which everyone involved brought, if not their best, then certainly their most, making *Geetaa Mera Naam* a keeper that's not to be missed.

QURBANI
"Sacrifice"

Released: 1980
Director: Feroz Khan
Stars: Feroz Khan, Vinod Khanna, Zeenat Aman, Amjad Khan, Aruna Irani, Amrish Puri, Shakti Kapoor, Dinesh Hingoo, Tun Tun, Viju Khote, Moolchand, Kader Khan, Mac Mohan, Bob Christo, Jagdeep, Narendra Nath, Natasha Chopra, Jagdeep, Raj Bharti, C.S. Aasie, Amjad Ali, Amarjeet, Azad, Bulbul, Ramesh Goyal, Harminder, Yusuf Irani, Irene, Jezebel, Ahmed Khan, Punnu, Rinchin, Sadiq, Sarwar, Sheron, Uttam Sodi, Surekha, Surjeet, Sunder Taneja, Yasmin
Writer: K.K. Shukla
Music: Kalyanji-Anandji (Kalyanji Virji Shah & Anandji Virji Shah)
Lyrics: Indeevar, Farooq Qaisar
Action Co-ordinator: Ravi Khanna

Rajesh (Feroz Khan) is a former motorcycle daredevil who has moved on to greater thrills in the world of high stakes thievery. Apprehended in the course of a daring burglary, Rajesh is sent up for a three year stretch, leaving his disco singer girlfriend Sheela (Zeenat Aman) vulnerable to the attentions of Amar (Vinod Khanna), a former driver for the criminal kingpin Rakka (Amrish Puri). Sheela stays true to Rajesh, however, and Amar, though clearly smitten, accepts the situation with manly stoicism, though he and Sheela continue to maintain a close friendship. In a stunning coincidence, Rajesh, upon his release from prison, happens upon Amar in a sticky situation and saves his life. The two, who have not previously met, establish a deep friendship, which deepens even further when Rajesh saves Amar's life a second time. Meanwhile, a creepily unhinged brother and sister duo (Aruna Irani and Shakti Kapoor) seek to entice Rajesh to steal back a fortune in jewels that Rakka has stolen from them. When Rajesh double crosses the pair, it leads to a situation that puts both Rajesh and Amar in mortal danger, as well as to the sacrifice of the film's title.

WATCHING FEROZ KHAN and Vinod Khanna in *Qurbani*, you might conclude that their characters are simply too confident in their rugged masculinity to have any qualms about being overtly demonstrative in their affections for one another. However, if you consider that it's the knee-weakeningly gorgeous Zeenat Aman, the alleged love interest of both men, who's being wholly ignored during all this tender hugging, shoulder rubbing and cheek tugging, you might be lead to another conclusion altogether. Of course, men in Bollywood movies are famously free in their capacity for brotherly PDA. That the tendency seems to stand out in especially stark relief in this case is most likely due to the musky, grease-stained backdrop of balls-out, testosterone wafting mayhem that *Qurbani* provides for it to play out against.

The world of *Qurbani* is one in which mechanic Bob Christo keeps a free standing brick wall in his auto body shop just so he

can demonstrate the power of his fists to any doubter who happens by, and a hay stack sits at the end of a jetty for the sole purpose of having a speeding car suddenly burst out from underneath it for no apparent reason. The fact that its hero is a famous motorcycle daredevil who's coupled with a famous disco diva sets the film in a sort of idealized 1970s universe reigned over by the perfect union of Evel Knievel and Donna Summer. And while, in keeping with Bollywood tradition, the film slows down during its middle third to focus on relationship drama, its bulk is so over-saturated with methed-up male aggression that it can't go five minutes without busting out into a fist fight, death-defying physical stunt or car chase. All of which is to say that, with *Qurbani*, director/star Feroz Khan, here making his third directorial effort, has reached his apotheosis.

With his early films, the task confronting Khan seems to have been that of reconciling the conventions of action films, as understood everywhere else in the world, with the peculiar narrative rhythms of Indian cinema, which didn't typically lend themselves to the kind of wall-to-wall thrills necessary to pleasing your run-of-the-mill genre fan. There were, of course, thrills to be had in mainstream Indian films, but often, thanks to all of the other narrative boxes that needed to be ticked off, they were delivered at too stingy a pace to satisfy viewers too impatient to wait for them. *Qurbani*, however, sets itself apart in that its high points are always well worth the wait, and stick with you enough to make the wait one marked more by anticipation than restlessness. Complementing this is the fact that, in the best Bollywood tradition, there is almost always an outlandish '70s outfit, garish bit of production design, over-the-top performance or skewed musical number on screen to keep you occupied when nothing's exploding.

Still—and as much as it pains me to say it—*Qurbani*, for all its strengths, does suffer from a bit of sloppy plotting. Most obviously, the love triangle between Rajesh, Amar and Sheela, though somewhat laboriously established, never gets to bear much dramatic fruit, since the film ultimately ends up being more about the love between Rajesh and Amar. As such, the romantic obstacles that would typically be thrown between male and female leads are here thrown between our two men of action, and the dramatic tension of the last act hinges largely on whether the two will mend their friendship and fall back into each others' arms before the film's pyrotechnic finale. Because of this, Zeenat Aman's character is reduced to being both window dressing (few opportunities are missed to have her get soaked with water) and a serially-imperiled pawn in the power plays between the heavies and heroes. In other words, anyone hoping to see her take part in any of the kung fu bad-assery she did in *Don* will be somewhat

disappointed—until she's doused with water, that is, at which point all previous expectations will be quickly forgotten.

In the plus column, the film benefits from a couple clever instances of misdirectional casting, including Amrish Puri's turn as a red herring villain who disappears from the action much sooner than expected. Another heavy on hand is Amjad Khan, the actor who played Bollywood's most iconic villain, *Sholay*'s Gabbar Singh. Yet here Khan is cast against type as a dogged police inspector who, having first put Rajesh away, is now tracking his every move in hopes of a misstep—and who also, in a curious touch of meta humor, is named Amjad Khan. Of course, Khan's mere presence gives the character a menacing edge, but we eventually see that the inspector, while having little faith in Rajesh's ability to reform, is more interested in justice than he is in harassment for its own sake. It's a performance that Khan clearly has fun with, playing off his own imposing demeanor with welcome injections of humor, and it's fun for us to watch as well, especially when we're treated to the rare sight of the actor sharing a goofy musical number with Aman.

Another of *Qurbani*'s greatest strengths, as anyone who's seen it will tell you, is its music. Scored by the team of Kalyanji-Anandji, the film boasts a hard hitting Hindi-funk soundtrack that almost makes all of those wide collars and questionably-patterned, tight-fitting flares look good. Furthermore, Zeenat Aman's disco numbers are as catchy as their picturizations are gaudy (although it should be noted that the best remembered among them, "Aap Jaisa Koi," was a non Kalyanji-Anandji track that became a breakthrough hit for its real vocalist, the then teenaged Pakistani singer Nazia Hassan). Aman's Sheela seems to have a new back-up band for every performance, including an all female ensemble whose incompetent miming on their instruments prefigures Robert Palmer's "Addicted to Love" video by a good few years.

Qurbani, not surprisingly, ends in a hail of flame and bullets, orchestrated in part by a wild eyed Aruna Irani in a rare, scenery-chewing dragon lady role. Yet, while suspense is evoked, there's a gleefulness to the destruction, as well. As with an earlier scene, in which a Mercedes Benz is introduced only to be systematically destroyed in a game of parking lot demolition derby, we get the sense that what we're really watching is Feroz Khan playing with some very expensive toys… and having an awesome time while he's at it.

AMAR AKBAR ANTHONY

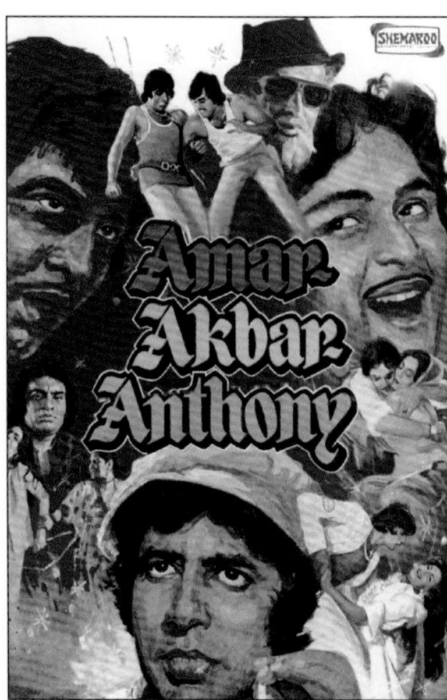

Released: 1977
Director: Manmohan Desai
Stars: Amitabh Bachchan, Vinod Khanna, Rishi Kapoor, Parveen Babi, Neetu Singh, Shabana Azmi, Jeevan, Pran, Nirupa Roy, Nasir Hussain, Ranjeet, Yusuf Khan, Kamal Kapoor, Shivraj, Helen, Mukri, Hercules, Pratima Devi, Moolchand, Master Bittoo, Master Ravi, Sabina, Master Tito, Nadira, Madhumati
Writers: Prayag Raj, Smt. Jeevanprabha M. Desai, Kader Khan, Pushpa Sharma, K.K. Shukla
Music: Laxmikant-Pyarelal (Laxmikant Shantaram Kudalkar & Pyarelal Ramprasad Sharma)
Lyrics: Anand Bakshi
Action Composer: Ravi Khanna

Okay, you might want to sit down for this one…

Wealthy sociopath Robert (Jeevan) convinces his loyal chauffeur Kishanlal (Pran) to take the fall for a hit and run death he caused, promising to care for Kishanlal's wife and children while he's in prison. Later, upon his release, Kishanlal finds that Robert has not been true to his word, that his wife is suffering from untreated TB, and that his three young sons are near starvation. When Kishanlal goes to confront the cruelly indifferent Robert, things do not go well, forcing him to make his escape by stealing a car that Robert exclaims is "filled with gold."

Meanwhile, Kishanlal's wife Bharati (Nirupa Roy) decides to commit suicide. Kishanlal returns home to find her note and, fearing the imminent arrival of Robert and his men, gathers up his sons and deposits them in front of a mosque for safety. A high speed chase follows, which ends with Kishanlal crashing the car. The effort-averse officers who arrive on the scene then take a cursory glance at the flaming car and make the determination that Kishanlal and his sons are all dead. Kishanlal, however, is very much alive and steals off with a crate full of Robert's gold that falls from the car's trunk.

His sons, meanwhile, have become separated. Little Anthony wanders into a Catholic church, where he is taken in by the priest. Akbar is found by a Muslim man. And Amar gets hit by a car and is rescued by the passing police superintendent. Since all available evidence points to them being orphans, a "finders keepers" rule seems to apply as far as these stray children are concerned. We also see that the boys' mother is not in fact dead, but is instead running madly through the woods for some reason, until she gets whacked in the head by a falling branch and is permanently blinded.

Twenty-two years later, Anthony (Amitabh Bachchan) has grown up to be a troublemaking street brawler making his living as a bootlegger and black marketer, and also a Catholic. Amar has become a tough-as-nails police inspector and a Hindu, and the lighthearted Akbar (Rishi Kapoor) seems to be mostly about wooing pretty lady doctor Salma (Neetu Singh) while being a Muslim. The three are united after Bharati suffers an accident and a call is put out for donors who match her rare blood type. The experience of sharing their blood in this manner creates a bond between the men, as well as between them and the old woman, who, despite

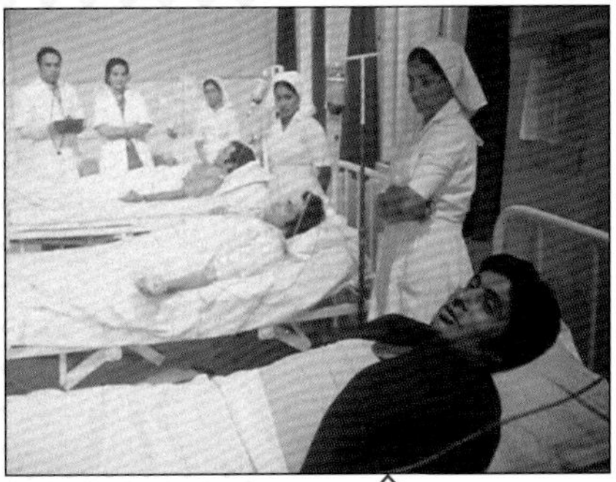

not knowing their true connection, comes to refer to them as her "sons." Meanwhile (there's that word again), we find that Kishanlal, thanks to his sudden infusion of wealth, has in the ensuing years turned the tables on Robert, and is now in control of his empire, with Robert groveling abjectly at his feet.

Part of Kishanlal's successful scheme to gain leverage over Robert involved the abduction of his young daughter, Jenny, whom he then sent abroad to prevent contact with her father. Now back in India, the adult Jenny (Parveen Babi) falls victim to an obsessive plot by Robert to steal her back. In this he is aided by Jenny's corrupt bodyguard Zebisko (Yusuf Khan), who has developed romantic designs on the girl. Unfortunately for these rascals, Jenny, since her return, has fallen hard for Anthony. It is now up to Anthony, with the help of his two undercover brothers, to effect a rescue. In the process, all connections will ultimately be revealed.

FOR MANY SEASONED LOVERS of Bollywood, *Amar Akbar Anthony* encapsulates all of the joys of classic Masala cinema at its most manic and convoluted—a fact which likely accounts for it being the most fondly remembered title from Manmohan Desai's 1977 quartet of "super hits" (the other three being *Parvarish*, *Chacha Bhatija* and the bipolar period epic *Dharam Veer*).

For Bollywood novices, however, *Amar Akbar Anthony* might prove to be something of an acid test. One's reaction to it can be a pretty clear indication of whether he or she should venture further into this branch of world cinema or simply close the gate and turn away.

Perhaps most indicative of *AAA*'s narrative extremes is the performance by Amitabh Bachchan, who goes from wearing a floppy pimp hat and literally punching people through walls one minute to jumping out of a giant Easter egg and performing a novelty song in which he walks on air the next. Furthermore, the film's surfeit of over-the-top melodrama insures that that performance looks not unlike an awards show highlight reel, with Bachchan jumping from one big, emotive showcase moment to the next. He even gives us that time tested number in which the angry hero, confronted by tragedy, calls the Almighty on the carpet and demands a miracle (which he, of course, gets).

It should be noted, however, that it's Vinod Khanna, rather than Bachchan, who is put front and center in a pivotal reunion scene. Thus it can't be said that the whole show belongs to the Big B alone, even if it is pretty clear who the top dog is. Nevertheless, Khanna's role is, by comparison, less dimensional than that of his co-star, as is that of Rishi Kapoor, who mostly seems relegated to the Mickey Dolenz role of tackling comic relief and lighthearted song and dance bits. Fortunately, all three are bolstered by a terrific supporting cast, treating us to the joy of seeing career character actors like Jeevan, Pran, Nasir Hussain, Nirupa Roy and Ranjeet doing what they were seemingly born to do. Also deserving note is Indian art cinema star Shabana Azmi, who is gravely underutilized as a lady grifter with a hard luck story who somehow (as in, mostly off-screen) wins the heart of Khanna's tough cop.

Unlike me, you don't have to write a detailed synopsis of *Amar Akbar Anthony*, which means that you're free to just sit back and let its ludicrously serpentine plot wash over you like the hurriedly unreeling tone poem of a sleep talking madman. This, at least, is what I recommend. Nonetheless, I would be remiss if I didn't warn you that, despite its frantic pacing and energetic performances, watching it can be an exhausting experience. Manmohan Desai's desire to entertain is no doubt fervent and sincere, but he nonetheless often seems as if he doesn't know when to let go of his audience's lapels. Thus a denouement that is more or less generically preordained is won only at the expense of sitting through a long, antic masquerade sequence reminiscent of an extended Marx Brothers skit—after which, of course, there is a long and protracted fist fight to settle things once and for all.

So out of control is Desai's drive to stuff *Amar Akbar Anthony* to bursting that the film ends up containing instances of what seem like orphaned elements from previous drafts, such as the pointless, eleventh hour introduction of a twin brother for Jeevan's character. Happily, the director's underlying message of unity and tolerance manages to survive above the mix. Pointed reference is made to the brothers' initial separation taking place on Independence Day, the date marking India's freedom from British rule and the subsequent partitioning of India and Pakistan. This adds symbolic—if characteristically unsubtle—weight to the moment, at the film's conclusions, when the three heroes of different faiths realize their true and literal brotherhood.

Amar Akbar Anthony's ending also neatly demonstrates the foundational philosophy of the Indian "lost and found" films as a whole. As in other movies of its type, the separation of *AAA's* central family creates such a profound imbalance that the entire universe seems to collude in creating a series of spuriously outlandish coincidences in order to set things right. As the viewer, it's up to you whether to throw up your hands and roll along with this or to turn the page. For instance, if you have not surrendered to *Amar Akbar Anthony*'s logic by the time of seeing a blind Nirupa Roy crawling on her hands and knees across a crowded temple to a shrine to the saint Sai Baba, *which then magically restores her sight*, I think it's safe to say you're barking up the wrong cinematic tree.

INTERNATIONAL CROOK

Released: 1974
Director: Pachhi
Stars: Dharmendra, Saira Banu, Feroz Khan, Om Prakash, Hiralal, Rajan Haksar, Susheela, Rathod, Sunder, Manorama, Raj Mehra, Jayshree T., Habib, Sulochana Chatterjee, Jagdeep, Jagdish Raj, M.B. Shetty
Writers: R.S. Choudhury, Aziz Kashmiri, Pachhi
Music: Shankar-Jaikishan (Shankarsingh Raghuwanshi & Jaikishan Dayabhai Pankal)
Lyrics: Aziz Kashmiri

Policeman Rajesh (Feroz Khan) is sent to the coastal city of Alibag to break up a nest of smugglers that is operating there. Once there, he reunites with his beloved school friend Shekhar (Dharmendra), who is now the General Manager of a shipping company. At the same time, Shekhar reunites with his childhood sweetheart Seema (Saira Banu), who happens to be the daughter of the Chief Customs Inspector (Raj Mehra). Shekhar and Seema both seem interested in rekindling their romance, but when Rajesh confesses that he too has feelings for Seema, the two men start trying to outdo one another in terms of honor and loyalty, each insisting that the other marry Seema—regardless of whatever Seema might want were she actually given say in the matter. Eventually it is Shekhar who marries Seema, and the two set off to Europe for their honeymoon, where Seema soon begins to suspect that there is more to Shekhar than meets the eye. And indeed, upon returning home, she discovers that Shekhar is secretly operating as the notorious smuggler Tiger Singh, conducting his gang's dirty business from a cave lair beneath their home. Shekhar is harboring an even deeper secret, however, one that involves his quest for revenge against the smugglers who murdered his family years ago.

IT'S A FACT THAT MANY BOLLYWOOD productions of the '70s were independent affairs, bereft of corporate backing and, thanks to the reluctance of India's banks to throw their lot in with the entertainment industry, such niceties as completion bonds. As a result, it was not unheard of for the money to occasionally run out and for production to be halted until more could be raised, sometimes leading to production times that extended from months into years. Now, I'm not saying that this was necessarily the case with *International Crook*. Nonetheless, there are unmistakable signs that its wrap time occurred quite a long time after its first day's traditional coconut breaking ritual.

Among the most telltale of those signs are the changes throughout to the hair styles, fashions and waistlines of *International Crooks*'s two stars, Dharmendra and Feroz Khan, who actually switch between 1960s and 1970s versions of themselves from one scene to the next. This culminates in more time travel paradoxes than the average episode of *Doctor Who*, with one scene depicting 1960s Dharmendra stepping into a car and then stepping out of it as 1970s Dharmendra, and another showing 1970s Feroz Khan having a phone conversation with 1960s Dharmendra. One benefit of this quirk is that it gives us a handy way to compare the shifting ideal of the Bollywood hero from one decade to the next. 1960s Dhamendra and Feroz are every Indian mother's dream, crisp and flawlessly clean cut, with haircuts you can set your watch by (thanks, Grandpa Simpson), while their 1970s incarnations are shaggy haired and defiantly open shirted.

All of this is not to say that *International Crook* might be a significantly better film if not for its time-lapse leading men. To the contrary, I must sadly report that that particular flaw is merely just a symptom of a larger pattern of haphazard neglect evidenced in *International Crook*'s overall half-assed construction. Nonetheless, there are bright spots. Shankar-Jaikishan's theme song is amazing, consisting of the word "crook" sung incessantly, like someone held a dark mirror up to the *Batman* theme. Also, Saira Bannu, while not a commanding presence in herself, models some pretty amazing clothes, such as one number that combines fishnet knee-highs and hot pants with a yellow pirate blouse and matching headband. (To be fair, given Khan and Dharmendra's simmering bromanticism here, it's possible such peacockery was necessary for her to register at all.)

Had *International Crook* not suffered whatever delays beset it and seen release without the assemblage of anachronistic inserts and dodgy process shots that now holds it together, it would have greeted the world as a fairly average 1960s Indian "Social" drama featuring lots of to-die-for atomic furniture. At the same time, though, it's an example of a whole other Indian sub-genre: the "Patriotic" film. As such, it suffers no lack of people looking into the camera and passionately decrying the smugglers as "traitors" whose activities are a dagger in the heart of Mother India. There's also no dearth of the typical Patriotic films' xenophobia, with appearances by a host of suspicious and uncouth Arabs, Turks, East Asians, and white Europeans. These last, as is so often the case in Indian films from this period, are largely portrayed by glassy-eyed flower children who are apparently taking a break from their drug tourism to pick up a couple extra dollars as extras.

Probably the best thing that I can say about *International Crook* is that someone loved it enough to finish it. That person may have been its director, Pachhi, an actor and producer who apparently has only one other directorial credit to his name. Whatever the case, it was obviously a process that involved no little work, including the unenviable task of wresting an increasingly middle aged Dharmendra and Feroz Khan away from other projects to read lines written for heroes of a type they'd long ago left behind. All in all, it speaks to a level of dedication that is admirable, although perhaps not altogether advisable.

ZANJEER
"The Chain"

Released: 1973
Director: Prakash Mehra
Stars: Amitabh Bachchan, Jaya Bhaduri, Pran, Om Prakash, Ajit, Bindu, Iftekhar, Keshto Mukherjee, Randhir, Gulshan Bawra, Ram Mohan, Yunus Parvez, B.B. Bhalla, Sanjana, Purnima, M. Rajan, Goga Kapoor, Tiger, Kirti Sethi, Sushil, Bhushan Tiwari, Gulloo, Omkar, Nandita Thakur, Satyendra Kapoor, D.K. Sapru, Amrit Pal, Master Rajesh, Dhanraj, Javed Khan, Raju, Makarnai, Ranvir Raj, Maqbool, Ramnath, Yograj, Krishan Dhawan, Ashalata Wabgaonkar, Subhash, Narayan, Mac Mohan, Ram P. Sethi
Writers: Salim-Javed (Salim Khan & Javed Akhtar)
Music: Kalyanji-Anandji (Kalyanji Virji Shah & Anandji Virji Shah)
Lyrics: Gulshan Bawra
Fights: Ravi Khanna

Ranjit, a low level thug, returns from prison to find that his infant daughter has succumbed to the very bootleg medicine manufactured by his criminal employer, Mr. Patel. He resigns, prompting Patel to dispatch his right hand man, Teja (Ajit), to tie up loose ends. Teja shoots Ranjit and his wife dead in front of their young son, Vijay, who, from his hiding place, is only able to see the chain on Teja's wrist, which bears a distinctive horse charm. The orphaned Vijay is then taken into the home of the police chief, where he grows up haunted by the charm's image.

Skip forward twenty-odd years, and Vijay (Amitabh Bachchan) is now a police officer with a troubled disciplinary history who is starting over in a new precinct. He inaugurates his tour of duty by kindling an unlikely friendship with Sher Khan (Pran), a Muslim gambling lord to whom he serves notice in the form of a sound beating. Recognizing Vijay as a fellow "Tiger," Sher Khan agrees on the spot to close down his dens and swears his lifelong friendship. Sometime later, Vijay starts to receive anonymous tips about truck loads of rotgut hooch being run by Teja and his gang. He manages to intercept the first shipment with little difficulty, but, on the second occasion, the truck leads them on a chase and strikes a group of school children, killing five of them. A scrappy young knife sharpener, Mala (Jaya Bhaduri), witnesses the accident and, despite efforts by Teja's men to buy her silence, is able to identify the driver, Goga (Goga Kapoor), to the police.

When Teja's men seek payback against Mala, she seeks shelter with Vijay, who takes her in. A tentative romance between the two lonely souls starts to bloom. Meanwhile, Vijay subjects Goga to ever tougher interrogations and is coming close to exposing the whole operation. In order to shut this down, Teja pays a small time thief to whom Vijay has made a business loan (Keshto Mukherjee) to frame him for bribery. The result is a six month prison stay for Vijay, who, though stripped of his badge, emerges from stir with a feverish resolve to hunt Teja down. He shadows the high living bandit at every opportunity, never missing a chance to personally deliver an ominous threat.

Meanwhile, Mala, eager to settle down to a quiet family life with Vijay, finds his obsession with justice an obstacle, and begs him to forget his vendetta against Teja. Out of love for her, he agrees, and meets with the kingpin to arrange a truce. However, the curtain of domesticity soon begins to chafe against Vijay, as he is still all too well aware of all of the corruption and murder that lies beyond it. Given no choice, Mala urges him to get it out of his system and follow his vengeful desires. In this, Vijay finds an unexpected ally in his formerly anonymous tipster, who is revealed to be D'Silva (Om Prakash), a Catholic man who has lost three of his sons to Teja's toxic moonshine.

***ZANJEER*, WHICH WAS ONE OF INDIA'S** top films of 1973, was the movie that blew it all up for Amitabh Bachchan, ending a period of struggle in under-recognized romantic roles and putting him well on the fast track to superstardom, as well as—thanks to the machinations of up and coming screen scribes Salim-Javed—introducing his trademark "Angry Young Man" character to Hindi audiences. (It was also, I should add, the first of a series of nineteen films in which he would adopt the character name Vijay.) Not only this, but *Zanjeer* also bears the heavy onus of being the picture that wrested once and for all the tropes of the action genre out of the ghetto of B grade "Stunt" pictures and into the Indian mainstream.

It's hard to imagine that this last development left audiences of the day unmoved, as *Zanjeer* throughout strives to put its most violent foot forward. In its opening minutes we see a young married couple bloodily riddled with bullets in front of their own child, and then a musical number in which the future Mrs. Bachchan, Jaya Bahduri, extols the benefits of a sharp knife while repeatedly lunging at the camera with one. In keeping with this, the mean streets of *Zanjeer* are mean indeed, with their grime, sweat and dirt palpable in every frame. In fact, one almost gets the sense of a grittiness being lost later in the decade when the genre gave itself over more to lavish lairs, kung fu battles and Bondian trappings.

At the same time, in terms of the development of the Angry Young Man, *Zanjeer* is a bit of a baby step. Unlike the more traditional antiheroes that Bachchan would play in later years, this Vijay starts out as a staunch believer in law and order—much like the typically upright police heroes of 1960s Bollywood thrillers—and only takes things into his own hands once he has been Pushed Too Far. It's also worth noting that this outlaw version of him is far from the iconized badass that we would see in films like *Don*, and that Vijay, after his release from prison, is instead presented as a good man crippled by rage. So miserable

is he in the modest suburban Eden that his loving wife has created for him that she must practically push him out the door with gun in hand to get the job done.

Because it occurs at the beginning of the Bachchan phenomenon, *Zanjeer* benefits greatly from a consistently sober tone. Not yet required to provide something for everyone, the star is free from the clowning and pandering that he was increasingly required to do in subsequent films, instead relying on the smoldering intensity to which he is so naturally inclined. The film is additionally energized by a fantastic supporting cast. Jaya Bhaduri and Pran both shine, while admittedly playing characters that are somewhat generic. Mala is the charmingly scrappy yet vulnerable street brawler, and dignifies the turn with spark and humanity. Pran's Sher Khan, for his part, is something of the picture's heart and soul, both a criminal and a man of faith, flawed but with a huge heart, who generously sings us into the third act maelstrom with an upbeat traditional about the value of friendship and brotherhood.

As for Ajit, it was his role as Teja in *Zanjeer* that—in much the same way that Amjad Khan's turn as Gabbar Singh in *Sholay* did for him—cemented the template for countless villain portrayals to come. Everything you see here is pretty much emblematic of the Ajit brand as it went forward: the crisp tuxedo, ever present snifter, the purring self regard—all put paid by the iconic moment when Teja shrugs off the depredations of his killer hooch by simply saying "I drink Scotch." This serves to stoke all the more our thirst for that climactic moment when our everyman hero, who elsewhere refers to Teja as "a highly respected big shot," beats the tar out of the well-heeled heel while dragging him up and down the length of his Olympic size swimming pool.

The last thing that needs to be said about *Zanjeer* is that, as an action film, it is rousingly successful. The aforementioned consistency of tone is partially responsible for this, leaving it with a narrative that is less load-bearing and more economical than many of the Masala pictures that were to come, allowing us to hit all the necessary dramatic points while still affording room for a steady parade of well directed chases and brutal fights. The total makes for a surprisingly brisk 145 minutes, as well as a bracing entryway into the glorious age of Bachchan.

APRADH
"Crime"

Released: 1972
Director: Feroz Khan
Stars: Feroz Khan, Mumtaz, Prem Chopra, Siddhu, Faryal, Iftekhar, Kuljeet, Shyam Kumar, Brahm Bhardwaj, Shetty, Habib, Bhushan Tiwari, Helen, Tun Tun, Madan Puri, Polson, Ranvir Raj, Pahelwan, Khursheed Khan, Hercules, Mukri, Randhir, Kishan Mehta, Jagdish Raj
Writers: Akhtar-Ul-Iman, Omkar Sahib and "F.K. International's Story Dept."
Music: Kalyanji-Anandji (Kalyanji Virji Shah & Anandji Virji Shah)
Lyrics: Indeevar
Fights: Mohammad Ali

Meena (Mumtaz), a young Indian woman living in Germany, makes off with a necklace worth 1.5 million Rs. after pulling an elaborate scam. When the police pick up her trail, she is forced to abandon her car and, in order to complete her getaway, must flag down a passing motorist. This is Ram (Feroz Khan), a celebrated Indian formula racer who is in Germany for a tournament—and who doesn't seem to need much persuading when it comes to giving a lift to a pretty stranger. When their car approaches a border checkpoint, Meena surreptitiously slips the necklace into Ram's pocket, but is later unable to retrieve it. When informed of this, the leader of Meena's gang, Nath (Siddhu), angrily dispatches gang member Fifi (Faryal) to Ram's hotel room disguised as a maid to find it. Fifi comes back empty handed, but Ram soon thereafter turns up at Meena's door bearing the necklace. This necklace, however, later proves to be fake, burdening Meena with finding the real article under threat of death from the gang. Meanwhile, love has blossomed between her and Ram, and the two begin making plans to return to India together. But first, Ram exposes Fifi as the real thief of the necklace, after which she is murdered by Nath and Ricky, Nath's right hand man. At the final race of the tournament, the gang turns up to finish off Ram and Meena, but Ram turns the tables on them, leaving Nath and Ricky locked in the trunk of his car.

Ram and Meena next prepare to leave Germany, but first Ram is handed a package at the airport by a stranger who claims that it's medicine for Ram's brother Harnam. Upon arriving in India, Ram finds that it is instead smuggled jewels which a rival of Harnam's named "Arab Sheikh" has planted in order to frame him. Ram is hauled off by the police and, despite his protestations of innocence, is summarily tried, convicted, and thrown in jail, only to emerge some months later to start life anew with Meena. It is at this point that the felonious Harnam (Prem Chopra) turns up on his doorstep, pressuring him to join his gang. Ram, determined to walk the narrow path, refuses, but when Ranjit (Shyam Kumar), a rogue member of Harnam's gang, sees fit to frame Ram for looting his employers' foundry, he reconsiders. He and Ram then plot to steal a cache of Arab Sheikh's smuggled gold as an act of revenge, though, in the event, Harnam also kills the Sheikh for good measure. The hijackers are then afforded only a brief honeymoon with the gold, as Ranjit soon thereafter kidnaps Meena and demands that Ram deliver the entirety of it to him as ransom. Harnam tries in vain to dissuade Ram from this course of action, telling him that sacrificing Meena will leave him rich enough to buy many more wives. True love, however, wins out, with the result a chaotic shootout involving Ranjit and his gang, a squad of policemen led by Superintendent Das (Iftekhar), and the two once again estranged brothers.

MAKING HIS DEBUT HERE as producer and director, triple threat Feroz Khan lets us know from *Apradh*'s opening moments that he has no intention of sticking to Bollywood business-as-usual. The choice of a music-free title sequence is indeed a radical one, and letting the credits play to the roar of the engines of the racing cars on screen has a distinct "New Hollywood" feel to it.

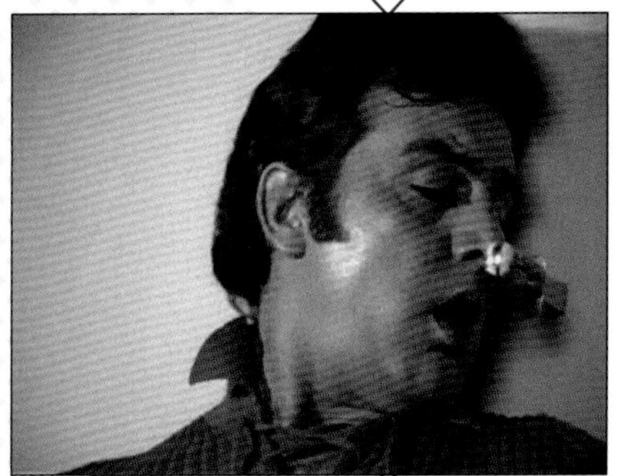

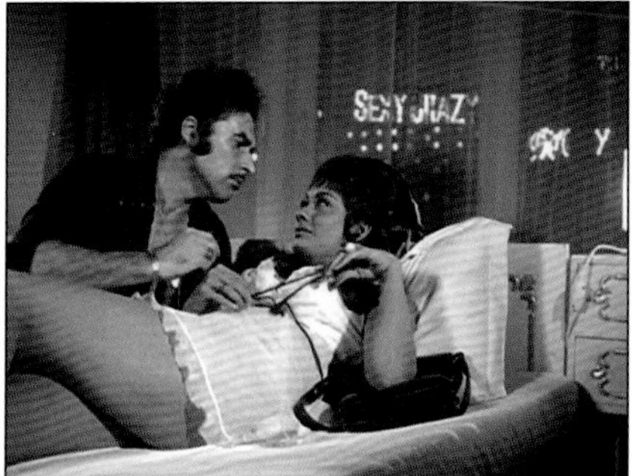

In addition, the German setting of the film's first half gives it a modish, European flavor not often found in Indian films of the era—one that Khan gives added immediacy through an abundant use of location shooting and intimate handheld camera work. The resulting naturalism makes the interwoven soundstage bound scenes, with their views overlooking patently phony model skylines, look more like self conscious artifice than the industry standard that they are.

It also must be said that the bad guys in *Apradh*'s German section, made up of some lesser known faces from the filmi rogues gallery, are just about the most believably nasty you'll find in '70s Hindi cinema. Nath and his crew are one sweaty, twitchy bunch—one might even venture meth-addled—and as a result project a real air of depravity and menace that suggests Frank Booth and his *Blue Velvet* cronies come to Frankfurt via Bombay. Nath's right hand man Ricky (Kuljeet), a giggling psychopath in bug-like sunglasses, cannot contain his arousal while murdering Fifi in her bathtub, turning both spigots on full blast in an act of ecstatic release as she gasps her last breath. (Khan, an enemy of subtlety, then drives his point home by giving us a shot of Fifi's death visage framed in milky white bath fluid.) Nath, for his part, seems on the constant verge of flying into a drug and rage fueled conniption, while Fifi, in life, is turned on by the violence around her to the point of essaying a perpetual Hindi-funk version of Dorothy Malone's Dance of Death from *Written on the Wind*.

The baddies in *Apradh*'s India-based section, on the other hand, are much more what we're used to. At their head we have the familiar face of Prem Chopra, a cozy vessel of trope-dependent villainy if there ever was

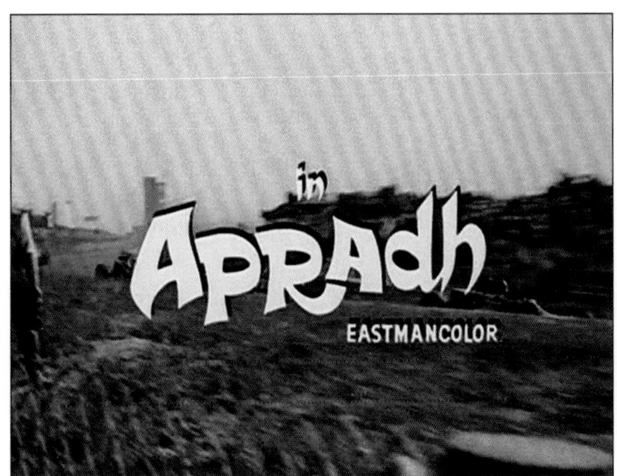

one, and among their ranks such trustworthy gunsels as Shetty, Shyam Kumar and, as the requisite moll/nautch girl, Helen. Harnam even has the expected lair, a combination casino and artificial grotto filled with stoned-looking Caucasian bikini girls, gaudy taxidermy and erotic statuary, and which comes complete with a pointlessly rotating bar and in-house psychedelic mariachi band. It is here, in fact, that Helen mimes to Asha Bhosle's take on Kalyanji-Anandji's "Ae Naujawan Hai Sab," a big hit that would later relieve the Black Eyed Peas of having to write their own hook for "Don't Phunk with My Heart."

Apradh's odd bifurcated structure calls into question whether Khan, who aspired toward the international market, in fact intended to make a movie that could be neatly divided into separate Euro- and Indian-friendly wholes. The two sections truly have nothing to do with one another, with Feroz and Mumtaz's characters—sexy and adventurous in one, pious and bland in the other—maintaining little consistency from one half to the next. True, the Indian episode does keep pace, thanks to a regular infusion of car chases and fist fights, but loses the rough exploitation edge of what preceded it, instead focusing on a fairly typical bit of brother-versus-brother masala melodrama.

Where Khan *is* consistent, however, is in pushing, throughout *Apradh*, the Indian censor's stringent limits on sex and violence. In addition to the aforementioned death by bukkake, we have a scene where a bare-chested Ram lies atop Meena in the couple's marital bed, the covers leaving to our imagination the extent of contact taking place. In another scene, Khan suggests a jarring level of mayhem by quick cutting between Fifi's frenzied dancing and snippets of Meena being beaten and tortured by the gang. All of this is part and parcel of the director/star's aggressively masculine screen universe, one that sees his distractible camera ogling muscle cars and women's asses with equal ardor. The only thing as reliable is Khan's fondness for gimmicky camera compositions, be they shot through keyholes, car mirrors, or the fancy latticework that Indian directors seem so unable to leave unexamined.

In the end, *Apradh* engages us as much as a mystery than as a thriller—the mystery being what Feroz Khan and his writers, Akhtar-Ul-Iman and Omkar Sahib, intended in making it. True, Indian cinema is rife with uneven, patchwork creations, but it's to Khan's credit—and the high level of craftsmanship evident throughout his work as a director—that one suspects there was a method to his madness here. And really, it is that madness that makes *Apradh* overall an enjoyable ride despite the bumps along the way. Khan might not have hit the sweet spot until two films later, with *Qurbani*, but we can still see unmistakably here the work of a genre visionary with a passion for action.

SAAZISH
"Conspiracy"

Released: 1975
Director: Kalidas
Stars: Saira Banu, Dharmendra, David Abraham, Brahm Bhardwaj, Helen, Iftekhar, Dev Kumar, Murad, Rajendra Nath, Paintal, Madan Puri, Jagdish Raj
Writers: Ranjan Bose, Ramesh Pant
Music: Shankar-Jaikishan (Shankarsingh Raghuwanshi & Jaikishan Dayabhai Pankal)
Lyrics: Hasrat Jaipuri
Fights: Master Munna

Indian beauty queen Sunita (Saira Banu) has just won the title of Miss Cosmos at a pageant in Hong Kong. With barely enough time to bask in the warm attentions of the world press, she is whisked away to her first important order of duty—presenting the trophy at an international racing competition! Here she meets and instantly falls in love with hunky race car driver Jai (Dharmendra). After a brief courtship which essentially involves Sunita chasing him all over the island and singing at him, Jai finally relents to Sunita's charms. Everything goes swimmingly for a while, until a fateful ferry ride results in Sunita stumbling upon an international gang's plot to smuggle two billion dollars' worth of stolen gold out of the country. This, in turn, results in Sunita being relentlessly hunted down by the gang. Meanwhile, Jai is captured and taken to the inner sanctum of the gang's mysterious masked leader, where he shockingly offers to kill Sunita in exchange for his life and a sizeable payoff. Is it a ruse? Later, Jai convinces Sunita to flee the country with him, only to have the cruise ship on which they've booked passage turn out to be the very one on which the gold is being smuggled.

***SAAZISH* MAKES A FITTING** companion piece to *International Crook*, in that both films are haphazard mid '70s Dharmendra vehicles marked by conspicuous evidence of haste and underfunding. *Saazish* even shows similar signs of having been filmed on a delayed schedule, with Dharmendra's girth and hairstyle changing dramatically from shot to shot. Mind you, this practice isn't radical to the point of providing the dizzying sense of decade hopping that it does in *International Crook*, but it nonetheless contributes to the film having a cobbled together feel. Further adding to the air of negligence are the lazy rear projection shots, which at one point make Saira Banu's car appear to be traveling sideways through traffic, and the opening car race, which offers some of the most ham-handed blending of stock and studio footage I've seen. Then of course there are the cruise ship passengers played by extras who stare ahead affectlessly as a moaning, blood soaked murder victim staggers across deck and dies in Saira Banu's arms.

Yet, unlike *International Crook*, which merely consumes the viewer with speculation about what went wrong, *Saazish* has a trashy energy that goes hand in hand with its trashy execution. The result is something like an Indian action movie stripped to its skivvies; unburdened by any lofty social concerns—or intelligence, for that matter—and rife with ridiculous, poverty row comic book trappings. Primary among these is the film's masked villain, who—with his blue, featureless visage—is an undisguised appropriation of the *fin de siecle* fictional French master criminal Fantomas, in particular as depicted in the tongue-in-cheek late '60s film series from director Andre Hunebelle. More archaic is faux Fantomas's right arm, an orientalist henchman named Mr. Wong, portrayed by Madan Puri in a yellow-face turn that comes off more like something out of an uninhibitedly racist wartime American serial.

Thankfully, anchoring all of this B movie detritus firmly in the 1970s is Dharmendra, who does his best to puff out his chest and bellow defiantly at these rickety spook house inhabitants as if they actually constituted some kind of threat. Unfortunately, no amount of bellowing can prevent the shrill and irksome performance by the top billed Saira Banu from taking the wind out of the movie's sails a bit. As happy as I was in theory to see a turning of the gender tables in *Saazish*'s presentation of the usual courtship-by-relentless-stalking scenario, Banu's off key strivings at reinventing herself as a cartoonish sex kitten were too hair raising to make it enjoyable in any way.

Given much of the above, it's hard to deny that *Saazish* is a pretty terrible film, and for that reason I don't fault Keith Allison, my colleague over at Teleport City, for hating it passionately. Still, I have to confess to having a soft spot for it. For one thing, I admire *Saazish*'s consistency; it's unerringly dumb from first frame to last, never hinting at any quality that might unfairly raise our expectations. Even the songs are dumb, with the most memorable number being the novelty tune "How Sweet Dadaji," which starts with Saira Banu jumping out of her own birthday cake (and, given her character's intelligence, probably surprising herself, as well). Furthermore, the clear sense you get that the film was made up by its makers as they went hastily along gives it an appealingly scrappy, seat-of-the-pants charm.

For its second half, *Saazish* leaves behind its somewhat underutilized Hong Kong locations and shifts into a sort of trash take on Agatha Christie, placing Dharmendra and Saira on a cruise ship with a rogue's gallery of potential suspects and an ever increasing pile of murdered bodies. Among the former are Helen, doing a delicious femme fatale turn as the ship's dancer Madam Lola, comic relief bumbler Rajendra Nath, and Dev Kumar as an eccentric Buddhist priest called Mr. Han. All end up taking part in an epically incoherent climactic fist fight and gun battle on the ship's deck, during which literally everyone on board is revealed to be either in cahoots with the bad guys or an Interpol agent in disguise.

This last scene also contains what some female viewers of *Saazish* consider to be its sole saving grace, as well as what accounts for it sometimes being referred to by them as "the one with Dharmendra in his chaddies." That is to say that Dharmendra performs much of his derring-do in this final dust-up pantsless but for his tighty whiteys. While personally unmoved by the sight, I appreciate *Saazish*'s egalitarian approach to providing its viewers with eye candy, even if, in some cases, it's better seen than heard.

WARRANT

Released: 1975
Director: Pramod Chakravorty
Stars: Dev Anand, Zeenat Aman, Pran, Dara Singh, Ajit, Satish Kaul, Birbal, Arpana Choudhary, Jankidas, Seema Kapoor, Viju Khote, Sujit Kumar, Sulochana Latkar, Lalita Pawar, Madan Puri, Barbara Shankar, Joginder, M.B. Shetty
Writers: Sachin Bhowmick, Vrajendra Gaur
Music: Rahul Dev Burman (R.D. Burman)
Lyrics: Anand Bakshi
Fights: Veeru Devgan

Arun, a conscientious jailer (Dev Anand), is saved during a prison riot by Dinesh (Satish Kaul), an inmate who has been sentenced to death for a murder he says he did not commit. Arun becomes convinced of Dinesh's innocence and, when he cannot postpone the execution by legal means, breaks him out of prison, becoming a fugitive himself in the process. Unfortunately, Arun's by-the-book police chief father (Pran) is not about to let family feeling stand in the way of his harsh conception of justice, and so issues a warrant ordering that Arun be captured dead or alive. Meanwhile, a white-suited Mr. Big by the name of The Master (Ajit)—the mastermind behind the murder Dinesh was framed for—puts a hit out on Arun and Dinesh in order to prevent them from discovering the truth. To this end he hires Rita (Zeenat Aman), a stylish assassin so ruthlessly efficient that she only loads her pistol with one bullet for each intended victim. As a result, Arun and Dinesh must conduct their search for The Real Killer while being hunted from all sides—a state of affairs which forces them to resort to the use of a number of putatively clever disguises, mostly involving mustaches.

DEV ANAND ESTABLISHED HIMSELF as a Bollywood icon in the late '40s and '50s by playing the suave protagonist of noir thrillers like Guru Dutt's *Baazi*. By the time he made *Warrant*, however, he'd grown a bit long in the tooth (for example, Pran, who plays Anand's father in the film, was only three years his senior at the time). Nonetheless, he seemed determined, not only to hold onto his leading man status, but also to reinvent himself as a 1970s style action hero in the mold of Amitabh Bachchan.

Part of the strategy for granting Anand eternal youth was casting him opposite much younger starlets like Parveen Babi and, as here, Zeenat Aman, an actress who had gotten her first big break from Anand in his 1971 directorial effort *Hare Rama Hare Krishna*. Your results may vary, but I tend to find something irredeemably creepy about Anand in these later films. He has a smug self-regard that might come across as roguish and intriguing in a younger actor, but which instead comes across as unctuous and insinuating, especially when he's pawing over a woman young enough to be his daughter.

Still, if you are able to get past this, later vehicles like *Warrant* surround him with all of the thrilling bells and whistles of the action genre, and can actually be great fun despite him.

And, to be sure, Zeenat Aman is nothing if not thrilling in her role here as the hit woman Rita. So much so, that it pains one to see her succumb, as she inevitably must, to Arun/Anand's charms. Yet succumb she does, leaving Ajit's Master and his minions to step up as the principle threat to the protagonists. Oh, and what minions these are, including among their number a small army of Smurf-like, blue-suited goons, an assortment of numerically designated lackeys and, most memorably, a hot pants clad, perpetually roller skating femme fatale by the name of Saloni (Barbara Shankar).

Warrant, despite not being a spy film, is a good example of the sway that 1970s Bollywood was held under by the James Bond series. In fact, so bright does its desire to be a Bond film burn that its proponents are blinded to some fairly glaring logical and aesthetic considerations. For Instance, why does Dev Anand's character, being only a humble jailer, come equipped with a watch that's tricked out with fancy secret gimmicks? And why does R.D. Burman compromise what is otherwise a typically original and accomplished bit of soundtrack work by incorporating immediately identifiable elements of the 007 theme into his score? The mind reels.

Warrant even goes one step further than most Indian Bond imitators by incorporating as its own a good deal of actual footage from the 1967 Bond entry *You Only Live Twice*. For those who spot it, this intrusion by parts of a completely different movie is a significant rupture in whatever success *Warrant* has had

at world building up to that point. At the same time, however, the theft is indicative of the reckless disregard that gives the film so much of its enjoyably trashy vigor. As such, much of what is original to *Warrant* is as deserving of praise as its thievery is of censure, with The Master's cavernous, trap laden lair being a key example. This includes among its diabolical tortures a room full of thrift store clocks, the combined ticking of which, when amplified through a pair of earphones, drives its occupant to madness. (The Master refers to this set-up as his "latest scientific invention," though I'm not sure what exactly he is claiming to have invented. Clocks? The idea of sound amplification?)

Lastly, *Warrant* deserves recommendation for its inclusion of a guest role for former wrestler and Bollywood "Stunt King" Dara Singh. Singh was a hero of action films back when they were the ghettoized realm of India's B movie industry, and, once they became part of the mainstream, his cameos throughout the '70s and '80s seem to have often served as homages to their influence. (Manmohan Desai, for instance, cast him as the father of the ultimate he-man played by Amitabh Bachchan in his wild stunt film pastiche *Mard*.) As elsewhere, his substantial role here seems an indication of a rough and tumble, stunt film heart beating at the center of *Warrant*, and that, its distasteful leading man aside, makes the film an easy one to like.

DEEWAAR
"Wall"

Released: 1975
Director: Yash Chopra
Stars: Shashi Kapoor, Amitabh Bachchan, Neetu Singh, Nirupa Roy, Parveen Babi, Manmohan Krishna, Madan Puri, Iftekhar, Satyendra Kapoor, Sudhir, Rajpal, Jagdish Raj, Kuljit Singh, Raj Kishore, Yunus Parvez, Sarveshwar, Mohan Sherry, Alankar Joshi, Master Raju, Shakeel, Raman Kumar, Rajan Verma, Vikas Anand, Radheshyam, H.L. Pardesi, Chandu Allahabadi, A.K. Hangal, Dulari, D.K. Sapru, Kamal Kapoor, Aruna Irani
Writers: Salim-Javed (Salim Khan & Javed Akhtar)
Music: Rahul Dev Burman (R.D. Burman)
Lyrics: Sahir
Fights: Shetty

Anand Verma (Satyendra Kapoor), a charismatic labor organizer, is forced to throw the negotiations of a miners' strike when the mine owner kidnaps his wife and young sons. News that he has sold the miners out travels fast and he becomes a public disgrace, subject to cat calls and heckling in the street. Shattered, he takes to the rails, mutely riding the train in an endless journey to "nowhere." Meanwhile, freed from captivity, his son Vijay is accosted by a group of angry miners and forced to have the words "My father is a thief" tattooed on his arm. Vijay's mother, Sumitra (Nirupa Roy), wanting to escape such persecution, takes Vijay and his brother Ravi to Bombay, where she struggles to provide for them. When Ravi starts to show an interest in education, Vijay resolves to help his mother pay for his schooling and, foregoing his own education, takes a full-time job as a shoe shine boy.

Vijay and Ravi's hardscrabble upbringing has different effects on the brothers. Vijay (Amitabh Bachchan) grows up angry and rebellious. He rejects God, and will only wait outside the temple for his mother on her daily visits, never going inside. When we catch up with him twenty some years later, he has taken a job on the docks. One of his coworkers tells him that his badge number, 786, is considered a good omen in the Muslim faith, and the steel plate bearing it indeed proves to save Vijay on a few occasions by deflecting bullets and the like. When the men of Samant (Madan Puri), a local gangster, come around to collect their regular protection money from the workers, Vijay refuses, and delivers a sound thrashing to the hoods when they try to shake him down. This impresses Davar (Iftekhar), a rival gangster, who hires Vijay to protect his latest shipment of smuggled gold, having had three previous shipments stolen by Samant. In the event, Vijay ends up selling the location of Davar's gold to Samant for a cool half million, then stealing it back from his men once they've stolen it and returning it to Davar for his agreed upon fee. He uses the resulting windfall to buy an opulent house for his mother, Ravi and himself to live in. Samant, for his part, begrudgingly congratulates Vijay for his treachery, but resolves to "finish the game."

Meanwhile, college graduate Ravi (Shashi Kapoor) has become passionate for social justice and, thanks to his girlfriend Veera (Neetu Singh), the daughter of the D.C.P., has landed a job with the police force, putting him on the fast track to becoming an inspector. This coincides with the ambitious Vijay's rise through Davar's organization. Wanting to place a mole within Samant's gang, he offers to put himself up as bait, sending another gang member to Samant with information on his whereabouts so that a hit can be set up. At the agreed upon bar, Vijay meets Anita (Parveen Babi), a cool headed and beautiful young woman who flirts with him. Forgetting his badge at the bar, he is saved once again when Anita brings it to him, stopping him short of walking into a sniper's bullet. Vijay's success in this mission results in Davar turning the day to day operations of the gang over to him. Vijay celebrates his new pay scale by lavishing both Anita and his mother with luxuries, though his mother worries at what the source of his sudden wealth might be.

Finally, the activities of Davar come to the attention of the police, and Ravi's superior calls him in on the case, specifically naming Vijay as a person of interest. The stunned Ravi refuses to take the case, admitting that Vijay is his brother. Later, however, he shoots a boy fleeing from a robbery only to find that he was stealing bread for his family. When the boy's mother castigates him for persecuting the poor in lieu of the real bad guys who prey upon them, he returns and accepts the case against Vijay. His first move then is to inform on Vijay's activities to his mother, who, outraged, disowns Vijay and moves out of the house he has provided for them. He then asks Vijay to sign an agreement to become a police informant. Vijay refuses, questioning why he should be punished when those responsible for his fate—the man who disgraced their father, the ones who tattooed him—have not been.

Vijay sees a change of heart when his mother takes desperately ill. Making his first trip to temple, he calls Vishnu to the carpet, demanding that his mother be spared in exchange for himself. His mother miraculously recovers, and Vijay returns home to Anita, who informs him that she is pregnant with his child. She tells him that he does not need to marry her, but that she nonetheless wants to raise the child as her own so that she can give it a better life than the one they've had. Vijay says that he will marry her immediately and then turn himself in to the police. He then calls his mother and asks her to meet him at the temple so that she may give him her blessing. Ravi, meanwhile, also has his mother's blessing in hunting Vijay down (to the extent of her handing him his gun and holster and advising him to shoot straight) and is sweeping the town in search of him. Samant, alerted by this to Vijay's presence in town, arrives at Anita's apartment and attempts to beat information about Vijay's whereabouts out of her. Vijay returns to have her die in his arms, then goes to Samant's high rise apartment and throws him out the window.

Vijay exits Samant's apartment to find the building surrounded by Ravi and his men. He flees and Ravi pursues. When he loses his badge, Ravi shoots him. Mortally wounded, he staggers to the temple and dies in his mother's arms. Later, when Ravi is given an award by the police for outstanding service, he insists that his mother accept it in his stead.

THE SECOND BILLED
Amitabh Bachchan was filming *Sholay* at the time of *Deewaar*'s release and groundbreaking success, meaning that that already much anticipated film came to market boasting among its cast the most famous man in India.

Deewaar, a fine film with another airtight Salim-Javed Script, went on to be one of the top five grossing films of 1975 and win multiple Filmfare awards, including best picture.

Genre film fans won't fail to identify *Deewaar*'s pedigree. It's a classic criminal "rise and fall" tale in the mold of Larry Cohen's *Black Caesar* or any version of *Scarface* you care to choose, though one informed by Indian popular cinema's trademark emphasis on themes of community and family connectedness to have a uniquely tragic dimension. For truly there is nothing sadder in Hindi cinema than the story of a man who gains the world but loses the love of his own mother.

After the "baby steps" of *Zanjeer*, in which Bachchan played the upright but disillusioned police officer, the star emerges full blown here as the Angry Young Man. As such, we get the first undiluted glimpses of him as the smoldering badass that would become ritualized into Canon in films like *Don*. The scene of a furious Bachchan in the temple angrily telling the idol of Vishnu exactly what time it is is an iconic representation of this, as is his distinctly matter of fact defenestration of Samant. All of this makes it very hard to take one's eyes off of the young star, especially in combination with his leading lady, Parveen Babi, who here gives an impressive demonstration of her transgressive appeal, playing a liberated young woman who smokes, drinks and admits without guilt to being pregnant out of wedlock. The film further pushes the bounds of propriety by showing a post coital Babi and Bachchan in bed sharing a cigarette.

As for top billed Shashi Kapoor, who was more or less a superstar at the time, a somewhat vanilla role as the "virtuous" brother leaves him ill equipped to wrest from the charismatic Bachchan the perception of being the film's true star. To be honest, in addition to giving voice to the film's moral dilemmas in a series of soulful soliloquies, one of Kapoor's major purposes here seems to be to, along with costar Neetu Singh, provide the smiling faces upon which R.D. Burman's romantic songs can be picturized. Granted, one welcome exception to this is an item number in which Aruna Irani rolls around in a pile of money on the floor of Davar's lair, but at some point a decision seems to have been made to keep the songs in *Deewaar* to a minimum, perhaps out of intent to preserve its serious and unabashedly political tone. In any case, Kapoor's performance is solid, and would lead to him being paired with Bachchan in a subsequent eleven films.

If anything sets *Deewaar* apart from the other films in this book, it is its aforementioned political nature. If it is indeed the quintessential Angry Young Man film, that is because it is itself an angry film, released just ahead of the State of Emergency declared by Indian president Fakhruddin Ali Ahmed in the tumultuous summer of 1975. Its sympathies render it admirably gray in its moral shading for a Bollywood film of its time—especially in comparison to the black and white proselytizing of the day's myriad "patriotic" and "social" dramas—with each of its characters being shown as deserving of sympathy despite not getting off the hook for their choices. Still, there is no denying the emotional violence implicit in the portrayal of a loving and conscientious Indian mother acquiescing to the murder of one son by another. In this sense, *Deewaar*, while delivering a crime thriller of iconic dimensions, also provides a disturbing portrait of a world gone off the rails.

THE BURNING TRAIN

Released: 1980
Director: Ravi Chopra
Stars: Dharmendra, Vinod Khanna, Jeetendra, Vinod Mehra, Hema Malini, Parveen Babi, Simi Garewal, Navin Nischol, Danny Denzongpa, Neetu Singh, Sujit Kumar, Ranjeet, Iftekhar, Nasir Hussain, Satyendra Kapoor, Padma Khanna, Rajendra Nath, Mukri, Paintal, Gufi Paintal, Nana Palsikar, Madan Puri, Jagdish Raj, Urmila Bhatt, Chadrashekhar, T.P. Jain, Jankidas, Padmini Kapila, Ravindra Kapoor, Manmauji, Mac Mohan, Indrani Mukherjee, Keshto Mukherjee, Yunus Parvez, Payal, Shammi, Anil Sharma, Ramesh Sharma, Romesh Sharma, Om Shivpuri, Dinesh Thakur, Komilla Wirk
Writers: Ravi Chopra, Kamleshwar
Music: Rahul Dev Burman (R.D. Burman)
Lyrics: Sahir
Action Co-ordinator: A. Mansoor

Ashok (Dharmendra), Vinod (Vinod Khanna) and Randhir (Danny Denzongpa) have shared a fascination with trains since childhood, which makes it no surprise that they've all come to work for the railroad as adults. However, while Ashok and Vinod have been inseparable friends throughout, the hot tempered Randhir has always found himself on the outside. When the railroad commission approves development of a revolutionary "Super Express" luxury train, Randhir is confident that his design for the vehicle will win out over those submitted by his two friends, which makes the sting that much worse when Vinod takes the prize. To compound matters, upon finally working up the nerve to ask out his crush Sheetal (Parveen Babi), Randhir learns that she is already engaged to Vinod. Ashok has also become engaged, to Seema (Hema Malini), but when family tragedy changes his financial fortunes, she sends him a letter abruptly calling it off. Shattered, Ashok takes to the road, disappearing from the lives of friends and family.

Six years later, Vinod still pines for the loss of his friend, while also losing hold of his marriage to Sheetal thanks to the demands of building the Super Express. Finally, the day of the inaugural journey arrives, and Ashok, wanting to honor his friend's achievement, quietly includes himself among the throng of boarding passengers. These also include the expected cross section of humanity, among them Madhu (Neetu Singh), a young woman fleeing an arranged marriage, Ravi (Jeetendra), a pickpocket with untapped reserves of bravery, a pompous military officer (Asrani), Chander (Ranjeet), a diamond smuggler, representatives of each of India's major faiths, a tragic couple, a bunch of school kids on a field trip, a goofy stowaway (Keshto Mukherjee) and an extremely pregnant lady, to name but a few. Also on board is Vinod's young son, Raju, whom Sheetal is sending to her parents in order to spare him the strife at home, and, to Ashok's consternation, Seema.

Undoubtedly the most fateful name on the passenger manifest, however, is that of Randhir, who seeks to revenge himself upon Vinod by planting a time bomb in the engine compartment, taking the further precaution of disabling the vacuum brakes so that the riders won't be able to stop the train themselves. During a stopover, he lets word of this plot slip to Ashok, prompting Ashok to punch him repeatedly and then tear off after the train on a succession of stolen vehicles. Unfortunately, Ashok is just slightly too late. The bomb explodes, killing the engine crew and sending the train and all of the assembled Bollywood talent aboard careening down the track at over a hundred miles per hour. As further proof that the gods are not smiling upon the Super Express, a totally unrelated gas explosion then causes a massive, rapidly traveling fire to erupt in the passenger section. It is left to Vinod and his team, back at the railroad's control center, to roll up their shirtsleeves and find a solution to the problem, while, on board, the passengers try to improvise while continually having to move further back into the train to escape the advancing inferno.

WHILE BOLLYWOOD DIRECTORS like Manmohan Desai and Rajkumar Kohli adopted the Hollywood disaster movie's "multi-starrer" format—and Desai cribbed from Irwin Allen's *The Towering Inferno* for the climax to his 1981 *Naseeb*—*The Burning Train* appears to be the first Indian picture to adhere closely to the disaster film template overall. Given those American films' tendency toward bloat, that might seem like cause for some trepidation. But given the taste of both Bollywood and the producers of films like *Earthquake* for epic length, archetypal characters, and blunt karmic moralizing, the marriage turns out to be one made in heaven. Which is to say that *The Burning Train*, while perhaps no *Titanic* (thank God), is one very solidly entertaining film.

Of course, the producers cut few corners in making *The Train* competitive within its chosen genre. In addition to the marquee busting cast, the production imported Hollywood talent Paul Wurtzel and Gerald Endler—the latter of whom worked on both *The Towering Inferno* and *Apocalypse Now*—to handle the copious special effects work. And while the local crew appears to have provided a couple of chintzy model shots for the climax, elsewhere the pro level pyrotechnic work achieves a harrowing verisimilitude. It was difficult in those pre-CGI days to portray the threat of imminent immolation without putting some of your actors in close proximity to the real thing. As such, it's difficult to imagine some of the stars here didn't more than once come home with singed eyebrows.

Since *The Burning Train* is able to deliver fully on the carnage promised by both its title and theme song (a classic bit of R.D. Burman freak funk employing the composer's distinct Cookie Monster vocal stylings to repeat the title to mnemonic immortality), it seems to take a more relaxed approach in the buildup to it. Gone are much of the grim portentousness and blood thirsty schadenfreude of its Western counterparts, replaced by a somewhat breezy depiction of the romantic relationships between Ashok and Vinod and their respective love interests, and indeed between Ashok and Vinod themselves, as few more bromantic pairings will be seen in these films. Granted, we also have Danny Denzongpa on hand to trash his office in a fit of bitter rage whenever we need a reminder of the coming storm.

Perhaps true to its origins, *The Burning Train* also struck me as being much more philosophical than the typical Irwin Allen joint. During a penultimate moment, when all hope of rescue seems lost, the film takes a quiet moment with each of the members of its seemingly doomed ensemble as they stoically contemplate and come to terms with the inevitable. Even stronger is an earlier scene, a diegetic musical number in which the assembled passengers, accompanied by a band of itinerant musicians, share a song together. The song, "Pal do Pal ka Saath," is in a Sufi folk style known as a qawwali, and treats the train journey as a metaphor for the journey of life. The travelers, the song exhorts, will only be together for a short time, and so should make the best of it. Ironically, at this point the passengers are unaware of the bomb in their midst that is only minutes away from going off.

This above song sequence is intercut with one of *The Burning Train*'s most dynamic stunt sequences, during which Ashok desperately races—first in a stolen car, and then on a stolen motorcycle—to catch up with the endangered train. Director Ravi Chopra (son of B.R. and nephew of Yash, both also producer/directors) expertly exploits the tension between the serenely celebratory song and the chaotic violence of the chase scene, bringing the interplay to a crescendo as Ashok races onto the platform and makes a leap for the train, barely grabbing hold of the side as the motorcycle is crushed under its wheels. Granted, it's not that anything similar hasn't been done before, but anyone willing to hold their cynicism at bay for the sake of enjoying a good old fashioned thrill will be well rewarded.

One of the rules of disaster cinema is that the disaster must be transformative.

One of the rules of disaster cinema is that the disaster must be transformative, in some way or another, for each of the characters. While some are made heroes, others are martyred; and while some are redeemed, others, recognizing their sins too late, are punished. (And then there are the innocents who are sacrificed simply to show that sometimes bad things happen to good people, God works in mysterious ways, shit happens, etc.) *The Burning Train*, with its company of clearly defined stock types, follows this rule implicitly. Ravi, the pickpocket played by

Jeetendra, steals onto the train in pursuit of the jewels carried by Neetu Singh's Madhu, but instead falls in love with his mark and ends up reaching ever greater heights of heroism in his efforts to save her and the other passengers. Jeetendra is late billed in the credits as one of the film's many guest artists, but is actually one of the triumvirate of male stars who drive its action. Come the final moment, when desperate measures are called for and the men must cleave from the boys, it is Dharmendra, Vinod Khanna, and Jeetendra who stand shoulder to shoulder against the inferno.

Further hewing to tradition, the disaster ends up acting as a sort of tough love marriage counselor for the other remaining protagonists. Ashok and Seema, trapped in close quarters with death lapping at their heels, are forced to get real with one another, Seema revealing a secret that casts new light on her actions. Sheetal gets to see firsthand the life and death nature of Vinod's work, and comes to appreciate it as more than just an obstacle to her happiness. Sadly, Parveen Babi finds herself once again underserved in *The Burning Train*, playing a character whose big epiphany seems to be that she needs to STFU. At the same time, it was refreshing to see a marriage in a Bollywood movie—where relationships are typically shattered by spectacular betrayals—dissolving through mundane attrition and neglect like the kind of troubled unions most of us are used to seeing in life.

Dealing in archetypes, *The Burning Train* has the advantage of playing to its stars' greatest strengths. As Ashok, Dharmendra is cast as the brooding, wounded tough guy, a part that he has repeatedly proven himself very good at. As such, he's also the film's primary actor when it comes to dishing out the violence, showing up to the picnic with a basket full of knuckle sandwiches for anyone who's asking for it. Appropriately, however, it is Vinod, the father of the Super Express, who ultimately sends the villain Randhir hurtling toward his just desserts. As Vinod, Khanna is the John Galt of the piece, a two-fisted captain of industry who, in the face of trouble, is not reluctant to roll up his sleeves and get down in the trenches. Alternately, the soulfully intense star also lets us in on Vinod's private anguish over his estrangement from wife and best friend alike, making it hard not to root for him. Such sharp casting continues all the way down through the ranks of supporting players, from the affable holy man played by Rajendra Nath to the comical drunken stowaway who could only have been played by Keshto (*hic*) Mukherjee.

If you're wondering why Bollywood didn't produce more films in the mold of *The Burning Train*, the answer could lie in the fact that the undoubtedly quite expensive film ended up being something of a disappointment at the Indian box office. While today's fans of 1970s Indian cinema might trill with excitement at the thought of that era's greatest stars all being placed on a passenger train turned into a fiery missile, contemporary audiences were apparently less moved. Perhaps this is due to the Hollywood productions that inspired the film being too recent in memory. In any case, having seen the film, I can only conclude that the problems were circumstantial rather than content-based. *The Burning Train* is a textbook example of classic Bollywood's ability to deliver on a high concept with peerless gusto, a colorful collision of stars, stunts, and Sturm und Drang that holds you in its goofy grip until absolutely everything that can be blown up, crashed, or razed to the ground has splintered to an end.

KALABAAZ
"Acrobat"

Released: 1977
Director: Ashok Roy
Stars: Dev Anand, Zeenat Aman, Asrani, Pradeep Kumar, Dev Kumar, Mohammed Ali, Major Anand, Vikas Anand, Darshan Arora, Gopal Raj Bhutani, Manik Dutt, Tarun Ghosh, Ramesh Goyal, Rajan Haksar, A.K. Hangal, Hercules, Ambika Johar, H.N. Kalla, Rajan Kapoor, Sujit Kumar, Lalita Kumari, Ram Mohan, Rajpuri, Keshav Rana, Maruti Rao, Probir Roy, Madhup Sharma, Mohan Sherry, Shobha, Subhash
Writers: Kaul Tarun Sen, S.M. Abbas, Tarun Ghosh
Music: Kalyanji-Anandji (Kalyanji Virji Shah & Anandji Virji Shah)
Lyrics: Anand Bakshi
Fights: Mansoor

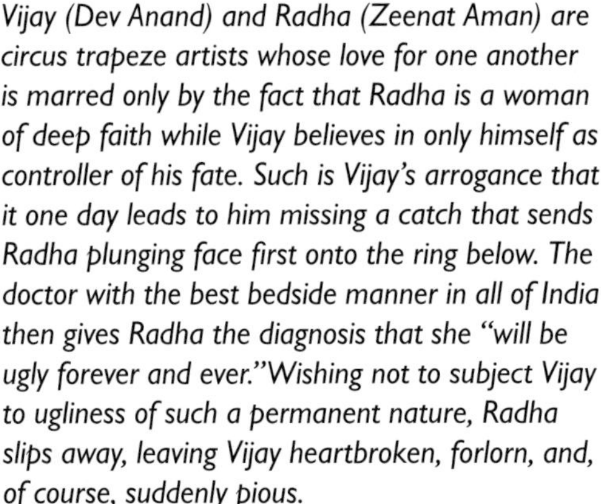

Vijay (Dev Anand) and Radha (Zeenat Aman) are circus trapeze artists whose love for one another is marred only by the fact that Radha is a woman of deep faith while Vijay believes in only himself as controller of his fate. Such is Vijay's arrogance that it one day leads to him missing a catch that sends Radha plunging face first onto the ring below. The doctor with the best bedside manner in all of India then gives Radha the diagnosis that she "will be ugly forever and ever." Wishing not to subject Vijay to ugliness of such a permanent nature, Radha slips away, leaving Vijay heartbroken, forlorn, and, of course, suddenly pious.

When a pair of valuable idols disappears from a temple that is of special importance to Radha's family, Vijay sees an opportunity both to redeem himself in her eyes and to prove his newfound faith. Recruiting a trio of his circus pals, he goes after the bandits, eventually finding a culprit in the person of flamboyant gangster King Mong (Dev Kumar). It turns out, however, that, before King Mong could get his hands on the idols, a priest had hidden them in a secret location somewhere in the treacherous mountain region between India and Burma. An expedition is then mounted that includes, in addition to Vijay and his men, Radha's father (Pradeep Kumar) and a facially reconstructed Radha posing as Radha's cousin.

Every step of the way, King Mong and his men are hot on the explorers' heels, leading to a climax in which Vijay and Radha must fall back upon the acrobatic skills that trauma and tragedy have led them to abandon.

THE SERPENTINE NATURE of most Bollywood movies' plots ensures that you often end up with a very different movie from the one you started out with. This leads to something that some of my blogging colleagues refer to as "the curse of the second half," whereby an Indian movie that starts out promisingly reneges spectacularly on that promise once you've had your midway bathroom break. With *Kalabaaz*, however, we have the opposite problem, in that the movie's tail end actually rewards you for your lead footed slog through its initial hour-plus of whatever happened while you were sleeping.

A lot of what makes *Kalabaaz*'s opening act uninvolving is its chronicling of the romance between Vijay and Radha. This mostly consists of an elderly Dev Anand wooing the pulchritudinous Zeenat Aman in that off-putting, boy-meets-girl-boy-relentlessly-stalks-girl manner so often seen in older Indian films. (See my review of *Warrant* for more on my feelings toward Dev Anand.) The problem with this device is that, no matter how happy the couple ends up being in the end, one can never be sure whether its female half didn't just get worn down or succumb to Stockholm Syndrome. Also slowing things down is the tone of solemnity lent by this portion's somewhat heavy handed examination of faith.

The thing is, however, that once the wooing ends, Zeenat does her game changing face plant, and those pivotal idols have been stolen, *Kalabaaz* inexplicably takes off at a run, displaying a rowdiness and verve that none of its preceding scenes have prepared us for. The attempts by Anand and his circus cronies to flush out King Mong involve them going to a series of psychedelic underworld watering holes and getting into wild bar fights filled with all kinds of ridiculous acrobatic stunts. And when they finally find Mong, he turns out to be the hulking, Lurch-like actor Dev Kumar sporting some truly fearsome mutton chops, a lime green velvet leisure suit, and a pet leopard on a leash. Truly, fans of over-the-top Bollywood villains will find much to weep with joy over here.

And yet, *Kalabaaz* has more in store. Once the setting of the film switches to the perilous peaks of India's northeast, it becomes a ripping adventure yarn marked by thrill-a-minute pacing. Upping the danger and intrigue, it soon becomes apparent that, in addition to the competing expeditions mounted by Vijay and King Mong, there is a third, mysterious party competing for the same prize, and that they will stop at nothing—nothing, I tell you!—to get it. It's almost enough to make you forgive the filmmakers' odd choice in representing Radha's post-reconstructive surgery look, which is to give Zeenat Aman seriously plucked eyebrows and lipstick that make her lips the same color as her skin.

Sealing the deal with *Kalabaaz* is yet another thumping, incessantly catchy score from Kalyanji-Anandji. To me, their tunes were the saving grace of that sleepy first act, especially during the number where Dev stalks Zeenat through the streets of Bombay on the back of an elephant. For those of you who choose to brave this one, I say, stick with it; you'll be surprised how worth it the wait turns out to be.

BESHARAM
"Shameless"

Released: 1978
Director: Deven Verma
Stars: Amitabh Bachchan, Sharmila Tagore, Amjad Khan, Bindu, Nirupa Roy, A.K. Hangal, Iftekhar, Jagdish Raj, Dhumal, Mohan Choti, Uma Dhawan, Helen, Jayshree T., Urmila Bhatt, Imtiaz, Deven Verma
Writers: Nerupama, Rahi Masum Raja, Nayyar Jehan
Music: Kalyanji-Anandji (Kalyanji Virji Shah & Anandji Virji Shah)
Lyrics: Yogesh
Fight composers: Mohammed Ali, Mansoor Ali

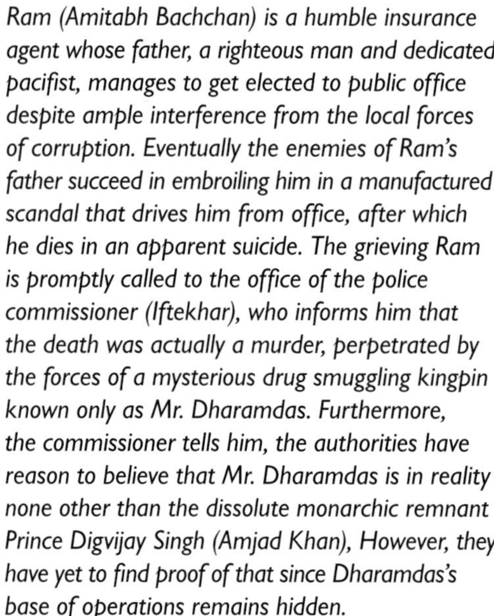

Ram (Amitabh Bachchan) is a humble insurance agent whose father, a righteous man and dedicated pacifist, manages to get elected to public office despite ample interference from the local forces of corruption. Eventually the enemies of Ram's father succeed in embroiling him in a manufactured scandal that drives him from office, after which he dies in an apparent suicide. The grieving Ram is promptly called to the office of the police commissioner (Iftekhar), who informs him that the death was actually a murder, perpetrated by the forces of a mysterious drug smuggling kingpin known only as Mr. Dharamdas. Furthermore, the commissioner tells him, the authorities have reason to believe that Mr. Dharamdas is in reality none other than the dissolute monarchic remnant Prince Digvijay Singh (Amjad Khan), However, they have yet to find proof of that since Dharamdas's base of operations remains hidden.

Because the grieving son of a murder victim who has no training in law enforcement is the ideal choice to take part in a delicate undercover operation, the commissioner asks Ram to pose as a fellow hoodlum in order to gain the Prince's confidence. Soon thereafter, Ram emerges in the guise of Chandrashekar, a South African diamond smuggler who glides effortlessly through the upper reaches of Bombay's underworld swathed in an array of hip-hugging '70s finery. Everyone is fooled, including the Prince's sister Rinku (Sharmila Tagore), despite the fact that the Prince himself had her romantically insinuate herself into Ram's life as a means of keeping tabs on him (perhaps, having seen too many Bollywood films, Rinku is unfazed by the idea that two unrelated people could be exact duplicates of one another).

Ram then sets his sights on romancing both Rinku and the Prince's mistress Manju (Bindu) in order to gain access to the inner circle, thus setting the stage for a violent confrontation with the Prince.

MOST AMITABH BACHCHAN vehicles from the late '70s model themselves upon one of his earlier breakthrough hits, but *Besharam* has the distinction of borrowing liberally from three of the most iconic. As in *Deewaar*, we have the theme of the martyred father, his life taken and good name tarnished by the forces of corruption, whose fate motivates the actions of the protagonist.

Also deserving mention is his lair, which is located underneath a cemetery and gives prominence to a tiger pit.

Like *Don*, we have a tale, set against a funky urban backdrop, of a peaceful innocent masquerading as a suave underworld figure. And, finally, as in *Sholay*, we have Bachchan pitted against a larger-than-life, seemingly unstoppable villain, here as in that case played by the great Amjad Khan.

However, unlike those films, *Besharam* doesn't seem to have much in the way of larger themes that it wants to put across. As such, it simply uses its resemblance to them as a sort of terse signifier of those themes—the fetters of family honor, the value of friendship and community, etc.—while it goes briskly about its real business of being a violent and somewhat trashy potboiler. This, of course, gives the movie something of a throwaway feel, but that just contributes all the more to it being such a fun experience. After all, if you're reading this book in the first place, you're probably aware that a movie doesn't need to be a classic to be great. And while *Besharam* is certainly no substitute for *Deewaar* or *Sholay*, there is something to be said for how it so compactly serves up the undiluted joys of Amitabh at his most funky and fighting-est.

That aside, many of the pulpy thrills that make up the wild heart of *Besharam* come to us courtesy of Amjad Khan, who here gives a performance that's as much a distillation of his métier as *Besharam* is of Bachchan's oeuvre as a whole. Digvijay Singh is a winning amalgam of all Khan's most time-tested villainous tics, blessed with a sweaty brow, leering eyes, a tendency toward bouts of unhinged giggling, and, needless to say, an explosive temper. On top of that, we have those flourishes and accoutrements that provide Digvijay Singh with his own signature ignominy, not the least being his heavy reliance upon live cobras to dispatch enemy and turncoat minion alike. Also deserving mention is his lair, which is located underneath a cemetery and gives prominence to a tiger pit, above which, during the movie's feverish climax, can be found dangling none other than Amitabh's long suffering old mom (Nirupa Roy, of course).

Yet to say that *Besharam* is unusually lean and fast moving for a 1970s masala film—which it is—is not to say that it doesn't have its share of narrative digressions. Chief among these is a comedic subplot that director/actor Deven Verma creates for himself in which he—perhaps anticipating Eddie Murphy's later career—plays an entire family, mother included. None of this seems to have much utility in terms of the actual story, nor does its comedy seem all that necessary in a film in which Amitabh Bachchan wears a polka dot tuxedo with a straight face. Nonetheless, Verma deserves credit for the streamlining he does elsewhere, especially in terms of the film's family drama—usually something of a narrative logjam in Indian action films—which is here nicely integrated within the larger plot.

Of course, scattered among the cobra killings, fistfights, and Amitabh's modeling of the latest fashions, *Besharam*'s most welcome digressions are its musical numbers. The duo Kalyanji-Anandji, known for their driving, wah-wah drenched instrumentals, also had a knack for writing extremely catchy, Western pop flavored songs, of which many of their tunes for *Besharam* are fine examples. "Mere Kis Kaam Ki" in particular is an earworm that will stick with you for days. Perhaps counting on that fact, Verma's picturization—featuring a tense dance of seduction between Bindu and a cruelly aloof Bachchan in a small hotel room—seems specifically intended to conjure happy associations with *Don*'s standout hit "Ye Mera Dil."

In terms of presentation, however, my favorite tune in *Besharam* has got to be "Iraade Dil Tumhara," which provides a brief showcase for Helen in a fiery cameo. Leading us into the film's explosive final act, this bit follows in the tradition of what I like to call the "prophetic item number": a staged performance that our hero passively takes in at the cusp of everything going pear-shaped, featuring an anonymous cabaret girl who pointedly sings about all of the bad things that are about to happen to him. Strangely enough, this song follows not too far on the heels of one in which Ram similarly watches Rinku performing in a pageant and is struck by the fact that she is singing about how she has seen through his disguise. Helen, in the same spirit, sings of how Ram's cover has been blown—and with much more at stake—but this time the message is lost on him.

THE *FUNKY BOLLYWOOD* PLAYLIST:

"Yeh Mera Dil Yaar ka Deewana"
From: DON
Writers: Kalyanji-Anandji, Lalji Pandey, Indeevar
Singer: Asha Bhosle

"Mohabbat Hi Mohabbat Hai"
From: GEETAA MERA NAAM
Writers: Laxmikant-Pyarelal, Rajendra Krishan
Singer: Mohammad Rafi

"Oh Meri Jaan Maine Kaha"
From: THE TRAIN
Writers: R.D. Burman, Anand Bakshi
Singers: Asha Bhosle and R.D. Burman

"Lekar Hum Deewana Dil"
From: YAADON KI BAARAAT
Writers: R.D. Burman, Majrooh Sultanpuri
Singers: Asha Bhosle and Kishore Kumar

"Aap Jaisa Koi"
From: QURBANI
Writer: Biddu
Singer: Nazia Hassan

YAADON KI BAARAAT
"Procession of Memories"

Released: 1973
Director: Nasir Hussain
Stars: Dharmendra, Zeenat Aman, Vijay Arora, Ajit, Imtiaz Khan, Tariq, Ravindra Kapoor, Satyendra Kapoor, Nasir Khan, Shyam Kumar, Shetty, Anamika, Sanjana, Ashoo, Pompi, Sofia, Mona Saxena, Kamal, Murad, Shivraj, Prem Sagar, Bhushan Tiwari, Ram Avtar, Dhanna, Ahmed Ali, Keshav Rana, Surendra Shetty, Moolchand, Uma Dutt, Raj Rani, H. Prakash, Navin Kumar, Manjeet, Ravi, Sopariwala, Lamba, Banerji, Jagdish, Bihari, Nawab, Gafoor, Neetu Singh, Jalal Agha, Master Rajesh, Master Sailesh, Master Ravi, Aamir Khan
Writers: Salim-Javed (Salim Khan & Javed Akhtar)
Music: Rahul Dev Burman (R.D. Burman)
Lyrics: Majrooh Sultanpuri
Fights: Shetty

The family of Gulzar the artist enjoys an idyllic scene, gathering at the birthday of one of his three young sons to sing together a festive song known only to them. Later that same evening, Gulzar witnesses the aftermath of a robbery and murder committed by the criminal mastermind Shakhaal (Ajit) and his gang. Gulzar goes to the police and offers to paint a portrait of Shakhaal, having gotten quite a good look at him. Back at his studio, however, Shakhaal and his men, disguised behind kerchiefs, interrupt Gulzar's process and shoot both him and his wife to death before he can finish the canvas. Gulzar's three sons, witnessing the carnage, flee and are helped by Jack (Satyendra Kapoor); a henchman of Shakhaal's who is having second thoughts. Jack ends up being captured by police for his trouble.

The two eldest boys, Shankar and Vijay, take off after a passing train, but Shankar is unable to grab hold and falls behind. Collapsing, he later comes to in the city and is taken under the wing of Usman, a street savvy urchin. Ratan, the youngest child, remains in the care of his nanny and ends up being raised by her as her own.

Flash forward fifteen years and Shankar (Dharmendra) and Usman (Ravindra Kapoor) are now part of a criminal gang. Shakhaal, on the other hand, is now head of an elaborate organization headquartered in the swank Park Hotel, and takes an interest in Shankar when the daring young thief makes off with a valuable royal necklace that his own men had had their sights on. Vijay (Vijay Arora), for his part, is living the life of a middle class student, having been raised the son of the manager of a campus house owned by the father of wealthy Sunita (Zeenat Aman). Vijay puts on wealthy airs to woo the pampered Sunita, leading to a courtship marked by constant pranking and deception.

And as for Ratan (Tariq), he has assumed the flamboyant guise of Prince Monto, a dynamic nightclub entertainer who combines the art of song and dance with the furious surf guitar

above: **Cover for the Thai DVD release of *Yaadon Ki Baaraat***

stylings of Dick Dale. Ratan marks every performance with a rendition of the song that his family sang together on that fateful night fifteen years ago, in the hope that one of his brothers might be in the audience and can complete the melody. But—although Monto's fame and ubiquity has assured that both Shankar and Vijay have been present at one of his performances or another—the timing has never worked out quite right.

Meanwhile, the grim Shankar, swearing revenge as his only purpose in life, has spent the interim years repeatedly trying to gain access to the imprisoned Jack, feeling that he is the only one who can reveal the identity of his parents' killer. When Shakhaal comes into possession of a letter that Jack has written Shankar in which he reveals all, he uses it to pressure Shankar into performing ever darker deeds at his bidding, from stealing a valuable idol from a museum to kidnapping Sunita in an effort to extort from her father. All the while, Ratan/Prince Monto, in residency at the Park Hotel, provides a soundtrack to the action, with only a matter of time remaining before Vijay—now working at the hotel as a steward—or Shankar, who lives there, hears his fateful tune.

ONE OF THE PITFALLS of the Bollywood "lost and found" film is that, once the first act groundwork has been set and the subject family has been scattered to the winds—as they are so very efficiently by Salim-Javed's tight script for *Yaadon Ki Baaraat* —the narrative itself also scatters, and we are left with parallel threads that are not always of equal interest. Fortunately, *Yaadon Ki Baaraat* represents a rare exception to this trend, focusing primarily on divergent stories that, while quite different in tone, are both just as involving—and which, even more impressively, end up re-entwining in a thoroughly satisfying manner.

Those not familiar with director Nasir Hussain's success with youth oriented features like *Teesri Manzil* might be surprised by just how much of *Yaadon Ki Baaraat*'s screen time is given over to the college hijinks of young stars Vijay Arora and Zeenat Aman. Yet I imagine this is in part a key to the film's phenomenal success at the Indian box office. As with *Teesri Manzil*, Hussain brings a colorful, Western influenced pop sensibility to these scenes. But, whereas *Teesri Manzil* came off like an Elvis movie directed by Hitchcock, *Yaadon*'s teen scene is an *Archie* comic book brought to life, with Zeenat playing the role of the spoiled, manipulative Veronica to a tee.

Yet the teen romance of Vijay and Sunita involves less of a romance than it does a weirdly obsessive juvenile rivalry, involving some fairly cruel pranks on the part of both parties. This mean spiritedness adds some welcome vinegar to what could easily have been a typically saccharine Bollywood tale of young love, and also provides interest as we watch how each becomes trapped by their own deceptions once feelings for one another that they are, at first, only feigning turn out to be real. It also doesn't hurt that both stars

are disarmingly appealing here (and, in Aman's case, even more kittenish than usual), a fact which makes it easy to root for them to overcome the well-orchestrated odds that the screenwriters have so meticulously lined up against them.

Hussain and his two writers also make very good use of Dharmendra, who, as in *The Burning Train*, is well capitalized upon as a businesslike distributor of punches. Of course, the performance could easily just boil down to Dharmendra's typical badass shtick, but the star really seems to be putting a lot of soul behind it in this instance, portraying it more as behavior arising from character than from Dharam just being Dharam. His Shankar is one of those movie thieves who somehow honors a strict moral code while being unable to separate himself from his troubled past, and there's a resulting tortured intensity that feeds all the more into the long delayed climactic reunion being one of particularly satisfying emotional potency.

And then, last but not least, is Tariq, the nephew of director Hussain, who with this film launched him on an abbreviated trajectory through the Bollywood firmament that would last only a handful of films. As Ratan/Monto, the young actor doesn't get much of a chance to show his chops, but there is nonetheless an oddball appeal to his bug eyed look and weirdly aggressive take on rocking out on the guitar that makes his scenes difficult to ignore. Compounding this is the fact that those scenes tend to center around some of composer R.D. Burman's more mind bendingly psychedelic tunes of the era, and feature such extras as starlet Neetu Singh making a cameo as an enthusiastically scat singing item girl. Burman's score overall is iconic, with the Asha Bhosle/Mohammad Rafi sung "Chura Liya Hai Tumne Jo Dil Ko" and the title tune remaining evergreens to this very day.

Perhaps as important a character in *Yaadon Ki Baaraat*, however, is the Park Hotel itself, which, in becoming the locus of absolutely all of the film's third act goings on, neatly underscores the role of the "International Hotel" in the Bollywood demimonde. One gets the sense of the place as a malevolent, shape shifting labyrinth—at once glamorous and foreboding—capable of housing both the grand ballroom in which Prince Monto wows his audience, the opulent rooms of its many inhabitants, and the requisite lair of Shakhaal. This last resembles a cross between a wood paneled basement rec room in a 1970s suburban home and the bridge of the starship Enterprise, and is well suited to the reign of Ajit, who here—with his silver cowboy vest, omnipresent gloves and cigarette holder—completes the villainous one/two punch that he started with *Zanjeer* earlier in the year.

"Lost and found" films are, of course, formula films, and, as such, *Yaadon Ki Baaraat* is no less predictable than other films of its type. Yet director Hussain, aided by a phenomenal Salim-Javed script, manages to hit all of the requisite beats in an especially satisfying manner, honoring at the same time all of the story's conflicting tones—from melodramatic set up to breezy rom com middle section to violent conclusion—with measured jurisprudence. The result is a shining example of the form—a template, if you will—capable of making the emotions of even the most hardened cult movie blogger dance like an especially eager-to-please organ grinder's monkey (not that I'm mentioning any names, mind you.)

RANI MERA NAAM
"Rani Is My Name"

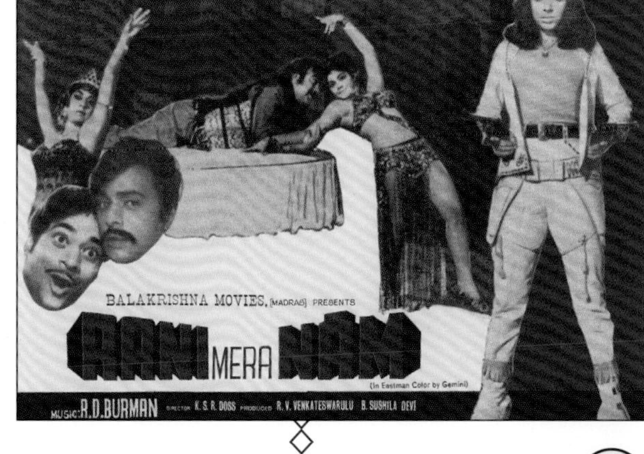

Released: 1972
Director: K.S.R. Doss
Stars: Vijaya Lalitha, Ajit, Madan Puri, Anwar Hussain, Natraj, Vinod Mehra, Iftekhar, Jagdeep, Jayshree T., Prem Nath, Om Prakash, Sulochana, Nasir Hussain, Sridevi
Writers: R.K. Nayyar, Madan Joshi, Baby Seema
Music: Rahul Dev Burman (R.D. Burman)
Lyrics: Majrooh Sultanpuri
Stunts: Madhavan

One dark night, little Rani, from a secure hiding place, watches in horror as her entire family is murdered by a gang of grotesque bandits. From her vantage point, she is only able to catch isolated glimpses of the villains' identifying features—a lone bulging eye here; a tattoo of playing cards there; a head tumor; a gold skull necklace—but those details are burned indelibly into her brain for future reference. Also sitting out the massacre is the family's faithful manservant (Iftekhar), who from that point on raises Rani as his own, training her in martial arts and weaponry so that she may be that much better equipped once the time for vengeance arrives. And arrive it does, setting the adult Rani (Vijaya Lalitha) off on a quest to find and ruthlessly eliminate the four men who orphaned her.

These men, we soon learn, have all done quite well for themselves in the intervening years, each becoming a criminal kingpin in his own right, complete with his own elaborate cave lair and army of minions. Rani undoes the first of these, a crooked casino owner (Ajit), by donning a series of disguises, including those of a mustached prince and a ninja-like henchman. From there she goes on, helped as much by coincidence as cunning, to work her way down the list, cracking the mask of a supposedly benevolent politician (Madan Puri) to expose him as the bulge-eyed man, and putting an end to the head tumor guy's career as a rural dacoit. In every case, Rani dispatches these villains with pitiless brutality, going into a rage fueled frenzy driven by psychedelic flashbacks to the night of her family's deaths.

All the while, the dwindling cadre of bad guys tries to throw obstacles in Rani's path in the form of an assortment of exotic hired killers, including a hot pants clad lesbian assassin and a guy with a clawed Freddy Krueger glove. Still, Rani's righteous fists and superior ka-ra-te persevere. Until, that is, she encounters her final bullet point, the owner of that gold skull necklace, who lures her into an agonizing web of torture and abuse. This treatment, of course, only qualifies this dirty dog for the worst fate of all once Rani gets the upper hand. Her thirst for payback then sated, she turns herself over to the authorities, stoically accepting that she, like her victims, is not immune to the consequences of her actions.

DIRECTOR K.S.R. DOSS, in later years, referred to his 1970 Telegu language hit *Rowdy Rani* as India's first "100% action film," by which he meant that he eschewed Indian cinema's typical hodgepodge of genre production. It boasted songs by the then red hot R.D. Burman and featured a top notch supporting cast that included a triumvirate of premium grade heavies in Ajit, Madan Puri and Anwar Hussain.

Is it trashy? Stupid? Gaudy? Lurid? Indeed it is. But, also like its heroine, it commits these crimes in pursuit of a worthy goal.

elements in order to give his audience a virtually nonstop procession of fistfights, chases and crazy stunts. Such a formula was rarely, if ever, seen outside of the "Stunt" films of Bollywood's B movie industry, which likely means that, once the film had been remade in Hindi as *Rani Mera Naam*, it dropped a few jaws. After all, while definitely on the trashy side, *Rani Mera Naam* was no poverty row

BALAKRISHNA MOVIES (Madras)
Presents
"RANI MERA NĀM"
(HINDI) EASTMANCOLOUR

Cast
PREMNATH, AJIT
MADANPURI, ANWAR HUSSAIN
IFTEKAR, NATARAJAN
and
JAGDEEP
VIJAYALALITHA, JAYASHREE T.
FARYAL, BABY SRIDEVI

Guest Artistes :
NAZIR HUSSAIN, SULOCHANA
PANDARI BAI

Special Appearance :
VINOD MEHRA

Friendly Appearance :
ASHOK KUMAR, OMPRAKASH

TECHNICIANS :

Dialogues :	RAJ BALDEVRAJ
Lyrics :	MAJROOH SULTANPURI
Play Back :	ASHA BHONSLEY MANNADEY
Dances :	B. HIRALAL
Art :	S. KRISHNA RAO
Camera :	M. KANNAPPA
Music :	R. D. BURMAN
Laboratory :	GEMINI COLOR LAB

Editing & Direction :
K. S. R. DOSS

Produced by :
R. N. VENKATESWARLU
&
B. SUSHILA DEVI

Vadapalani Press, Madras-26.

In fact, *Rani*'s transition from Tollywood to Bollywood saw a complete turnover in all of its main actors except for one: its diminutive titular star Vijaya Lalitha. Why this was is easy to surmise. It's unlikely that any of the female stars of Hindi cinema at the time would have been willing to commit to the film's physical stunts to the degree Lalitha did. Yet here we see Lalitha—who had become a star of Telegu films as much for her dancing as her willingness to take a punch—enthusiastically leaping, kicking and rolling in the dirt with her opponents, often taking them down with a flying scissor hold or other bone-crunching wrestling maneuver. Adding to this spectacle's impact is Lalitha's appearance: small and bird-like in her movements, with large, anime girl eyes and an immovable helmet of red hair, she is, if not an unlikely action heroine, then certainly an unforgettable one. And this is without even mentioning her dancing, which is almost as violent as her fighting.

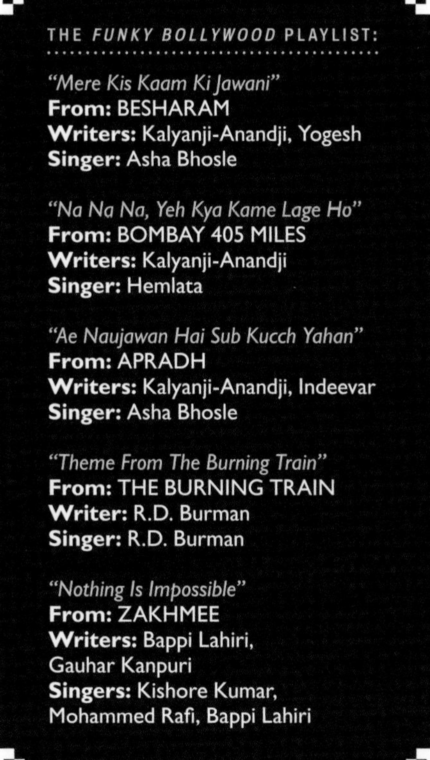
THE *FUNKY BOLLYWOOD* PLAYLIST:

"Mere Kis Kaam Ki Jawani"
From: BESHARAM
Writers: Kalyanji-Anandji, Yogesh
Singer: Asha Bhosle

"Na Na Na, Yeh Kya Kame Lage Ho"
From: BOMBAY 405 MILES
Writers: Kalyanji-Anandji
Singer: Hemlata

"Ae Naujawan Hai Sub Kucch Yahan"
From: APRADH
Writers: Kalyanji-Anandji, Indeevar
Singer: Asha Bhosle

"Theme From The Burning Train"
From: THE BURNING TRAIN
Writer: R.D. Burman
Singer: R.D. Burman

"Nothing Is Impossible"
From: ZAKHMEE
Writers: Bappi Lahiri, Gauhar Kanpuri
Singers: Kishore Kumar, Mohammed Rafi, Bappi Lahiri

Doss here tones down some of the familiar elements from his Telegu work, most noticeably his raunchy approach to filming dance numbers, with none of the upskirt shots that were so prevalent in films like *Pistolwali* and *James Bond 777*. His approach to action, however, remains as raw and reckless as ever. In addition to under-cranking everything, Doss puts his audience in the middle of *Rani*'s fight scenes by tumbling his camera side over side as if it were a participant in the melee. We get another one of his trademarks in the obviously rear projected motorcycle chase scene. With two hours plus to fill with "100 percent action," there is actually more than one of these, giving us the chance to see an assortment of cast members doing their best to look like they're really riding a motorcycle as an anonymous stretch of highway spools out on the flickering screen behind them.

K.S.R. Doss's films tend to tax my vocabulary, as there are only so many ways one can describe a film as cartoonish and comic book-like, and I've just, with this sentence, exhausted both of them. The problem is that those two phrases sum up the look and feel of his movies so succinctly that to use alternates would sacrifice clarity. True to form, *Rani*'s sped up violence, hyper-real color schemes, and caricatured grotesquery serve to transport its action out of any universe recognizable as our own and into that of an especially bloody *Tom and Jerry* one reeler. And my lexicon isn't given any further breaks by Doss's drawing upon some equally comic book influenced European films for *Rani*'s overall style, bringing to mind, among others, *Modesty Blaise*, Mario Bava's *Danger: Diabolik*, and even, to some extent, a bit of Jess Franco's "Red Lips" films. The debt to Spaghetti Westerns is also obvious, in particular Giulio Petroni's *Death Rides a Horse*, of which *Rani* is essentially a gender-switched remake.

Like its heroine, *Rani Mera Naam* is guilty of many sins. Is it trashy? Stupid? Gaudy? Lurid? Indeed it is. But, also like its heroine, it commits these crimes in pursuit of a worthy goal. Along with all of Doss's best work, it's pure cinema, a riot of outlandish action and hyperbolic style, and for those willing to let go of their pretensions, its pleasures are pure also. In short, if loving *Rani Mera Naam* is wrong, I don't want to be right.

BADA KABUTAR
"Big Pigeon"

Released: 1973
Director: Deven Verma
Stars: Ashok Kumar, Rehana Sultan, Deven Verma, Pinchoo Kapoor, Ashoo, Keshto Mukherjee, Subroto Mahapatra, Paul Sharma, Sunder, Leela Mishra, Helen, Nikhilesh, Sajan, Kailash Sharma, Samina, Golu, Madan Puri
Writers: Akhtar-Ul-Imam
Music: Rahul Dev Burman (R.D. Burman)
Lyrics: Yogesh
Fights: Shetty, Mohammed Ali, Surendra

A group of four more or less bumbling crooks led by Rampuri (Ashok Kumar) stages a daring late night burglary. Waiting outside in his car—a jalopy that, for undisclosed reasons, he has named "Big Pigeon"—Rampuri gets spooked by sirens and takes off, leaving his nephew Bhola (Deven Verma) behind to fall into the clutches of the police. Months later, Bhola is released from prison only to be told by Rampuri that he is brewing a new scheme. Having already been jailed seven times as a result of his uncle's plotting, Bhola is anxious to avoid him.

This turns out to be a losing battle for Bhola, as his aging mother (Leela Mishra), wanting him to return to the criminal fold, plots with Rampuri to feign a serious illness. Rampuri then recruits a friend to pose as a doctor and tell Bhola that his mother is in immediate need of an expensive operation. Thus does Bhola agree to take part in Rampuri's next caper, which promises him a 50,000 Rs. payday. Rampuri then brings in the other two members of the gang, Abdul, a drunkard (Keshto Mukherjee) and Subroto, a dry cleaner (Subbu). He also hires Navin (Nikhilesh), a pole vaulter, and Rita (Rehana Sultan), a cabaret dancer. Navin and Rita's assignment is to pose as man and wife, and to complete the bogus family portrait, Rampuri rents an infant child named Golu (billed as "Golu—A Wonder Child") from an oddball underworld figure by the name of Tiger Sando.

Rampuri finally reveals that his plot is to kidnap the infant son of Dharamdas (Pinchoo Kapoor), a millionaire who, when we first meet him, is murdering a rival in cold blood. Because the baby is the only child of the unmarried Dharamdas, it is constantly surrounded by bodyguards and nursing staff, which means that the gang will have to wait vigilantly for an opportunity to strike. Fortunately, Rampuri has an inside man within Dharamdas's organization in the person of Bhuta Singh (Paul Sharma), his chief body guard.

Before Rampuri can put his plan in motion, he learns that Gaffur (Madan Puri), another old associate who has done time on his behalf, is out of prison and looking to settle a grudge. Gaffur seizes the first opportunity to kidnap baby Golu and hold him hostage, only to be thwarted by Navin, who vaults into his hideout and thrashes his men. This episode takes away valuable rehearsal time from the gang and, when they learn from Bhuta Singh that Dharamdas's son is to be sent on an outing to a public park with his nurse and chauffeur the following day, they are forced to act with little preparation. It is at this time that Rampuri explains to Rita and Navin that his plan involves them bringing Golu to the park in a stroller identical to that of Dharamdas's baby and exchanging the two children. The only problem with this plan is that, in the course of playing house, Rita and Navin have developed real feelings both for each other and for their rented child. Rita refuses, only to agree once Rampuri guarantees her that Golu will only be gone for a couple of days. determines that what they need to do is invade Dharamdas's mansion and steal Golu back.

The opportunity for said snatch comes when Dharamdas throws a lavish birthday party for his son—in absentia, of course—which will feature among its attractions an item number by Helen. Bhuta Singh clues the gang in to a secret entrance to the place and they successfully make off with Golu. A madcap relay follows in which Bhola, then Abdul, then an interfering Gaffur, then Bhola's mom have the child. Then, back home, all involved must hide the

In the event, it is Rita and Bhola who pull off the switch of the two children, only to have Dharamdas's nurse and chauffeur immediately recognize the child as not being the right one. They give chase, and Bhola hands the baby off to Navin, who, strapping the child to his back, pole vaults over the park wall. Later, Rampuri calls Dharamdas and identifies himself as a member of the "Big Pigeon Gang," demanding a ransom of three lakh rupees and the return of Golu in exchange for his son. Unknown to Rampuri, Rita, unable to contain herself, has already called Dharamdas and inquired after Golu's welfare. Clued in that Golu will be missed, the cunning Dharamdas tells Rampuri that he's happy to leave things as is and keep the child he's been given. With this, the Big Pigeon Gang

presence of two babies within Navin and Rita's home as, meanwhile, Dharamdas's men scour the town for information about the mysterious Big Pigeon Gang. Finally Dharamdas, signaling defeat, contacts Rampuri to make arrangements for dropping off payment, but it is really an attempt to lure the gang into a trap. Come time for the meet, Rampuri fools the tycoon's men with mannequins, after which Dharamdas learns exactly why the gang's car is called Big Pigeon: it comes armed with an egg canon.

WITH THE EXCELLENT *BESHARAM*, Deven Verma proved that, despite his background as a comedic actor, he had a good

I only kept watching to see what awful things its "lovable" leads would do next.

head for action—even if the comic subplot he created for himself in that film provided some of its few rough spots. However, while *Besharam* was a straight ahead actioner, *Bada Kabutar*, is something altogether different: an "action comedy." This means, among other things, that its many fights are largely played as slapstick, with only the handsome newcomer Nikhilesh allowed to present anything resembling a credible physical threat. It also means that it takes place in a world where its protagonists can be despicable in both motive and action and still be presented as lovable underdogs.

Seriously, how much you enjoy *Bada Kabutar* may be determined by just how high your tolerance is for watching flagrant child neglect. Rita may develop maternal feelings for little Golu, but that's not before she's let him wander into the street and get hit by a car, or set his nursery ablaze with a carelessly discarded match. As with the superior *Bombay 405 Miles*, *Bada Kabutar*'s producers are as mercenary and exploitive as the film's putative protagonists when it comes to manipulating audience sympathies through promiscuous imperilment of its toddler stars. (Which is not to say that Golu himself is any walk in the park, either, given that his dialog consists of the same crying loop repeated over and over again.)

Perhaps the most enjoyable thing about *Bada Kabutar* for me was the preponderance of unfamiliar faces in its cast. Stars Rehana Sultan, Nikhilesh, and Dara Singh lookalike Paul Sharma all had less than a dozen credits between them at the time. As Bhola, director Verma gives himself a fairly prominent role this time, but he turns out to be one of those insipid man-children who provide little interest. Pinchoo Kapoor, who I was also unacquainted with, bore a distracting resemblance to Orson Welles. Overall—and with the exception of elder golden age star Ashok Kumar—you have to take notice of a film in which the most recognizable faces are those of career drunkard Keshto Mukherjee and uncredited perpetual "Boss" Madan Puri.

As one would expect, R.D. Burman's songs are also an asset to *Bada Kabutar*, as catchy and energetic as ever. We also get a rare diegetic intrusion by western pop music in a scene where Rita shimmies to The Equals' 1967 hit "Hold Me Closer." For the most part, Burman's tunes serve to underscore the budding romance between Rita and Navin, but there is also a welcome number from Helen, during which she sings a song of congratulations at the birthday fete for Dharamdas's son. It's a bit sexy for the occasion, and nicely illustrates how, despite all his professions of love for his child, this venal fat cat is really all about his own desires.

In a way, the repellent actions of its main characters lend *Bada Kabutar* a kind of outrageous appeal. I think I only kept watching to see what awful things its "lovable" leads would do next, and to see just how winsomely it would seek to portray those atrocities. Suffice it to say it was not unsatisfying when virtually every character on screen ended up getting hauled off to prison during the finale. It couldn't have happened to a nicer bunch of guys.

AZAAD
"Free"

Released: 1978
Director: Pramod Chakravorty
Stars: Dharmendra, Hema Malini, Prem Chopra, Sulochana Latkar, Keshto Mukherjee, Randhir, Jankidas, Master Bhagwan, Mohan Choti, Birbal, Viju Khote, Kuljeet, Roohi Berde, Kanu Roy, Bihari, Jagdish Raj, Manmauji, Madhup Sharma, Farooq, Madhu Chauhan, C.S. Dubey, Lalita Kumari, Abhi Bhattacharya, Pinchoo Kapoor, Om Shivpuri, Shoma Anand, Ajit, Amol Sen, M.B. Shetty
Writers: Sachin Bhowmick, Gulshan Nanda, Ehsan Rizvi
Music: Rahul Dev Burman (R.D. Burman)
Lyrics: Anand Bakshi
"Thrills": Mansoor

Ashok (Dharmendra), who seems old enough to know better, spends his abundant free time posing as a masked cavalier called Azaad and righting the wrongs of his community. Unfortunately, in Ashok's small village of Gangapur there is little in the way of true evil for him to oppose. Thus he busies himself with projects like trying to derail the arranged marriage of an elderly money lender to a girl whom Ashok deems inappropriately young.

One day Ashok comes upon a grain field set ablaze and finds that the culprit is a haughty young woman named Seema (Hema Malini), who started the fire so that she could paint it. Ashok throws her painting into the fire and lectures her on the importance of the field to the people of the village. She orders her body guards to attack him. Ashok thrashes them. Later he learns from the police that Seema is the Princess of Raigadh. The police are quite cross with Ashok over the incident, as they feel they are perfectly equipped to handle the infractions of visiting royals without him.

This incident also proves the final straw for Ashok's long suffering sister-in-law Sarla (Sulochana Latkar), who has been caring for him since his policeman older brother disappeared a couple of years previously. She boards the train out of town, washing her hands of his antics, only to have a desperate Ashok chase the train down and stop it. He instead proposes that he leave town, upon which she gifts him with a pendant that belonged to his brother and a letter of introduction to her brother Ramesh (Keshto Mukherjee) who lives in the city.

Upon arriving at the home of Ramesh and his sister Rekha (Shoma Anand), Ashok is taken by Ramesh to the Raigadh Palace, where he is greeted coolly by none other than Seema. Most of the industry in town, it turns out, is run by the mysterious King Company, which is owned by Seema and administered by her uncle Ajit Singh (Ajit) and his spoiled son Prem (Prem Chopra). Ashok despairs of finding a job with the company if it is Seema who is making the decision, but, much to his surprise, she gives him work at the same distillery where Ramesh is employed. Little does he know, but she is only doing this so that she can exact revenge for the humiliation she suffered at his hands in Gangapur.

What follows are a series of cruel pranks on Seema's part, most of which are thwarted by Ashok's inherent mightiness. She orders him to ride an unruly horse to which she's fed a bottle of whisky, only to have him tame and claim the animal as his own. Later, Ashok interferes with a hunt she's on by showing up in a shabby bear costume. He then takes Seema hostage and determines to "make a woman" out of her by forcing her to cook for him and perform other menial domestic tasks. Seema responds to this by pushing him down a well, at which point she is attacked by a wild tiger. Ashok struggles out of the well to wrestle the tiger, at great injury to himself, and saves Seema's life. She falls in love with him.

This romantic development is bad news for Prem, who was hoping to marry Seema, giving him and his father greater access to her fortune. Nonetheless, a breach with the Singhs is inevitable for Ashok, as it is soon revealed that they are responsible for pretty much everything bad that has happened in Azaad. A flashback tells us that it was Ajit who murdered Ashok's policeman brother. And, as it was Seema's father (Om Shivpuri) who witnessed the crime and threatened to tell the authorities, Ajit had him declared insane, imprisoning him in a tower where he has kept him confused and docile all these years with constant injections of intravenous drugs. Not only that, but Ajit and Prem are also involved in the illegal drug trade, using the King Company's fishery to smuggle hashish, which they hide inside blocks of ice.

This last racket is accidentally stumbled upon by Ramesh, who naively goes to Ajit Singh with the news. Ajit feigns ignorance of the drug operation and thanks Ramesh for his heroism, then ushers him into the "Machine of Hell," a funhouse style gauntlet of torture devices hidden within the recesses of the palace, where he dies. His sister Rekha later shows up at the palace looking for him and Prem attempts to rape her, only to have her escape and send Ashok back to give him a brutal beating. Ajit later finds Ashok's pendant, which bears a picture of his brother, and, realizing who he is, lures him back to the palace, where he, too, is subjected to the Machine of Hell. Ashok, however, proves well matched to the various devilish contraptions and escapes, killing one of Ajit's vicious dogs in the process. Ajit, in a last ditch effort, then kidnaps Rekha and Ashok's sister-in-law and imprisons them in the torture chamber. Thus is Ashok forced to take on the Machine of Hell one last time.

INDIA'S B "STUNT" FILMS—taking their cue from American serials and Douglas Fairbanks's early screen adventures—were awash with Tarzan figures and swashbuckling heroes of the people. Seen in that context, *Azaad* could be viewed as something of a gentle parody. In his guise as Azaad, Dharmendra's Ashok not only looks like an off-brand Zorro, but also swings from vines and lets out a throaty jungle yell in a manner identical to Johnny Weissmuller's Jungle Lord. Could it be that Ashok has simply watched too many old Dara Singh movies?

It's also true that, when viewed in this light, *Azaad* comes across as something of a bait and switch, as the colorful figure of Azaad only appears in its opening minutes, never to be seen again for the rest of the film. This opens the possibility that *Azaad* is meant to be some kind of coming-of-age story, which also doesn't work—and for two reasons.

First of all, Dharmendra, well north of forty, is simply too old here to portray the callow youth that such a story would require. Secondly, his character, by the end of the film, really hasn't undergone any kind of identifiable "arc"; he has merely performed a bunch of awesome feats involving a lot of stunt-doubled leaping and back flipping. This leaves us with the conclusion that *Azaad* is simply just another dumb mid-to-late-'70s Dharmendra action vehicle, in which it is not alone (yes, I'm looking at you, *Saazish*. You too, *International Crook*.)

The Machine of Hell is perhaps the most convoluted and insane death trap of all.

All of which is not to say that *Azaad* is not without its charms. Ajit Singh may be an autopilot role for the great Ajit, but casting Prem Chopra as his whiny daddy's boy of a son is truly inspired. R.D. Burman's score is strong, and there is a wonderful drunk song in "Jaan ki Kasam Sach Kaite Hain," sung by Lata Mangeshkar, which occurs after Ashok and Seema unwittingly drink spiked buttermilk (it's a long story, but suffice it to say that Keshto Mukherjee's character is involved). None of this makes up for the repellent spectacle of Dharmendra "taming" Hema Malini's Seema through forced housewifery, which had become something of a ritual in Dharmendra's movies at this point, an identical scenario having played out with Zeenat Aman's haughty princess in 1975's *Dharam Veer.*

And then, of course, there is the "Machine of Hell." If I have so far neglected to mention that a highlight of the elaborate lairs haunted by Bollywood's villains is the convoluted death traps that often hide within their recesses, now is the time, because the Machine of Hell is perhaps the most convoluted and insane of them all. Granted, the death trap in *Main Balwaan*, another Dharmendra film—albeit from the '80s—features giant busy box gears that grind its live victims into mincemeat, but the Machine has the added bonus of featuring little aesthetic touches that serve to accentuate its wealthy owners' decadence. These include dancing puppets in Victorian garb and a stuffed bear holding a bottle of Vat 69.

On the more practical side, the Machine of Death includes dozens of swinging spiked balls arrayed around a lava pit like a deadly game of Skittle Bowl, a tunnel lined with spinning buzz saw blades on sticks leading to a giant industrial fan with saw toothed blades, and a cavernous hall that shakes, dislodging hundreds of empty glass bottles to shatter down on whoever passes through. This last, in particular, while seeming to boast formidable killing power, also strikes me as potentially being extremely troublesome to set up again once sprung, much like the old Mouse Trap game.

I also found it charming how, once the Machine of Hell was introduced, during the film's eleventh hour, it pretty much became the star of the whole show, with the script coming up with ever new reasons to return to it again and again. It's as if *Azaad* was so slight that even its own makers couldn't help but be distracted from it by the appearance of a new toy.

BULLET

Released: 1976
Director: Vijay Anand
Stars: Dev Anand, Parveen Babi, Rakesh Roshan, Kabir Bedi, Jyoti Bakshi, Shreeram Lagoo, Sonia Sahni, Jagdeep, Ranjan, Murad, Mohan Sherry, Ranjana Sachdev, Sheela, Barkha Madan, Shahana, Shefali, Zarina Ratna, Ratna, Jezebel, Julie, Teresa, Shirley, Latif, Moolchand, Deepak Raj, Mamaji, Misra, Omi, Babu, Sudarshan Sethi, Kalla, Yusuf, Roy, Uttamraj, Ramesh, Jaswant, Mehra, Jullianin, Krishna
Writers: Vijay Anand, Suraj Sanim
Music: Rahul Dev Burman (R.D. Burman)
Lyrics: Anand Bakshi
Action: Mansoor Ali

Sapna (Parveen Babi), personal secretary to an international shipping magnate, discovers that her new boyfriend Dharam (Dev Anand) is an inspector with the police force. Confronted, Dharam tells her that her boss, Durga (Kabir Bedi), is being investigated both for conducting criminal activity under his company facade and for defrauding poor investors with millions of dollars in phony stocks. Sapna defends Durga at first, but when Durga tries to pimp her out to a business associate, she reconsiders and divulges to Dharam the location of some incriminating files. Dharam breaks into the office and steals the files, but is photographed in the process. Durga then sends some goons to apprehend Dharam before he can take the files to his superiors, and they stage what looks like a drunken hit and run car accident for which Dharam ends up being sentenced to "two years of rigorous imprisonment."

Upon his release, Dharam is determined to continue his pursuit of Durga despite being stripped of his badge. He takes to carrying a solitary bullet in his breast pocket, telling Durga "It'll remain near my heart til I lodge it in yours." Such is Dharam's campaign of harassment that the beleaguered executive ends up becoming obsessed with the bullet itself, ordering his minions to attack Dharam and steal it from him. This fails, and Dharam, with Sapna's help, is eventually able to intercept a large cache of currency that Durga is trying to smuggle out of the country. Things go downhill for Sapna's boss from there, and his passport is seized by the authorities in lieu of a sizable unpaid tax debt.

Meanwhile, Durga has entrusted the dirty files to his accountant, Zafurullah (Jagdeep), who has hidden them in his home. Zafurullah has taken up with the widow of one of Durga's jilted stockholders, but has since decided that he would rather marry the woman's comely teenage daughter. The mother agrees, but only if Zafurullah will pay a dowry of $50,000. Desperate, Zafurullah goes to Dharam and offers him the files at that price, but Dharam is unable to come up with the money. At the same time, Durga contacts his lover Mala (Sonia Sahni), wife of the wealthy Mr. Ghanshyamdas

(Shreeram Lagoo), and asks if she can come up with the cash necessary to pay his tax bill. Together they come up with a plot to stage a fake kidnapping of Ghanshyamdas's teenage daughter Roshni (Jyoti Bakshi) in order to extort the needed amount from the miser.

To complete the circle, Mala approaches Dharam about playing the kidnapper in their plan, not telling him of Durga's involvement. As the payment she offers would cover Zafurullah's asking price for the files, he reluctantly agrees. As for Roshni, being a rebellious tearaway with a full menu of chemical dependencies and what are clinically referred to as "serious daddy issues," she needs little convincing to take part. Unfortunately, come the night of the scam, Durga sneaks into the safe house where Roshni is waiting for the ransom to be delivered and murders her. Mala, meanwhile, has secretly replaced Ghanshyamdas's cash-stuffed briefcase with one stuffed with newspaper and delivered the loot to Durga. Because Dharam has not considered himself to be participating in an actual crime, he has made little effort to cover his tracks, and so the significance is not lost upon him when he comes upon Roshni's corpse. As fate would have it, it is at this time that the police see fit to reinstate Dharam and put him in charge of the investigation of Roshni's disappearance.

From this point Dharam is consumed with trying to hide his involvement in Roshni's death from his partner Rajesh (Rakesh Roshan), who loved her, while trying to figure out a way to point the finger of blame back at Durga. This he finally does by siphoning word to Durga that Roshni has actually survived his attack, luring the criminal forth to silence this unexpected witness. All leads to a final confrontation at a hospital, during which Durga threatens a maternity ward full of newborns with a briefcase filled with hand grenades.

LIKE A LOT OF BOLLYWOOD MOVIES, *Bullet* starts out with a straightforward concept and ends up with an awful lot of business on its hands. But what's impressive is just how well—at least in terms of sheer plot mechanics—it handles that business. From its interval point on, the film piles on one classic film noir plot twist on top of another, leaving no stone unturned in making sure that our protagonist is thoroughly entangled in a strangling Chinese puzzle of implication and compromise. Perhaps director and screenwriter Vijay Anand just wanted to prove to his big brother Dev what a clever boy he was, and it's hard to imagine he wasn't successful. The attention to detail is amazing. I especially like how Dharam's ass covering measures—such as having Mala and Roshni sign an affidavit outlining the plot—actually end up incriminating him deeper once Roshni turns up dead.

Unfortunately, amid the raveling and, by necessity, equally laborious unraveling of all these schemes, other things gets lost. Among them is Parveen Babi, who, already underused, disappears from the narrative completely for a substantial length, only to be called back for some thankless woman-in-peril work in the eleventh hour. Fortunately, we have *Bullet*'s titular motif on hand to keep

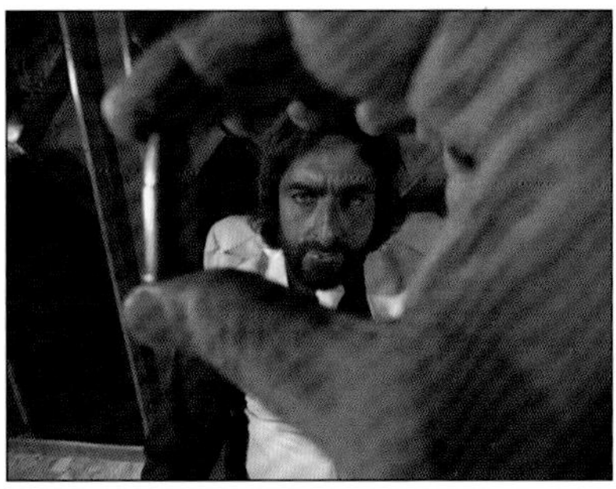

us from completely careening, *Apradh*-like, into full blown movie schizophrenia. It would be obnoxious to call Dharam's bullet the "star" of the film, but it can't be argued that it doesn't loom large over the proceedings. Especially fascinating is the scene following the gang's attempt to rob Dharam of the shell, during which Dharam goes to a bar patronized by Durga and, with the help of a chorus of hoochie coochie girls, reenacts the scene in dance as if it were a tableau from the religious epics (complete with a cooed refrain of "boo-LET boo-LET boo-LET!).

As for Dev Anand, despite him being once again paired with a stunning actress many years his junior, I was unable to find him nearly as unctuous as I generally feel obligated to. Perhaps that's because he's up against a distasteful subplot in which Jagdeep's desire to marry his adopted teenage daughter is played for laughs. It could also be that the surfeit of calamity poured upon his head lead to an exhaustion of schadenfreude on my part. In any case, I was willing to extend him credit for all of his legitimately suave portrayals of the '50s and '60s and accept a minimum of smirking and just a few ridiculously doubled back flips in return.

Also among the business that the already overburdened *Bullet* has on its plate is the introduction of teenaged starlet Jyoti Bakshi, who plays Roshni. Interestingly, Roshni is very similar to Janice, the rebellious stoner played by Zeenat Aman in Dev Anand's early directorial effort *Hare Raama Hare Krishna*. But while Janice was the recipient of all manner of condescending moralizing on Anand's part in that film, a scene in *Bullet* where Roshni and Dharam drop acid together is played for laughs, and even becomes the occasion for a Disney-esque musical number filled with naïve special effects. Sadly, because she's burdened with representing everything that's wrong with Indian youth (did I mention that she gambles as well as smokes, drops pills and drinks?), Roshni's ultimate fate in *Bullet* is to be reduced, in death, to being nothing more than an inconvenient obstacle to be unceremoniously disposed of. Even sadder is the fact that dependency problems appear to have been a part of Bakshi's life off-screen, and would eventually contribute to her early death.

Of course, you'd think that for a film like *Bullet* to succeed, it would require an audience willing to follow along with all of its myriad crosses and double crosses. But the good news for those of us with shorter attention spans is that the film also boasts all the bells and whistles typical of '70s Bollywood fare. R.D. Burman's great song score, a fantastic psychedelic nightclub set complete with skulls and giant spider webs, and a number of fight scenes involving a spindly looking older gentlemen improbably twirling end over end, are just a few of the colorful distractions to keep us onboard through the complicated bits. And, let's be honest: no matter how many of those complications turn up, there's not a soul watching who would doubt for a moment that the film will end with Dev getting Durga intimately acquainted with that bullet. Say hello to my little friend, indeed.

BOMBAY TO GOA

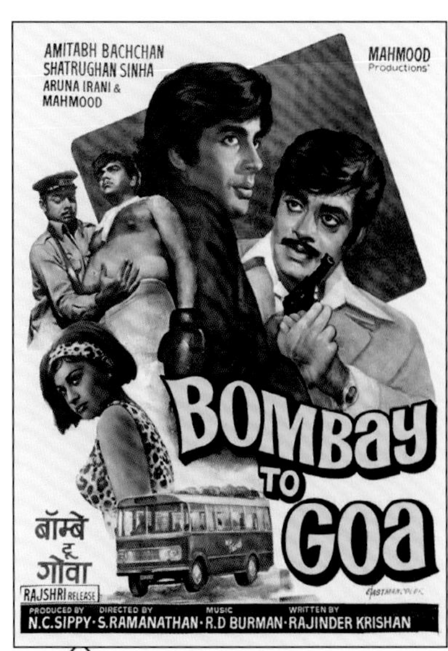

Released: 1972
Director: S. Ramanathan
Stars: Amitabh Bachchan, Aruna Irani, Shatrughan Sinha, Mehmood, Anwar Ali, Kishore Kumar, Lalita Pawar, Monorama, Keshto Mukherjee, Kukri, Agha, Manmohan, Nasir Hussain, Sunder, Asit Sen, Mehmood Jr., Randhir, Rah Kishore, Darshan, Muniraj, Sheikh, Yashraj, Somender, Oscar Unger, Hanuman, Robert, Babban, Misrilal, Suresh Desai, Vijoo, Reddy, Mirchandani, Saul, Birbal, Mohan Singh, Moqsood, Ahmed, Noshir, Jerry, Master Javed, Kader, Dilip Dutt, Sushil Dutt, Shobha, Praveen Paul, Dulari, Gene, Kammo, Mona Saxena, Indira Bansal, Mary, Trezu, Neeru, Usha Iyer, Yusuf Khan
Writers: Rajendra Krishan, Usilai Somanathan
Music: Rahul Dev Burman (R.D. Burman)
Lyrics: Rajendra Krishan
Fights: Tiruvarur Das

Mala (Aruna Irani) is a college girl about to be married off by her wealthy parents to the son of a family friend she has yet to meet. She is also movie mad. When two con men posing as movie producers, Sharma (Shatrughan Sinha) and Verma (Manmohan), "discover" her at a local swimming pool, she is all too quick to agree to star as the heroine in their entirely invented film. The two scoundrels then take her on the town, wining, dining and pampering her in a manner befitting a star, but somehow manage to forget their wallets each time. Meanwhile, Ravi (Amitabh Bachchan), a tall and mysterious stranger, starts to repeatedly turn up in Mala's shadow, frequently—and much to her irritation—antagonizing the two con men and showing no aversion to throwing punches when doing so.

When a mildly racy publicity photo of Mala appears in a movie magazine, her parents, outraged that she would disgrace the family by embracing such a lowly profession, threaten to withdraw her from college and accelerate her wedding plans. Hearing of this, Sharma encourages Mala to run away from home, but asks that she first steal as much as she can get her hands on. This she does, making off with a small fortune in jewelry from the family safe.

Of course, soon thereafter, Sharma claims need of a substantial cash infusion in order to hire a male star for his film who is equal to Mala's luster. Mala dutifully complies, but the division of the money between Sharma and the rest of his gang, who number several men in addition to Verma, causes discord. As a result, Mala walks in just as Sharma is knifing Verma to death, and flees the hideout with the gang in close pursuit. After a long night of evading the goons through the streets of Bombay, she hops aboard a cross country bus and buys a ticket for the last stop in Goa.

The bus is staffed by Khanna (Mehmood), the irascible and sharp tongued conductor, and Rajesh, the good natured but dimwitted driver (played by

Mehmood's brother, Anwar Ali), with a passenger list made up of a large cast of eccentrics. These include, among others, a domineering former stage diva (Manorama) and her daughter, two lecherous old scholars, a narcoleptic drunk (Keshto Mukherjee, naturally), a Brahmin couple with a son who is a mewling fat mutant, and a surly boxer with a wooden leg (Yusuf Khan). Along the way, they also pick up famed actor and playback singer Kishore Kumar (Kishore Kumar), whose car has broken down on the way to a film shoot. Cajoled by the star-struck passengers, he regales them with the film's theme song.

Meanwhile, Sharma and his men, following in their car, are gaining ground on the bus, and eventually manage to get an armed representative of their number on board. Fortunately for Mala, none other than Ravi soon thereafter flags the vehicle down and, after being surreptitiously alerted by her to the hit man's presence, manages to quash this first attempt on her life. By this time the audience has been made privy to the fact that, unknown to Mala, Ravi is actually that son of a family friend to whom she has been involuntarily betrothed, and is tailing her in order to get some sense of what he's getting himself into.

The gang's attempts on Mala continue, only to be repeatedly thwarted by Ravi's wits and fighting skills. Finally, Sharma himself takes it upon himself to board the bus, managing to overpower Ravi and spirit Mala away. Ravi takes off after the gang's car on foot, leading to a confrontation in which he is hopelessly outnumbered. At this point, the passengers rally and head off to join him. A protracted and chaotic free-for-all follows in which the hoodlums are ultimately defeated. Everyone sings the theme song. The End.

***BOMBAY TO GOA* GETS OFF TO** a great start: a woman screams and flees into the night. The gang of killers takes off in pursuit, and a long, wordless chase ensues through the forebodingly darkened streets of Bombay. All the while, a mysterious Amitabh Bachchan watches silently from the shadows. No exposition, either verbal or visual, is provided to orient us within the action, no clues as to who any of these people are or what their relationship to one another might be. In their place is only action and ominous, free floating mood. It's a bold stylistic approach that, all in all, feels impeccably modern.

And then day breaks… and *Bombay to Goa* suddenly starts to seem like something from another era entirely. This is perhaps due in part to the involvement of Mehmood, a widely popular screen comedian with roots in the previous decade, who produced the film and is even credited by some sources as its director (although the screen credit goes to S. Ramanathan). The result is that *Bombay to Goa* ends up being somewhat at war with itself; a film with a hard, contemporary crime thriller shell and a goofy and dated comic escapade at its center.

For, despite its moody, noir-ish setup, what the film ends up being is that most time tested of comic staples: the road picture—and, not only that, but a road picture in which the journey is largely padded out by comedic episodes that serve in no way to move the larger plot forward. A chicken smuggled aboard the bus escapes, leading to a hapless and pratfall ridden hunt through the countryside. Someone accidentally dumps a box of snuff, causing all of the passengers to sneeze. An obese child, obsessed with "fried snacks," turns into a howling monster until being forcibly gagged. And all of this is projected by a cast of veteran comedic actors with a level of cartoonish mugging that, at its best, merely limns the grotesque—all the better for Mehmood to react with his arsenal of barbed put downs and pained takes, and all else involved to quarrel, quarrel, quarrel.

In such an unabashedly slapstick context, Amitabh Bachchan—here granted an early leading man turn in the days leading up to his breakout in *Zanjeer*—is largely relegated to playing the potentially awesome Ravi as a mischievous, wisecracking scallywag, padding the blows of his lightning fists with a heavy dose of family friendly tomfoolery. Not that we wouldn't see this side of Bachchan in later films, but it at least makes us appreciate what his subsequent icon status for the most part freed him from, while at the same time making us admire his professionalism. The swarthy Shatrughan Sinha, for his part, impresses less as a villain than he would in other films as an unlikely hero, being a far cry from the Anglo ideal represented by most Bollywood leading men. Meanwhile, Aruna Irani, a favorite of Mehmood's, manages to be appealing while showing little of the fire that would make her the shoulda-been superstar she was. Mala is clearly more of a waylaid innocent than an actual bad girl and, as such, gives the actress little to bite into.

Another way in which *Bombay to Goa* gives the appearance of being at war with itself is in how it seems to embody the Indian public's very real moral ambivalence toward its country's film industry. Its depiction of that industry as providing the context for a vicious flimflam artist like Sharma would seem to support Mala's parents' view of it as inherently disreputable. Yet Mala and other characters are also given the opportunity

It is a film with a hard, contemporary crime thriller shell and a goofy and dated comic escapade at its center.

to rebut that view (Mala, for her part, woundedly claims that the tame cheesecake shots of her were "artistic" in nature). There is also the extent to which the film comes off as a love letter to show business itself, as well as to show business fandom. The characters of Rajesh and Khanna, we learn, have named themselves in homage to the then phenomenally popular star Rajesh Khanna, and later enthusiastically display an encyclopedic knowledge of Kishore Kumar's work as a playback singer. Popular Indian jazz singer Usha Iyer turns up as herself in a nightclub number in which she frantically races through a medley of English language hits—"Listen to the Pouring Rain," "Fever" and "Be-Bop-a-Lula" among them. And then there is the fourth wall breaking cameo by Kishore Kumar himself, with his diegetic showcase of the film's theme song—which, I must point out, brazenly appropriates the entire melody of the Beach Boys' "Help Me Rhonda" to its own ends without adding much musically to stake claim on it as its own.

BIO:

SHATRUGHAN SINHA

Appears in: *Bombay to Goa, Kalicharan, Shareef Budmaash, Bombay 405 Miles, Shaan*

Watch 1972's *Bombay to Goa* and you'll see Shatrughan Sinha in the type of role to which Indian audiences of the time had become accustomed to seeing him: that of a menacing, predatory thug, a scourge to the defenseless heroine, who must seek protection from him in the arms of the heroic Amitabh Bachchan. Skip forward a little and you'll start to see that character softening at the edges a bit: in *Bombay 405 Miles*, a kidnapper with a heart of gold, in *Kalicharan*, a principled bandit, intense yet sympathetic. That he would eventually make the transition to romantic hero is one of the most fascinating aspects of Sinha's career. Swarthy, mustached, and with a rough, lived-in face, he is anything but the typical Bollywood hero, yet that he became one nonetheless is a refreshing reminder that, in the age of the "angry young man", there was wiggle room in even the most fixed of Indian cinema conventions. Sinha would go on to further buck Bollywood trends by not only having a political career, but an actually successful one, holding two cabinet ministries between 2003 and 2004. He is currently the head of the Bharatiya Janata Party's Culture and Arts Department.

Aside from that last mentioned bit of plunderphonics, R.D. Burman's score is perfectly agreeable, and ended up providing evergreen hits with songs like the upbeat "Dekha Na Hai Re Socha," which was sung by—who else?—Kishore Kumar to be picturized on an antic Bachchan. (*Bombay to Goa*, itself a remake of a 1966 Tamil film, is today enough of an evergreen itself to have been remade in 2007.) All nonetheless contribute to a film that is less concerned with being a comedy, a thriller, or a musical than it is with entertaining its restless audience at all costs. That said—and as much as I might like to—*Bombay to Goa*'s action element can't be ignored. Indeed, so prevalent are acrobatic stunts and kinetic punch-ups within its desperately crowd-pleasing confines that one could only see it as indicative of the increasing importance of those elements as the '70s dawned. And that would only become more so as time progressed.

KHOON KHOON
"Blood Blood"

Released: 1973
Director: Mohammed Hussain
Stars: Mahendra Sandhu, Danny Denzongpa, Jagdeep, Rekha, Murad, Helen, Faryal, Agha, Karan Dewan, Madan Puri, Dev Kumar, Rajan Kapoor, Padma Khanna, Manmohan Krishna, Asit Sen, Shyama, Habib, Sabeena, Brahm Bhardwaj, Ratan Gaurang
Writer: Umesh Mehra, Vrajendra Gaur
Music: Vijay Singh
Lyrics: Hasrat Jaipuri, Dev Kohli, Gajinder
Fights: Gani

A psychotic sniper (Danny Denzongpa) is holding the city in a grip of fear, picking off innocent citizens seemingly at random. As the body count rises, it becomes clear that his targets are not limited to hotsy totsy dancers and that even children and holy men are not safe. Eventually, in the course of a series of taunting phone calls to the Police Commissioner (Murad), the killer makes a ransom demand, requiring lead investigator Anand (Mahendra Sandhu) and his tomfoolery prone partner (Jagdeep) to make an exhausting relay from one end of the city to the other. Nonetheless, Anand seems to get the last laugh when he tracks the killer down, tracing him to the sports arena where he works as a live-in caretaker and arresting him after a tense scuffle. Sadly, the madman proves deft at gaming the system and not only wins his freedom but also frames Anand for police brutality in the process. Finally, when the killer hijacks a bus full of school children, Anand realizes it's time to take the gloves off.

IF THE ABOVE SYNOPSIS sounds familiar, congratulations; you have seen *Dirty Harry*, Don Siegel's masterpiece of gritty 1970s noir that was also a successful vehicle for a post-spaghetti western Clint Eastwood. *Khoon Khoon* director Mohammed Hussain, a prolific denizen of Bollywood's B movie industry, was no stranger to adapting Western source material, having been one of the first directors to bring Superman to India's screens and also, with *Aaya Toofan*, reworking Nathan Juran's *Jack the Giant Killer* as a vehicle for wrestler Dara Singh. Even Hussain's 1963 jungle adventure *Shikari* can trace its origins to *King Kong* by way of *Doctor Cyclops*.

With *Khoon Khoon*, Hussain sticks pretty close to his inspiration, even recreating some of *Dirty Harry*'s scenes in near shot-for-shot detail—although he makes one significant departure. At the time of *Khoon Khoon*'s production, Amitabh Bachchan had yet to popularize the image of the angry young antihero, and, as a result, Indian movie audiences may not have been considered ready for a protagonist of such deep moral ambiguity as Clint Eastwood's Harry Callahan. It is perhaps for this reason that newcomer

Mahendra Sandhu's character is more representative of the type of screen heroes that preceded—and perhaps even necessitated—Bachchan.

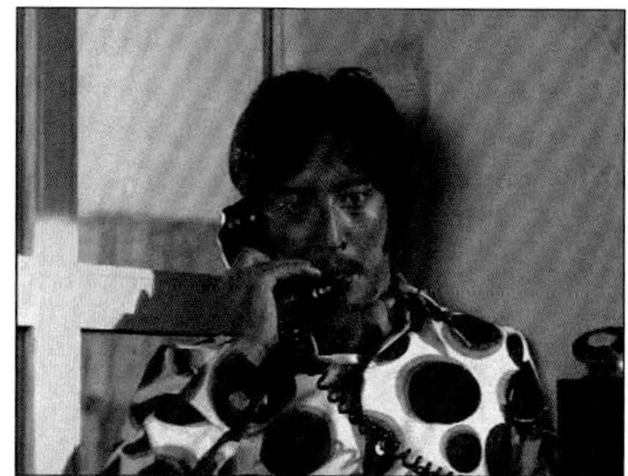

Like many Bollywood policeman of his day, Sandhu's Anand is an upright and honorable caretaker of the public will, one who enjoys both the respect of his peers and the support of his superiors, and who comes home each night to a loving family comprised of his beautiful wife (Rekha, in a "special appearance"), doll-like daughter, and doting live-in parents. Gone is the volatile Callahan driven by his wife's murder and, with him, much of *Dirty Harry*'s elements of character study. In their place is a story stripped to its police procedural bones, fleshed out instead by the usual musical numbers and episodes of comic relief from Jagdeep. Thankfully, Jagdeep's comedy here is less rooted than usual in simple bumbling, allowing him to be an effective partner to Anand when the action requires it and less of a potential annoyance as a result. (He also gains extra points for scoring Helen as his love interest.)

Compensating for the lack of grit that the film's neutering of Anand achieves is the performance of Danny Denzongpa. Though perennial bad guy Prem Chopra is more of a ringer for *Dirty Harry*'s original psycho killer, actor Andrew Robinson, I can't think of another Bollywood actor of the era more suited to the part. The dashing young Denzongpa here gives a performance that is as compelling as it is lacking in vanity, swinging unpredictably from grandiosity, to sniveling cowardice, to impotent rage without ever losing the character's air of unhinged menace. Hussain and screenwriter Vrajendra Gaur seem to have realized that Denzongpa's serial sniper was the real star of the show, providing a prologue in which we catch a glimpse of the character as a child—an obvious bad seed who, after being caught trying to stab his baby brother with a kitchen knife, escapes from the mental institution to which he's been remanded.

Stylistically, *Khoon Khoon* is about as perfect a collision of the disparate sensibilities of 1970s Bollywood and Hollywood as one could imagine. In the many location shot scenes, Hussain scrupulously mimics Segal's harsh realist approach, but, in the set bound sequences, seems to offset that with an even heavier than usual reliance on artifice. The resulting combination clashes in all the right ways, as with the opening murder, in which

the female victim dramatically falls back across her blinding chartreuse bed spread with a flower of fire engine red blood blossoming on the front of her nightgown. Terror has come to Candyland, Hussain seems to be saying, and no cozy genre expectations can be relied upon to protect you.

Khoon Khoon's "Bollywood-izing" of *Dirty Harry* also employs a good deal of cleverness in terms of how the requisite song and dance numbers are integrated. In most cases, these are segregated from the action by placing them within flashbacks or nightclub numbers, but, at other times, a more adventurous approach is taken. (The songs, by the way, are credited to Vijay Singh, though the movie's instrumental score relies heavily on needle drops from Lalo Schifrin's original *Dirty Harry* score.) One of the more daring song stagings takes place in the scene—lifted off a piece from the original film—in which Denzongpa's killer, having hijacked the bus full of children, attempts to engage his young captives in a sing-along to stave off panic. In contrast to the tense rendition of "Row, Row, Row Your Boat" seen in *Dirty Harry*, *Khoon Khoon* uses this circumstance as the opportunity for a full-fledged musical number, with Denzongpa and the kids joining together in a chipper little ditty to full instrumental accompaniment. As awful as that sounds, it's actually kind of effective, introducing an element of the nightmarishly surreal into the sequence that is all the more jarring once a violent outburst from Denzongpa abruptly snaps us back into the ugly reality of the situation.

It is this merging and chafing of sensibilities that makes *Khoon Khoon*, regardless of its origins, a singular and fascinating film, and far from the haphazard carbon copy that other Westerners might lazily dismiss it as.

Like other Indian adaptations of Hollywood films, it less apes its source material than holds a funhouse mirror up to it.

Like other Indian adaptations of Hollywood films, it less apes its source material than holds a funhouse mirror up to it, casting it in an entirely different light and dimension. I should also mention that it reimagines *Dirty Harry* as what K.S.R. Doss might call a "100 percent action film," goosing up the proceedings to include that much more in terms of car chases and fist fights. Even Madan Puri is called forth for a cameo as a typical Bollywood "Boss" type so that Mahendra Sandhu and Jagdeep can have a bunch of anonymous suited goons to punch and be punched by.

All of which is to say that, even though it helps in deciphering the film when watching it without English subtitles (as I had to), one does not need to see *Dirty Harry* in order to enjoy *Khoon Khoon*. In fact, seeing it without any knowledge of its Hollywood lineage might just highlight all that is unique about it that much more.

FAKIRA
"Sage"

Released: 1976
Director: C.P. Dixit
Stars: Shashi Kapoor, Shabana Azmi, Asrani, Aruna Irani, Danny Denzongpa, Madan Puri, Iftekhar, Achala Sachdev, Asit Sen, Satyendra Kapoor, Purnima, Ramesh Deo, Ranjan, Mukri, Jagdish Raj, Rajan Haksar, Shetty, Jankidas, Chaman Puri, Ram Avtar, Birbal, Brahmachari, Moolchand, Bijnore, Jugnu, Aslam Khan, Kishin Punjabi, Prakash, Surjeet Redi, Prabhakar, Sarwar, Premji, Kamu, Master Ratan, Master Chicoo, Master Bittoo, Master Rajesh Valecha, Master Ravi
Writers: Dhruva Chatterjee, R.K. Bannerjee, S.M. Abbas
Music: Ravindra Jain
Lyrics: Ravindra Jain, Rajkani Tulsi
Fights: S. Azimbhai

The upright father of little Vijay and Ajay informs the police of their neighbors' smuggling activities. In response, those neighbors, in an effort to cover their tracks, torch the tenement in which they live, and Vijay and Ajay can only watch helplessly as both of their parents die inside. Later, aided by their friend Popat, the kids stage a sort of guerilla attack on the bad guys in an attempt at revenge. In the ensuing melee, Ajay gets separated from them and ends up being taken in by a benevolent stranger who takes pity on him, not to be seen by his family for many years.

Vijay (Sashi Kapoor) comes to adulthood as Fakira, a cunning robber who lives in a fantastic underground lair with his assistants, the quarrelsome Popat (now played by Asrani) and Neelam (Aruna Irani), using a gift for disguise and trickery to steal the loot of smugglers and redistribute it to the poor. When we join them, the trio's latest mark is Chimanlai (Madan Puri), a smuggler who uses the Honesty Jewelers store as a front to fence stolen diamonds and gold. Masquerading as a nawab and his entourage, Vijay, Popat and Neelam manage to make off with a necklace worth 400,000. Upon returning to their base, Vijay finds, hiding in the trunk of his car, "Geetaa" (Shabana Azmi), an apparent orphan who tells him a hard luck story about being exploited by an older man. Vijay agrees to help her and lets her stay in the lair, much to the chagrin of Neelam, who has unreciprocated feelings for Vijay.

Meanwhile, Chimanlai vows revenge against Fakira and approaches the fearsome bandit Toofan (Danny Denzongpa) in hopes of putting a hit on the vigilante. Toofan, however, will only agree to capture, not kill, Fakira. In a subsequent meeting, the two men display their feathers to one another while still showing some signs of grudging respect, but when Toofan draws a gun in Vijay's car, Vijay uses the ejector seat to launch him to the curbside. His ego bruised, Toofan swears to kill Fakira.

Neelam is at the same time keeping a close eye on Geetaa, and inadvertently discovers that she is, in fact, Neeta, the daughter of the Police Commissioner (Iftekhar) and acting as an undercover agent to bring Fakira to justice. Informed of this, Vijay responds by performing a marriage ritual on Geetaa/Neeta. This, he says, will make life more complicated for the Commissioner, as he will no longer be just Fakira, but also the Commissioner's son-in-law. Soon thereafter, a gang of hoods disguised as police burst into Vijay's lair and cart him off to Toofan's hideout, where Vijay also finds Neelam, who has sold him out. After refusing Chimanlai's offer to join his gang, he is brought to a large hall where he is attacked by sword wielding henchmen swinging from the rafters by ropes. The unconscious Vijay is then taken out to sea and dumped by Toofan.

Finally, Toofan comes home to his adoptive father, and we see that it is the same man who took in little Ajay all those years ago. Told of what Toofan has done to Fakira, the man tells him that he has committed a terrible sin, given all the good that Fakira has done for the people. Toofan then finds a childhood picture of him and Vijay together and somehow puts together that they are brothers. He rushes to collect Popat and the two of them rescue Vijay, who, thanks to his yoga training, is able to hold his breath for up to thirty minutes. Then it is time for revenge.

The opportunity for this comes when Chimanlai, wanting to set a trap for Fakira, advertises a fiftieth birthday party for himself at which the cake will be laden with contraband gold and diamonds. Come the day, not only do Vijay, Popat and Toofan show up in silly musician disguises, but the police as well. After a bizarre scene in which Chimanlai auctions off every stitch of his clothing, Popat kills the electricity and, in the ensuing panic, Fakira's gang makes off with not only the cake, but also all of the proceeds. In a desperate, last ditch effort, Chimanlai kidnaps Neeta and ties her up inside a gargantuan effigy of Rama during the Dussehra Festival. This leads to a frantic race against time for Vijay, for at sundown the effigy will be set alight.

THE ROBIN HOOD FIGURE is pretty much inescapable throughout world popular cinema. In India alone we've already seen the Dharmendra vehicles *Azaad* and *Jugnu*, not to mention that latter film's Tamil remake *Guru*. Everyone likes to see a cheeky upstart hero stick it to the man. But what may set *Fakira* apart is the fact that it allows its audience to at once cheer that hero's populist heroics while at the same time thrilling to his Bondian excesses. With its underground ramp entrance, sliding circular doors and omnipresent red track lighting, Fakira's lair (which I'm assuming is the creation of Art Director S.S. Samel) is one of the most arrestingly mod in Indian popular film. If not a direct inspiration of, it is certainly a spiritual sibling to that of the Italian fumetti antihero Diabolik in Mario Bava's *Danger: Diabolik* and, as such, serves as a signal of *Fakira's* comic book aspirations.

And within that context, heartthrob Shashi Kapoor does a fine job at what is essentially the film's Batman role; balancing his motorcycle riding man of action portrayal with a strong measure of both brooding

intensity and haunted introspection. He also brings more than a little strut and swagger to the part; the scene where he and Danny Denzongpa's Toofan first meet is a joy to behold, the two of them lustily trading imperious, third person declarations of their own ferocity as all around scurry to get away from the impending brawl. Of course, *Fakira* is also very much a love story, with considerable time given over to Kapoor and Shabana Azmi giving voice to their feeling via Ravindra Jain's romantic tunes. Happily, the chemistry between the two stars is good and Azmi, known as much for her work in theater and Indian art cinema as Bollywood, is an appealingly modern presence, coming across as very much the liberated 1970s woman. This seems to encourage the filmmakers to get a little racier than they might get otherwise, as we're treated, not only to some simulated kissing between the two, but also a scene of them apparently nude in bed together.

Of course, it's always a pleasure to see the oft sidelined Aruna Irani in a substantial role, and here her Neelam traces a character arc that approaches Greek tragedy in its dimensions. The woman scorned, her jealousy drives her to the debased state of being little more than a cheap moll to the odious Chimanlai who, like many Bollywood vamps before her, can only redeem herself by giving her life to save the hero.

As for Asrani's Popat, the less said the better, for he's a stock comic relief character in a film in little need of one. For all its themes of revenge and families torn asunder, *Fakira* is actually a fairly lightweight picture, perhaps unable to take itself all that seriously. For proof, look at some of its whimsical set pieces: Aruna Irani and Shabana Azmi have a cat fight in which their traded slaps keep turning the lights in Fakira's lair—which operate on the "Clapper" principle—on and off; during the climactic fight with Chinmanlai's gang, Popat releases a flock of ridiculous looking, exploding robot birds. And then the film itself literally ends with a wink. And that is not to mention those moments where *Fakira* just can't be bothered to make sense, such as when Danny Denzongpa's Toofan divines his true relationship to Vijay apparently just because it was the point in the screenplay where that was supposed to happen.

In saying all of this, I don't mean to imply that *Fakira* disappoints; it is for the most part engagingly colorful and action packed, with charming performances from most of its stars. I do, however, think that the movie's flirtations with self parody are indicative of the state of the "masala" film at the dawn of the late '70s. It was getting to the point where those behind the camera could no longer help but be conscious of its excesses, and it would only get worse.

RAM BHAROSE
"God's Grace"

Released: 1977
Director: Anand Sagar
Stars: Randhir Kapoor, Rekha, Amjad Khan, Dara Singh, Keshto Mukherjee, Kanan Kaushal, Madan Puri, Nasir Hussain, Suijt Kumar, Raza Murad, Tom Alter, Sailesh Kumar, Gajanan Jagirdar, Jagdish Raj, Chaman Puri, Master Baboo, Javed Khan, Shivraj, Parshuram, Sole, Shahid Bijnori, Ram Murthy, Deepak Raj, Shetty
Writers: Moti Sagar, Krishnan Chander
Music: Ravindra Jain
Lyrics: Ravindra Jain, Hasrat Jaipuri, Dev Kohli, Taj Dar Taj
Fights: Shetty

Growing up in dire straits has left brothers Ram (Randhir Kapoor) and Bhanu (Amjad Khan) with very different approaches to life. Ram, open hearted and devout, has embraced the cause of justice, and intends to follow in his late father's footsteps by joining the police force, even though he is by all appearances retarded and has no aptitude for the task. Bhanu, by contrast, is cynical and ruthlessly materialistic, worshiping money at the expense of God and Mother India. This has lead Bhanu to, without his family's knowledge, take employment with one of those many Indian movie baddies who is known only as "Boss" (Madan Puri) and serve the interests of some unnamed and nefarious "foreign country" represented by token Caucasian weasel Tom Alter.

When C.I.B. Agent 1107 (Dara Singh) steals out of said foreign country with an incriminating microfilm, Boss and his goons are hot on his tail, finally forcing a wounded 1107 to pass the film off to the hapless Ram during a chance encounter. Thus is set in motion the string of events that will lead the brothers to face each other from opposite sides of the law, and ultimately offer Bhanu a final chance at redemption.

R*AM BHAROSE* OFFERS A LESSON in the pitfalls of star cameos. Like *Warrant* before it, it seems to be making a nod to its roots by including a supporting role for wrestler-turned-1960s-"stunt"-film-king Dara Singh. While Singh was essentially India's answer to Steve Reeves, portraying figures like Hercules and Samson in a string of low budget sword and sandal romps, he also did his share of Bondian knock-offs. None of these, however, was as handsomely funded as the obviously "A" list *Ram Bharose*, and, as such, his presence here only leads us to wonder what might have been had the appealing star been given it all.

What we get instead is a standard "reluctant secret agent" spoof fronted by lesser Kapoor family scion Randhir (son of the legendary director/star Raj, father to '90s sirens Karisma and Kareena) who's certainly no Dara Singh, much less a Sean Connery. As a result, while *Ram Bharose*, at least superficially, stacks its moral debate in favor of Kapoor's Ram, it ultimately doesn't make a very good case for virtue. I think we're meant to be charmed

by what director Anand Sagar and Randhir Kapoor himself consider to be Ram's child-like innocence. But what he comes across as is a freakish, creepily desexualized man-child, basically Baby Huey without the diaper. Thus, whenever he does one of his wide-eyed takes at the oh so mysterious workings of the adult world, or uncomprehendingly lets one of the femme fatale's obvious come-ons fall clatteringly to the floor in the space between, all we want to do is smack him across his stupid face.

By contrast, it is Amjad Khan's Bhanu, the more complex of the two lead characters, who provides most of the film's real heat and excitement. And it's nice to see the often underutilized Khan playing a somewhat more dimensional version of his usual heavy—one who, despite being bad, is at least given reasons for being so, as well as a chance at redemption, even if that ultimately involves his heart's icicles being unconvincingly melted by Ram's insipid goodness.

Also on hand here is Rekha as Kiran, the daughter of one of Boss's enemies whom the villain kidnapped in infancy and raised to be a kung fu fighting "Mafia Queen." It's a fun bad girl role that sees her tasked with vamping the coveted microfilm away from the naïve Ram, at one point by disguising herself in a sexy nurse's outfit. Of course, Kiran's background makes her also ripe for redemption and, sadly, ultimately not immune to Ram's Keane-eyed guilelessness. Another performer worth noting for receiving a little more of the limelight than usual here is Keshto Mukherjee, 1970s Bollywood's favorite comedy drunkard, who gets a fairly meaty sidekick role opposite Kapoor (albeit one that requires him to act drunk a good portion of the time).

As for Dara Singh, *Ram Bharose*'s action keeps him confined to the Boss's underground dungeon for a good portion of the film, though not without affording him a nice iconic moment during the climax. A good few years past his *Hercules* days, the star proves still adept at pretending to bust heavy chains with his heaving pectorals, just as he did during the final moments of countless Bollywood proxy peplums during the previous decade. In this sense, Dara is here in *Ram Bharose* to play what is essentially a quote from a Dara Singh movie, and that fact in turn testifies to his beloved status within Indian popular culture. It's a wise choice by the filmmakers in this case, because, to my mind, his appearance is one of the few things that make this otherwise unremarkable masala worth mentioning.

INKAAR
"Denial"

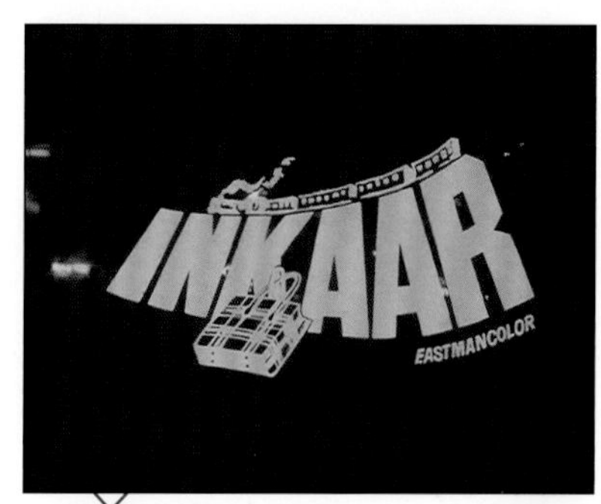

Released: 1977
Director: Raj N. Sippy
Stars: Vinod Khanna, Vidya Sinha, Shreeram Lagoo, Sadhu Meher, Amjad Khan, M. Rajan, Lily Chakravarty, Master Rajesh, Bharat Kapoor, Master Raju, Ranjita Thakur, Sheetal, Harish Magon, Shekhar Purohit, Kamaldeep, Siddharth, Chopra, Dharamvir, H.L. Pardesi, Chandu, Ranvir Raj, Ratna, Helen, Keshto Mukherjee, Rakesh Roshan, Prem Sagar, Gurbachchan Singh
Writers: Jyoti Swaroop, Sagar Sarhadi
Music: Rajesh Roshan
Lyrics: Majrooh Sultanpuri
Fights: Veeru Devgun

Choudhury (Shreeram Lagoo), the wealthy chief executive of the National Shoe Company, faced with the threat of ouster by a rebellious board of directors, is on the verge of a dramatic takeover of the company using company funds he has secretly borrowed. Before he can complete the stock purchase, however, he receives word that his son has been kidnapped, with the abductors setting the ransom at the exact amount needed for the buyout.

Be that as it may, it turns out that the kidnappers have made a major mistake and, rather than snatching Choudhury's son Guddu (Master Rajesh), have instead ended up with Bansi (Master Raju), the son of Choudhury's faithful chauffeur (Sadhu Meher). Once this is established, Choudhury initially refuses to pay the ransom, but is soon driven by his conscience to change his mind, thus putting the financial future of the company he has struggled to build from the ground up in serious jeopardy. His only hope is that CID Inspector Amar Gill (Vinod Khanna) and his men, who have made his home their base of operations, can track down the culprit, a disgruntled former employee named Raj Singh (Amjad Khan), and recover both the child and the money before it is too late. For Inspector Gill, the only obstacle is an emotional one: the fact that Choudhury's sister Geetaa (Vidya Sinha), who lives in the executive's house, is a former lover of his to whom Choudhury refused marriage due to the policeman's modest means.

AKIRA KUROSAWA'S *HIGH AND LOW*— itself adapted from the Ed McBain novel *King's Ransom*—may not strike one as the most obvious inspiration for a 1970s Bollywood thriller, yet it nonetheless serves *Inkaar* well. Director Raj N. Sippy and screenwriter Jyoti Swaroop stick fairly close to their source material here, only really mixing things up with the introduction of a two-fisted, take-no-prisoners police detective in the person of Vinod Khanna's Inspector Gill, who provides quite a contrast to the super-efficient but relatively faceless group of law enforcement functionaries in Kurosawa's original (and who comes with a love story attached, no less, albeit one largely

told in flashback). The effect is to combine the Japanese master's sprawling, Dickensian social drama—an examination of those inevitable points where the various strata of society, giving the lie to the façade of mutual exclusivity, meet and fret like overlapping tectonic plates—with a *Dirty Harry* style police actioner, a marriage of disparate elements that ends up being surprisingly successful.

Inkaar's close adherence to its model makes for a much grittier type of crime film than you'd typically see coming out of Bollywood in the '70s. The underworld that its bad guys inhabit is a far cry from the glamorous demimonde of other such films, exemplified by the fact that Amjad Khan's hideout, rather than the lavishly appointed lair we're used to seeing, is nothing more than a dingy bungalow, and his haunts, rather than the gaudy monuments to decadence that usually stand in for the underworld denizens' habitat of choice, are simply squalid little dives (one of which plays host to a wonderful and appropriately debauched item number from Helen in the role of a trashy barmaid). Furthermore, this is a Bollywood crime film in which we get to see its detectives doing actual detective work—though, of course, not at the expense of them also doling out a liberal amount of the old "dishoom dishoom"—which is quite striking. Amar and his men analyze tire and finger prints, pore over crime scene photos, and subject their suspects to brutal interrogations, all of which makes their victory seem more hard won once the noose inevitably begins to tighten around Raj Singh's neck. That, combined with a generous amount of grimy location shooting, gives *Inkaar* an exhilarating feeling of authenticity that makes it really stand out from other contemporary examples of its genre.

At times, *Inkaar*'s makers see fit to simply follow Kurosawa's film shot-for-shot, as with the taut, haunting sequence in which the executive Choudhury makes delivery of the ransom by tossing it from a moving train to the kidnapper's emissary standing on an embankment below. It's hard to argue with this choice, because to do otherwise would be an attempt to improve upon perfection. What's important is that, whether sticking to the template or veering from it, the creative team devises a consistent look—marked in some places by a very Leone-esque reliance on intense, sweaty close-ups—that never undermines the narrative or jars with the maintenance of cohesive tone. Finally, credit also has to go to Rajesh Roshan for his instrumental score, a tense funk built on reverbed-out, staccato guitar jabs that Kalyanji-Anandji would have been proud to put their names on.

A Bollywood remake of *High and Low*, by its nature, is guaranteed to be such a completely different animal that any qualitative comparison between it and its inspiration would be largely pointless. Suffice it to say, however, that *Inkaar* has far from replaced the original in my heart. Nonetheless, it is to my mind something of an ideal remake: respectful of the original, but at the same time adding enough of its own elements to enable it to stand alone. It's also a solid example of '70s Bollywood action cinema at its best, and one that I would recommend to anyone, regardless of whether they've seen the classic it was modeled upon.

GADDAAR
"Traitor"

Released: 1973
Director: Harmesh Malhotra
Stars: Vinod Khanna, Yogeeta Bali, Pran, Madan Puri, Anwar Hussain, Manmohan, Iftekhar, Ram Mohan, Ranjeet, Satyendra Kapoor, Varsha, V. Gopal, Master Raju, Ratan Gaurang, Nishan, Rajni Bala, Aarti, Shefali, Leena Das, Oscar Unger, Padma Khanna, Jankidas, Ajit
Writer: Ravi Kapoor
Music: Laxmikant-Pyarelal (Laxmikant Shantaram Kudalkar & Pyarelal Ramprasad Sharma)
Lyrics: Anand Bakshi
"Thrills": Ravi Khanna

A gang of seven men led by B.K. (Pran) steal a royal fortune of forty lakhs from an electrified palace safe in a meticulously planned robbery. Their number includes Sampat (Anwar Hussain), an acrobat; Professor (Iftekhar), the science guy; Babu (Ranjeet), who punches people; Kanhaiya (Madan Puri), the driver; John (Ram Mohan) and Mohan (Manmohan). Just as it seems the gang is going to get away free, a guard pulls an alarm and a shootout ensues. B.K. is wounded and the gang is separated. Later, everyone makes it back to the hideout except for Kanhaiya, who was carrying the money. The men wait, becoming more quarrelsome by the moment.

Night falls and the gang make their way to Kanhaiya's apartment. There they come upon Raja (Vinod Khanna), a small time thief, in the process of an attempted burglary. Raja knows who they are and asks for a cut of the loot in exchange for his silence and his assistance in tracking down Kanhaiya. Before B.K. can answer, he escapes. Later the men go to see a cabaret dancer (Padma Khanna) who is a known consort of Kanhaiya's. Raja shows up again and takes the woman into his custody, again asking the gang for a guaranty of a cut. B.K. agrees, and Raja strong arms the dancer into divulging that Kanhaiya had planned a world tour with a first stop in Madras. Raja then shoots the woman in cold blood.

Raja heads to Madras, where Kanhaiya's trail leads to the gang of Brother Akhtar (Nishan). Kanhaiya has paid the gang to kill Raja, but Raja makes quick work of them. Akhtar tells Raja that Kanhaiya has gone to a village called Rampur in the snowy Himachal Pradesh region of Northern India. Arriving in Rampur, Raja gets lost in a snow storm and comes upon the isolated Hotel Mansaro. This turns out to have been recently purchased by Kanhaiya, who lives there with his daughter Reshma (Yogeeta Bali) and young son Tito (Master Raju). The hotel is otherwise empty for the off season, with the only other guests being Mathur (Satyendra Kapoor), an alcoholic doctor, his wife, and Shankar (V. Gopal), the hotel's porter.

Meanwhile, the rest of the gang is hiding out in a cave near the hotel, with B.K. overcome by a racking, consumptive cough that gets worse by the minute. Informed by Raja of Kanhaiya's presence, they make their way to what they

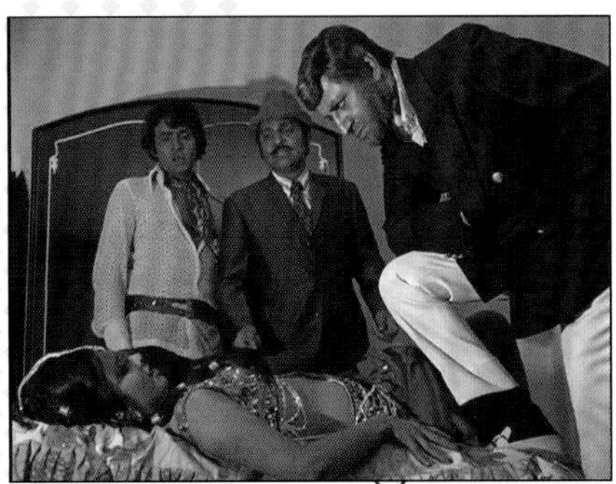

think is an abandoned barn on the property, where an armed guard seriously wounds Sampat before being shot dead by them. The men then descend upon the hotel and take the staff and guests hostage. After B.K. threatens little Tito with torture, Kanhaiya reveals that thirty five remaining lakhs of the treasure are buried in a cave nearby. B.K. and Professor follow him there, only to find that the cave is the very one that they had just been hiding in. Kanhaiya begins to dig up the strong box, but then pulls a gun and shoots Professor. As he dies, Professor asks B.K. to promise him that there will be no bloodshed.

Back at the hotel, Babu pressures Mathur to operate on the wounded Sampat, whose leg needs to be amputated. Sampat grabs a gun and holds them off, but Raja talks him down with promises that he will invest in Sampat's idea for a circus. Soothed by Raja's promise that his leg will not be amputated, Sampat goes to sleep and wakes up minus one leg, whereupon he shoots himself. Mohan, meanwhile, has developed rapey designs on Reshma—already once thwarted by B.K.—and forces himself upon her, only to receive a thrashing from Raja.

Hauling the strong box through the snow, B.K., raving, stops and begins to burn handfuls of the cash. Kanhaiya grabs the box and tries to run off, but B.K. shoots him in the back. Kanhaiya nonetheless survives to return to the hotel, where he attacks Raja and runs off with Reshma. He then goes back for Tito, killing Babu in the process. B.K. finally confronts Kanhaiya and kills him outright, though not before Kanhaiya cryptically claims to have recognized Raja. Things then get worse between the four remaining thieves, with Mohan convinced that Raja and John are plotting to kill him and B.K. Raja then shoots John, revealing to the others that he is, in fact, Inspector Rajkumar of the CBI (the murder of the dancer was faked). Mohan tries to gun everyone down and B.K. escapes into the snow with the loot. Raja follows him and, after a brutal fist fight in the stable, gets the drop on the progressively sickly boss. Ultimately, B.K.'s pride won't let him live a captive and, despite Raja's efforts to save him, he throws himself off a cliff.

FEW INDIAN CRIME FILMS are as pure as *Gaddaar*. Within seconds of its opening credits, we are right in the middle of a thrilling depiction of its central crime and meeting our criminals. And what criminals they are—brutalizing women, children and the elderly with equal abandon, murdering innocent witnesses, attempting rape. These are hard, awful men.

And what a cast playing those hard, awful men! While *Gaddaar* provides a good showcase for star Vinod Khanna and his matinee idol good looks—here sporting an oversized swastika necklace and the apparently then-popular belted turtleneck look—its arguable main attraction is the first rate assemblage of Bollywood character actors who portray its crooks. Not only do we have career bad guys like Madan Puri and Ranjeet doing what they do absolutely best—even if Ranjeet's wardrobe is a bit disappointingly sedate—but MVP's like Iftekhar taking a rare step outside his usual police official roles to essay the part of the noble villain. And then there is B.K., probably one of the all time great Pran roles. Prone to referring to himself in the third person and making extravagant claims of infallibility, B.K. is a figure at once ridiculous, imposing, and tragic, ultimately undone by his own ego.

The musical sequences include a strange, Egyptian-themed nightclub number that involves white hippie girls and lots of eating.

Like any great "heist gone wrong" tale, *Gaddaar* descend into greater and greater violence as it goes along, depicting the erosion of trust between the criminals in fairly unflinching detail as the bullets fly with increasing frequency. Leavening this somewhat are Laxmikant-Pyarelal's musical sequences, which include a strange, Egyptian-themed nightclub number that involves white hippie girls and a lot of eating. Overall, the duo's song score here is pleasantly heavy on the tribal rhythms and traditional melodies, while the film's instrumental score relies heavily on needle dropped cues from Ennio Morricone's score to *For a Few Dollars More*. Anand Bakshi's lyrics are also clever. Upon learning of the remaining loot, the gang archly celebrates Madan Puri's Kanhaiya with a rousing rendition of the theme song:

> *"You are a traitor after all*
> *you are a cheat after all*
> *you are our old friend*
> *At least you love money."*

Gaddaar was apparently only the second film as director—and the first as producer—for Harmesh Malhotra, a career director whose work included 1986's fanciful "snake lady" film *Nagina*. His talent is nonetheless well in evidence, from his arresting use of bold primary colors, and his shrewd, atmospheric use of the snowy Himachal Pradesh locations, to his taut staging of the opening heist. True, there is room for all kinds of films under the Bollywood action umbrella, from the sober social drama of *Deewaar* to the comic book histrionics of a *Maha Badmaash*. But it is films like *Gaddaar* that hold down the rare generic middle ground. As such, it is one that I'd recommend to any fan of either great caper films or crime films of an international nature, whether or not they've yet gotten their Indian cinema training wheels.

BOMBAY 405 MILES

Released: 1980
Director: Brij Sadanah (as Brij)
Stars: Vinod Khanna, Shatrughan Sinha, Zeenat Aman, Pran, Amjad Khan, Deven Verma, Iftekhar, Master Bhagwan, Birbal, Helen, Manmauji, Mac Mohan, Murad, Raza Murad, Chaman Puri, Shammi, Sudhir
Writers: K.A. Narayan, Kader Khan
Music: Kalyanji-Anandji (Kalyanji Virji Shah & Anandji Virji Shah)
Lyrics: Indeevar
Fights: Shetty, Khodi Irani

Masterji (Pran) enjoys a happy visit with his young daughter Sonu before returning to his business travels. The child is then returned to her uncle Mohan, with whom she lives during Masterji's absence, who takes her to the home of his employer, the wealthy Ranvir Singh (Iftekhar), who is departing on a trip to Singapore. Ranvir returns from his trip some days later, bearing a talking doll his little daughter Munni had requested as a gift, only to be greeted at his home by his insane adopted brother Veer (Amjad Khan) and his retinue of armed goons. Veer has murdered Ranvir's wife and two children as an act of revenge for being disowned, in response to his attempted rape of a servant, by Ranvir's father.

Shown the corpses, Ranvir sees that Veer has mistakenly killed Masterji's child Sonu rather than Munni, and surreptitiously presses the "record" button on the doll in order to capture the psycho's words. Veer then reveals a forged suicide note in Ranvir's hand that also confesses to the murders, after which he shoots Ranvir. The wounded Ranvir manages to escape long enough to find Mohan, to whom he hands the doll and begs to save Munni, who is safe at school, at all costs. Later, Veer's extravagant displays of grief for the benefit of the authorities prove all for naught when the seemingly dead Ranvir begins to show signs of life. Fortunately for Veer, he has apparently been driven mad by his ordeal and can only laugh dementedly—at least for the time being.

Meanwhile, in courtrooms in Delhi and Calcutta, Kanhaiya (Vinod Khanna), a forger, and Kishan (Shatrughan Sinha), a safecracker, are being banished by flustered judges from their respective states after repeated offenses. The two con men eventually meet up after being dropped at the same bus depot, where each separately decides upon Bombay as a destination. They also meet up with a third con artist, Radha (Zeenat Aman), who causes a stir when Kishan gets fresh, causing both men to flee. She turns up again shortly thereafter, once Kanhaiya and Kishan have decided to team up, and easily bilks them out of the take from their latest scam. Taken by both her beauty and criminal wiles, the two men beg her to join up with them, but Radha instead chooses to board the next train for Bombay and leave them in her dust.

Kanhaiya and Kishan next hop a freight train, only to find—running along the boxcar roofs with Munni under one arm, the talking doll under another, and Veer's goons in hot pursuit—a gravely wounded Mohan. The two give the goons a sound thrashing, after which Mohan, with his last breath, begs them to take care of Munni, saying that there are "crores at stake," by which he means millions of rupees. The two cons at first want nothing to do with the situation and hop the train, but later, driven in part by conscience, steal a motorcycle and hustle back to collect Munni, who is by now becoming ill from neglect. Also motivating them, of course, is the notion that Munni might be the victim of a botched kidnapping, and that there might be a rich ransom in store if they can only locate her parents.

Once in Bombay, Kanhaiya and Kishan take Munni to a barber and, in an effort to disguise her, have her hair cut to make her look like a boy. They then bilk the barber into signing an agreement designating them as renters of both his home and shop and throw him out. Meanwhile, Radha, fleeing from the authorities, takes refuge in Masterji's ashram. Masterji, it turns out, is also a con artist, specializing in a method of anonymous phone extortion by which he provokes random guilty parties into paying through vague intimations of holding knowledge of their secrets. Taken, Radha asks to be his disciple. Masterji also happens to be a friend of the barber and, after hearing his sob story, decides to employ his methods against Kanhaiya and Kishan as a means of payback.

BOMBAY
405
MILES

Meanwhile, Veer, having been alerted to his oversight, has his men scouring Bombay for Munni. When Kanhaiya and Kishan, in an attempt to locate the girl's parents, take out an ad in the paper, he responds, and the two naïve small time crooks, not knowing who they're dealing with, foolishly ask for the exorbitant sum of fifty lakhs for her return. Thus is set in motion a deadly game that can only end once the secrets held by either a mute madman or a talking doll have been spoken. At the same time, Masterji and Radha, having had their attempt to scam Kanhaiya and Kishan turned back upon them, have entered into a tenuous alliance with the two, exacerbated by the fact that both young men are in love with Radha. Masterji continues to shame both for their apparent eagerness to sell an innocent child for money. Yet it takes little Munni being run over by a car and in need of a risky, life saving operation for their hearts to finally thaw.

BOMBAY 405 MILES bears many similarities to the earlier *Bada Kabutar*, but comes out ahead due to a tighter script, more rocking tunes, and, quite frankly, a sexier cast. Nonetheless, both films suffer in light of contemporary standards that might not see the topic of child abduction as an appropriate subject for an action comedy. Granted, *Bombay* does manage to put a more convincing focus on its protagonists' change of heart where the subject tyke is concerned—and, thanks to the stubbornly hard edged and violent backdrop that it plays out against, manages to do so without descending completely into saccharine sentimentality.

Still, it has to be said that *Bombay 405 Miles*'s makers display an equal shamelessness to those of *Bada Kabutar*'s in the lengths that

they are willing to exploit child endangerment as a means of manipulating audience sympathy. The scene of Munni being run over by a car—graphic and bloody, if mercifully brief—is a particular jaw-dropper. And then there is the apparent rough treatment that the child actress who plays Munni herself gets, often hoisted on a protagonist's shoulder during one of the film's plentiful fistfights with blows landing mere centimeters from her head and, at one point, having a sweaty Amjad Khan angrily wrap his fingers around her pint-sized throat. There is also dark amusement to be had in those action scenes in which she is simply doubled by a life-sized doll, in which the actors haphazardly throw her around like an old duffel bag.

Such technical foibles aside, *Bombay 405 Miles*, as directed by Brij, is a conspicuously slick affair, with a relentlessly snappy pace and dynamic cinematography that is consistently fluid and alluring. Vinod Khanna and future cabinet minister Shatrughan Sinha make a great comedic team, and deliver Kader Khan's dialogue with an agreeable looseness that adds to the film overall having a hip and funny tone. Amjad Khan also needs to be commended for, with Veeru Singh, perhaps finding his most repellent villain yet, a gleeful child killer who is nonetheless prone to extravagant expressions of self pity. Add in a sly and lustrous Zeenat Aman and a game Pran—as well as staunch supporting players like Iftekhar and Raza Murad—and you have a true dream cast, even if Helen is somewhat wasted in a largely line free, non-dancing role.

But *Bombay 405 Miles*'s not-so-secret weapon may be Kalyanji-Anandji's musical score, which is truly one of the sibling duo's most unabashedly funktastic. Perhaps its most well known tune outside of India—thanks, at least, in part to its inclusion on hipster compilations like 2007's *Bombay Connection* CD—is "Na Na Na Ye Kya Karne Lage Ho," sung by Hemlata. A straight up "moaner and groaner" in the mold of Sylvia's "Pillow Talk," the song is picturized on Zeenat Aman in a climactic scene in which, from inside a curtained VW bus, she tries to distract Veer's men by convincing them that there is some really hot and heavy action going on. This has the quite convincing result of causing the men to clamor desperately all over the vehicle, fighting one another for a better peek.

Also helping the film is its commitment to the "action" part of its action comedy equation. For one thing, this helps smooth over the leaps in a script that is overwhelmingly coincidence dependent. But it also contributes to *Bombay 405 Miles* simply being an exciting and entertaining picture, even while it somehow delicately maintains a balance with the impression of it also being a very smartly conceived one. Thus, in between the snappy dialogue and comic set ups, we also get plenty of time for all of the chases, well choreographed brawls, exploding cars and elaborate booby traps that one might find in a less ambitious "stunt" film. All of the above adds up to *Bombay* being, if not necessarily one for the ages, then certainly one of the great entertainers of its era.

SEETA AUR GEETA
"Seeta and Geeta"

Released: 1972
Director: Ramesh Sippy
Stars: Hema Malini, Dharmendra, Sanjeev Kumar, Manorama, Pratima Devi, Satyendra Kapoor, Kamal Kapoor, Ratnamala, Radhika Rani, Honey Irani, Dev Kishan, Alankar Joshi, Roopesh Kumar, Keshav Rana, Mushtaq Merchant, Deepak, Shetty, Suresh, Master Ravi, Abhi Bhattacharya, Asit Sen, Dulari, Asrani, Ashoo
Writers: Salim-Javed (Salim Khan & Javed Akhtar), Satish Bhatnagar
Music: Rahul Dev Burman (R.D. Burman)
Lyrics: Anand Bakshi
Fights: Shetty

It is a dark and stormy night. A wealthy couple's car breaks down in route to the hospital, and the man and very pregnant wife are forced to take refuge in the modest slum dwelling inhabited by the childless Leela (Radhika Rani) and her husband. The men go off to fetch a doctor and return to find that a child has been born, a little girl. The next day, once the new parents have departed, Leela reveals another child, a twin baby girl, whom she has stashed away to keep for her own. Asked by her husband what they could provide for this child in quantity equal to what its wealthy parents could, Leela replies "love."

That spare child grows up to be Geeta (Hema Malini), a scrappy and confident street dancer who spends her days trading good natured barbs with Raka (Dharmendra), a hard drinking but big hearted ne'er-do-well with whom she concocts various schemes to draw in whatever cash they can. The other daughter, Seeta (Malini again), has, on the opposite hand, not quite had the deck stacked in her favor in the manner one might expect. Her wealthy parents have died in the intervening years, leaving her in the charge of her shrewish aunt Kaushalya (Manorama), who beats her and treats her as a servant while pocketing her monthly trust fund checks. According to her parents' will, Kaushalya's guardianship over Seeta will end once she has been married, but, given the material benefits of the arrangement, Kaushalya has no interest in seeing that happen. Thus, when a distinguished doctor, Ravi (Sanjeev Kumar), shows interest, Kaushalya sabotages the meeting with his parents by forcing the demure Seeta to dress in a hot pink mini dress that offends the elders' conservative values.

The final injury for Seeta occurs when Kaushalya's brother Ranjeet (Roopesh Kumar) attempts to rape her and, in retaliation for her rejection, frames her for stealing a purse belonging to his sister. Seeta disappears from the household, prompting Kaushalya to notify the police. Soon after, Geeta shows up at her local police station, wanting to report some scammers who have stolen a young boy's money, and the police think they recognize her from Seeta's photo. Their attempts to capture her, however, only result in the acrobatic Geeta laying waste to the entire station house. In escaping, she coincidentally ends

up hitching a ride with a passing Dr. Ravi, who, thinking she is Seeta, finds himself unexpectedly charmed by her.

Seeta, meanwhile, has chosen suicide, and throws herself from a bridge within view of Raka, who is fishing nearby. He saves her, and when she proves unable to recognize him or her mother, it is assumed that she is suffering from amnesia as a result of her trauma. Seeta quickly warms to living life as Geeta, and stuns those accustomed to her tomboyish sister's ways with the sewing and cooking skills she's developed as a virtual live-in slave to Kaushalya. Romance blooms between her and Raka, and she is later instrumental in him giving up the bottle.

After an episode involving some runaway roller skates, Geeta likewise ends up in Seeta's household, where the fit is not quite as harmonious. Geeta does not respond to Kaushalya's physical abuse in the same manner as the timid Seeta and, in fighting back, ends up terrorizing the harridan into submission, quickly coming to rule the house with an iron fist. Kaushalya puts up with this until Geeta/"Seeta" and Ravi announce their plan to marry, whereupon she calls in Ranjeet to return things to status quo. Though Ranjeet's initial attempts to rein Geeta in result in him receiving the whipping of his life, he ultimately, through a combination of stealth and happenstance, uncovers the existence of Seeta's twin. Employing a gang of thugs, he kidnaps Seeta and holds her captive as, at the same time, Geeta is arrested by the police for her masquerade and imprisoned. This leads to Raka having to stage a dangerous jailbreak, then working with Geeta to free her long lost sister so that everyone who has appeared on screen thus far in Seeta aur Geeta *can have a huge fight involving swords, chains, whips and shovels.*

***SEETA AUR GEETA* COMBINES TWO** of 1970s Bollywood's most oft used story devices—those of the double and the "lost and found" family drama—to create a narrative so convoluted as to almost defeat comprehension. Fortunately, the film's true pleasures lie not in deciphering its plot mechanics, but in the central performance of Hema Malini, who gets billing beneath Dharmendra and traditional leading man Sanjeev Kumar despite essaying the titular double role.

The film is truly more of a modern fairy tale than a crime film, yet that Malini's Geeta defines herself through action is undeniable. In doing so, she draws upon the tradition of rough and tumble heroines established through India's B "Stunt" films, in particular those of the phenomenally popular Fearless Nadia, whose whip wielding *Hunterwali* couldn't have been far from the writers' minds (as might have been Nadia's similar, twins-themed adventure from 1942, *Muqabla*.) Malini, who won a Filmfare award for her performance, gamely expands into the role, displaying a level of strut and swagger commensurate with a distaff Bachchan, and the result is electrifying. In those scenes where she is dishing out well deserved comeuppance to the horrible golems who lord over Seeta's household—a barrage of rapid fire slaps in the aunt's case, a table turning belt whipping in the rapey brother-in-law's—it's hard not to imagine the audience standing on their chairs and cheering. It should also be said that the fearsome looking Manorama, who made something of a career of these harpy roles, truly holds up her end of the equation as the rare female villain, making the payback all the more delicious.

Elsewhere in its cast roster, *Seeta aur Geeta* provides a showcase for everything that is great about Dharmendra. His Raka is the very type of brash, likeable rogue we're used to seeing him play so well, yet we're surprised when, at the movie's halfway point, his hard drinking, rather than just a rakish character note, is revealed to be an actual problem. R.D. Burman provides him with a great "drunk" song in "Abhi Toh Haath Mein Hai," but, as opposed to the whimsical or comedic tone such numbers usually take, this one is plaintive and melancholy. The actor follows it with a maudlin, tear-filled rant that makes clear that what we are seeing is Raka's "bottoming out" in the preface to embracing sobriety. Fortunately, he gets himself cleaned up in time to deliver some classic hero moments, such as when he crashes through a skylight to come to Geeta's rescue, or engages the bald pated fight coordinator Shetty in a brutal dust up employing chains and shovels. In short, you will see few films from the era that make better use of Dharam's combined physicality and fitful soulfulness.

Seeta aur Geeta benefits from some top rate behind-the-camera talent, many of whom—director Ramesh Sippy, screenwriters Salim-Javed, R.D. Burman—would also be involved in the groundbreaking *Sholay* a couple of years later. Thus the fact that it ultimately manages the feat of not toppling under its own narrative weight is not altogether surprising, even though, as with many Bollywood "lost twin" tales, keeping up with its constant masquerades and switcheroos can be a little exhausting. Again, this can be overcome by simply focusing on its appealing lead performances—which might even help you forgive that it ends with a dumb boudoir joke teasing the idea of Dharmendra and Sanjeev Kumar accidentally screwing each other's wife.

CHHAILLA BABU
"Cool Guy"

Released: 1977
Director: Joy Mukherjee
Stars: Rajesh Khanna, Zeenat Aman, Asrani, Om Shivpuri, Padma Khanna, Achala Sachdev, Ranjeet, P. Jairaj, Ravindra Kapoor, Mac Mohan, Manmohan, Gulshan Arora, Mohan Sherry, Ashim Kumar, Shyam, Guru Dharshan, Manik Dutt, Qureishi, Uttam, Yashraj, Vinod Thakkar, Haroon, Johnny Whisky, Dhanna, Salim, Aziz Asser, Raghuveer, Kader Khan, Yusuf Khan, D.K. Sapru
Writers: Kader Khan, Shomu Mukherjee, Sayed Sultan
Music: Laxmikant-Pyarelal (Laxmikant Shantaram Kudalkar & Pyarelal Ramprasad Sharma)
Lyrics: Anand Bakshi
Fights: Ravi Khanna

The mysterious Scorpion assembles a gang to rob an armored car of the Southern Bank, hoping to nab a treasure of eighty lakhs. Come the day of the heist, gang member Pratap (P. Jairaj), who is in charge of carrying the take, shoots the Scorpion's driver and makes preparations to leave the country with both the money and Lilly (Padma Khanna), the gang's lone female member. It turns out that Lilly has betrayed him, however, as, upon his arrival at the airport, he is shot by the gang. Collapsing into the arms of a policeman, Pratap only has time to tell the officer that the loot is in the hands of his daughter Rita and the code number "7203" before dying. Lilly overhears this and passes the information on to the Scorpion.

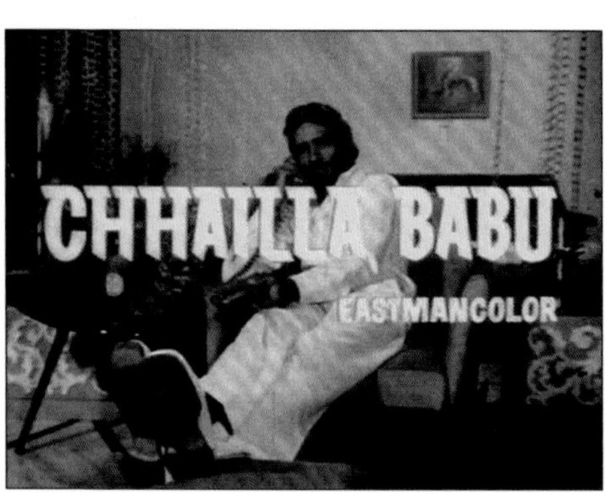

Meanwhile, Rita (Zeenat Aman) is on a skiing trip in Kashmir, where she starts to receive the repeated attentions of a mysterious figure who only calls himself Chhailla Babu (Rajesh Khanna). First appearing as a ski guide and then as a carriage driver, he tells her that he has a gift that allows him to "mold into any character." The two develop an instant attraction, and Chhailla Babu obliquely confides to Rita about a tragedy in his past in which he "lost everything" and was separated from his mother. Around the same time, the police commissioner (Om Shivpuri) arrives in Kashmir to inform Rita of her father's death. Convinced that Rita knows nothing about the stolen loot, he asks that she return to Bombay until the case can be solved.

Back in Bombay, Chhailla Babu helps thwart repeated attempts on Rita's life by the robbery gang, who are convinced that she is holding the money. At the same time, the Scorpion orders the gang to stop their search for the money, and threatens them with death if they don't comply. They don't, and the Scorpion begins to pick them off one by one, motivating them to also set their sights on the Scorpion, whom they are increasingly beginning to believe is Chhailla Babu. The police are likewise keeping a close eye on Rita and Chhailla Babu, and are also beginning to think that he is the Scorpion.

The commissioner voices his suspicions to Rita, and asks for her assistance in capturing Chhailla Babu, telling her that he is wooing her only to get at the money. To convince her, he takes her to a nightclub where she watches Chhailla Babu canoodle with Lilly and then perform a wild stage number as "Drummer Raju." Rita agrees to help. However, her feelings for Chhailla Babu are not so easy to turn off, and the two continue to dance in and out of each others' lives. Then they accidentally discover the case containing the robbery stash in a secret dartboard safe in Rita's father's house. They try to flee with the money, but the gang, having bugged the house, is not far behind, as also, we will find, is the Scorpion.

Also nearby—as she has been all along—is Chhailla Babu's long lost mother, who plays a major role in bringing the Scorpion into the light. It seems that our hero's father was the judge who hanged the original Scorpion, and that the current one is the Scorpion's brother, who murdered the judge in retaliation. This is the reason for the suspicious scorpion pendant that Chhailla Babu wears, as well as his thirst for vengeance against the faceless villain.

Oh, and we also learn who the Scorpion is. Just remember that it doesn't need to make sense.

***CHHAILLA BABU* IS A FUN FILM** that invests too much effort in preserving its central mystery at the expense of coherent

storytelling. To support that assertion, one need only consider that its entire "lost and found" storyline is covered within a flashback that hastily takes place during the picture's final *twenty minutes*, and even then is told in a series of freeze frames like a slideshow. Is giving your hero an actual name and meager back story really such a high price to pay for avoiding such sloppiness?

After all, as played by Rajesh Khanna, Chhailla Babu really isn't a figure who calls for being cloaked in a lot of mystique. He's a hale, expansively gesturing free spirit who sings his song with a wink in his eye and a tilt of his hat. This Chhailla Babu wants to be loved, not feared. And, in Zeenat Aman's Rita he finds a perfect match. Both characters are vigorous, strapping, and joyously physical, Rita often fighting alongside Chhailla Babu with a smile on her face like the Peel to his Steed. We root for them because of that.

On the other side of the equation, while *Chhailla Babu*, thanks to its cagey structure, suffers from something of a villain vacuum, it nonetheless boasts one of those all star casts of flunkies that make '70s crime films so enjoyable. Such welcome mugs as Mac Mohan, Manmohan, and a resplendently bearded Ranjeet are among the members of the Scorpion

From an audience standpoint, such deliberate withholding can't help but be seen as a bit punitive and churlish.

gang, with the added bonus of Padma Khanna playing a femme fatale who is at once sexy and vicious. Still, keeping its bad guy under wraps the way it does deprives the film of the Amjad Khan, Ajit, or Madan Puri who would otherwise provide *Chhailla Babu* with a villainous center of gravity for all of its action and drama to swirl around. Bollywood films do villains well, after all, and, from an audience standpoint, such deliberate withholding can't help but be seen as a bit punitive and churlish.

As for Laxmikant-Pyarelal, they can certainly take credit for composing a title song that is catchy to the point of obnoxiousness. But I'm not sure what else, because much of *Chhailla Babu*'s instrumental score is made up of needle dropped cues from filmland's greatest hits. Everything from Spaghetti western themes to "Diamonds Are Forever" to "Thus Spoke Zarathustra" from *2001* makes it into the mix, as well as the theme from *Enter the Dragon* complete with Bruce Lee's screaming. And then there's also some excellent, disco-y '70s cop show music that serves *Chhailla Babu*'s funky flavor especially well.

All told, *Chhailla Babu* was a huge hit at the Indian box office in 1977. Likely a deciding factor in this was the presence at its helm of two massively popular and appealing stars. But could a part also have been played by the film's long climactic car chase loaded with preposterous stunts (including a car balancing on two wheels for what seems like three city blocks)? How about the farcical chase through a cartoonish Native American festival that sees Zeenat Aman dressed as a sexy squaw and running from teepee to teepee with the suitcase full of loot? Whatever the case, *Chhailla Babu* seems to be bucking the constraints of the Masala formula. But, in the course of doing so, it falls victim to the same self mockery that afflicted other late '70s efforts within that genre like *Fakira*. Nonetheless, fans of Zeenat Aman and Rajesh Khanna will not be wasting their time.

CHOR MACHAYE SHOR
"Cry of a Thief"

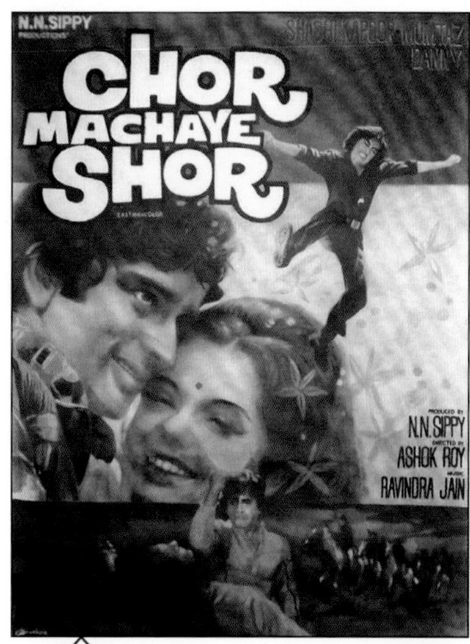

Released: 1974
Director: Ashok Roy
Stars: Shashi Kapoor, Mumtaz, Danny Denzongpa, Asrani, Tarun Ghosh, Madan Puri, Kamal Kapoor, Sajjan, Shyam Kumar, Asit Sen, Chaman Puri, Ram Mohan, C.L. Shah, Mahendra Dutt, Uma Dutt, Prakash, Meena T., Kamal, Master Chintu, Chandrima Bhaduri, Gulshan, Hangama, Moolchand
Writers: S.M. Abbas, Dhruva Chatterjee, Tarun Ghosh
Music: Ravindra Jain
Lyrics: Ravindra Jain, Raj Kavi Inderjeet Singh Tulsi
Fights: Mansoor

Vijay (Shashi Kapoor), a humble engineer, is in love with Rekha (Mumtaz) and wants to marry her. However, Rekha's wealthy father (Kamal Kapoor) is opposed to the marriage and instead plans to marry Rekha off to the son of Jamanadas (Madan Puri), a corrupt politician whose campaign he is financing. When Vijay refuses to make himself scarce, Jamanadas lures him into a trap in which a double of Rekha is used to put him in a compromising situation. When Rekha is unable to support his version of events, he is convicted of attempted rape and sent to prison. Convinced that she had a part in framing him, Vijay swears to take revenge upon Rekha upon his release.

Once incarcerated, Vijay immediately clashes with Raju Ustad (Danny Denzongpa), the self described "Don" of the prison. By maintaining a tough-as-nails demeanor, he quickly gains the hood's respect and is welcomed into Raju's gang, which also includes his two lieutenants, Bhalua (Asrani) and Kalua (Tarun Ghosh). Afterward, the resourceful Vijay manages to wrangle the group a coveted spot on an off-site work project. This affords them the opportunity to make an escape. Pursued by the authorities, Vijay then makes his way to Rekha's home, where he makes plain his attention to rape her in earnest as revenge for her perceived betrayal. Rekha manages to appeal to his senses, enlightening him to the fact that it was Jamanadas and not her who framed him. Ashamed, Vijay vows to disappear from her life, but Rekha insists on joining him.

Vijay and Rekha join with Raju, Bhalua and Kalua and board a train for the small village of Shantinagan, which is the farthest stop on the line. Meanwhile, Jamanadas, who has substantial land holdings in Shantinagan, dispatches four cronies to the village to pose as social workers and woo the villagers with promised improvements in the lead up to the election. The train on which the cronies are riding derails and, when the separate train carrying Vijay and his fellow fugitives arrives in the town, they are mistaken by the villagers for the social workers. The group decides to take advantage of this ready-made disguise, but, not being aware of the chicanery involved, take it upon themselves to implement actual improvements in the lives of the disadvantaged inhabitants, the most ambitious being a canal project that will divert water into the chronically parched region.

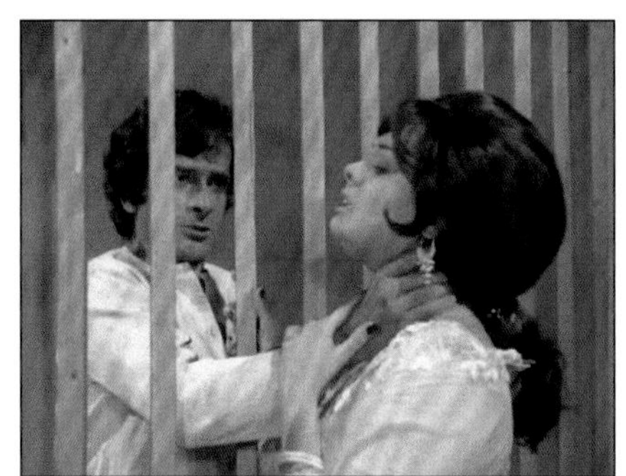

Jamanadas learns of the good works being done by Vijay and company around the same time that he learns that his own "social workers" never made it to Shantinagan, and decides to visit the place in order to get to the bottom of things. Once there, we find that Jamanadas in is league with the local bandit Rupa Singh (Shyam Kumar) and his gang to rob the region of artifacts, and that they in fact plan to use the cover of the election to steal a priceless idol from a local temple. Furthermore, Jamanadas has already engaged the bandits, come election time, to violently suppress the opposition vote. Meanwhile, Vijay keeps silent about his knowledge of Jamanadas's role in his frame-up, all the while plotting his revenge.

THE SUCCESS OF *CHOR MACHAYE SHOR* was in part responsible for the genesis of 1976's also successful *Fakira*, another film in which Shashi Kapoor and Danny Denzongpa enjoyed a troubled bromance set to the tunes of Rajindra Jain. But where *Fakira* was a somewhat silly—in fact, almost self mocking—masala romp, *Chor Machaye Shor* comes across as something altogether more earnest; both a serious social and prison drama in addition to being a film that ends with a drawn out and stunt-filled shootout with a gang of elaborately mustached bandits.

Chor Machaye Shor also proves to be admirably strong stomached in presenting its protagonists at both their moral best and worst. It's hard to imagine the spectacle of heartthrob Shashi Kapoor declaring his wild eyed intention to revenge rape Bollywood sweetheart Mumtaz—a starlet who literally grew up before the eyes of her audience—failing to shock. Equally shocking, I imagine, was the moment when, in response, Mumtaz, back to camera, bares her breasts to him in an attempt to kick start his sense of shame. (Shashi, proving himself a good Indian boy, immediately covers his eyes and insists she cover up.)

In fact—and perhaps in an attempt to score the virtuous divide between city and country—*Chor Machaye Shor* proves to have something of an obsession with rape. Raju falls for Chandramukhi (Meena T.), Shantinagan's village belle, and can't think of any better way to express it than to spirit her away to a quiet place and start forcibly removing her clothing. This, of course, is part of the struggle with his baser impulses that comprises much of Danny Denzongpa's storyline within the film, contrasting unflatteringly with his chivalrous treatment of Rekha, whom he actually quite touchingly embraces as a sister. (Vijay, who righteously steps in to prevent Raju's defilement of

Chandramukhi, seems to have had less of a struggle with his inner rapist, having apparently settled it all in that one cathartic moment with Rekha.) On the irredeemable far side of this moral equator is the bandit Rupa, who, in a climactic scene, is ordered by Jamanadas to rape Rekha before the eyes of all and sundry.

Also noteworthy about *Chor Machaye Shor* is its resemblance to the landmark Amitabh Bachchan blockbuster *Sholay*, which was still a year off, as well as to other "curry westerns" like *Khotte Sikkay*. Like them, it is a tale of hard men softened by the humble bonds of community and connection to the land to which they are exposed by life in a rural village. That the film presents this metamorphosis as a somewhat tortuous one, causing repeated fractures within the core group of fugitives, lends it that much more resonance.

And, as suggested above, Danny Denzongpa's portrayal of that tortured becoming is especially moving, if nonetheless melodramatic. Addled by drink and inarticulate rage, Raju pathetically yearns for acceptance within his new adopted family—by Vijay and Rekha, in particular—but also feels driven by his criminal code to assert himself as an alpha dog at all times. It's a great demonstration of the actor's talent, and strong enough for me to give a pass to the film's predictably teary conclusion, during which the fugitives bid a weepy farewell to the grateful villagers, as well earned. As for Shashi Kapoor, he does a good job with a lot of righteous and bellow-y moral proclamations, giving Dharmendra a run for his money. Meanwhile, he and Mumtaz, in their quiet moments, enjoy a type of relaxed and jokey rapport that is uncommon among Bollywood's typically over-ardent screen lovers, and, as a result, make Vijay and Rekha paradoxically easy to root for.

Addled by drink and inarticulate rage, Raju pathetically yearns for acceptance within his new adopted family.

And finally, there is Madan Puri's Jamanadas, whose portrayal serves as a reminder that, wherever you looked during the mid '70s—be it the "new" Hollywood, Bollywood, or beyond—it was nearly impossible to find a career politician who wasn't presented as an irredeemable heel. This, given the events of the time, is understandable, of course. But Jamanadas's humiliation at Vijay's hands—duped into a forced march through the village during which he's showered with the issue of incontinent toddlers and cattle alike—actually made me feel a little sorry for him. But this was the "angry" Bollywood of the 1970s, after all, and Jamanadas was just one of countless fat cats, fixers and martinets (many of them played by Madan Puri) lined up for comeuppance at the hands of a newly empowered Everyman.

INTERVAL

THE CHALLENGE THAT THE AVERAGE BOLLYWOOD FILM'S two-and-a-half to three hour running time presents to the human bladder makes the interval—what we in the West would call an intermission—an essential part of the Indian theatergoing experience. Almost all Bollywood films made in the 1970s featured an interval—usually occurring as a cliffhanger at the film's midpoint, following on the heels of some game-changing plot twist or revelation —and some, like 1972's *Mera Naam Joker*, even had two. This break would allow audience members not only to relieve themselves, but also to hit the snack bar – which featured such international standards as popcorn and soda (Thums Up Cola and Gold Spot being the favored Indian brands) along with hot chai and homegrown treats like samosas and vada, a donut-like fried savory. Back in the theater itself, advertisements would play on the screen as patrons walked the aisles, chatting and visiting with friends and neighbors. At the end of it all, after maybe 15 minutes or so, a bell would sound, notifying the crowd that it was time to return to their seats and enjoy the remainder of the film.

So, at this point in *Funky Bollywood*, I'd like to offer you the opportunity to stretch, say hello to your neighbor, have a wee, and perhaps sample some of those spicy treats that are available in your kitchen (or the local Indian takeout, as is more likely the case). We've got a lot more films to cover, and I want you to be rested up and well fed for the big finale.

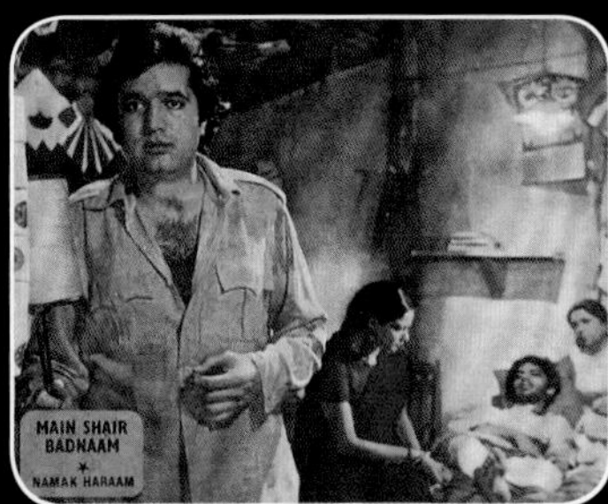

DON

Pran's Tightrope Walk to Freedom!

opposite page: Telegu heroine Vijaya Lalitha plays the title role in *Revolver Rani* (1971), a female-driven South Indian revenge Western.
below: A colorful assortment of goons menace Mumtaz in *Apradh* (1972).

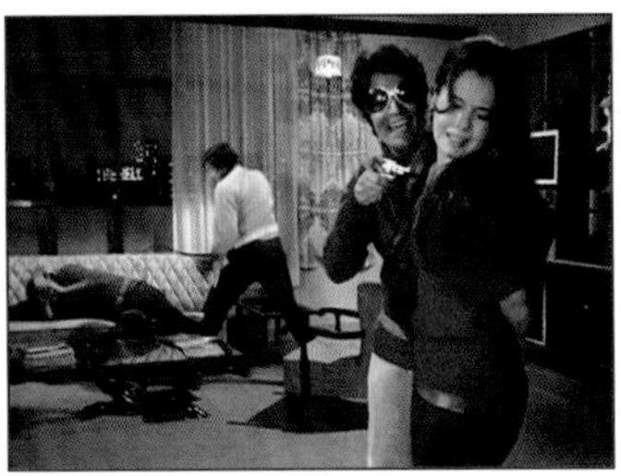

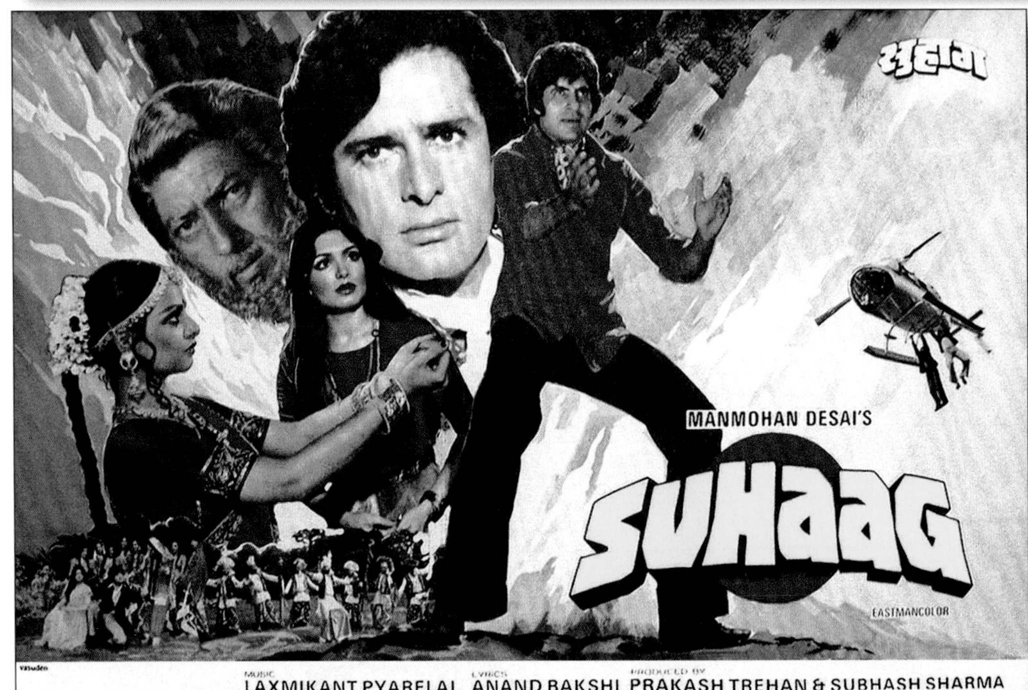

CONTINENTAL FILMS PRESENT
VIJAYALALITHA IN
REVOLVER Rani
Director K. V. S. KUTUMBA RAO Music SATYAN

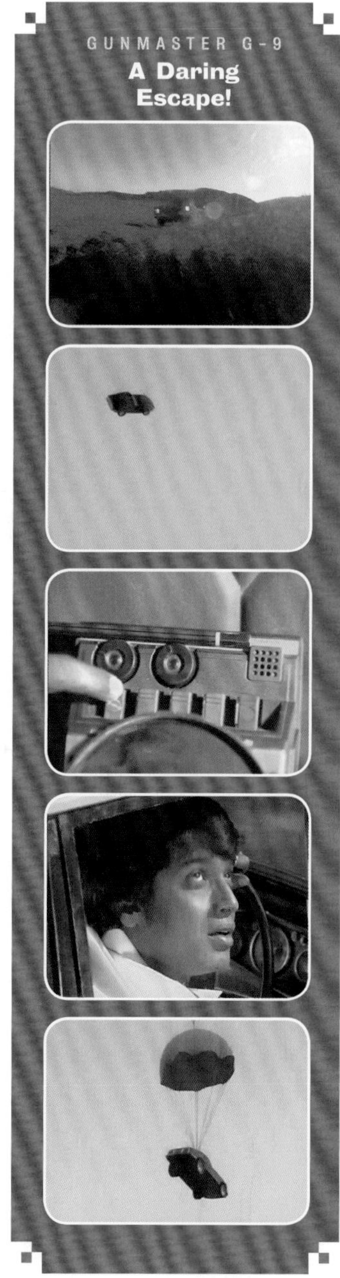
GUNMASTER G-9
A Daring Escape!

Polydor
2392 095
Fortune Films'
Darling Darling

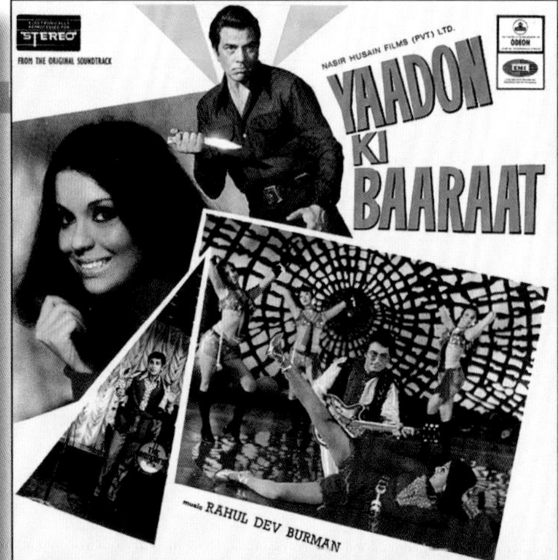
STEREO
FROM THE ORIGINAL SOUNDTRACK
NASIR HUSAIN FILMS (PVT) LTD.
ODEON
EMI
YAADON KI BAARAAT
music RAHUL DEV BURMAN

EMI
MUQADDAR KA SIKANDAR
Music: KALYANJI ANANDJI
Lyrics: ANJAAN • PRAKASH MEHRA
FROM THE ORIGINAL SOUNDTRACK

Polydor
premium
TOPAZ
T. M. BIHARI'S
PROFESSOR PYARELAL

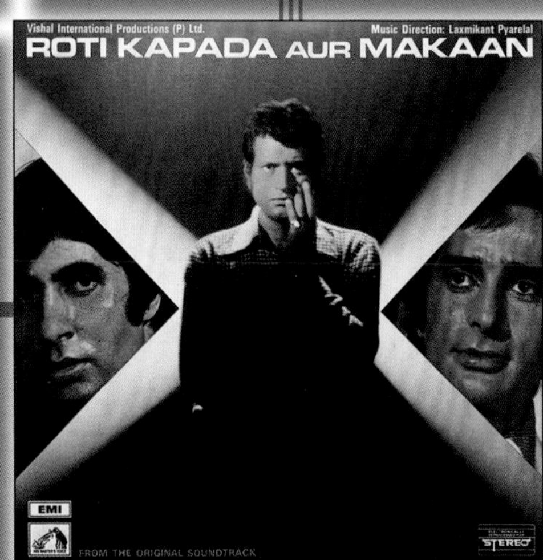
Vishal International Productions (P) Ltd.
Music Direction: Laxmikant Pyarelal
ROTI KAPADA AUR MAKAAN
EMI
FROM THE ORIGINAL SOUNDTRACK
STEREO

DEEWAAR

Polydor
2392 103
Mukerji Bros.
chailla babu

EMI
STEREO
B.R.CHOPRA'S
THE BURNING TRAIN
STORY & DIRECTION BY RAVI CHOPRA
LYRICS: SAHIR
MUSIC: RAHUL DEV BURMAN

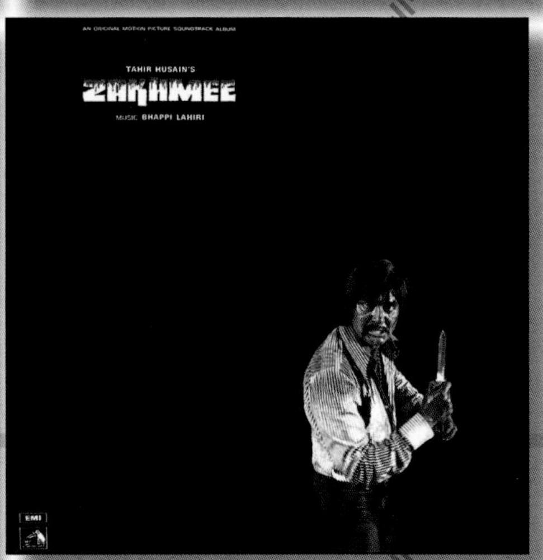
AN ORIGINAL MOTION PICTURE SOUNDTRACK ALBUM
TAHIR HUSAIN'S
ZAKHMEE
MUSIC BHAPPI LAHIRI
EMI

PHILIPS
GEETA MERA NAAM

EMI ORIGINAL SOUNDTRACK RECORDING
45 RPM
SAROJINI ARTS
CHEPPINDI CHESTAA (TELUGU)
MUSIC: SATHYAM

PARASMANI CHITRASHALA
EMI
MUSIC:
KALYANJI ANANDJI
Farishta
-Ya-Qatil
FROM THE ORIGINAL SOUNDTRACK

KRISHNA SHAH'S
SHALIMAR
PRODUCER: SURESH SHAH • DIRECTOR: KRISHNA SHAH • MUSIC: R.D. BURMAN • LYRICS: ANAND BAKSHI
EXECUTIVE PRODUCERS: RANVEER SINGH & BHUPENDRA SHAH

FROM THE ORIGINAL SOUNDTRACK
RANI
MERA
NAM

ASSOCIATED FILMS & FINANCE CORPORATION
THE GREAT GAMBLER
Music
Rahul Dev Burman
Lyrics
Anand Bakshi
EMI
From the Original Soundtrack

ORIGINAL SOUNDTRACK RECORDING
MUSIC KALYANJI ANANDJI
PURAB AUR PACHHIM

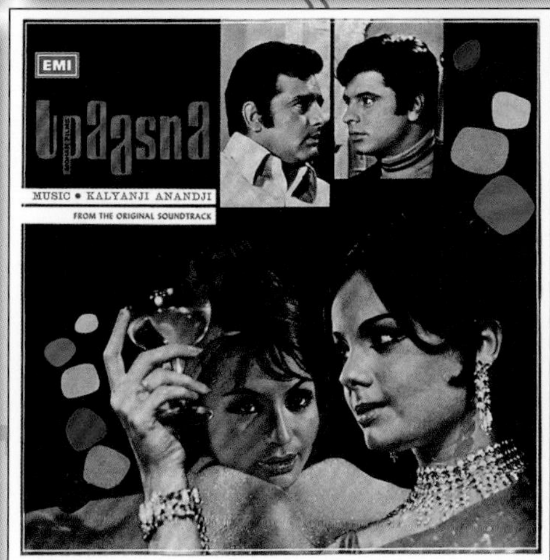
EMI
Upaasna
MUSIC • KALYANJI ANANDJI
FROM THE ORIGINAL SOUNDTRACK

Polydor
PREMIUM
G.P. SIPPY'S
SHOLAY
70 mm

AMITABH BACHCHAN

G.P. SIPPY'S

SHOLAY

DIRECTED BY RAMESH SIPPY

70mm

शोले

SALIM JAVED

R.D.BURMAN

ANAND BAKSHI

DWARKA DIVECHA

opposite top: Gatefold, *Qurbani* soundtrack album (1980); **right:** Zeenat Aman lights up in *Hare Raama Hare Krishna* (1971); **bottom right:** Helen torments Reena Roy in *Zakhmee* (1975); **below:** Amitabh Bachchan and Parveen Babi in *Shaan* (1980); **opposite bottom right:** Action was a staple genre throughout India's numerous regional cinemas. Soundtrack album to the Karnatakan thriller *Operation Diamond Racket*; **opposite centre right:** Dharmendra and Hema Malini in a tight spot. *Azaad* (1978); **opposite bottom left:** Bros before ho's: Amitabh Bachchan and Dharmendra in *Sholay* (1975).

SHAAN

Amitabh vs Alligator!

THE GREAT GAMBLER

Released: 1979
Director: Shakti Samanta
Stars: Amitabh Bachchan, Zeenat Aman, Neetu Singh, Prem Chopra, Utpal Dutt, Madan Puri, Om Shivpuri, Iftekhar, Sujit Kumar, Roopesh Kumar, Helen, Madhu Malhotra, Jagdish Raj, Keshav Rana, Brahm Bhardwaj, Rajan Kapoor, Prem Sagar, Ranjit Sood, S.C. Pandey, R.A. Rehman, Chandrashekhar, Gulshan, Shetty, Sarla Yeolekar
Writers: Ranjan Bose, Vrajendra Gaur, C.J. Pavri, Shakti Samanta
(Based on a novel by Vikramaditya)
Music: Rahul Dev Burman (R.D. Burman)
Lyrics: Anand Bakshi
Fights: Shetty

Jai (Amitabh Bachchan), a back alley card sharp, is recruited by Ratandas (Madan Puri), owner of a swanky upscale casino, to be his in-house player. Jai's formidable skills allow Ratandas, who is secretly a member of an international spy network, to force his influential customers into his debt, thus making it easier for him to pry lucrative secrets from them. Such is the case with Nath (Jagdish Raj), an Indian government worker whom Ratandas pressures into providing the documentation for Plan K2, a highly classified project involving a radar controlled death ray. Ratandas and his crew then communicate with their superiors and foreign clients by way of encoded films that feature the dancer Monica (Helen) doing specialized routines against a backdrop of flashing lights.

When one of the coded films is intercepted by the C.I.D., agent Vijay (Bachchan again), by chance an exact double of Jai, is assigned to track Monica down. Vijay does find Monica, only to have her gunned down by a sniper before she can reveal the nature of the code. That sniper, Sethi (Roopesh Kumar), escapes, but not without being seen by Vijay. As a result he becomes a liability to his organization. Ratandas dispatches Sethi to Rome to lay low, not telling him that the gang's Italian operative Marconi (Sujit Kumar) has instructions to kill him upon his arrival. In the event, Sethi overpowers Marconi and makes off with the gang's codebook. As an act of vengeance, he offers the book to the C.I.D. for a price, with a hand-off meeting arranged in Venice for a few days hence.

Vijay is tasked with making the assignation in Venice, and fatefully given the alias Jai for the purpose, along with the codename "Delhi Friend." Meanwhile, Ratandas has intercepted Sethi's communications with the agency and assigns his man Ramesh (Prem Chopra) to follow Vijay. Also along for the ride will be Ramesh's fiance Shabnam (Zeenat Aman), a cabaret dancer who has been hired to replace Monica. At the same time, Ratandas informs Jai that he has approved an arranged marriage between him and the daughter of Deepchand (Iftekhar) a wealthy friend of his who lives in Lisbon, explaining that Jai is the closest thing to a son that he has. Jai balks, but, when told that

the marriage is a scheme to get hold of Deepchand's money, agrees to fly to Lisbon to meet the girl.

Come the day, Vijay, Jai, Ramesh and Shabnam all end up booked on the same flight, but Vijay misses it. Ramesh, mistaking Jai for Vijay, attempts to set a honey trap for him by having Shabnam sit next to him and flirt. When a bomb threat grounds their flight in Cairo, Jai and Shabnam end up spending a romantic night of sightseeing together. Meanwhile, Vijay boards another flight and, during a stopover in Rome, is greeted by Mala (Neetu Singh), the daughter of Deepchand, who mistakes him for Jai. Troubled by the implication that he has a double out there somewhere, Vijay decides to play along in order to find out as much about Jai as possible. As a result, he and Mala end up spending a romantic evening of sightseeing together.

Once in Rome, Ramesh and Shabnam, now joined by Marconi, put the screws to Jai, only to learn that he is not, in fact, Vijay. The trio then decides to use his resemblance to Vijay to get their hands on the code book. This results in a race against time between the two lookalikes to see who can get to Sethi first. Ultimately, the chase leads to the island lair of Saxena (Utpal Dutt), the criminal organization's leader, where, amid explosions and plumes of poison gas, it just may be revealed that Jai and Vijay's resemblance is more than coincidental.

"**HEY FOLKS!** Watch him! He's a gambler. The *great* gambler!"

The Great Gambler is about as generous a combination of '70s kitsch and pulp absurdity as Bollywood could offer. Where else will you see Zeenat Aman getting down to KC and the Sunshine Band's "Get Down Tonight," Amitabh Bachchan attempting kung fu in a black satin tuxedo and zebra print tie, or Prem Chopra essaying the role of a medallion sporting disco dude? Then we have R.D. Burman's theme song, quoted above, which consists largely of a drunk sounding woman enthusing in fairly uncertain terms about the virtues of our titular card shark. And let's not forget fight composer Shetty's eleventh hour appearance, in which he's dressed as a slaughterhouse attendant and appears to be channeling *Plan 9 from Outer Space*'s Tor Johnson, during which he and the Big B fight it out in a meat locker filled with gory animal carcasses. And why again is he painted black?

Which is not to say that *The Great Gambler* is a B movie by any stretch of the imagination. Like the following year's *The Burning Train*, the picture seems like part of a sub-trend of Indian action films of the period that strove to be competitive, in terms of production value, with their Western counterparts. The result is a relatively pricey looking affair whose evidence of conspicuous consumption includes a host of international locations, a thrilling speedboat chase through the canals of Venice, and two extended car chases. Also like *The Burning Train*, *The Great Gambler*'s producers recruited some Western talent for their stunt team, this time in the persons of stunt coordinators Roy Alon (*The Spy Who Loved Me*, *Superman III*), Dicky Beer (*A Bridge Too Far*, *Return of the Jedi*) and Jalil Jay Lynch (*New Jack City*, *The Last Action Hero*). Nonetheless, there is still some evidence of budget shortfall in the film's action scenes; The car chases, for the most part, are of the type that take place on Italian back roads that are empty save for the occasional stunt car, and, while exciting, come across more like watching a pair of Hot Wheels race around the track than, say, *The Italian Job*.

Ultimately, and despite all these slam bang trappings, *The Great Gambler*, in obeisance to its Bollywood DNA, can't help but become a

fantasy about romantic destiny. Once the real Jai finally makes it to Lisbon for his long delayed meeting with Mala, he's shamed by the obvious love she feels for Vijay and comes clean, thus freeing himself to pursue his romance with Shabnam. And this is as it should be. As the designated bad kids, Jai and Shabnam have a relationship that is barbed and sexy, while Vijay and Mala are earnest, soul searching and boring (the usually effervescent Neetu Singh seems to have been tranquilized for her role). This also allows *The Great Gambler*, in the wake of its climactic gun battles, death traps and lair exploding, to close out its running time with that cheesiest of filmic conventions, the double wedding.

Perhaps among *The Great Gambler*'s greatest liabilities are the labyrinthine tendrils spread by its combining the time tested plot devices of the double and the "lost and found" family drama, the result a baffling and top-heavy construct that requires such patent unlikelihoods as Vijay coincidentally being given the alias "Jai" and people who clearly should be aware of Jai's existence being somehow completely ignorant of it. Still, it's hard to say that the movie doesn't make up for its pitfalls with its eye candy. The milieu of the glamorous, high stakes casino makes for a near endless pageant of '70s excess. Zeenat Aman's introductory number, meant to be a nightclub act that is occurring in real time, involves her changing from one colorful costume to the next almost every five seconds. The film's copious nods to the disco era also make for some unforgettable instances of ill-advised sartorial adventuring.

In terms of its cast, *The Great Gambler* is another film that benefits from a generous abundance of seasoned screen villainy, with both Madan Puri and Prem Chopra bringing their worst to tailor made roles. Still, its most noteworthy casting may be represented by an absence: that of the great Amjad Khan, who, after a serious accident on the set, had to be replaced by Utpal Dutt in the role of Saxena. One can only marvel at what might have been.

As for Amitabh Bachchan, *The Great Gambler* might be seen as an example of him moving away from the angry young man archetype, the traditionally less sympathetic Jai being the closest to a representation of that character we see in the film. Yet, so strong is the association that even the sophisticated spy Vijay is represented in a way that pays homage to it: a gum chewing James Bond with the moves of a street brawler. There's nonetheless no denying that this is Bachchan in a decidedly more frivolous mode. Sending that down easy is the fact that, unlike earlier double films, the technology was by this time available to have Vijay and Jai appear on screen together, making for a thrilling spectacle once they team up at the end to fight the bad guys. Perhaps today second only to *Don* in terms of cult status, *The Great Gambler* earns its stripes by truly giving us double the Bachchan for our buck.

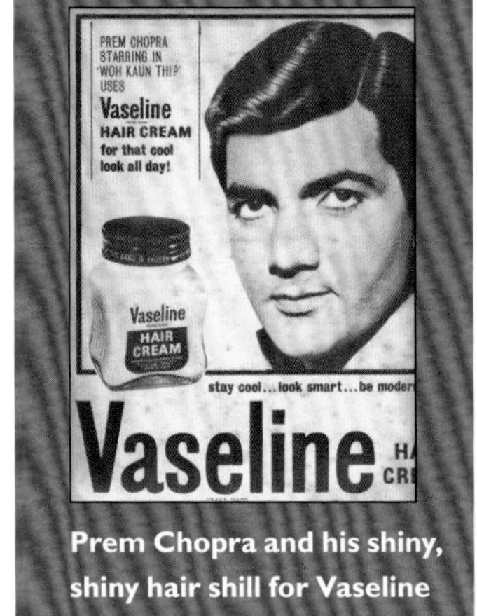

Prem Chopra and his shiny, shiny hair shill for Vaseline

SHALIMAR

Released: 1978
Director: Krishna Shah
Stars: Dharmendra, Zeenat Aman, Rex Harrison, Sylvia Miles, John Saxon, O.P. Ralhan, Shammi Kapoor, Prem Nath, Shreeram Lagoo, Aruna Irani, Clyde Chai-Fa, M.B. Shetty, Phunsok Ladhakhi, Anita, Jayamalini, Kader Khan
Writers: Krishna Shah, Stanford Sherman, Kader Khan, Momin Khan
Music: Rahul Dev Burman (R.D. Burman)
Lyrics: Anand Bakshi
Fights: Shetty

Kumar (Dharmendra), a small time thief who manages a gambling club, finds that he's in debt to the club's owners, who suspect him of skimming the take. After a patron takes a bullet intended for him, Kumar finds an invitation in the man's pocket for a gathering on the private island of Sir John Locksley (Rex Harrison). Posing as the man's son, Kumar heads for the island with the intention of robbing Locksley.

It turns out that Locksley is a master thief who has assembled for the occasion a collection of the world's greatest thieves. These include Colonel Columbus, a mute former military man (John Saxon); Countess Rasmussen, an acrobat and trapeze artist (Sylvia Miles); Dr. Bukhari, a religious con man (Shammi Kapoor); and Romeo (O.P. Ralhan). Also present is Locksley's private nurse, Sheila (Zeenat Aman), with whom Kumar has a romantic history.

Locksley tells the gathered thieves that he is in possession of the Shalimar Ruby, "the most precious stone in the world." He also tells them that he is dying of cancer and that, in order to determine a worthy inheritor of the Shalimar, he has decided to hold a contest to see who among the gathered hoods can steal it. This, of course, will prove no easy task, as the ruby is protected by Locksley's army of heavily armed native guards, land mines, a laser alarm system and assorted booby traps.

Columbus and the Countess are the first and second of the guests to try for the stone and are both killed within inches of reaching it. Convinced that an attempt to steal the ruby means certain death, Kumar tries to dissuade Bukhari—whom it is revealed is Sheila's godfather—from trying. The older man proceeds anyway and, by all appearances, ends up being executed in cold blood by the guards.

Romeo then tries to withdraw from the competition but is murdered outright by Locksley. It now becomes clear that Locksley is a madman who is simply trying to wipe out his competition. Plotting an escape, Kumar and Sheila are forced by Locksley to make the final attempt on the ruby together.

SHALIMAR WAS AN EARLY experiment in Bollywood/Hollywood synergy and, as such, failed spectacularly in two languages on two continents simultaneously. It was directed by Krishna Shah, an Indian American director with a history in American television, whose Judson Productions co-produced it. Another veteran of American television, Stanford Sherman, co-wrote the story. Of course, the most conspicuous evidence of Western involvement in *Shalimar* is the presence of stars Rex Harrison, Sylvia Miles and John Saxon (the latter no stranger to international co-productions, having starred in numerous Euro-genre pictures over the years and, perhaps most notably, the U.S./Hong Kong produced *Enter the Dragon* five years earlier).

At first, *Shalimar* does make for a disorienting collision of worlds. It is admittedly weird to watch Dharmendra righteously yelling at Dr. Dolittle. Naturally, the screenwriters compensate by making Sir Locksley a classist bad guy in the classic Bollywood mode, a decadent product of the upper crust who takes pot shots at his native servants for fun. Harrison brings little energy to the role, which provides an interesting contrast to the salivating mania of the Amjad Khan, Ajit or Prem Chopra who would have essayed it otherwise. Miles, for her part, is saddled with both a role and a Shirley Temple wig that are conspicuously inappropriate for her age, but proceeds enthusiastically. John Saxon, playing a mute, is spared the indignities of the Hindi dubbing job given the others and gets to relive some of his *Enter the Dragon* glory in a scene where he fights off a squadron of guards with his lightning fists.

An early experiment in Bollywood/ Hollywood synergy, it failed spectacularly in two languages on two continents simultaneously.

Still, while entertaining, *Shalimar* in many ways underscores the ways in which the sensibilities of the two industries shall never meet. Its economical, Hollywood-style middle section makes its convoluted prologue and endlessly deferred climax seem like needless padding—something that would be true in an American film, but which, in an Indian film, would simply be a matter of storytelling style. R.D. Burman's song score (Kersi Lord composed the instrumental) makes few concessions to an English speaking audience and was likely edited out of the Anglo version. One exception is an English Language song about doing the Cha Cha which incorporates parts of KC and the Sunshine Band's "That's the Way I Like It," sung by dance instructor Aruna Irani in an early scene. This bit comes off as irresistibly kitschy today, thought it's tough to judge how an American audience would have reacted to it at the time.

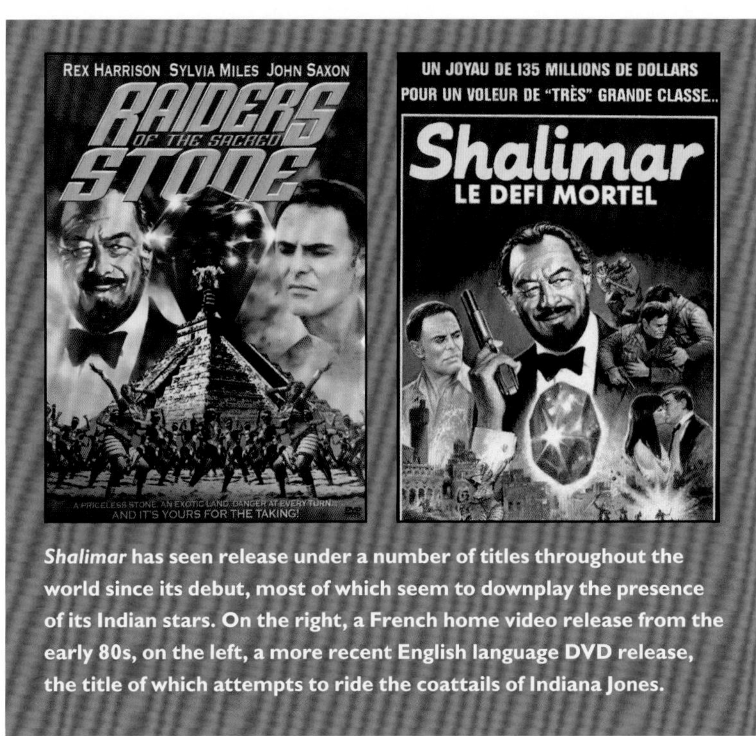

Shalimar **has seen release under a number of titles throughout the world since its debut, most of which seem to downplay the presence of its Indian stars. On the right, a French home video release from the early 80s, on the left, a more recent English language DVD release, the title of which attempts to ride the coattails of Indiana Jones.**

The film's light is also dimmed by the treatment of its native characters, which harkens back to the minstrelsy of '30s films like *King Kong* (an attempt at naive exoticism to appeal to the colonialist mindset? Perhaps). In any case, Locksley's islander guards are presented as cartoonish and outrageously expendable; each contestant in the game gleefully throws them from turrets and onto land mines by the several without so much as a look backward, while the death of one of the thieves is always treated with the utmost solemnity. The natives and their spooky, primal beliefs are also the subject of a particularly eerie sequence in which they paint Columbus's dead body to serve as an idol and start worshipping him as a god.

Dharmendra and Zeenat Aman, meanwhile, are their normal glamorous selves. In fact, it's hard to imagine that, were the desire there, these two stars couldn't have made the crossover to Hollywood themselves. Heaven knows we've endured our share of monosyllabic, foreign born action heroes over the years, and it's unlikely that Dharam could do much worse. Then again, it's true that his strength lies in his oratory—as evidenced by the scorching takedown he delivers to Locksley and his entire class ("Your faces differ, but your laughter is the same!") during *Shalimar*'s final half. It would be a shame to lose that.

CHORI MERA KAAM
"To Steal Is My Job"

Released: 1975
Director: Brij
Stars: Ashok Kumar, Shashi Kapoor, Zeenat Aman, Pran, Anwar Hussain, David Abraham, Deven Verma, Iftekhar, Raza Murad, Shetty, Maruti Rao, Asha Potdar, Komilla Wirk, Urmila Bhatt, Anoop Kumar, Appi Umrani, Chaman Puri, Jankidas, Khursheed Khan, Fazal, Lamba, Harbans Darshan M. Arora, Birbal
Writers: K.A. Narayan, Ehsan Rizvi
Music: Kalyanji-Anandji (Kalyanji Virji Shah & Anandji Virji Shah)
Lyrics: Varma Malik
Fights: Shetty

Upright police inspector Kumar (Pran), about to present damning evidence in the trial of kidnapper Amarchand (Anwar Hussain), is notified that his own small son, Munna, has been abducted, with the named ransom his withholding of that evidence. Kumar defiantly follows through with his duty, telling Amarchand that he would gladly sacrifice both of his sons in order to protect all of the children of India from the likes of him. Meanwhile, little Munna, just about to have his throat cut by one of Amarchand's gang, is rescued by the chance intervention of Shankar (Ashok Kumar), a gentle hearted petty criminal. Shankar intends to take Munna home, but, in transit, is intercepted by his bitter criminal rival John (David Abraham), who seizes the first opportunity to abscond with Munna, whom he assumes to be Shankar's own child.

Twenty years later, Munna, raised by John into a life of crime, has grown up to be Bhola (Shashi Kapoor), a small time thief who works in partnership with Sharmili (Zeenat Aman), another carefree pickpocket, prowler and con artist. Shyam (Raza Murad), Inspector Kumar's other son, has grown up to join the police department, and has just been named a sub-inspector. As for Amarchand, he has become the mysterious criminal mastermind No.7, commanding a gang that is responsible for a series of brazen and meticulously planned robberies at which a tile bearing the number 7—Amarchand's prison number following his conviction—is always left behind. Inspector Kumar, meanwhile, appears unaged and as upright and dedicated to upholding the law as ever.

One night during their criminal rounds, Bhola and Sharmili break into an apartment—which we later learn belongs to Shankar—and steal a briefcase from the safe. To their disappointment, this turns out to contain, rather than cash, a manuscript titled To Steal Is My Job*, which is basically an in-depth criminal memoir and "how to" guide that Shankar has written. Later, after being thrown out of a restaurant, the pair shakes down Pravin (Deven Verma), a passing motorist, by having Sharmili pretend to be struck and killed by him. Bhola gets the shaken Pravin to agree to pay him 50,000 Rs. in return for not being turned in to the police and, showing up at his office the next* *day to collect, discovers that Bhola is a publisher. Bhola then adds to his demands that Pravin publish Shankar's manuscript, which he submits under his own name.*

To Steal Is My Job *ends up becoming a major best seller, requiring Bhola to go on the publicity circuit as a celebrated author. Making this problematic is the fact that the illiterate Bhola has neither read nor can read* To Steal Is My Job, *and is thus unequipped to answer the many questions posed about it by reporters and fans alike. It is perhaps fortunate, then, that Shankar has been shadowing him and Sharmili since the theft of the manuscript, and steps forward in the role of Bhola's secretary to field those questions for him—all for a cut of the take, of course. Meanwhile, Inspector Kumar has read the book and, based on the level of criminal expertise displayed, begins to suspect that Bhola is No.7. As for Amarchand/No.7, his takeaway from* To Steal Is My Job *is an obsession with finding a certain party mentioned therein who is capable of supplying criminals with fool proof disguises. He nabs Bhola and Shankar toward this end, but they manage to escape without giving him any substantial information.*

Said mask maker is ultimately revealed to be Sharmili's crippled father, Shambhu (Chaman Puri), whom Amarchand kidnaps and forces to do his bidding. The fruit of his labors is a mask that allows Amarchand to rob a jewelry auction of a fortune in gems disguised as Inspector Kumar. Kumar awakens to find himself a hunted man, and is arrested by Shyam, who proves to be as much of a stickler for duty as his old man. However, Kumar's imprisonment is soon revealed to be a ruse, as he is quickly freed to go undercover as the "infamous dacoit" (bandit) Shera to work his way into No.7's organization. At the same time, in an effort to free her father, Sharmili allows herself to be taken captive by the gang, while Bhola and Shankar go undercover as two American hoods interested in purchasing the take from the jewelry heist. During an epic brawl within the colorful confines of Amarchand's lair, the masks come off as the fists fly, and the true connections between all are ultimately revealed.

Chori mera kaam
ASHOK KUMAR
SHASHI KAPOOR
ZEENAT AMAN
PRODUCED BY: CHANDER SADANAH
DIRECTED BY: BRIJ
MUSIC: KALYANJI - ANANDJI

BY 1975, THE CLEAN CUT and morally upright heroes of the sixties—perhaps in *Chori Mera Kaam* best represented by Raza Murad's board-backed and frankly miserable looking Inspector Shyam Kumar—had been pretty much pushed to the sidelines in favor of protagonists of a more morally ambiguous cast. This still left room for some diversity, of course, because, for every tragic antihero in the vein of *Deewaar*'s Vijay, you also had carefree, lovable rogues in the mold of *Chori Mera Kaam*'s Bhola, Sharmili and Shankar. This trio, in fact, bears a lot of similarities to the central trio played by Vinod Khanna, Shatrugan Sinha and a returning Zeenat Aman in director Brij's later *Bombay 405 Miles*, although that film was more successful due to a more streamlined structure and consistent level of craft. Without a strong narrative, these "winsome thug" movies tend to gain little from what they sacrifice in believability.

suits to his multicolored, coliseum style lair. *Chori Mera Kaam* is also one of those films in which the fearsome, chrome domed Shetty—one of the most recognizable of all 1970s Bollywood's criminal cronies, as well as its most prolifically employed fight choreographer—actually plays a character named Shetty.

And speaking of fights, *Chori Mera Kaam* is one of the many, many 1970s masalas that ends with a protracted dustup involving virtually every member of its cast, this one augmented by lightning, stampeding horses, a wild tiger, and a lot of mud. So long is this particular row that it ends up comprising something of a hostage situation in itself. Such scenes are typically punctuated by slapstick gags, showcase stunts and one-liners, and remind me a lot of the kind of chaotic free-for-alls that closed out "wacky" 1960s comedies like Charles Feldman's *Casino Royale* and *What's New Pussycat?* In both cases, these fights often strike me as the equivalent of filmmakers throwing their hands up in surrender after having painted themselves into a corner by piling on too many baroque plot complications, like the toppling of an especially precarious house of cards. And *Chori Mera Kaam* is certainly guilty of such excess, compulsively adding new twists up to its closing moments, long after all potential for suspense has been exhausted.

Still, some could attribute such excesses to a generosity of spirit, which goes along with *Chori Mera Kaam* taking the trouble to provide a quirky storyline that goes beyond the simple unwinding of its "lost and found" plot mechanics. Director Brij, whose career was tragically cut short by suicide in 1990, certainly had better in him, yet *Chori Mera Kaam* nonetheless supports the case for his work overall being worthy of examination.

Still, *Chori Mera Kaam* succeeds in its lighthearted approach better than others, with the business between Shashi Kapoor and Zeenat Aman at times approaching a satisfying level of screwball comedy. The episode wherein Aman tries to spook Deven Verma's Pravin—first by impersonating a corpse and then a howling ghost—definitely had its amusements, as did the scene where, once discovered, she convinces him that she's the twin sister of the deceased, asking him "Haven't you watched *Seeta aur Geeta*?" I also have to say that I enjoyed Deven Verma's performance as Pravin, finding his preening character slightly more developed than that of your typical comic relief fraidy cat, and, along with it, the film's quaint portrait of the glamorous and decadent world of book publishing, with all its fancy soirees, literary groupies, paparazzo and intimations of a general public that actually cares about books.

Within the rest of the cast, we have yet another MVP performance by Pran, who shines especially in his moments as the massively moled and mustached bandit Shera, who sings us into the third act melee with Kalyanji-Anandji's driving "Meri Nazar Se." In his portrayal of No.7, Anwar Hussain seems to be channeling Madan Puri, which was probably the best choice, given the character screams Puri with everything from his immaculate white

DHARMATMA
"God Man"

Released: 1975
Director: Feroz Khan
Stars: Prem Nath, Feroz Khan, Hema Malini, Rekha, Danny Denzongpa, Farida Jalal, Ranjeet, Sudhir, Imtiaz Khan, Madan Puri, Jeevan, Satyendra Kapoor, Helen, Iftekhar, Faryal, Sulochana Latkar, Seema Kapoor, Jagdish Raj, Krishnakant, Habib, Anand Pal, Major Anand, Brahm Bhardwaj, V. Gopal, Hercules, Dhanraj, Rafiq, Zaheera, Nadira, Alka, P. Jairaj, Yashraj, Nana Palsikar, Nasir Hussain, Krishan Dhawan, Gurnam, Mohan Choti, Himmat Singh Chauhan, Dara Singh, Azad, Jankidas, Yusuf Khan
Writer: Kaushal Bharati
Music: Kalyanji-Anandji (Kalyanji Virji Shah & Anandji Virji Shah)
Lyrics: Indeevar
Fights: Mohammed Ali

"God Man" Dharamdas (Prem Nath) enjoys a reputation for altruism, despite sitting on a fortune amassed through the operation of gambling halls and other illegal enterprises. What he lacks, however, is an heir to his empire, being estranged from his only son Ranbir (Feroz Khan), who rejects his criminal activities. When his daughter Mona (Farida Jalal) becomes engaged to Kundan (Imtiaz Khan), the son of a recently deceased friend, Dharamdas welcomes him into the organization, hoping to groom him as a successor.

Ranbir, meanwhile, is in Afghanistan, working for his Uncle (Madan Puri). Visiting a gypsy encampment, he falls for Reshma (Hema Malini), touching off a vicious rivalry with one of her suitors from within the tribe, Jankura (Danny Denzongpa). Once this is settled, he and Reshma are engaged. Soon thereafter, word comes of Mona's upcoming nuptials and Ranbir reluctantly returns to India, where he is received coolly by his father.

Later, the brothers Anokhela (Jeevan) and Meghnao (Satyendra Kapoor), longstanding rivals of Dharamdas, approach him with a proposal to join forces in a drug dealing operation. Dharamdas, opposed to dealing drugs, rejects the offer, but the green Kundan makes the mistake of challenging his judgment and is fired by Dharamdas as a result. This leads to Kundan secretly joining forces with the brothers and plotting to kill Dharamdas, with the goal of Kundan rising to the head of the organization in service to the brothers' interests.

Of course, the conspirators realize that, in order to assure Kundan's ascension, they must also get Ranbir out of the way. And so, as an assassination attempt on Dharamdas is mounted in India, so too are a pair of hit men—the cousins Rishi (Ranjeet) and Natwar (Sudhir)—dispatched to Afghanistan. The attempt on Dharamdas results in him being hospitalized, while an attempt to bomb Ranbir's car results in the death of Reshma. Bent on revenge, the grieving Ranbir returns to India, where he provisionally takes over Dharamdas's organization.

Eventually, Kundan manages to finish the job and murder Dharamdas in his hospital room. However,

in his death agonies the old man grabs hold of Kundan's distinctive ring, which Ranbir later uses in his search for the killer. Ranbir is joined in this search by his father's faithful bodyguard Shakti Singh (Dara Singh) and aided by Dharamdas's vast fortune, which his mother has put at his disposal. Nonetheless, success is not guaranteed, as the closer Ranbir comes to tightening the noose around Kundan's neck, the more his enemies step up their ever more diabolical attempts to put him out of the picture.

COMING AFTER *APRADH* and before *Qurbani*, *Dharmatma* is the lesser of Feroz Khan's directorial efforts from the '70s, but still has things to recommend it. While it's widely regarded as a remake of *The Godfather*, it should be noted that it is a remake of *The Godfather* aimed squarely at those who felt Coppola's original suffered from a shortage of motorcycle stunts and explosions.

Dharmatma was the first Indian film to be shot on location in Afghanistan and—though Khan chose well from the local landscapes and filmed them beautifully—he also seems to have felt obligated to include a lot of local color and travelogue business that otherwise slows the picture down. Even the clash between Khan and Danny Denzongpa's characters bears little fruit—though it perhaps serves the *muy macho* Khan's larger goals by presenting us with a cock fight so epic that it threatens to bring the very sky crashing down around it. Elsewhere, a brutal game of Buzkashi—a sort of Central Asian version of polo on steroids—is filmed excitingly but accounts for little. I suppose, if you're not paying too close attention, all of this could serve to make what is essentially a pretty standard Bollywood revenge thriller seem like some kind of sprawling saga, but it otherwise leaves one wondering when exactly *Dharmatma* is going to start being about something.

Of course, as a stylist, Khan doesn't let us down. *Dharmatma* throughout looks great and is filled with visual invention. The director—working here, as in *Apradh*, with cinematographer Kamal Bose—seems allergic to setting up a conventional shot, and in his creative restlessness employs everything from fish-eye lenses to wild POV shots and unnatural looking color gels to get his desired effects. Occasionally this does get a bit much—a crazily spinning shot transitioning from the burning car in which Reshma has just died to her funeral pyre almost looks like something out of an old Hanna-Barbera cartoon—but it certainly can't be said that *Dharmatma* is ever boring to look at.

It also has to be said that, once *Dharmatma* finally settles into being that standard Bollywood revenge thriller that it was so born to be, Khan fully lives up to his promise as one of India's best action directors of the era. The scene in which Ranbir is attacked by a team of lasso-wielding, motorcycle assassins in fright masks is as thrilling as it is silly, and the assassination attempt on Dharamdas, set in the vaguely defined confines of his neon webbed casino, is both disorienting and effectively nerve wracking. Even the climactic item number, ushering us into the frenzied final confrontation, is handled like an action tour de force; in this case, it's a fevered tribal dance—set in a debauched cantina called "The Devil's Hut"—in which Helen seems to be literally trying to shake her way out of her own skin, and which appropriately reaches its crescendo when Khan comes crashing through the club's wall in his car.

BREAKDOWN:
Cycle Killers!

Khan also makes good on his tendency, demonstrated in *Apradh*, to provide us with villains who go above and beyond the Bollywood norm in their visceral grotesquerie. Even working with such cozily familiar faces of evil as Jeevan and Satyendra Kapoor, he manages to make the nervously cackling Anokhelal, with his ever present monocle, and Meghnao, with his neck brace and strangled voice, enough to make you want to run for the shower. Even more of a skin crawling triumph, however, is the hit man team of Rishi and Natwar, played by Ranjeet and Sudhir. A brilliant recurring gag is made of these murderous cousins' matching outfits, with the characteristically flamboyant Ranjeet wisely made the style setter of the two. These taste flaying get-ups range from matching aqua sport coats worn over bare chests, to matching skintight black mesh shirts, to a particularly fetching urban cowboy look modeled by both toward the picture's end. And finally, tying up a motif, Khan once again, as in *Apradh*, has a treacherous Faryal getting murdered in the bath.

As for the other performances in the film, they're strong overall, despite the fact that Khan seems to show a lot more interest in his male stars. Rekha, playing an old flame of Ranbir's back home, comes across as oddly mannequin-like and waiting for direction, while, as Reshma, Hema Malini seems to get by on her natural charisma and energy. Elsewhere, however, we have the great Iftekhar doing yet another noble turn as Dharamdas's doomed right hand man and Danny Denzongpa attacking the role of Jankura with his characteristic wounded ferocity. "Stunt King" Dara Singh, looking fit and imposing, also shows up for a welcome cameo in a role that is gratifyingly action oriented.

And then there is Feroz Khan, who, is clearly the star of *Dharmatma*, his second billing to Golden Age star Prem Nath notwithstanding. In keeping with the FK brand, his Ranbir may be a starry eyed idealist—perhaps, within the film's unique universe, even some kind of a pacifist—but he also comes with a lot of strut and swagger. The shirt comes off at regular intervals, as is that trademark look of cavalier sexual confidence, head cocked and winking, regularly deployed in a series of hip swiveling Kalyanji-Anandji numbers. For a career Milquetoast such as me, the temptation is to see a figure like Khan as an obnoxious proto-douchebag, yet the man so clearly enjoys being a boy that it's hard to begrudge him his good time.

It is likewise hard to deny that *Dharmatma*—amid all its hair tearing, histrionics, and tragedy—is also a good time. It may not come across as a great film when viewed in this day, but it was nonetheless a smash hit in its own. If received with an open heart, it's not hard to see why.

MAHA BADMAASH
"Great Scoundrel"

Released: 1977
Director: R.G. Thaker
Stars: Vinod Khanna, Neetu Singh, Nisar Ahmad Ansari, Bindu, Brahmachari, Rajan Haksar, Imtiaz, Pinchoo Kapoor, Inder Khosla, Shiv Kumar, Raza Murad, Praveen Paul, Shetty, Om Shivpuri, Nandita Thakur
Writer: Faiz Salim
Music: Ravindra Jain
Lyrics: Kulwant Jani, Noor Dewasi, Naqsh Lyallpuri

A shadowy criminal mastermind called Mogambo has a knack for getting others to do his dirty work, thus making it that much harder for the authorities to track him down. For his latest undisclosed plot, he determines that he must have the services of Bombay casino owner Ratan (Vinod Khanna), and dispatches his African henchman Mamba (Rajan Haksar) to make it so. Also tasked with recruiting Ratan is Pinky (Neetu Singh), a young woman coerced into service to Mogambo by the fact that he is holding her father hostage. Mamba arrives at Ratan's Flush Club to quickly get caught cheating by Ratan, who gives him a thrashing and throws him out onto the street. Later Mamba turns up dead and Pinky approaches Ratan with an incriminating photograph of the two men's fight. Ratan, who considers himself a thug with principles, nonetheless agrees to participate in Mogambo's scheme to ensure her silence.

At Pinky's instructions, Ratan checks into the Hotel Hilton and, without any details about the mission that Mogambo has in store for him, begins his training—which involves, among other things, holding his breath for a long time and sitting in a deep freeze. Ratan is also whisked away to a meeting with Mogambo, whom, thanks to his only appearing in silhouette, Ratan can only identify by the distinctive cane he carries. It turns out, however, that a lot of guests at the Hotel Hilton have that same cane, one of them being a man later revealed to be Police Commissioner Saxena (N.A. Ansari), who is keeping close tabs on Ratan and Pinky. Saxena eventually succeeds in apprehending Pinky, whereupon he substitutes in her place Seema (Neetu Singh again), Pinky's long lost twin sister. Seema, the more modest and pious of the two sisters, has her work cut out for her, seeing as she not only has to convince the suspicious Mogambo of her authenticity, but also Ratan and her boyfriend Mike, who is also part of Mogambo's crew.

Meanwhile, tensions rise as Ratan tries to find out the exact nature of the grand criminal scheme he's been recruited for, as well as the identity of the seemingly omnipresent Mogambo.

MAHA BADMAASH is a Hindi comic book film rife with mystery, intrigue and, sadly, naked racism potent enough to snap your head back like a well timed haymaker. It is also a film that features an early instance of a Bollywood villain being named Mogambo, a moniker that would rise to immortality with Amrish Puri's show stopping turn as the like named antagonist of 1987's monster smash *Mr. India*. However, as much as I might like to entertain the idea that Mogambo was Indian cinema's answer to Hannibal Lecter, the greater likelihood is that someone simply thought that Mogambo was too good of a villain name to use just once.

The Mogambo of *Maha Badmaash* is a villain whose identity, motives, and plans are not revealed until the movie's final moments, presenting the filmmakers with quite a challenge in terms of having to convince us, their audience, that we should give a toss in the first place. And it's a challenge that they prove for the most part unable to meet. Whatever scheme Mogambo has in mind, however, it is abundantly clear that he wants Vinod Khanna's Ratan to carry it out. To this end, he sends forth from his African hideout his "black" henchman, Mamba, who is portrayed by Indian actor Rajan Haksar sporting an Afro wig, fake muttonchops and green face paint.

Ratan has an idiotic comic relief sidekick named Reddy, played by Brahmachari, who astonishingly, out of all the idiotic comic relief sidekicks in Indian cinema, clearly stands head and shoulders above the rest in terms of his cretinous stupidity. Upon Mamba's arrival at the Flush Club, Reddy is quick to notify Ratan of the presence of a "negro" in his establishment. (Granted, I am relying here on the English subtitles to the DVD of *Maha Badmaash* and, given the Yoda-like syntax that they employ throughout the film, I certainly wouldn't vouch for their accuracy.) Ratan is quick to unmask Mamba as a card cheat and violently ejects him from the casino—while, according to the subs, repeatedly referring to him contemptuously as "black man." As cartoonish as the context may be, the ugliness of this sequence and Rajan Haksar's minstrelsy within it leaves a bad taste that the remainder of *Maha Badmaash* is ill equipped to wash way.

Brahmachari, astonishingly, out of all the idiotic comic relief sidekicks in Indian cinema, clearly stands head and shoulders above the rest in terms of his cretinous stupidity.

Though quite short at just two hours, *Maha Badmaash* still seems to spend a lot of its middle section spinning its wheels, and once the caper that it has not been doing a very good job of building anticipation for finally transpires, it turns out to be pretty much of a letdown. On top of that, the confusion of identities that results from the introduction into the plot of twins and numerous red herrings, rather than providing that loopy masala movie sense of fun that we might hope for, largely ends up taxing our ability to care. Not that they don't go down trying, mind you, leaving us with one of those mildly

desperate seeming madcap "everybody fights everybody" finales in which one mask after another is cast off and the tables are turned again and again and again.

As far as the performances go in *Maha Badmaash*, the extent to which they fail seems due largely to scripting and miscasting rather than the actors themselves. Ratan is suave but glacial, a man married to his work, and seems a waste of Vinod Khanna's ability to exude an easy, devilish charm. Neetu Singh—possessed of a more wholesome kind of sensuality than, say, Zeenat Aman or Rekha—seems less of an obvious choice to play a classic femme fatale, but nonetheless gives it her best. Her resulting arsenal of winks and come hither glances come off as, for the most part, awkward and, as with Khanna, undermines our enjoyment of an otherwise perfectly appealing performer. Furthermore, as a result of Mogambo's cipher-like status, the film suffers from a lack of the kind of anchoring bad guy turn that an old pro like Amjad Khan or Ajit could have provided.

Still, there are positive things to take away from *Maha Badmaash* if one so desires, though the more liberal minded among us might feel dirty for doing so. Mogambo's moon base style HQ is definitely one for the pages of *Better Lairs and Hideouts*, and the driving, guitar twang heavy instrumental score by Ravindra Jain is outstanding. Bindu also has an interesting role as Reena, the daughter of the Hotel Hilton's owner, whose primary purpose seems to be to launch into an exposition heavy item number whenever she enters a scene. At one point she recognizes Seema as an impostor and threatens, in song, to expose her, while Ratan, also in song, insists that she is mistaken. This takes place in front of an oblivious crowd that includes most of the film's major characters, and serves as yet another example of the interesting tendency for songs in Hindi movies to create subliminal dialogues within the larger narrative.

Maha Badmaash also, it should be noted—and in spite of the baroque rabbit holes of its plot—seems to have designs on being a straightforward action film. Its fights, chases, and stunt sequences are plentiful and frequent, and are staged with a lot of energy. (No one is credited as fight coordinator, though the presence of Shetty in the cast alone suggests it was likely him.) This, along with the film's colorful design, grants it the potential to be a lightweight but enjoyable piece of pulp entertainment—in essence, the exact type of film this book was meant to celebrate. Sadly, it falls one Mamba short of perfection, which turns out to be quite a deficit indeed.

TRISHUL

Released: 1978
Director: Yash Chopra
Stars: Amitabh Bachchan, Sanjeev Kumar, Shashi Kapoor, Hema Malini, Rakhee Gulzar, Waheeda Rehman, Prem Chopra, Poonam Dhillon, Sachin, Manmohan Krishna, Iftekhar, Yunus Parvez, Shetty, Manik Irani, Gita Siddharth, Jagdish Raj, Mohan Sherry
Writers: Salim-Javed (Salim Khan & Javed Akhtar)
Music: Khayyam
Lyrics: Sahir
Fights: Shetty

Gupta (Sanjeev Kumar) asks his mom to give her blessings to his engagement to working class Shanti (Waheeda Rehman). She says she approves, but in private insists that Gupta insure his financial future by marrying his wealthy boss's daughter Kamini (Gita Siddharth). Gupta complies with her wishes and, on the day of his wedding to Kamini, a devastated Shanti comes to his office to offer him her congratulations—and to notify him that she is pregnant with his child. Shanti refuses his offers of financial assistance and takes to the road, nurturing her bitterness toward Gupta for the next 25 years and instilling it in her child, Vijay (Amitabh Bachchan). On her deathbed, she makes Vijay promise her that he will never "become weak in life." He pledges to make sure that the one responsible for her suffering never finds peace.

Vijay's first step in his plot against Gupta, who has since become a wealthy construction magnate, is to offer him a pittance for a parcel of land rendered useless by a gang of bandits occupying it. Deed in hand, Vijay then ousts the bandits using the power of his fists, once again making the land a profitable source of capital. He then, in return for protecting him from a blackmailer, pressures Gupta's employee Bhandari (Yunus Parvez), into revealing his company's trade secrets. With this information, he is able to steal valuable contracts from beneath Gupta's nose by outbidding him by just one rupee. The furious Gupta suspects his loyal secretary Geeta (Rakhee Gulzar) of leaking this information and fires her, whereupon she goes to work for Vijay, for whom she has romantic feelings.

Meanwhile, Gupta's son Shekhar (Shashi Kapoor) returns from two years abroad to take his place beside his father in the company. Together, they watch in astonishment as, over the next two years, Vijay becomes a major competitor in their industry, clueless as to just what his very obvious grudge against them might be. Shekhar also meets and romances Sheetal (Hema Malini), the daughter of a wealthy associate and a formidable businesswoman in her own right. Shekhar's little sister Bubbli (Poonam Dhillon), at the same time, wants to marry young Ravi (Sachin) and is chafing at the restrictions of her father, who disapproves of the union. Vijay, who befriends Bubbli when he saves her from a car crash, encourages her to ignore her father's wishes and elope.

an uncharacteristically conservative role. Not only that, but, unless you count the leering and mugging of Prem Chopra, the film is refreshingly absent any comic relief characters or subplots. Only a bubble gummy musical number featuring youngsters Poonam Dhillon and Sachin seems calculated to lighten the mood.

Upon learning that Vijay has agreed to host Bubbli and Jai's clandestine wedding, a livid Shekhar seeks Vijay out at his apartment. A fight ensues and is broken up by Geeta, who fills Shekhar in on the reason for Vijay's ire against his father. Ashamed, Shekhar goes to his father and informs him that he and Bubbli are moving out of his house, further adding that he now supports Bubbli's marriage. In the event, Gupta enjoins a sleazy business rival, Balwant (Prem Chopra), and his minions to violently break up the ceremony, which they accomplish by busting in and kidnapping Ravi. However, by this time, Gupta has been made aware of his relationship to Vijay and rushes, along with Shekhar and Vijay, to set things right.

AMITABH BACHCHAN and Shashi Kapoor certainly have their charms, but does one really need to see *all* of the movies in which they starred together? Of course not, though some definitely are more worthwhile than others. Case in point: *Trishul*, which is a surprisingly earnest and even-toned take on Bollywood's age old family revenge tropes that, in hands other than director Yash Chopra's, might have been downright goofy. Even a 1978 vintage Bachchan, who, by this time, was no stranger to comic mugging and pandering, is unwaveringly serious, as is Hema Malini in

Even more interesting is the nature of the revenge that Vijay takes against Gupta. Though Vijay is demonstrated early and repeatedly to be good with his fists, his "war" against his erstwhile father is an economic one, each thrust and parry a maneuver on the stage of big business. After watching so many traditionally fisticuffs-based revengers grind inexorably to preordained conclusions like not-so-well oiled machines, this was a welcome change-up. The details of these intrigues also make *Trishul* a Bollywood film that rewards close attention beyond that needed to keep track of the usual shifting identities and motives.

Of course, all of *Trishul*'s earnestness does at times threaten to upend the whole show. By laboring to make herself a paragon of suffering, Vijay's mom—as played by Golden Age diva Waheeda Rehman—is a character bordering on the ridiculous, like a parody of all of those extravagantly wounded moms that litter Hindi cinema throughout its history. Even the portrait of her to whom Vijay monologues has a permanently aggrieved look. Fortunately, her faith in Vijay as an engine of her vengeance is not misplaced. Otherwise it's not hard to imagine her stepping out of that portrait and smacking him one.

RANI AUR JAANI
"Rani and Jaani"

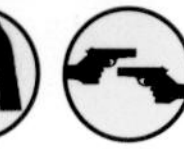

Released: 1973
Director: K.S.R. Doss
Stars: Aruna Irani, Jyothi Laxmi, Anil Dhawan, Narendra Nath, Jagdeep, Ramaprabha, Cocacola, Shetty, Shekhar, Prem Kumar, Arun Kumar, Master Ripple, Solochana Latkar, Uday Laxmi, Vijayalaxmi, Baby Dolly, Charulatha, Bindu, Brahm Bhardwaj
Writers: K.S.R. Doss, Prem Kapoor
Music: Satyam
Lyrics: Hasrat Jaipuri
Fights: K.S. Madhavan

The father of young Anu and Sona, a judge, raises them to be rough-housers, encouraging the girls to wail on each other in playful but nonetheless violent sparring matches at every opportunity. One night, the bandit Bhavani Singh, having escaped following his sentencing, steals into their home and murders the judge in an act of vengeance. Singh then tries to kidnap Anu and Sonu, but his man drops Anu when shot by pursuing police. The rest of the gang escapes, little Sonu vanishing with them.

Years later, Anu (Aruna Irani) is an inspector for the CID. In the course of an undercover operation, she comes into contact with Saajan (Anil Dhawan), a charming rogue with apparent underworld connections. One day, at a public pool, she sees Sajaan attacked by a pair of switch-blade wielding, bikini clad assassins and jumps in to rescue him. A flirtation between them develops, igniting a rivalry with Chanda (Jyothi Laxmi), Saajan's girlfriend, who takes the opportunity of a chance encounter with the two to make her displeasure known in no uncertain terms.

Meanwhile, we've learned that Chanda is one of Bhavani Singh's most trusted minions. When Anu later catches the bandit's gang in the commission of a horseback train robbery, she is shocked to recognize Chanda riding at their lead. Soon after, Chanda shows up at Anu's home and, only finding her mother home, brutally beats the old woman and kidnaps her. The family dog Peter manages to escape its bonds and chase after Chanda's car, and is thus, upon Anu's return, able to lead her, roaring off on her motorcycle, to the spot where her mother is held. After a wild fight with Chanda's men, Anu manages to free her mother.

Shortly thereafter, Anu and Chanda both show up at Saajan's house, only to have the lights suddenly go out and a shot fired. When the lights go on again, Saajan is revealed to be gravely wounded. The police arrest both women for the crime, but they manage to escape, using a passing train to sever the manacles that bind them together. Afterward, visiting Saajan in the hospital, Anu learns that he, too, is a police officer, and that his wooing of Chanda is just part of his attempts to get information about Bavani Singh's gang.

Anu doubles her efforts to track down Bavani Singh, and eventually catches him in the act of smuggling contraband in a truck loaded with

livestock. She brings the bandit to her home in the hope that her mother can identify him as the man who murdered her father, but the old woman fails to recognize him. The bandit then reveals that he is wearing a disguise and takes the two women hostage. Anu and her mother are taken to Singh's cave lair and put at the mercy of the whip wielding Chanda—only "Anu" reveals herself to be a masked impostor sent by Anu in her place.

Events finally come to a head at a birthday party for Saajan where a sing-off between Anu and Chanda turns ugly. Chanda tries to flee with Saajan, only to be confronted by him about her crimes. Anu then attempts to arrest Chanda, only to have her leap through a window. A wild motorcycle chase follows, ending in a field where Anu and Chanda engage in a violent punch up.

And it is only in the course of smacking each other silly that the two women recognize their true bond—that Chanda is, in fact, Sonu, and that they are indeed those same sisters who used to enthusiastically pummel each other for fun all those years ago. After a moment for tearful reunion, the two resolve to return to the lair in force and rescue their mother, Chanda dramatically turning her whip on Bavani Singh in the process.

RANI AUR JAANI IS YET ANOTHER trashy comic book thriller from Tollywood action director K.S.R. Doss, though this time one produced in the Hindi language. This change-up means that we have none of the towering pompadours or gyno-centric camera angles of his Telegu films, but a much greater number of familiar Bollywood faces in the form of Aruna Irani, Shetty, Jagdeep, etc.

More important, though, may be the fact that *Rani aur Jaani* represents a rare instance of one of 1970s Bollywood's most often trod narrative paths—that of long lost siblings meeting from opposite sides of a moral divide—being undertaken in women's shoes, with two sisters substituted for the usual brothers. Of course, in Doss's gleefully subtlety-averse hands, this means we're just a couple of drag queens away from something like *Deewaar* as imagined by a young John Waters.

Doss's perch at the helm also pretty much guarantees the presence within *Rani aur Jaani* of his apparent muse, "South Bomb" Jyothi Laxmi, the imposingly big boned Telegu item girl who fronted so many of his female driven actioners. With a bone chilling arsenal of ferocious grimaces, aggrieved scowls and piercing stink eyes, Laxmi has just the lack of vanity necessary to make the tragic figure of Sonu/

With a bone chilling arsenal of ferocious grimaces, aggrieved scowls and piercing stink eyes, Laxmi has just the lack of vanity necessary.

Chanda something akin to one of Danny Denzongpa's great wounded villains (see *Chor Machaye Shor, The Burning Train*). Well knowing that she's been cheated of the happy upbringing that was her birthright, Chanda is desperate for love and acceptance, but is separated from it by both her volcanic rage and inherent scariness.

Of course, the true star of *Rani aur Jaani*, despite Anil Dhawan's dubious top billing, is Aruna Irani, here given a rare and much deserved turn in the spotlight. I was happy to learn that the underused Irani later had a side career as a heroine in Gujarati language action films—and was regarded in that industry as sort of a female Bachchan—because in *Rani* she proves to be a scrappy and appealing protagonist. The career dancer's athleticism in particular serves her well, especially given that *Rani*'s fight choreography, in typical Doss fashion, is a lot more visceral than the dainty pantomimes you'd typically see Bollywood actresses asked to partake in. In their fight scenes together, Irani and the equally game Laxmi really appear to be beating the shit out of one another, something that Doss puts that much more in your face through his usual combination of quick cuts, shock zooms, and rolling camera moves.

BREAKDOWN:
The Motorcycle Chase!

Rani aur Jaani also deserves to be singled out for how it provides an example of an unusual convention of Indian action films wherein, when the gloves come off, everyone from little Munni and Munna to the family pet can often be found throwing themselves into the fray. Within the animal kingdom, this is often confined to the typical Rin Tin Tin style heroics, but Anu's dog Peter, during a fight scene between Irani and Shetty, takes it to the next level. Just as Shetty's hulking gunsel seems about to get the drop on Anu, she knocks the gun from his hand, whereupon Peter grabs it between his paws and fatally shoots him. Opposable thumbs be damned.

Despite some flaws and extraneous business (Jagdeep's comic subplot, for instance, seems so superfluous that it could be excised without constituting much of a sacrifice) *Rani aur Jaani* has all the makings of a cult classic. That is, if it were only more widely available beyond the un-subtitled VCDs that currently appear to be its sole legal domain. Until that is otherwise, I am happy to carry the torch for it as a personal favorite. Crude, camp, and unabashedly thrill-packed, it is what more shame-based individuals might call a "guilty pleasure," but what I simply call pure cinema at its most joyously unrefined.

DEEWAANGEE
"Madness"

Released: 1976
Director: Samir Ganguly
Stars: Shashi Kapoor, Zeenat Aman, Ranjeet, Helen, Mehmood Jr., Madan Puri, Master Raju, Narendra Nath, Manju Asrani, Viju Khote, Namab, Ranvir Raj, Paresh Nanda, Sujata, Raj Kishore, Shivraj, Lalita Kumari, Purnima, Krishnakant, Paintal, Brij Gopal, Rajan Haksar
Writers: Anand Dutta, Sneh Dutta
Music: Ravindra Jain, Sachin Dev Burman (S.D. Burman)
Lyrics: Ravindra Jain, Hasrat Jaipuri, Naqsh Lyallpuri, Anand Bakshi
Fights: Shetty

Ever since the untimely death of his devout mother, Shekhar (Shashi Kapoor) has been a hardened materialist, distrusting women and religion and focusing on enriching himself above his current subsistence level as an auto mechanic. The only reason he lets the beautiful Kanchan (Zeenat Aman) into his home is the 10,000 Rs. reward placed on her head by the domineering aunt from whom she ran away. Nonetheless, while waiting for his payday, Shekhar falls in love with the pious Kanchan, and ultimately marries her to free her from her aunt's grasp.

Shekhar and Kanchan share five years of wedded bliss and give birth to a son, Babloo (Master Raju). But eventually money worries resurface and Shekhar again begins to dream of sudden wealth. It is at this time that they receive a visit from Shekhar's old friend Bill (Paintal), whose purple finery speaks to him doing quite well for himself. Bill tells Shekhar of a job he has coming up that could pay Shekhar 25,000 Rs. He then makes a hasty exit, leaving behind a case he says he will pick up later. Almost immediately after, Bill is struck by a car and killed. A grieving Shekhar opens the case to find it loaded with a fortune in diamonds.

Seeing them as a gift from god, Shekhar has every intention of keeping the diamonds, but Kanchan begs him to leave them alone, fearing that they will only bring unhappiness. And sure enough, that very night, the gang

of hoodlums lead by Munne Khan (Narendra Nath) breaks into their home and ransacks it while they pretend to be asleep. They leave empty handed, but are followed by the gang of "George" (Madan Puri), who threaten Shekhar and his family with grave consequences should the diamonds turn out to be in their possession.

Shortly thereafter, Munne Khan's gang kidnaps little Babloo and demand the diamonds in return for his life. Amazingly, Shekhar is still reluctant to relinquish them, but finally relents. He goes to the house of his friend Harry (Ranjeet), where he has stashed the diamonds. Unfortunately, Harry's gold digging girlfriend, Miss Kitti (Helen), has stumbled upon the stash and seduces Harry into stealing away with it while she distracts Shekhar with a song and dance. Shekhar takes off after Harry and, after a fight atop the grain car of a moving train—which has been set on fire—wrests the case away from him. He returns the case to Munne, who, true to his word, returns Babloo.

Before they can get home, however, Shekhar and Babloo are intercepted by George's men, who inform him that they have kidnapped Kanchan. They will return her only after Shekhar has stolen the diamonds back from Munne and handed them over to them. This Shekhar does, at great peril to himself. But when he makes the delivery to George, George does not keep his word and instead throws Shekhar into a cell with his wife and child.

Once the diamonds have arrived in George's hideout, they set off a chain reaction of murderous venality. George's moll, Ruby (Manju Asrani), tricks the rest of George's men into a death trap in order to avoid paying their share. For the same reason, George ties Ruby to a chair and sets her on fire, only to be told by her that she has poisoned him. This massacre leaves Shekhar and his little family with the distinct predicament of being trapped in a cell with a time bomb and no criminals left alive who could free them even if they wanted to. Will the faith of Kanchan—who has a far more practical idea of providence than her husband—see them through?

***DEEWAANGEE* USES BOLLYWOOD'S** expansive mode of storytelling to turn what could have been a simple moral parable into an epic. Indeed, it does become a parade of nonstop action during its third act—quite a violent one—but that is seemingly our reward for paying attention through the first two. The seesawing courtship of Shekhar and Kanchan—during which Shekhar learns his first lesson about putting money before love—takes up the first hour of the film, and in that time you will see several characters come and go without much apparent utility (the Donny Osmond-like Mehmood Jr., playing Shekhar's teenage assistant, even makes his own exit from the story, as if he has realized he has nothing left to do with it).

Deewaangee is a rare attempt within Indian cinema of exploring a noir sensibility in a God fearing context.

Still, if one has the patience for it, *Deewaangee* is an interesting film, eschewing the many tendril-like plot digressions of the typical masala film in favor of telling a straight-forward tale that could easily have been as compact as a *Twilight Zone* episode. The case of diamonds is like a Pandora's Box, bringing

calamity to all who gaze upon its contents. Or, better yet, it is *Kiss Me Deadly*'s "Great Whatsit"—a similarity driven home by the appearance of an immolated woman during the climactic moments of both films. In either case, it is a rare attempt within Indian cinema of exploring a noir sensibility in a God fearing context.

Working in contrast to that noirish tone is Ravindra Jain's score, which is paradoxically upbeat and hummable. Especially toe tapping are the two numbers granted Helen, who here essays one of her classic vamp roles. The film is also given buoyancy by the performances of its two stars. Shashi Kapoor somehow manages to retain Shekhar's status as a sympathetic character despite his mind-blowingly poor decision making. At the same time, Zeenat Aman, while in doe eyed innocent mode, shows enough spark to allow for some sexy chemistry between the two—a scene in which they share a popsicle must have been especially scandalous at the time.

Such lightheartedness aside, there's no doubt that *Deewaangee* teaches a hard lesson. Nothing underscores this more than the final scene, in which Shekhar and his family stroll out of George's hideout through a sea of corpses. Diamonds are no substitute for happiness—and happiness is not being massacred by a bunch of bloodthirsty goons.

Sunil Dutt, Shatrughan Sinha, Dharmendra, and Hema Malini celebrate Sinha's birthday

RAJA JANI
"Prince of My Heart"

Released: 1972
Director: Mohan Segal
Stars: Dharmendra, Hema Malini, Prem Nath, Prem Chopra, Johnny Walker, Durga Khote, Nadira, Sajjan, Hiralal, Rajan Haksar, Lata Sinha, Jankidas, Madhup Sharma, Pal Sharma, Bhushan Tiwari, Mumtaj, Kamaldeep, C.S. Dubey, Bindu, Manmohan, Helen
Writers: Nabendu Ghosh, S. Ali Raza, Shahid Akberpuri
Music: Laxmikant-Pyarelal (Laxmikant Shantaram Kudalkar & Pyarelal Ramprasad Sharma)
Lyrics: Anand Bakshi
Fights: Ravi Khanna, M.S. Das

Raja (Dharmendra) is recruited by Diwan Gajendra Singh (Prem Nath), a member of the Queen's inner circle, to find a suitable girl to impersonate the Princess Ratna, who went missing years ago following the assassination of her parents. While most consider the Princess to be long dead, her grandmother, the Queen (Durga Khote), keeps a daily vigil, believing she'll return someday. If Diwan and Raja can present her with an heir, it will keep the aging queen's vast fortune in the "family" and closer to their grasp.

Raja thinks he has found a likely candidate in Shanno (Hema Malini), a poor street dancer. When he meets her, she is fleeing after stabbing a lustful john to whom her scheming parents sold her for 300 Rs. The john, however, was just a shill of Raja's and is very much alive. After Raja saves Shanno from a gang of ruffians on the train for Bombay, he convinces her to come back home with him, where, springing on her his knowledge of her "crime," he pretends that his plan to pass her off as the Princess is intended to hide her from the authorities.

Shanno, coarse mannered but innocent, is skeptical of the plan and suspects its true nature. Nonetheless, she is smitten by Raja and decides to go along with it, thinking it will afford her the opportunity to teach him the value of love over money. A crash course in royal comportment follows, after which Diwan introduces her to the Queen and her entourage. She is greeted with suspicion at first, especially by Diwan's son Pratap (Prem Chopra), the Princess's childhood sweetheart, who outright denounces her as a fraud. However, Shanno's presentation of a chronic cough, an affliction shared by the real princess, convinces the Queen beyond a doubt. Once the Queen has spoken, Pratap quickly tries to pick up with the "Princess" where they left off, though Shanno holds him at bay.

Once she has settled into the palace, Shanno, so used to being exploited by those close to her, finds herself deeply moved by the sincere love and affection that the Queen shows her, such that she feels incapable of going through with the plan. Meanwhile, Shanno's "real" parents, Panna (Nadira) and Khairati (Sajjan), see her in a royal procession and show up at the palace, where they are angrily ejected by Raja. Pratap, seeing this, becomes convinced of Raja's duplicity, after which he tries to convince his father that Raja is a liability

who must be eliminated. Meanwhile, Shanno starts to flirt with Pratap to make Raja jealous.

At a grand ceremony during which Shanno is presented with the keys to the royal treasure, the Queen announces that she has arranged for the Princess to be married to Pratap. This leaves Raja more devastated than he might have imagined and, coming to terms with his love for Shanno—which receives its fullest expression in him punching her in the face—decides the two should flee the palace together. Diwan overhears this plan and has Raja and Shanno captured by the palace guard, leading to an ugly stint in the dungeon, a battle for the precious key, and, ultimately, some surprising revelations.

Malini here gets to show off all of that whip wielding and fancy swordplay that makes her such a joy in films like Seeta aur Geeta.

***RAJA JANI* IS PURE BOLLYWOOD** fantasy, filled with glamour, absurd opulence and eye searing effusions of color (PURPLE! YELLOW! PINK!). Yet it is also a fantasy with a sinister edge, and that edge comes to us courtesy of none other than Dharmendra. Sure, we're used to seeing Dharam play a criminal, but that's usually in the perennial vein of the lovable con man or thief with a heart of gold. Here it's hard to tell whether his Raja has a good side at all. And as much as we enjoy seeing him and Hema Malini together and root for their romance to take flower, when we look at them through grown up glasses it's easy to see that Shanno's history of abuse is the only thing that makes her able to look at a heel like Raja with loving eyes. Need I repeat that his big emotional breakthrough happens when he *punches her in the face*?

Seeing Malini dominated in this way is all the more troubling for the fact that, in other parts of the picture, she is her usual scrappy, swashbuckling self. Ironically, Malini

In addition to Dharmendra's almost unwaveringly unsympathetic portrayal, *Raja Jani* offers another surprise in the portrayal of veteran comic relief fixture Johnny Walker as Raja's sleepwalking houseman Imartilal, which is admittedly hilarious. As distasteful as I often find this type of character in lesser hands, I have to bow to a true professional. Also providing a bit of a surprise is a trimmed down Prem Chopra, who actually plays someone who's believable as someone else's love interest—even though he transforms himself into the usual craven heel by the end.

is at once one of '70s Bollywood's most glamorous and most action oriented female stars, and she here gets to show off all of that whip wielding and fancy swordplay that made her such a joy in films like *Seeta aur Geeta*—a perhaps more manicured heir to Fearless Nadia. And to that point, it has to be said that Kavi Khanna and M.S. Das's fight choreography for *Raja Jani* is truly exceptional. A multi person brawl featuring bodies flipping and flying within a small train compartment calls to mind the similar sequence in *From Russia with Love*, but is all the more impressive for its coherence given the exponential number of participants. Likewise, the climactic battles in which Dharmendra and Malini repeatedly fight off an army of palace guards are at once chaotic and commendably legible, with some dizzying work on some very conveniently placed parallel bars by Dharam.

In the end, *Raja Jani* explodes into the usual masala climax rife with swordfights and surprise revelations. Along the way, we get an ecstatic dance number from Helen—which occurs mockingly right on the heels of Shanno's wedding announcement—and a guy in a rubber mask impersonating Raja to keep the fact that the real deal is being whipped in the dungeon under wraps. With all the attendant color and lavish design, it's enough to delight the senses, yet not enough to dispel the film's underlying darkness. The cynical betrayal of an old woman's love for her granddaughter, the fact that Shanno can love a man who callously exploits her the way Raja does (along with the fact that we're supposed to accept that), the way Diwan is so quick to viciously turn on his partner—all of this is a clear indication that all is not right in the palace. It sure is pretty, though.

HERA PHERI
"Monkey Business"

Released: 1976
Director: Prakash Mehra
Stars: Amitabh Bachchan, Vinod Khanna, Saira Banu, Sulakshana Pandit, Shreeram Lagoo, Pinchoo Kapoor, P. Jairaj, Yunus Parvez, MacMohan, Mohan Sherry, Urmila Bhatt, Goga Kapoor, Randhir, Vikas Anand, R.P. Sethi, Tarun Ghosh, Indu Mehta, Tun Tun, Padma Khanna, Asrani, Dev Kumar, Moolchand
Writers: Vijay Kaul, Satish Bhatnagar
Music: Kalyanji-Anandji (Kalyanji Virji Shah & Anandji Virji Shah)
Lyrics: Anjaan (Lalji Pandey), Indeevar
Fights: Manzoor, Mohamed Ali

Vijay (Amitabh Bachchan) and Ajay (Vinod Khanna) have been inseparable friends since Vijay rescued Ajay from a suicide attempt years earlier. Now making their living as con men, the pair's latest take comes from their posing as holy men to access the cash reserves of a gang who use the basement of a local temple as a stash. No sooner have they got the loot back to their shared apartment than they are visited by Kiran (Saira Banu), a young woman who claims to be fleeing rapists. The men allow her to spend the night, only to find in the morning that she has made off with the money. Vijay manages to track her down and scams back some of the money, a feat which impresses Kiran to the point that she presses both men to join her criminal group.

Kiran works for P.K. (Pinchoo Kapoor), who, years before, murdered Vijay's father and now wants to eliminate Vijay as a witness. Thanks to a photograph his father was holding when he died, Vijay knows that P.K. is the culprit, but what he does not know is that P.K. also goes under the guise of Mr. Ghanshyamdas, a respectable citizen who was a close friend of Vijay's father and family. P.K. now wants to do away with his criminal identity altogether and assume the role of Ghanshyamdas permanently, but first must kill Vijay and his mom, the only two remaining people capable of making the connection between the two. Vijay's mom, who was reduced to a catatonic state by the tragedy, is now being cared for by Vijay's sister in a location unknown to the crook. One person who is unaware of all of the above is Ajay, thanks to Vijay's secretiveness about his past. This leads to trouble when P.K. recognizes Ajay as the son he sold in infancy in order to buy medication for his ailing wife, leading to a rootless life as a displaced orphan for Ajay. Ajay has pined for genuine family affection his entire life, and so embraces P.K. wholeheartedly, pledging his lifelong love and loyalty. When Vijay recognizes who Ajay's newfound father figure is, cruel words—and blows—are exchanged between the friends and they part ways. Later, Vijay, mourning the friendship, goes out on a drunken tear and is found passed out in the street by a solicitous Kiran, who ushers him home.

P.K. hopes to use Kiran to get to Vijay and, through him, Vijay's mom. Unfortunately for him, she has fallen for Vijay in earnest and instead takes him to P.K.'s safe house on Madh Island for shelter. Learning of this, P.K. dispatches Ajay, who has volunteered for the job, to kill Vijay and Kiran. Vijay and Kiran manage to escape, but not before an eavesdropping Ajay has learned the location of Vijay's mother. In the confusion that follows, Vijay's mom regains consciousness and wanders out into the street, where she is hit by the car of Ajay and his men and captured. It now falls upon Vijay to rescue her and avenge his father, but he must first make his way through his enemy's staunchest defender, his former friend Ajay. But is Ajay's change of loyalties really on the level?

WITH ***HERA PHERI, ZANJEER*** director Prakash Mehra wisely uses the chemistry between stars Amitabh Bachchan and Vinod Khanna—here making the fourth of ten films together—to best advantage. Unlike the popular teaming of Bachchan with Shashi Kapoor, who often seemed to act the lukewarm water to Bachchan's fire, Bachchan and Khanna seem, in many ways, to be two of a kind, matching each other smolder for smolder. The two also share that masala star versatility necessary to finessing the film's progression from rakish comedy to high melodrama over the course of its running time.

Hera Pheri depends for much of its early comedic episodes on the "odd couple" relationship between the two characters, Khanna's Ajay being a bashful and deeply religious man and Bachchan's Vijay a defiantly non-believing and womanizing one. Yet both men have tragic pasts that make them prone to moodiness, and it is the volatility of their relationship that makes the moments of affection between them seem all the more real. It should also not be ignored that *Hera Pheri* doesn't shy away from milking the homoerotic potential of the pairing, presenting us with any number of domestic scenes in which the two roommates are pictured in various stages

Bachchan and Khanna seem, in many ways, to be two of a kind, matching each other smolder for smolder.

of undress (and Khanna, at one point, filling out a pretty tiny pair of man shorts).

Partly due to the above, *Hera Pheri* is one of those Bollywood movies that somehow sneaks up on you despite all of its obviousness. The break between Vijay and Ajay, when it comes, is unexpectedly devastating, and we can't help but join Amitabh in spirit as he makes his drunken, heartbroken crawl through the nocturnal streets of the city. Those sympathies also make the absurd switch-a-roo that takes place at the film's climax embarrassingly gratifying. Indeed, *Hera Pheri* may be cheese, but, in the hands of Mehra, it is exquisitely sliced.

Elsewhere among the film's performances, the sometimes grating Saira Banu does a fine job in the rare role of an Indian female who is actually a fully fledged villain rather than a wayward femme fatale—even if she must inevitably succumb to the hero's charms. Pinchoo Kapoor, for his part, is gifted with a novel role as P.K.—a Bollywood villain who wants not to conceal his secret identity but to obliterate it entirely—and goes the extra mile in contrasting his coldhearted murderousness with the undeniable tenderness he feels toward Ajay.

Mehta helps *Hera Pheri* go down easy by keeping its pacing tight and propulsive, with action that just keeps on coming. He also greases the narrative wheels by parsing out back story in a nonlinear fashion, sparing us the type of laborious prologue that often kicks off these kinds of "lost and found" tales. This also helps us to sympathize with Ajay's sense of betrayal once he learns of Vijay's secret past, which we also have just been made privy too. It's a rare gambit in 1970s Indian cinema that proves that, in the hands of a skilled director, one needn't have all of the story groundwork laid out in plain sight in order for a film to be both coherent and compelling.

JUGNU
"Firefly"

Released: 1973
Director: Pramod Chakravorty
Stars: Dharmendra, Hema Malini, Pran, Prem Chopra, Mehmood, Lalita Pawar, Shamim, Asha Potdar, Jayshree T., Manmohan, Raj Mehra, Nasir Hussain, Randhir, Brahm Bhardwaj, Kamal Kapoor, Alankar Joshi, Satyajeet, Master Ravi, Dhumal, Kanu Roy, Rajan Kapoor, Paresh Nanda, Birbal, Ratan Gaurang, Khurshid, Gauli, Ameer, Shyam Kumar, Sabina, Mona Saxena, Bhanumati, Parvez, Sandesh Kumar, Faquira, Akbar Bakshi, Rajan, Gemini Balu, Murthy, Sonia Sahni, Sujit Kumar, Ajit
Writers: Sachin Bhowmick, Gulshan Nanda, Ehsan Rizvi
Music: Sachin Dev Burman (S.D. Burman)
Lyrics: Anand Bakshi

1942, the early days of the anti-colonial Quit India Movement: Shyam (Pran), a revolutionary, bombs a railroad overpass and escapes home, only to be turned over to the police by his father (Nasir Hussain). With the help of his pregnant wife Parvati, he escapes the authorities' grasp and rides off into the night on his motorcycle, renouncing his father's name as he goes.

Several years later, Parvati and her now school-aged son Ashok, in the aftermath of Partition, have ended up on the Pakistani side of the divide, losing touch with father and grandfather alike. Parvati works for Thakur Ghansham Das (Sujit Kumar), who has unwholesome designs upon her. When he tries to rape Parvati, Ashok intervenes, only to have Parvati step between him and the bullet when Das tries to shoot him. His mother dead, Ashok beats Das to death with a rock, then rides off into the distance with Das's minions in pursuit. Meanwhile, back in India, Shyam's father bemoans his lack of an heir to bequeath his sizeable fortune to, to which his scheming accountant responds by finding a convenient boy, named Ramesh, to present to Shyam's father as his long lost grandson.

Some more years later, the adult Ashok (Dharmendra) has adopted the guise of the altruistic bandit Jugnu, who, using a variety of disguises, robs the criminal element of their ill gotten spoils. All of his plunder is put toward philanthropic ends, including a home for disadvantaged boys that he has named after his mother. One of Jugnu's biggest takes comes at the expense of a spy ring run by Boss (Ajit), whom—in a bold, train hopping heist—he relieves of both a large cache of jewels and the cash meant to be exchanged for it. As is his practice, in place of their treasure, Jugnu leaves as his calling card a golden bird figurine adorned with flashing colored lights.

Meanwhile, Ramesh (Prem Chopra) has grown up to be a disgrace to his family, a drunk and a card cheat who is habitually running up debts at the local casino. Ashok visits that casino out of a suspicion that it is a front for spy activity and overhears Ramesh being propositioned by the Boss's man Mike (Manmohan), who wants him to photograph military installations in the area for a payment of three lakhs. When Ramesh, an amateur helicopter pilot, undertakes that mission,

Ashok is there to make it as difficult as possible, buzzing him in a light plane and ultimately stealing both the film and his payment from him.

Also along for the flight with Ramesh is Seema (Hema Malini), the niece of the Inspector General (Raj Mehra), with whom Ashok has already begun one of those typically antagonistic flirtations so often seen in Indian movies. Seema ends up being the unwitting beneficiary of Ashok's larceny when he donates Ramesh's three lakhs to a charity event she is hosting. Later, after visiting the boys' home with Ashok and seeing the extent of his generosity, she begins to fall for him. Meanwhile, that stands there, confirming his suspicion that Ashok is his son. Worried that the statue will draw the authorities to Ashok, who is still wanted for the murder of Ghansham Das, he destroys it, only to suffer the wrath of a confused Ashok as a result of its discovery.

After learning that Seema is the daughter of Ghansham Das, and has been made fatherless as a result of his actions, Ashok has a crisis of conscience about his activities as Jugnu. He decides to quit and let Mahesh take over his day to day operations, but will first take on one last robbery in order to provide him with the

Ashok and his sidekick Mahesh (Mehmood) continue to make the lives of Ramesh and the Boss miserable. Ashok, in the guise of Jugnu, even manages to deal the Boss a permanent facial scar during a daring incursion into his lair.

Come the date of Seema's charity event, Ashok attends and is introduced to the distinguished academic Professor Chakravarty, who, unknown to both of them, is actually Ashok's dad Shyam. Also in attendance is Mike, who tries to shoot Ashok, but wounds Shyam instead. Desperate, the assassin kidnaps Seema and tears off, but Ashok, pursuing in his customized Jugnu-mobile, manages to rescue her. Later, Shyam, tipped off by a casual remark made by Ashok, visits the boys' home and sees the statue of his late wife

necessary capital. This will involve the theft of a bejeweled fish which is on display at the Sonu Mahal and protected by an array of high tech security measures. The Boss learns of Ashok's plan and alerts the authorities, with the result that, just as it seems he is going to get away scot free, the police arrive in force. Wounded in the ensuing pursuit, Ashok passes out on a river bank and is rescued by Shyam, who takes him back to his home. When the police arrive at his door, Shyam lies and tells them that it is he who is Jugnu.

Eventually, Ashok will be made aware of his relationship to Shyam, leading to a climax in which the two will face off against the Boss and his minions as father and son.

***JUGNU* WAS ONE** of 1973's top performers at the Indian box office, a fact which might account for its director, Pramod Chakravorty, helming the almost obsessively similar *Azaad* several years later, as well as for the existence of 1980's *Guru*, a faithful Tamil language remake. Judging from *Jugnu* and *Azaad*, Chakravorty doesn't strike me as being the most attentive of craftsmen.

Jugnu's equal commitment to providing as many goofy and comic book-ish Saturday matinee serial trappings as possible also doesn't hurt it.

Jugnu, for instance, is marked by sloppiness in the form of jarring interjections of song snippets, as well as flashbacks to scenes which took place immediately prior to them. There also appears to have been little effort to smooth over the disconnect between the film's broadly drawn comedic, melodramatic and thriller aspects. A subplot that involves beloved comedian Mehmood wooing a circus performer and getting chased around by tigers stands out like an extra thumb in particular.

Yet still, *Jugnu* charms. Part of that is thanks to it starring Dharmendra at his early '70s peak, when he was still capable of playing the lovable rogue, aggrieved people's champion and soulful outlaw—all of which are called upon here—with equal commitment. Indeed, as minor as the film might seem, Dharmendra gets a chance to do a lot of what Dharmendra does best in it, which includes making a lot of chest-thumping proclamations of defiance to corrupt holders of power and issuing bone-chilling threats of vengeance to same while referring to himself in the third person. It's things like that that make pictures like *Jugnu*, *Saazish* and *Azaad* palatable, like the enjoyable little stepping stones that took the appealing star from one more noteworthy 1970s success—*Yaadon Ki Baaraat*, or *Seeta aur Geeta,* for example—to the next. They can't all be *Sholay*, after all.

Jugnu's equal commitment to providing as many goofy and comic book-ish Saturday matinee serial trappings as possible also doesn't hurt it. As the Boss, Ajit sports a metal arm prosthetic that looks like an oversized cocktail shaker with all manner of nasty, pointy things extruding from it. And then there is Jugnu's absurdly elaborate bird-shaped calling card and, of course, the Jugnu-mobile, the main feature of which is a side mounted spotlight that projects the word "Jugnu" at whomever he is pursuing. As things pan out, he would have done better investing in a bullet proof windshield, but, as they say, it pays to advertise.

The film also engages in a lot of silliness that might also be the result of inattention on its makers' parts, but which nonetheless make it oddly endearing. Why is Hema Malini's

Seema, when we meet her, firing the words "I Love You" into a giant paper heart with a pistol? Was The Boss's big death trap, which is revealed to be a bunch of buzz-saw blades spinning on the ends of narrow poles like plates in a variety act, actually expected to appear menacing? And then there is the fact that, despite none of Jugnu's disguises in any way concealing Ashok's face, no one ever recognizes him. Other of the film's whimsies are more calculated, but nonetheless winning, such as "Jaane Kya Pilaaye," a delightful "drunk" song, sung by Lata Mangeshkar, that's picturized on Seema after she's slipped a mickey by Ramesh (the refrain: "I don't know what you gave me to drink, but it's great fun".)

Like a lot of Bollywood's action movies from the '70s, *Jugnu* owes an obvious debt to the James Bond series—one it explicitly acknowledges in a scene where Ashok says that the only two figures of comparable intelligence are "James Bond in the West, and Jugnu in the East." *Jugnu* is also the second Bollywood movie that I've seen—*Warrant* being the first—that incorporates actual footage lifted from the James Bond movie *You Only Live Twice* as its own. In this case it is the scene in which a helicopter uses a giant magnet to lift a car off of the road and drop it into the ocean. Of course, 007 wasn't the only victim of such pilfering, and the sequence above all serves as a reminder of the "wild west" mentality that seemed to prevail in India when it came to international copyrights. An even later Dharmendra film, *Charas*, took the more widely acceptable approach of simply stealing the *Idea* of that scene and recreating it within its own means.

On a more sober note, *Jugnu* deserves mention for how it explicitly ties in the "lost and found" theme with the event of Partition, and how, in doing so, it shines a light on why that theme might have resonated so with Indian audiences at the time. Because many families were indeed torn apart by that cleaving in two of their homeland—irreversibly in some cases, thanks to the violence and rioting that accompanied it. Later "patriotic" films would treat India and Pakistan as the ultimate separated siblings, now staring one another down, like the brothers in *Deewaar*, across a troubling moral chasm, though *Jugnu*, thankfully, doesn't stoop to such propaganda. Still, the grief is there, adding an unexpectedly mournful cadence to what would otherwise be a fairly frothy and routine Dharmendra potboiler.

GURU
"Teacher"

Released: 1980
Director: I.V. Sasi
Stars: Kamal Haasan, Sridevi, Muthuraman, Mohan Babu, M.N. Nambiar, Major Sundarrajan, Pandari Bai, Y. Gee Mahendra, Poornam Vishwanathan, Venniradai Nirmala, Jayamalini, Mohan Babu, Ceylon Manohar
Writers: Sachin Bhowmick, Gulshan Nanda, Ehsan Rizvi (adapted), Seakar Sharma (dialog)
Music: Ilaiyaraaja
Lyrics: Seakar Sharma
"Action": M.S. Doss

Ashok's father becomes a fugitive as a result of his anti-colonialist activities, leaving Ashok to be raised by his mother, who is later murdered in the course of a rape attempt by the landlord she works for. Ashok kills the man in retaliation and himself becomes a fugitive. Years later, the adult Ashok (Kamal Haasan) leads a double life as a philanthropist by day and as Guru, a Robin Hood like bandit, by night. His practice is to rob criminals of their ill gotten gains and then use the money to fund his altruistic pursuits, which include an orphanage that he has named after his mother.

Guru's activities bring him into contact with a criminal gang who are trading in India's secrets. Among their number is Ramesh, a spoiled young man, who, unknown to Ashok, is actually posing as the grandson and heir of Ramesh's own long lost grandfather. He also meets Sujatha (Sridevi), the niece of the police commissioner, to whom he takes an immediate shine, and through her meets a college professor (Muthuraman) who quickly takes a special interest in him. When that professor later falsely confesses to being Jugnu in order to protect Ashok, it sets the stage for a series of shocking revelations, as well as a prolonged punch-up in a slick villain's lair.

CROSSPOLLINATION BETWEEN Bollywood and India's many regional cinemas is a common practice to this very day, with Hindi language hits often remade in different tongues with stars nearer and dearer to the hearts of a particular local audience. The practice also goes in the opposite direction, with 1973's *Rani Mera Naam*, a Bollywood remake of K.S.R. Doss's Telegu language hit *Rowdy Rani*, being just one of many examples. The existence of a Hindi dub of the Tamil film *Guru* also indicates that, on occasion, Hindi speaking audiences could enjoy cheaper, idiosyncratic regional interpretations of films they'd already seen in their own language.

As a retelling of the 1973 Bollywood hit *Jugnu*, *Guru* sticks scrupulously to its source material, other than it substituting Tamil film superstar Kamal Haasan—essentially that industry's equivalent of Amitabh Bachchan—for the original's Dharmendra, and Sridevi, an actress whose superstar appeal crossed regional boundaries, for Hema Malini. Beyond that, I'm happy to say, *Jugnu*'s many cheesy comic book trappings

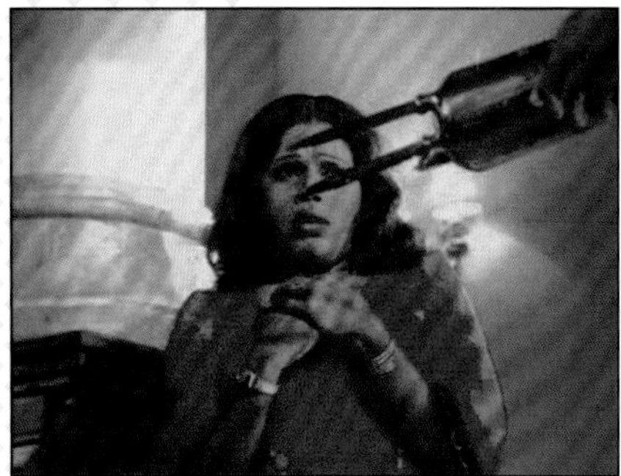

Jugnu's many cheesy comic book trappings are treated as sacrosanct. The villain still sports an ungainly metal hand prosthetic adorned with stabby appurtenances.

are treated as sacrosanct. M.N. Nambiar, its villain, like Ajit in the original, still sports an ungainly metal hand prosthetic adorned with stabby appurtenances. Guru still leaves a gaudy bird tchotchke as a calling card and drives the Jugnu-mobile. Naturally, the latter is now by necessity the Guru-mobile, but it still features the same side mounted spotlight to project Guru's name at whomever he's chasing down the road. *Guru* even steals the same footage from *You Only Live Twice* as its predecessor, not to mention some shots from *Jugnu* itself.

But where *Guru* can't help but depart from its inspiration is the manner in which it hews to the garish aesthetic of the dawning 1980s. It's really hard to imagine a film being any more pink. This is especially apparent in the scene where Guru invades the villain's lair—a task for which Dharmendra wore a daring yellow ensemble—during which the hero wears a full-on pink superhero costume. At least this Tamil version of Ashok has the sense to wear an actual mask, making all the more credible the fact that everyone fails to recognize him. Alas, this conceit is abandoned after the one sequence, leaving us to an otherwise fairly dutiful trotting out of the first film's plot convolutions.

What *Guru* does bring to the table are some quite nice Tamil language songs by Kamal Haasan favorite Ilaiyaraaja, which are sadly butchered in the Hindi dubbed version. Beyond that, those of us dependent upon subtitles in either case—and barring any particular devotion to Kamal Haasan or Sridevi, both stars whose considerable charisma is not in question—are probably best served by that which came first.

ZAKHMEE
"Injured"

Released: 1975
Director: Raja Thakur
Stars: Sunil Dutt, Asha Parekh, Rakesh Roshan, Reena Roy, Tariq, Helen, Johnny Walker, Imtiaz, Yunus Parvez, Jankidas, Habib, Madhup Sharma, Shyam Kumar, D.S. Rana, Abhimanyu Sharma, Babul, Gulam Hussain, Khursheed Khan, Jerry Raja, Babubhai, Navin Kumar, Sujata Rubener, Shahzad Malik, Vikrant, Vijayakanth, Shahid Bijnori, B. Chandrashekhar, Kamal Kapoor, Iftekhar, Baby Pinky, Piloo J. Wadia, Usha Thakur, Ruhi Khan, Agha
Writers: Humayun Mirza, Madan Joshi
Music: Bappi Lahiri
Lyrics: Gauhar Kanpuri
Fights: Azim Bhai

Anand (Sunil Dutt) is pulled away from his wedding ceremony by a call from his business partner Mohan, who demands that he come to their office immediately. When Anand arrives he finds a gang of armed thugs led by Tiger (Imtiaz) standing over the bound body of Mohan. Tiger tells Anand that, with Mohan's help, his gang has been using their business as a front for drug smuggling, but that Mohan has been cheating them. Tiger stabs Mohan to death, telling Anand that he must take the blame, lest he want any harm to come to his family. When Anand is questioned about the crime by authorities, he stays tight lipped and is thrown in jail to await trial.

Back home, Anand's family—which consists of his younger brothers Amar (Rakesh Roshan) and Pawan (Tariq) and his baby sister Tina (Baby Pinky), all of whom he's been charged with caring for since his parents' death, along with his bride-to-be Asha (Asha Parekh)—are convinced of his innocence, especially Amar and Pawan. Armed with more enthusiasm than intelligence or cogent planning, the two decide to pursue the judge in the case, Ganguly (Iftekhar). They first try to do this, unsuccessfully, by wooing the judge's free spirited daughter Nisha (Reena Roy), a hot pants wearing, motorcycle riding young hellion. When an attempt to bribe the judge directly by shoving handfuls of cash at him ends in them having to throw themselves from a moving car, they decide to instead simply kidnap Nisha in return for Anand's release. This plan backfires when Nisha, by all appearances, is delighted to be kidnapped, taking a shine to both of her hapless captors, Amar in particular.

Meanwhile, Anand, with the help of his new prison buddy Johnny (Johnny Walker), escapes from stir and sets out to be the bane of Tiger's existence, starting out by torching one of his drug laden warehouses. Furthermore, he sows seeds of distrust within the gang that result in the murder of Jankidas (Jankidas) the traitorous manager of Anand and Mohan's company. With Anand becoming more determined to uncover the identity of the gang's mysterious

boss "Chief"—and Tiger determined to prevent that from happening—the criminal vows to "destroy" Anand's family. The abduction of Amar, Pawan, Asha, and baby Tina follows. But when the fiery Nisha is added to the captive roll call, it looks more likely that the villains have sown the seeds of their own resounding ass kicking than they have revenge.

***ZAKHMEE* IS A STRAIGHTFORWARDLY** plotted Bollywood actioner that's held together by what would otherwise seem like a fairly digressive middle section. The spectacle of the puppyish Amar and Pawan (and what actor of the day could be more puppy-ish than the bug-eyed Tariq?) trying to pass themselves off as hardened kidnappers is one that can't help but bear rich comedic fruit, especially when that pair is pitted against a gleefully volatile cat girl in the mold of Reena Roy's Nisha. Thus director Raja Thakur is wise to devote much of the film's screen time to this trio's antics.

As with many Bollywood heroes and heroines, the solemn virtue of Sunil Dutt's Anand and Asha Parekh's "Asha" makes them more than a little boring and sanctimonious. Thus Thakur takes pains to show us just how much fun those on the other side of the moral divide are having: Back in Tiger's digs, Helen does a go-go dance to Steam's "Na Na Hey Hey Kiss Him Goodbye" on the villain's bed. In the colorful nightclub where Reena Roy's Nisha hangs out, both she and the all girl band rock out frenziedly to a Bappi Lahiri composition called "Nothing is Impossible" which, despite being chaotic to the point of being nonmusical, is nonetheless infectious and debauchedly celebratory (plus it affords Tariq the opportunity to reprise some of his bugged out guitar flailing from *Yaadon Ki Baaraat*).

And speaking of Reena Roy, if this isn't her shining moment as an action heroine, I have a lot of catching up to do. One need only witness Nisha's entrance during the climactic brawl, crashing her motorcycle through a picture window to then whomp every minion in her path while popping some mean wheelies, to wonder why it is Dutt, rather than her, that gets top billing. Furthermore, this same sequence incorporates a clothes ripping, Sapphic cat fight between Roy and Helen that's kinky even by the furiously sublimating standards of old Bollywood. Clearly, *Zakhmee* should stand beside *Nagin* as an essential representation of this underappreciated starlet's unique talents and appeal.

With colorful lairs, wild costuming (check out the mesh peek-a-boo windows on Tiger's minions' shirts), frenetic action, Helen as a classic moll turned angel of death, and tantalizing glimpses of a pop-driven psychedelic demimonde, *Zakhmee* is no game changer in the world of Indian action cinema, but it certainly provides almost everything you might want from it. Just don't pay too much attention to those nice people who are its ostensible protagonists; it is within Reena Roy's shiny go-go boots that this film's trashy, pulp addled heart truly lies.

THE TRAIN

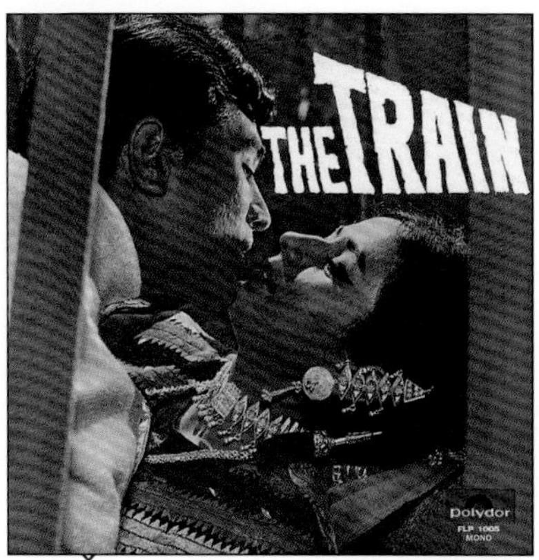

Released: 1970
Director: Ravikant Nagaich
Stars: Rajesh Khanna, Nanda, Helen, Rajendra Nath, Madan Puri, Sunder, Randhir, Iftekhar, Chaman Puri, Shetty, Mumtaz Begum, Raje, Mamaji, Ranvir Raj, John, Kalam, Nivrati, Ramu, Shinde, Radheshyam, Navin Parekh, Gurnam, Rajpal, Aruna Irani, Shammi, Tun Tun
Writers: Arudra, V.D. Puranik, Raj Baldev Raj
Music: Rahul Dev Burman (R.D. Burman)
Lyrics: Anand Bakshi
Fights: M.B. Shetty

Jewelers are being murdered aboard the Kolkata Express and their wares stolen, the killer making his escape by jumping from the moving train and off an overpass into the river below. CBI officer Shyam (Rajesh Khanna) is assigned to the case. The killers' trail leads him to the Hilltop Hotel, where his old college flame Lily (Helen) works as a dancer. Little does he know that Lily is part of the gang responsible for the killings, which also consists of No.1 (Madan Puri) and the scarred strong-arm man Joggie (Shetty), all of whom report to an unseen Mr. Big. Lily, who still has feelings for Shyam, is under orders from the boss to use her feminine wiles to distract him from his investigation.

Shyam's heart, however, belongs to Nita (Nanda), whose father, wrongfully convicted of murder years before, makes an unexpected appearance at her home after escaping from jail. Shyam comes upon the scene and, despite the pleadings of Nanda and her mother, feels duty bound to turn him over to the authorities. Nita banishes Shyam from the house, telling him she never wants to see him again. Shortly thereafter, No.1 shows up at the home posing as an old friend of Nita's father and offers her a job as a receptionist at the Hilltop.

Comes the time for another robbery and the gang's mark, another jeweler, finds himself sharing a compartment with frivolous wayfarer Pyare (Rajendra Nath). Also joining them is a woman who by all appearances is Nita, yet who introduces herself as "Kalavati" and is later found to have bought her ticket under the name Geeta. Geeta flirts with the receptive Pyare and, when the train stops, invites him to join her for lunch at the station. He misses the train as a result, leaving the gang's target unattended and naked to the ravages of Joggie's blade.

When Pyare is arrested under suspicion of committing the murder, he tells Shyam of the mysterious Geeta, and the two of them set off to find her, though with disappointing results. Meanwhile, No.1 and Joggie continue their attempts to get Shyam out of the way. Finally, Pyare sees Shyam's wallet photo of Nita and, to Shyam's shock, identifies her as the woman they're after.

It is determined that the only course of action is for Shyam and Pyare to ride the Express in disguise, Pyare masquerading as a jeweler with a case of priceless gems and Shyam as his

Beatle-wigged seat mate. As hoped, the gang, Geeta included, make their appearance. In the ensuing melee, Shyam apprehends Geeta and confronts her with her treachery, only to have No.1 shoot her before she can talk. With her dying breath, she removes her mask to reveal that she is, in fact, Lily, who was hoping, by her impersonation, to soil Nita in Shyam's eyes.

***THE TRAIN* COULD BE SEEN** as a sort of transitional film, a halfway point between the glitzy Bollywood thrillers of the '60s and the more reckless and violent Indian films of the '70s. Its protagonist, Shyam, is certainly a Bollywood hero in the 1960s, pre-Bachchan mode: a clean cut teetotaler with a steady girl. So unwavering is his sense of duty that he cannot resist returning Nita's father to the authorities who wrongfully imprisoned him, even at the cost of losing her affections forever.

As for the film's gauzy, old school sense of underworld glamour, that's best exemplified in the scenes that take place in the Hilltop Hotel's lounge, where Helen's Lily performs her frenetic musical numbers. Aiding these sequences immeasurably is R.D. Burman, who contributes one of his most iconic—and subsequently most frequently anthologized—scores. If you want proof that Burman was a genius, I don't think you need look any further than "Meri Jaan Maine Kaha." It's a head-spinning masterpiece of cartoon futurism, sounding like a cross between the *Munsters* theme and "Eep Opp Ork Ah-ah" from *The Jetsons* sung in part by a scat-singing, Hindi version of Louis Armstrong (in fact Burman himself, although in the movie it's lip-synched by a little guy who looks like the love child of Prince and Jagdeep.)

Director Ravikant Nagaich gives the film the Hitchcockian flavor favored by numerous 1960s Indian thrillers—*Teesri Manzil, Gumnaam*—by infusing it with voyeurism and paranoia. Throughout the first half especially, character are constantly seen peering at one another from hiding, or are seen through apertures in set elements like latticework and keyholes. Even some of the camera angles have a surreptitious feel to them, as if we are watching the action at a remove from a concealed vantage point. Meanwhile, the gang, in their threats to the police, stress their all-seeing omnipotence. All of this makes it especially ironic once it appears that the one person whom Shyam trusts, Nita, is living an elaborate double life.

But where *The Train* truly steps into the freewheeling spirit of '70s Bollywood is in its employment of outrageous plot twists and complications. Once you see the lack of resemblance between Nanda and Helen, it's easy to appreciate all the more the absurdity of her masquerade, or the likelihood that she had access to the mask-makers from *Mission Impossible*. It should also go without saying that Shyam, in the course of putting the lockdown on the robbery gang, discovers a convenient connection that handily solves the murder for which Nita's father was wrongfully convicted. Now all you need is a bow.

SHAREEF BUDMAASH
"The Gentleman Scoundrel"

Released: 1973
Director: Raj Khosla
Stars: Dev Anand, Hema Malini, Ajit, Jeevan, Trilok Kapoor, Helen, Master Bhagwan, Jankidas, D.K. Sapru, Sudhir, Asrani, Birbal, Hercules, Viju Khote, Manmohan, Mac Mohan, Gurbachchan Singh, Shatrughan Sinha
Writer: K.A. Narayan
Music: Rahul Dev Burman (R.D. Burman)
Lyrics: Anand Bakshi
Fights: Ravi Khanna

A microfilm containing plans for a revolutionary new fighter jet is stolen in transit to the Ministry of Defense and the scientists transporting it murdered. The film ends up in the possession of the traitorous Diwan (Jeevan), who hides it inside a case containing 50 lakhs worth of stolen jewelry. Ajit (Sudhir), Diwan's adopted son, steals the case and is thrown in jail, but claims that the case was in turn stolen from him.

It is around this time that a succession of criminal types start approaching Sustram (Dev Anand), insisting that he is "Rocky," a notorious jail breaker who has been thought dead for the past five years. Sustram denies being Rocky to all, until Diwan offers the entire 50 lakhs to him in return for retrieving the case—the idea being for Rocky to break Ajit out of jail so he can lead them to the case's whereabouts.

Sustram/Rocky's plan is to seduce Seema (Hema Malini), a cabaret dancer with whom the jailer of the prison where Ajit is held is in love. This ends up taking Sustram to Kashmir, where Seema performs a striptease act with another dancer, Carmen (Helen). After a long campaign of wooing and deception, Seema admits to Sustram that she, too, has her eye on the 50 lakhs worth of missing jewels.

Sustram pretends to burglarize Seema's apartment and is thrown in jail, whereupon, with the jailer's help, he breaks Ajit out. However, it is ultimately revealed that the case is actually in the possession of criminal mastermind Ranjit (Ajit), who has been unable to find the film's well concealed hiding place within the case. Sustram, Seema and Diwan make their way to Ranjit's subterranean mansion, where shocking revelations are made about the relationship between them all.

FEW BOLLYWOOD THRILLERS are as cut and dried as *Shareef Budmaash*. Within the first five minutes, we are introduced to the McGuffin, meet our villains, and, though there is some confusion as to our hero's identity—he'll go by three different names before film's end—the fact that he's played by Dev Anand orients him pretty firmly within the film's moral universe.

Yet, as refreshing as it is to find a 1970s Bollywood film that doesn't require us to start out a full generation before the commencement of its central plot, there is little to support the wisdom of trying to introduce "lost and found" elements during a movie's final moments, as *Shareef Budmaash* does, with no kind of preface at all. In short, *Shareef Budmaash* tries to stun us with revelations of things found that we had no idea were lost in the first place. When the missing relatives we've never heard of suddenly start to pop out of the woodwork, it's enough to boggle the mind. Mind you, this is not necessarily the *most* nonsensical thing about the film: it's doubtful that any amount of explaining could convincingly elucidate why Jeevan decides to hide a coveted microfilm in a case containing a fortune in jewels.

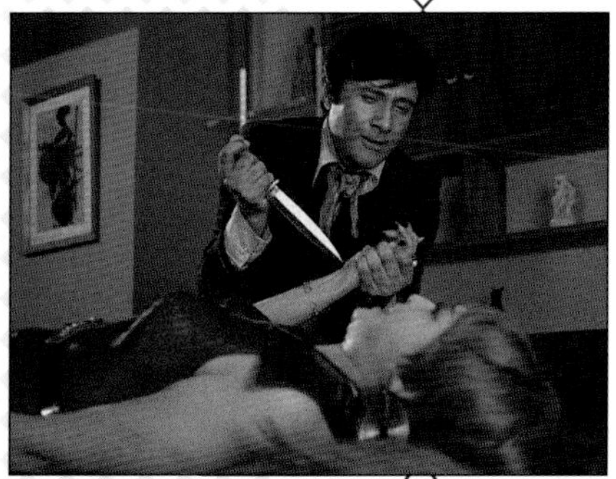

Producer and star Anand plays Sustram/Rocky as a mischievous rogue, leaving out a lot of the smug preening that made other of his 1970s heroes so unappealing. This does not compensate, however, for the fact that there is little to no chemistry between him and Hema Malini. Malini, in facts, appears here to be dialed down considerably, with even the item numbers composed for her by R.D. Burman striking one as unusually sedate. It is a racy choice to make Seema a burlesque dancer rather than a simple nautch girl (a profession already considered disreputable enough in the world of 1970s Indian cinema), but her "striptease" numbers are so coy that it's almost impossible to tell whether she is actually putting on more clothes rather than taking them off. Still, those looking for kink will find it in a surprisingly frank number in which Helen and Malini drunkenly flirt with each other while lying together on a bed.

Sapphic shenanigans aside, *Shareef Budmaash* provides enough entertainment within its slight confines to warrant a cursory look. The outfits are gaudy—check out Dev Anand's salmon shirt and pink fishing hat combo—and there's never anything wrong with seeing two old pros like Ajit and Jeevan facing off in juicy villain roles. Furthermore, Ajit's lair, a combination of Gothic excess and campy spy-fi trappings located somewhere within the bowels of the Earth, is as fine a piece of evil real estate as one can hope for in such a picture. There's even a last minute cameo by Shatgrughan Sinha for absolutely no reason, which, given the addled state the movie leaves us in, seems somehow strangely appropriate.

MR. NATWARLAL

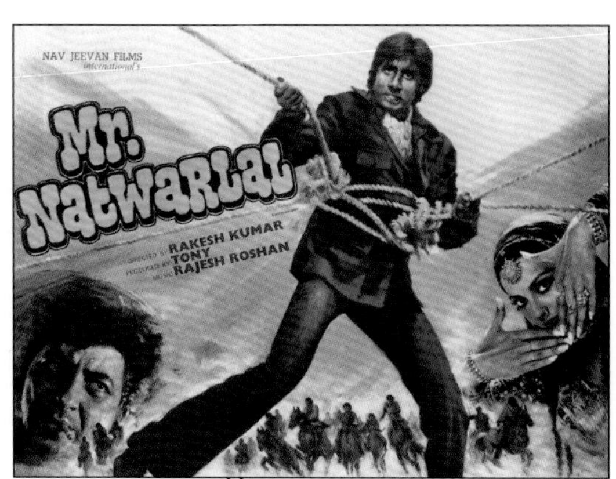

Released: 1979
Director: Rakesh Kumar
Stars: Amitabh Bachchan, Rekha, Ajit, Amjad Khan, Kader Khan, Rajni Sharma, Indrani Mukherjee, Satyendra Kapoor, Iftekhar, Yunus Parvez, Gurbachchan Singh, Vikas Anand, Goga Kapoor, Hiralal, Veeru Devgan, Gyanji, Moolchand, Ratan Gaurang, Rekha Chauvan, Wali Khan, Raj Mata, Ravi Mehra, Sahib Singh, Master Ravi, Master Bittoo, Master Laddu, Bharathi, Manik Irani
Writers: Rakesh Kumar, Kader Khan, Sayed Sultan
Music: Rajesh Roshan
Lyrics: Anand Bakshi
"Action": Veeru Devgun

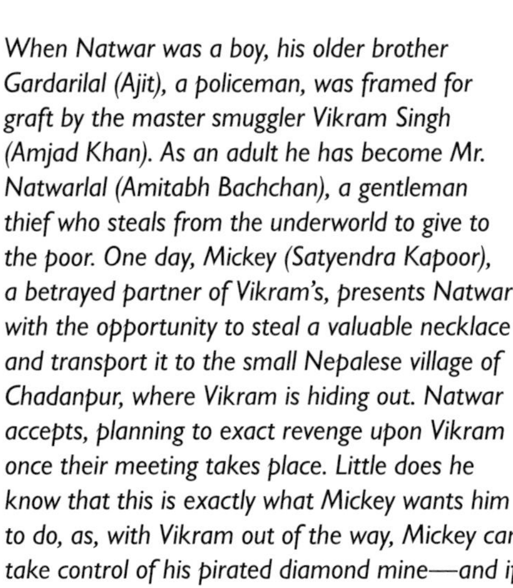

When Natwar was a boy, his older brother Gardarilal (Ajit), a policeman, was framed for graft by the master smuggler Vikram Singh (Amjad Khan). As an adult he has become Mr. Natwarlal (Amitabh Bachchan), a gentleman thief who steals from the underworld to give to the poor. One day, Mickey (Satyendra Kapoor), a betrayed partner of Vikram's, presents Natwar with the opportunity to steal a valuable necklace and transport it to the small Nepalese village of Chadanpur, where Vikram is hiding out. Natwar accepts, planning to exact revenge upon Vikram once their meeting takes place. Little does he know that this is exactly what Mickey wants him to do, as, with Vikram out of the way, Mickey can take control of his pirated diamond mine—and if Vikram kills Natwar in the process, all the better.

Meanwhile, the residents of Chadanpur are being terrorized by what they think is a wild tiger, with their men folk steadily disappearing in groups of three. Unknown to them, however, it is not the tiger that is to blame, but Vikram, who has been kidnapping the men to work as slave labor in his mine while using the tiger as cover for his actions. The village elder sends out for a famed hunter, Avtar Singh, to rid them of the tiger. Unfortunately, while on his way to the village, the hunter is captured by Vikram and killed. Natwar then arrives in the village and is mistaken for Avtar Singh, a confusion of identity that he decides to roll with.

At first, the villager's simple ways chafe on Natwar, causing him to consider scuttling his plan and returning home—until, that is, he falls for the elder's beautiful daughter, Shanno (Rekha). Meanwhile, Vikram learns that, due to an administrative hold up, there will be a lapse in the Border Security Forces' patrols of the area, and so starts kidnapping the villagers wholesale. Now seeing the full picture, Natwar realizes that he must lead the villagers in a revolt against Vikram and his army of goons, with the result a pitched battle.

M*R. NATWARLAL* IS NAMED for a legendary Indian con man whose name has since become synonymous with practitioners of the grift. However, the film is much less concerned

with the con than it is with revenge, romance, and, perhaps above all, redemption. Indian audiences loved to see Amitabh Bachchan play the bad boy, but they also needed to see him have his big “come to Vishnu” moment. As in *Deewaar* and other films, our hero has a fractious relationship with the deity, as evidenced by some one-sided conversations in which he churlishly scolds the god for his indifference. But in the final act, when the chips are down and defeat looks certain, it is Natwar who comes dewy eyed to the shrine. In this way, *Mr. Natwarlal* shares a lot with the “curry westerns” of its day by showing the spiritual awakening of Natwar, a city boy, as resulting from of his immersion in the simpler existence of a rural community.

As directed by Rakesh Kumar, *Mr. Natwarlal* is a well made and good looking film. The production values are high, the beautiful natural locations are put to good use, and the large scale action scenes are suitably spectacular. The film also benefits from a well drawn love story between Bachchan and Rekha, which is developed with some care and humor, as opposed to the obligatory treatment such romantic subplots often got in similar pictures. The two actors—who were rumored to be lovers in real life—bring a real chemistry to the screen, such that even the initial loutishness of Bachchan’s character fails to break their spell. Amjad Khan, for his part, while clearly exhibiting his late career bloat, gives us another of his great tyrannical man-child villains, a sweaty ball of craven cowardice and belligerent sadism (a scene where he gingerly tiptoes to freedom through a minefield he’s laid out as his doomed captives watch is the distillation of the Amjad Khan villain). Ajit, by contrast, faces off against Khan in a rare (for the ’70s) righteous good guy role.

If *Mr. Natwarlal* has a fatal flaw it is its over-complicated and fragmentary prologue (you know when a Bollywood film resorts to still frames for exposition that a lot ended up on the cutting room floor). It just seems like it takes too long to get Natwar to Chadanpur, where the film’s real story lies. Once he arrives, however, *Mr. Natwarlal* becomes quite a charming and engaging movie, with a hard charging, action drenched third act it’s hard not to be roused by—even if it does lead to yet another climax in which the entire cast somehow ends up crowded into the villain’s lair. In other words, this is one that’s worth enduring the longueurs for.

NAGIN
"Snake Woman"

Released: 1976
Director: Rajkumar Kohli
Stars: Sunil Dutt, Feroz Khan, Vinod Mehra, Kabir Bedi, Anil Dhawan, Sanjay Khan, Rekha, Yogeeta Bali, Prema Narayan, Neelam Mehra, Reena Roy, Prem Nath, Aruna Irani, Ranjeet, Heena Kausar, Roopesh Kumar, Komilla Wirk, Sulochana Latkar, Maruti Rao, Gulshan Arora, Tun Tun, Satish Arora, Master Bittoo, Anita Guha, Rajan Sethi, Jeetendra, Mumtaz, Harbans Darshan M. Arora, Jagdeep
Writers: Inder Raj Anand, Jaggi Rampal, Charandas Shokh, Rajendra Singh 'Atish'
Music: Laxmikant-Pyarelal (Laxmikant Shantaram Kudalkar & Pyarelal Ramprasad Sharma)
Lyrics: Varma Malik
Fights: A. Gani

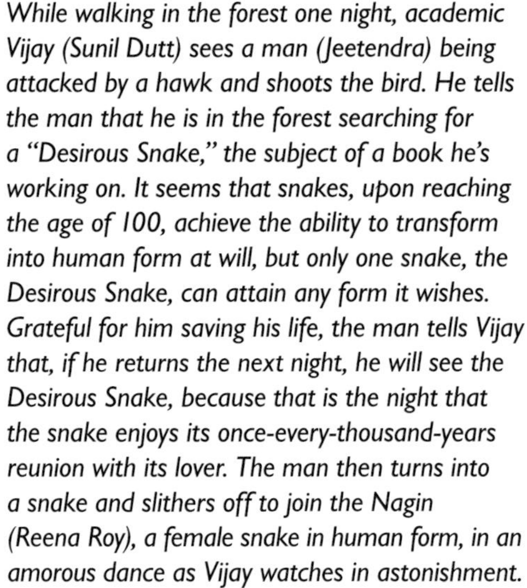

While walking in the forest one night, academic Vijay (Sunil Dutt) sees a man (Jeetendra) being attacked by a hawk and shoots the bird. He tells the man that he is in the forest searching for a "Desirous Snake," the subject of a book he's working on. It seems that snakes, upon reaching the age of 100, achieve the ability to transform into human form at will, but only one snake, the Desirous Snake, can attain any form it wishes. Grateful for him saving his life, the man tells Vijay that, if he returns the next night, he will see the Desirous Snake, because that is the night that the snake enjoys its once-every-thousand-years reunion with its lover. The man then turns into a snake and slithers off to join the Nagin (Reena Roy), a female snake in human form, in an amorous dance as Vijay watches in astonishment.

Vijay summons a group of his well-to-do male friends to share with them what he has seen. They laugh, until they hear the song of the Nagin. Stepping outside, they see the Nagin dancing, and the Desirous Snake, in his snake form, rushing to join her. One of the men, Kiran (Anil Dhawan), misinterprets the scene and fires his gun at the snake, thinking he is protecting the woman. As it dies, the snake transforms into the man that Vijay had met the night before. Aware that the Nagin is now certain to exact mortal revenge against its lover's killers, Vijay urges his friends to flee. But it is too late; the Nagin has already memorized their faces and sworn her blood oath.

Soon enough, the grief stricken Nagin is picking off the men one-by-one, doing so by taking on a series of seductive female guises. First comes Kiran and then Rajesh (Vinod Mehra), whom the snake lures by posing as his fiancée Rita (Yogeeta Bali). In the wake of these killings, the four remaining men—Vijay, Raj (Feroz Khan), Suraj (Sanjay Khan), and Uday (Kabir Bedi)—meet to plan some kind of defense. Vijay takes them to a shaman (Prem Nath), who gives each of them an amulet bearing the Om symbol that he says will act as a barrier to the Nagin. Uday, an atheist, at first rejects the amulet, until the shaman demonstrates how a live cobra ignores the three men wearing it but attacks Uday. This signifies a "come to Om" moment for Uday, much to the delight of his deeply religious wife Sheela (Neelam Mehra).

With this, the challenge for the Nagin becomes, not just killing the remaining men, but first getting the amulets off of them so that she can do so. In Uday's case, she convinces a hot tempered construction worker (Ranjeet) that Uday is her abusive husband and that Sheela is his prostitute mistress. The worker storms Uday's house and beats him, tearing off the amulet in the process, at which point the Nagin strikes. The Nagin then confronts the shaman himself, who captures her and traps her in a basket. The men try to buy the Nagin from the shaman so that they can kill her. When the shaman refuses, they pay his bumbling apprentice Bhopali (Jagdeep) to steal it for them. Once the deed is done, Raj shoots the snake and watches it burst into flames.

That the snake they killed was not actually the Nagin becomes apparent when the Nagin kidnaps Suraj's little daughter Anu (Master Bittoo). She demands that Suraj remove his amulet in return for the child's safety. He complies, at which point the Nagin fatally bites him. This leaves only Raj and Vijay to battle this supernatural nemesis. Unfortunately, Raj chooses this time to confront Vijay with his suspicions about Vijay doing some shady dealings vis-a-vis a joint investment between the group of friends. This argument devolves into a physical fight before the two are able to smooth over the misunderstanding. A penitent Raj then insists that he confront the Nagin alone, a confrontation that does not end well for Raj. This means that the final confrontation with the Nagin will be Vijay's, which leads to Vijay and little Anu hanging perilously from a line stretched between two skyscrapers as the Nagin slithers ever closer to them.

IN 1976, DIRECTOR AND PRODUCER Rajkumar Kohli did the impossible by turning a horror film—traditionally a disreputable and ghettoized genre within Indian cinema—into a mainstream Bollywood hit. This he did by top loading his cast with grade "A" Bollywood beefcake like Sunil Dutt, Feroz Khan, Jeetendra, and Kabir Bedi, as well as top line starlets like Rekha, Yogeeta Bali, Reena Roy, and Mumtaz (here making her alleged "last film," though the release of *Aaina* would follow the next year). Such an assemblage of two-fisted he-men in his cast behooved Kohli to put as much of an emphasis on action as scares, and the combination serves *Nagin* very well indeed.

With *Nagin*, Kohli opted to forego the labyrinthine plot mechanics so typical in Indian films at the time and instead adopt a propulsive, event driven structure more similar to that of Hollywood's "body count" horror films of the '70s and '80s. Throughout the picture, Dutt's Vijay and whoever of his friends are left alive race to save the next victim, only to have the Nagin beat them by displaying some evermore fearsome, previously unrevealed supernatural power. Between these episodes there is plenty of gunplay and fistfights, making for an entertainment that is pleasingly fast paced, if not always as atmospheric as one might hope for from their mystical thrillers.

Also making *Nagin* crackle is Kohli's dramatic—and some might say garish—use of color. Fluorescent primary colors flood the screen throughout, either in the form of otherworldly lighting gels or Reena Roy's flamboyant, heavy on the green wardrobe. This creates a backdrop of surreal fantasy against which the film's horrific events are all the more jarring. Furthermore, the film's transformation effects, done by pioneering Indian FX man Babhubai Mistry, are of the very particular Bollywood variety that are disconcertingly bizarre more due to, than in spite of, their crudity.

BREAKDOWN:
Man Into Snake!

Reena Roy, who began her career as a sort of B movie sexpot, does a fine job portraying the Nagin, modulating between grief and fury while at the same time displaying an over the top sexuality appropriate to the film's feeling of queasy gynophobia. Of course, as the Nagin performs much of her dirty work in the guise of other female characters, Rekha, Mumtaz and Yogeeta Bali also get their opportunity to act the murderous vamp. As awful as her deeds are, however, there's no doubt that the Nagin is meant to be, in part, a sympathetic character. Roy is repeatedly haunted by the love song that she and her serpent lover sang during their brief moment of bliss, and decries the unfairness of her fate. If only she hadn't crossed paths with a group of guys as heavily armed as Vijay and his friends apparently tend to be.

Nagin ends with an overheated masala movie climax that's as absurd as any, as Vijay, little baby Anu clinging to his belt and the Nagin in hot pursuit, tries to make his way along a rope strung between two skyscrapers, a breathless crowd that includes most of the surviving cast watching from below. Suffice it to say that the Nagin is allowed a few poignant last words and dies with relative dignity. Still, despite the litany of poor decisions and unhappy consequences on display, *Nagin* offers little in the way of moral lessons. What it does offer, however, is a very potent dose of '70s Bollywood at its most baldly entertaining.

KHEL KHILARI KA
"The Player's Game"

Released: 1977
Director: Arjun Hingorani
Stars: Dharmendra, Shabana Azmi, Dhruv, Dev Kumar, Narendra Nath, Mehmood Jr., Komilla Wirk, Ravi, Johnny Walker, Sujata Bakshi, Bharat Bhushan, Shyama, Sajjan, Hiralal, Jankidas, Ranvir Raj, Anand Bihari, Ramesh Kumar, Hari Shivdasani, Birbal, Makarnai, Harbans Darshan M. Arora, Master Bhagwan, Sunder, Rajan Haksar, C.S. Dubey, Uday Kumar, Deepak, H.L. Pardesi, Hangama, Mahendra, Maruti Rao, Polson, Ashok Razdan, Mukhtar Ahmed, Deepak Raj, Padmini Kapila, Upendra Trivedi, Helen, Ashoo, Shakti Kapoor, Master Suhail, Arjun Hingorani, Hema Malini, Uday Chandra, Ravi Kumar, Phunsok Ladhakhi, Keshav Rana, Prem Sagar
Writer: S.M. Abbas
Music: Kalyanji-Anandji (Kalyanji Virji Shah & Anandji Virji Shah)
Lyrics: Rajindra Krishan
"Thrills composer": Makrani

What a difference a day makes. A happy trip to the Diwali fair turns into a nightmare for young Ajit when gold toothed madman Sangram Singh (Dev Kumar) and his two companions design to rape Ajit's sister Laxmi (Padmini Kapila). Ajit's father tries to intervene, but is stabbed in the heart, dropping Ajit's baby brother Munna into the rapidly flowing river as he dies. After the rape, Laxmi follows the only course laid open to rape victims in old Bollywood movies and kills herself, using the same dagger that was used to slay her pa. With her dying breath, she hands the dagger to Ajit, asking that, once he is old enough to hold his own, he avenge their family.

Ajit immediately makes good on his promise, killing one of Sangram's two accomplices when he comes upon him in the forest. Chased by the remaining two men, he hops a train and ends up in the city, where he is befriended by a street urchin named Mohan who ushers him into a life of petty crime. One day, after one such caper, the two are separated while fleeing the authorities. Mohan stumbles into a temple, where he is shielded from the cops by an aged pandit. Mohan is so moved by this act of kindness that he swears off his dishonest ways on the spot, vowing to take the spiritual path. Meanwhile, we see that baby Munna is found by Khairatilal (Johnny Walker), a boozy, childless farmer, and his wife, who take him on as their own and name him Shankar.

Some twenty years later, Mohan (played by director Arjun Hingorani) has become a dedicated teacher at a school for wayward boys. Ajit (Dharmendra) meanwhile, has come to be known as wealthy citizen Raja Saheb, while at the same time masquerading as the "Sakhi Robber," an altruistic thief who robs the rich for the benefit of the poor. As for Shankar/Munna, he starts matriculating at Mohan's school, where he falls in with a gang of young toughs led by Tony (Shakti Kapoor). As their teacher, Mohan tries to steer the boys along the right path, but is flustered by the fact that they idolize Raja/Ajit, who is widely suspected of being the Sakhi Robber.

Throughout all, Ajit has not forgotten his mission of vengeance, still carrying the fateful dagger in an ankle sheath wherever he goes. When a telltale scar identifies an associate of his as one of the rapists, he brutally dispatches him, wounding him in a way that will ensure a slow, painful death. Ajit has also not forgotten about his missing baby brother, and freely asserts his belief that the boy is alive to all and sundry. Thus old golden teeth himself, Sangram Singh, tiring of Raja's criminal competition, decides to put forward his own son (Narendra Nath) as the missing Munna in order to gain intelligence on Raja's operations. Thanks to a forged tattoo, Ajit embraces the imposter upon their arranged "accidental" meeting, letting him move into his house.

In short order, the imposter determines that Shankar—who, along with his gang, has taken to helping Raja in his capers—is the actual Munna, and makes it his first order of business to soil Shankar in Raja's eyes. This he does in resoundingly successful fashion by making it appear that a drunken Shankar has embezzled the take from a recent heist. Furious, Raja disavows Shankar and sends him out into the streets. Sangram's son also learns of Ajit's mission of vengeance against a man with golden teeth and is quick to inform his father. Based on this, Sangram Singh determines that it is time to rid himself of Raja altogether. All that is needed is a lair stocked with lascivious item girls, a diabolical death trap, and the abduction of Shankar and his entire adopted family. In the thrill packed climax, all secrets will be revealed.

JUDGING BY THE NUMBER of backslashes I had to employ to identify the characters in *Khel Khilari Ka*, you can probably guess that it is a fairly worshipful rendering of the lost and found template, although it is also one that gains a darker edge thanks to the attachment of a rape revenge plot to its exploded family histrionics. Absent is the grinning, swashbuckling Dharmendra of other films, replaced by a grim avenger who cannot even allow himself the simple joys of Diwali until his mission is accomplished.

So fixed in his rancor is Dharmendra's Ajit that the film cannot even afford him a love interest, which makes even stranger the stunt casting of Hema Malini (in a "special appearance") as a sort of Sakhi Robber groupie. After a couple of brief scenes, her character vanishes from the movie without

Dharmendra is so dependable a masala movie protagonist that he could have been genetically bred for the purpose.

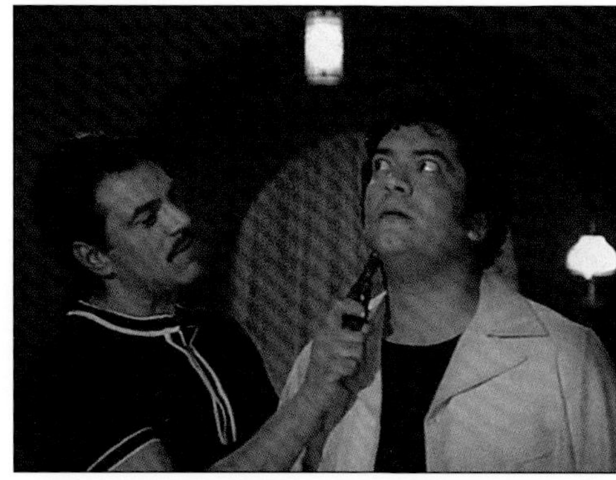

providing much in the way of utility, other than perhaps that Dharmendra was able to spend a little extra time with the future Mrs. Dharmendra during shooting. Instead, the romantic heat is provided by the star-crossed coupling of newcomer Dhruv as Shankar and the always welcome Shabana Azmi as Sangram Singh's niece Rachna. The film spends an awful lot of time on the antics of Shankar and his teenaged pals, and it's easy to assume that someone was trying to put forward the doe-eye Dhruv as some kind of teen idol. Judging by the fact that his subsequent filmography could easily be inscribed on the head of a pin, the attempt was unsuccessful.

In truth, *Khel Khilari Ka* provides a lot of pleasures that can be found in many other similar films—many of which star Dharmendra, so dependable a masala movie protagonist that he could have been genetically bred for the purpose. But if one is really looking for a reason to stick with *Khel Khilari Ka* in particular—and one is, like me, a junkie for the debauched thrills of the villainous life as portrayed by Indian popular cinema—it is its climax. Here we have the young Dhruv suspended above a pit of ruby red coals, the only thing preventing him from becoming human tandoori being the brute strength of Dharmendra, who clings desperately to the other end of the rope. Enter Helen and another item girl (whom I unfortunately can't identify), who proceed to make Ajit's job as difficult as possible, adding their weight to Shankar's by wildly swinging back and forth across the pit on ropes that are attached to his. And, of course, all of this can't be accomplished without a song: "Dekhenge Khel Khilari Ka," which Helen and her partner mime with malicious relish as they go about their murderous routine. It's insane.

Lastly, *Khel Khilari Ka* gives me the opportunity to spotlight the role of the child actors in these lost and found movies, who have the thankless task of portraying the younger versions of the stars during the chaotic prologue. Generally, we only see as little of them as this pre-credits set up requires, but it struck me that, in *Khel Khilari Ka*, we end up spending an awful lot of time with young Ajit. Not only that, but the young actor who plays him is actually quite good, giving us a credible, ten year old version of the elder Dharmendra's intensity. Sadly, I'm not sure what that actor's name is (is it Master Suhail? Anybody?), but, regardless, once he disappeared from the screen, it was one instance where I wished a masala film had spent more time on a hero's journey from boy to man.

PARVARISH
"Upbringing"

Released: 1977
Director: Manmohan Desai
Stars: Amitabh Bachchan, Vinod Khanna, Shammi Kapoor, Neetu Singh, Shabana Azmi, Kader Khan, Amjad Khan, Dev Kumar, Indrani Mukherjee, Heena Kausar, Master Ratan, Master Tito, Chand Usmani, Shaikh, Viju Khote, Bhushan Tiwari, Yusuf Khan, Tom Alter, Baby Deepali, Baby Shalu, Moolchand, Dilip, Ekram Kashmiri, Meena T., Shyam Varma, Ram P. Sethi
Writers: Kader Khan, Prayag Raj, K.K. Shukla
Music: Laxmikant-Pyarelal (Laxmikant Shantaram Kudalkar & Pyarelal Ramprasad Sharma)
Lyrics: Majrooh Sultanpuri
Fights: Ravi Khanna

His encampment surrounded by police, the bandit Mangal Singh (Amjad Khan) escapes by using his pregnant wife as a human shield. The woman subsequently dies in childbirth, but, before she does, gives her newborn son to Police D.S.P. Shamsher Singh (Shammi Kapoor) to raise as his own. Shamsher later expresses to his wife (Indrani Mukherjee) concern that the boy, who they've named Amit, is doomed by his parentage to grow up bad. She replies that raising him with the same love and care that they do their natural born son, Kishan, will be enough to instill good character in him. Years later, when Mangal Singh learns of Amit's whereabouts, he goes to Shamsher asking for his return. Shamsher refuses, but young Kishan, now school aged, misunderstands something that he overhears his father saying and wrongly concludes that he is Mangal Singh's son. He follows after the bandit and proclaims himself to be his child, whereupon the vengeful Mangal Singh tells him to return home, where he can act as Mangal Singh's agent within Shamsher's family.

Years later, Mangal Singh is a slick professional criminal with a wardrobe of crisp suits, a small army of goons and a palatial underground lair; Shamsher Singh is police commissioner, and Kishan (Vinod Khanna) runs a school for the blind by day and, unknown to his family, is a key part of Mangal Singh's smuggling operation by night. Perhaps most surprisingly, Amit (Amitabh Bachchan), in defiance of his birthright, is a dedicated and virtuous police officer. Amit has come close to catching Kishan in the act in the past, but has failed due to the fact that someone on the inside seems to be tipping off Mangal Singh to the police's plans. Meanwhile, the two brothers meet their romantic match in Neetu (Neetu Singh) and Shabu (Shabana Azmi), a con woman sister act who sideline in pick pocketing and petty thievery. After arresting her, Amit eventually succumbs to the fast talking Neetu's charms, while Shabu's aggressive pursuit of Kishan likewise bears fruit.

Amit eventually comes up with a plan to catch the smugglers that involves a fake diamond-encrusted clock fitted with a tracking device. He flaunts the clock while checking into the Holiday Inn disguised as a long haired international traveler, and soon both Neetu—disguised as a hotel maid, but wearing something closer to a milk maid's outfit—and

Kishan are breaching his room to get their hands on it. After a scuffle in the dark that ends with him shooting Kishan in the leg, Amit finally comes face to face with the fact that his brother is a member of the smuggling gang. He keeps this information to himself at first, pressuring Kishan to reveal who he is working for, but, when that proves fruitless, outs Kishan to his parents. This backfires when Kishan is able to disguise the bullet wound that would prove Amit's story, and alienates Amit from his parents as a result.

Later, Amit witnesses an enemy of Kishan's planting a time bomb in his car. He races after Kishan to warn him, but his brother, assuming he's trying to arrest him, leads him on a chase. When Amit jumps into Kishan's car, the bomb explodes, critically injuring him. Upon his recovery, Amit pretends to be blind and moves into Kishan's school in order to keep closer tabs on him. Meanwhile, Neetu and Shabu also are revealed to have a connection to Mangal Singh; he murdered their parents when they were children and thus, according to them, is responsible for them being the wayward criminals that they are today. They attempt to assassinate Singh at a qawwali performance at which he is a guest of honor, but fail and are subsequently captured by the gang.

Amit and Kishan's rescue of Neetu and Shabu, when it comes, involves pulling them from a torture pit in Mangal Singh's lair that's equipped with lava-like quicksand and advancing spiked walls. There then follows a thrilling pursuit in which the two brothers, finally united in purpose and piloting a mini sub, take off after Mangal Singh, who is making his escape in an obvious toy submarine.

ONE OF MANMOHAN DESAI'S quartet of "super hits" from 1977, *Parvarish* takes an interesting detour from the well exercised "lost and found" formula, in that its subject siblings, Amit and Kishan, are more lost to themselves than anyone else, each entertaining a false idea of who they are and where they've come from. By then putting these two under the same roof, the film really taps into the inflammatory potential of this situation, especially once Amit has discovered Kishan's secret and the two must act out their bitter antagonism while maintaining, for the sake of their parents, the illusion of family harmony. Uncomfortable family dynamics are further explored later in the picture, when we see Amit's adoptive mom and dad showing signs of resenting him as an interloping "other" within the family. On top of that, its falling down fairly soundly on the "nurture" side of the nature vs. nurture debate puts *Parvarish* somewhat at odds with the near mystical characterization of the family bond that is the typical "lost and found" film's stock in trade.

But above all else, of course, *Parvarish* is one of Manmohan Desai's trademark entertainers, which means that the director is somewhat over generous in stuffing it with business. The results of this, as always, are hit or miss. The top heavy cast means that some very capable performers are given very little to do, and the need to alternate crowd pleasing shenanigans with the intense drama at the story's center may result in vertigo for some viewers. Still, there is good to be had among the movie's many side attractions.

In particular, we get a couple of especially clever visualizations of Laxmikant-Pyarelal's songs. For "Jaate Ho Jane Hana," there's a darkly comic episode in which the sisters Neetu and Shabu, having threatened suicide to manipulate Amit and Kishan's affections, are chased from one potential death scenario to the next by the brothers, who, pursuing them on motor cycles, cheerfully goad them on. "Aayi Woh Raat Aayi" occurs during the scene in which Neetu and Shabu go to the qawwali performance with the intention of killing Mangal Singh—an act which involves them performing an Annie Oakley style song and dance number that ends with them firing their guns into the audience. Much as Zeenat Aman did in *Don* with "Jiska Mujhe Tha Intezar," the two sing in no uncertain terms of their plan to off Singh ("The night is here… either you die or we do") while, in the audience, their mark nods along in a state of happy obliviousness.

As Shabhu, Shabana Azmi, a fine actress, is here reduced to playing something of a madcap, but, to her credit, does a good job of it. More impressive is Indrani Mukherjee, a youthful and beautiful actress who nonetheless ended up in a lot of mother roles during this period. In contrast to the doleful martyrs often played by the likes of Nirupa Roy, however, Mukherjee, as the mother of Amit and Kishan, plays the Indian matriarch as a fierce and formidable protector. And lord help her sons when her plentiful reserves of righteous anger are turned upon them. Playing her husband, Shamsher Singh—and getting honorary top billing—is '60s heartthrob Shammi Kapoor, who, though almost unrecognizable in his beardy middle age, still exhibits some of his patented goofy charm in a couple of showcase musical numbers.

As for Amjad Khan, his Mangal is essentially just the type of craven maniac the actor excelled at, but is afforded the odd moment of dignity and even, with his (presumed) son, tenderness. More important, perhaps, is that Khan is here appointed with what just may be the greatest lair in the history of Bollywood villainy: a palatial, glacially themed hall bedecked with icicles and equipped with both a centrally located torture pit and a colored scrim behind which a backlit troupe of nautch girls shimmies apparently 24/7.

Personally, my favorite aspect of *Parvarish* is its climactic submarine chase. I'm undecided as to whether Bollywood special effects during this period were crude by necessity or simply represented a different standard of verisimilitude on the part of Indian filmmakers—the result, perhaps, of an audience more willing to work with them in terms of suspending disbelief. It is nonetheless striking to see a film made in the same year as *Star Wars* that tries to put forward what is very obviously a child's plastic bathtub toy as a real submarine. It's also kind of charming. Against the backdrop of the relatively heavy themes that the movie touches upon, ending it in this manner comes across like an invitation to play, an exultation to not take anything that has preceded it all too seriously. Granted, this is a Manmohan Desai masala film, so whether such exultations are necessary is certainly open to question.

And lest I forget to mention Amitabh Bachchan and Vinod Khanna, the pair once again make for a winning team. The truth is that, by this point, the two had proven themselves so adept at playing the kinds of roles they play here that it's all too easy to overlook just how good they are in them. As the son whose tireless efforts to live up to his parents' expectations only end up placing a wall between him and their affections, Amit charts a tragic trajectory that we've seen Amitabh's characters follow before, and not always with the most happy results. Ironically, Amit is only what his parents have made him, a sad fact which the actor underlines with a measured infusion of soulful dignity. As for Kishan, Vinod Khanna manages to show us enough of the pain behind his smirking resentment to stop us just short of finding him unsympathetic, even when he's at his worst. Perhaps most impressive is how the film's schizoid structure requires both actors, even at the height of their characters' mutual enmity, to together take part in no small amount of rakish tomfoolery during the many song picturizations in which they're involved—a feat which they manage while, in most cases, actually appearing to have a lot of fun.

Of course, at the end of *Parvarish*, all the issues of confused parentage are sorted out, with all involved being markedly relieved at the fact—and the villains being all too magnanimous about being brought to justice as a result. Manmohan Desai, having had a very busy year, would then give the "lost and found" trope a well deserved rest, not to return to it until 1979's *Suhaag*, for which Amitabh Bachchan would again be dutifully at the ready. And such was inevitable. Bollywood, as long as there are brothers born, will likely always find a way to tear them asunder, but I feel confident in saying that few ever did so as gleefully as Desai.

BREAKDOWN:

The Submarine Chase!

RAFOO CHAKKAR

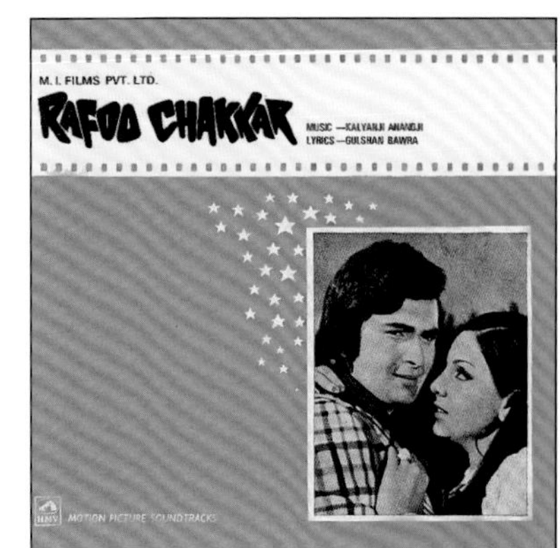

Released: 1975
Director: Narendra Bedi
Stars: Rishi Kapoor, Neetu Singh, Rajendra Nath, Faryal, Asrani, Master Chicoo, Paintal, Madan Puri, Anwar Hussain, Sulochana Latkar, Mumtaz Begum, Shetty, Viju Khote, Shamim, Surendra Shetty, K.N. Singh, Sudhir, Master Bhagwan, Mac Mohan, Manmohan, Habib, Jankidas, M. Rajan, Ramayan Tiwari, Mohan Sherry, Hiralal, Rajan Haksar, Goga Kapoor, Dalpat, D.K. Sapru, Kamran, Uma Dutt, Kamran Khan, Lalita Kumari, Narendra Nath, Bachchan Singh, Bhushan Tiwari
Writers: Jayant Dharmadhikari, Kader Khan, K.K. Shukla, Rajkumar Bedi
Music: Kalyanji-Anandji (Kalyanji Virji Shah & Anandji Virji Shah)
Lyrics: Gulshan Bawra
Fights: S. Azim

Dev (Rishi Kapoor) and Salim (Paintal), two young musicians, are desperate to find work to feed their impoverished families. When they inadvertently witness a hit by the gang of Prakash (Madan Puri) and Ranjit (Anwar Hussain), they hurriedly join up with an all girl band, disguising themselves as women—Devi and Salma—for the purpose. Dev falls for the singer of the band, Ritu (Neetu Singh), who is looking for a rich man to marry, and, when the band arrives at their destination of Kashmir, disguises himself as a wealthy young oil baron to win her over. At the same time, Salim/Salma is wooed by an aging tycoon played by Rajendra Nath. Meanwhile, Prakash and Ranjit are heading to Kashmir for an international meeting of smugglers, which will also be attended by their mysterious boss, who is known only as "Chief." Once these rogues discover that the two witnesses to their crime are right under their noses, they will stop at nothing to silence them forever.

NARENDRA BEDI MAY BE no Billy Wilder, but he nonetheless does a good job of committing the events of Wilder's *Some Like It Hot* to the screen in the most breakneck manner possible. With *Rafoo Chakkar*, the director somehow manages what is almost a scene-for-scene remake of the original in what seems like double time. This is all for the best, of course, as, once the plot of *Some Like It Hot* has been exhausted, the gods of Indian action cinema must be appeased. This means that, where *Some* ends, *Rafoo Chakkar* adds secret lairs with torture chambers, cackling, Blofeld-like madmen holding our heroes' sweet old mothers hostage, revelations of previously unknown parentage and, of course, a knock-down-drag-out fight featuring the entire cast, sweet old mothers included, dishoom dishooming, sword fighting, and chandelier swinging through the opposition.

Westerners watching *Rafoo Chakkar* would do well to remind themselves that those involved probably didn't care about how well the Indian performers approximated the performances of *Some Like It Hot*'s original stars.

Sure, Rishi Kapoor and Paintal may be no Tony Curtis and Jack Lemmon, but the point was to populate the story of a beloved international hit with Indian faces that were familiar and beloved to the South Asian audience. In this sense, Indian "copy" films are one part homage and one part appropriation. It must be said, however, that Neetu Singh does exhibit a combination of naiveté and unwitting sex appeal that's indeed reminiscent of Marilyn Monroe in *Some* and, like Monroe, also delivers a handful of scintillating song and dance numbers, but this is as much a reflection of Singh's comparable role within Indian cinema as it is any kind of imitation. That aside, *Rafoo Chakkar* has no illusions that it's fooling anybody; at one point, Rishi Kapoor's Dev, asked why he doesn't see Hindi films, replies, "Because they are a copy of English films."

Awkward in construction by its very nature, *Rafoo Chakkar* is not an example of a great Indian action film, but instead a great example of how, in the Bollywood of the 1970s, the elements of the Indian action film were irrepressible. Were audience expectations such by 1974 that not even a remake of a madcap American romantic comedy could be free of a sadistic villain in a Nehru jacket with a cat in his lap? In any case, I can't say it's entirely successful, but it does go down relatively easy, thanks in large part to a spritely pace and a wise adherence to the original's gags.

As for the film's transgender elements, they are handled with a refreshingly light touch. I'd even say that, compared to Curtis and Lemmon—who tended to play up the awkwardness of their masquerade for slapstick effect—Kapoor and Paintal take to drag like a pair of old pros. During their song numbers, which are dubbed by female playback singers, the two camp it up with abandon, by all appearances having the time of their lives. Were India ready for a Bollywood version of *Priscilla, Queen of the Desert*, this could have been a jumping off point. As an explanation for this, I can only offer that, hey, it was the '70s and, even in conservative India, people were beginning to relax about this stuff a bit. The original's final aphorism, "Nobody's perfect"—here spoken by Rajendra Nath in response to Salim revealing his true gender—is also kept intact in this version. Needless to say, neither version shows us where things go from there.

DUS NUMBRI
"Number 10"

Released: 1976
Director: Madan Mohla
Stars: Manoj Kumar, Hema Malini, Prem Nath, Pran, Bindu, Kamini Kaushal, Om Shivpuri, David Abraham, Sajjan, Abhi Bhattacharya, Shyam Kumar, Ram Mohan, Shivraj, Kumud Tripathi, Rajan Haksar, Madhup Sharma, Dev Kishan, Hercules, Rajan Kapoor, V. Gopal, Azad, Pahelwan, C.S. Dubey, Kamaldeep, Keshav Rana, Kamal, Rajni Bala, Master Raju, Imtiaz Khan, Kuljeet, Usha Thakur
Writers: Dhruva Chatterjee, S. Ali Raza, Shahid Akberpuri
Music: Laxmikant-Pyarelal (Laxmikant Shantaram Kudalkar & Pyarelal Ramprasad Sharma)
Lyrics: Majrooh Sultanpuri
Fights: Veeru Devgan

In the course of arresting a string of suspects for passing counterfeit bills, policeman Shivnath (Abhi Bhattacharya) notices that all of them have some personal connection to his fellow officer Karamchand (Om Shivpuri). Shivnath mentions this to Karamchand, who responds by having one of his criminal associates plant a fortune in counterfeit money in Shivnath's home, with the result that Shivnath is arrested and thrown in jail. Shivnath's wife Radha (Kamini Kaushal) goes mad from the trauma of this and his young son, Arjun, is thrown out on the street to fend for himself. Later, Karamchand's wife Sundari (Hema Malini), a friend of Radha's, tells him that she knows he framed Shivnath and that she is considering telling the authorities. Soon thereafter, a mysterious figure orders a hit on her and she is stabbed to death in her car. Also in the car is her infant daughter, whom the assassins take with them.

Young Arjun's first run in with the authorities happens after he brains another child with a rock for calling his mom "mad." There follows a long string of incarcerations for various infractions and, by the time we catch up with him twenty years later, Arjun (now played by Manoj Kumar) has embraced his undesirable status, adopting the moniker Number 10 (it says so on his shirt), a common, largely pejorative term for a habitual criminal. Number 10, with a gift for appearing seemingly out of thin air, uses his might to extract a punishing "tax" on the ill gotten gains of any criminal operating in his area, which is then used to help the needy. It is through these vigilante activities that he comes into contact with Rosy (Hema Malini again), a savvy street hustler who is actually Karamchand and Sundari's child grown up. Rosy initially responds to Arjun's shutting down of her street card game operation by hiring thugs to kill him, but after seeing him handily dispatch those thugs, falls in love with him.

Aside from economic redistribution, Arjun's other passions include (1) proving his father's innocence and (2) curing his mom of her dementia. When his mother, meeting Rosy, mistakes her for Sundari, Arjun starts to see her as the key to his mother's recovery. Radha also lets slip that Sundari had evidence of his father's innocence. Arjun, with some difficulty, then tracks down his father in a

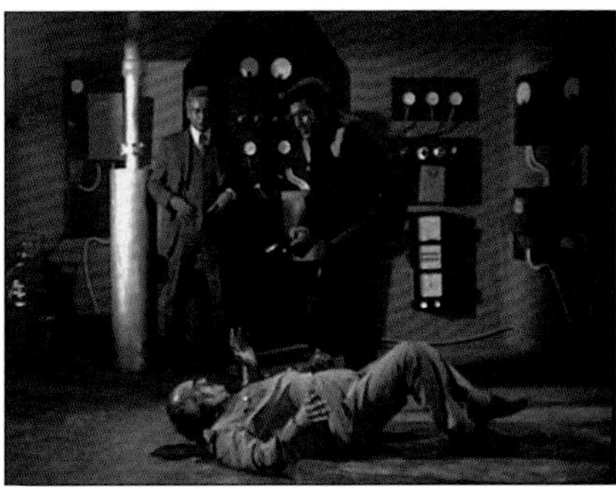

jail in Calcutta, where he learns the truth that Karamchand was the actual counterfeiter. He then recruits the help of Constable Karan Singh (Pran), a corrupt but kind hearted police officer, in nailing Karamchand.

In order to draw Karamchand out, Arjun and Karan Singh go into business with "Dilruba from Delhi" (Bindu), a dancer and madam who runs a formidable counterfeiting operation out of her basement. Karamchand's associate, Police Inspector Jaichan, begins an aggressive crack down on the operation, finally staging a raid on Dilruba's home. Arjun, however, manages to escape with the plates before the police can grab them. Jaichan, we soon learn, is the mastermind of the whole counterfeiting operation that led to Arjun's dad's incarceration, and is now obsessed with getting those plates due to their rare quality. To get them, he will stop at nothing, including torture and the kidnapping of Arjun's addled mom.

AH, THE ALTRUISTIC THIEF. So far we've seen him in *Jugnu, Guru, Fakira,* and now *Dus Numbri.* Out of all of these, Dus Numbri might strike the most fear into the hearts of his less civic minded criminal brethren, thanks in no small part to his customized logo tee and omnipresent beret and sun glasses ("to hide the tears"), not to mention star Manoj Kumar's mumbly, monotonic portrayal of him.

Known throughout the '60s as a hero of "Patriotic" films, the stone faced Kumar provides *Dus Numbri* with a center that doesn't necessarily hold. Thankfully, other of its stars seem more in tune with the film's reckless silliness. Hema Malini plays another in a long line of sharp tongued, street smart beauties, and is even given a whip at one point so that she can summon the past glories of *Seeta aur Geeta.* Pran, as seems often the case with his more comedic roles, is given the opportunity to ham it up in a series of "wacky" disguises. As much as this kind of typecasting might put these stars on auto pilot, there's no question that they nonetheless light up the screen whenever upon it, providing a welcome

Hema Malini plays another in a long line of sharp tongued, street smart beauties.

contrast to the lead footed heaviness of Kumar's turn as the tortured, albeit whimsically attired, hero.

As for our villains, *Dus Numbri* continues the steadfastly populist tradition of Indian action cinema by making the primary proof of their evil be the fact that they are members of the moneyed classes. The generously proportioned Prem Nath is perfect for this kind of role, a literal fat cat who looks like he eats orphans sandwiched between 1000 rupee notes for breakfast. He also comes equipped with a lair that, thanks to some sloppy editing, appears to have its own rapidly self assembling gas chamber.

Other signs of sloppiness put *Dus Numbri* in an interesting position—somewhere between hastily assembled B thrillers like *Saazish* and the more lavish crowd pleasers of a Manmohan Desai or Nasir Hussain. *Dus Numbri*'s labyrinthine plot certainly has the ambitions of those latter films, but there seems something rushed and corner-cutting about its telling that makes it at times hard to follow—especially once its doubles are doubled and allegiances start to switch with every new, and frequent, revelation of a character's hidden identity.

Of course, not really caring whether or not you understand the plot is often a key asset in enjoying these types of masala films, and, if that's you, there's no reason not to watch *Dus Numbri*. For one, it has a great selection of upbeat songs from Laxmikant-Pyarelal. Manoj Kumar has a classic "I'm going to sing about how I'm going to kill you in front of everyone and you're going to nod along like a fat idiot" number, which is rapidly becoming my very favorite genre of Bollywood tune. Furthermore, during one of Kumar and Pran's disguised escapades, they sing the antic "Na Tum Ho Yaar Aloo," the lyrics of which spin a ridiculous shaggy dog story about finding a missing washer woman.

Also, if you're a fan of Hema Malini-based meta humor, *Dus Numbri* will scratch that very peculiar itch. The visit by Malini's Rosy to the mental hospital where Arjun's mom is housed brings her face to face with a patient who imagines herself to be… Hema Malini (another thinks she's Rekha) and, later, during the aforementioned jokey musical number, Ashok produces a snapshot of the actress Hema Malini he boasts of finding in a wallet. All of these are indications that not everyone involved in *Dus Numbri* took it entirely seriously. If you follow suit, the film will likely provide some modest rewards.

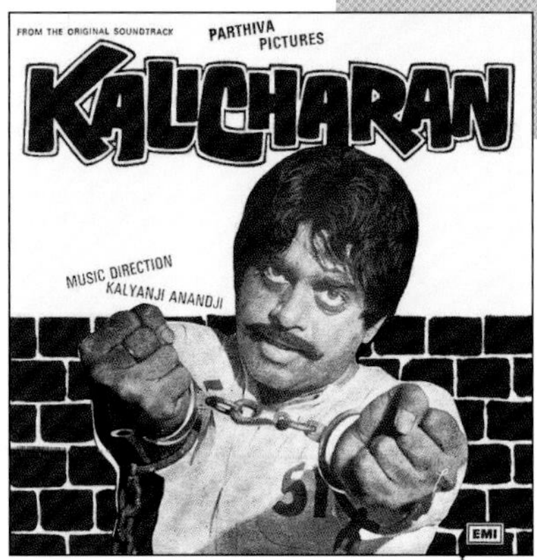

KALICHARAN

Released: 1976
Director: Subhash Ghai
Stars: Shatrughan Sinha, Reena Roy, Ajit, Prem Nath, Danny Denzongpa, Helen, Madan Puri, David Abraham, Krishan Dhawan, Leela Mishra, Dinesh Thakur, Sailesh Kumar, Alka, Bittoo, Manik Irani
Writer: Jainendra Jain
Music: Kalyanji-Anandji (Kalyanji Virji Shah & Anandji Virji Shah)
Lyrics: Ravindra Jain, Raj Kavi Tulsi
Fights: Shetty

A criminal gang is hoarding grains and other staples in order to drive up the market, leaving India's poor to suffer the resulting famine and rioting. Inspector General Khanna (Prem Nath) assigns to the case Prabhakar (Shatrughan Sinha), an officer whose name will "send shivers down the spines" of the evildoers. Prabhakar's first move it to apprehend one of the gang's truck drivers and, in a brutal interrogation, force the name of the gang's leader out of him.

This turns out to be Mr. Deendayal (Ajit), a wealthy philanthropist whose heroism has earned him the name "The Lion" among the people. Prabhakar doesn't believe this at first, but in a later confrontation with The Lion, becomes convinced of his guilt. The Lion responds by having one of his minions force Prabhakar off the road on his motorcycle. He sustains mortal injuries and later dies in hospital, but not before managing to scrawl the word "LION" on one of his charts. Unfortunately, he has written the word upside down, so when I.G. Khanna and his men find it, they read it as NO 17".

At the same time, a visiting jailer (David Abraham) recognizes Prabhakar's exact resemblance to a prisoner in his charge, Kalicharan. Hatching an idea, I.G. Khanna asks the doctors to hold off on announcing Prabhakar's death and asks to be taken to Kalicharan. Khanna's plan to replace Prabhakar with Kalicharan will prove difficult, however, as the prisoner (Sinha again) is a violent, incorrigible wild man. Nonetheless, Khanna takes him back to Prabhakar's house to live with Prabhakar's sister Anju (Alka) and two children, Chinki and Pinky (the latter played by child actor Master Bittoo in female drag).

Kalicharan immediately begins a repeated pattern of flight and capture. He confides in Anju that his urge to escape is fueled by his need to exact revenge against Shetty (Shetty), the last surviving member of a gang who raped his sister and drove her to suicide. Anju eventually appeals to Kalicharan's better nature and he agrees to take on Prabhakar's identity and uniform. His first move in this guise is to overzealously arrest anyone with the slightest connection—birthday, license plate, address—to the number 17. Meanwhile, hoping to silence Prabhakar/Kalicharan, The Lion steps forward to woo him. This includes an invitation to a swank reception at the kingpin's Lion Hotel, where a rotating "LION" sign finally clues Kalicharan in to what was really written by Prabhakar on that chart.

BIO:
PREM NATH

Appears in: *Rani Mera Naam, Raja Jani, Roti Kapada aur Makaan, Pran Jaye Par Vachan Na Jaye, Dharmatma, Nagin, Kalicharan, Dus Numbri, Shalimar*

Casting Prem Nath in a thriller or action film brought with it a desirable sort of tension. As a villain, he bore a Wellesian gravitas that lent disconcerting power to his already considerable menace. As a more ostensibly "positive" character—a staunch police commissioner, say, or a respected captain of industry—he had a sinister air that left you feeling that he was not to be trusted. When the final dust up came and all the masks came off, his was the character you were least surprised to find had been on the dark side all along. Born in the Peshawar region of Pakistan, Nath forged a career that spanned the length of Bollywood's golden age, starting with Mehboob Khan's *Aurat* in 1940 and running through 1985's *Hum Dono*, in which he appeared with Rajesh Khanna and Hema Malini. While not as light of touch as his younger brother, comedic actor Rajendra Nath, Nath also essayed his share of sympathetic characters—think the helpful shaman in *Nagin*, or the bear-like protector of Moushum Chatterjee's character in *Roti Kapada aur Makaan*. His well roundedness as a character actor made him an inescapable presence in the Indian popular cinema of his era, in the process earning him four Filmfare award nominations.

Kalicharan determines that the best course of action is for him to pretend to offer The Lion his clandestine assistance. The Lion gladly accepts, and his first job is to use his badge to gain access to a tightly secured grain warehouse. His accomplice in this assignment: SHETTY!

WITH CORRUPT AUTHORITIES exploiting the common man behind a mask of propriety, and a common man—a common criminal, even—assuming a mask of authority in order to topple them, few films encapsulate the class politics of funky Bollywood as well as *Kalicharan*. (A speech given by Prem Nath about the importance of roti in the common Indian's life even echoes words made famous by Zulfikar Ali Bhutto in the lead up the Pakistani general election of 1970.) And, fittingly, Shatrughan Sinha's Kalicharan—bellowing, wild eyed, and punching his way through all obstacles—is enough of an angry young man for two Amitabh Bachchans.

All of which is not to simplify *Kalicharan*, of course. Missing from the synopsis above are the appearance of Danny Denzongpa as yet another cheerful savage/bromancer, a lavish Helen dance number during a surreal masked ball, a subplot involving a mute, acrobatic killer, Madan Puri as "a dangerous dog from South India," and a performance by Reena Roy as Sinha's love interest. Still, it surely was, at least in part, the pointed way in which *Kalicharan* spoke to simmering class resentments of its day that contributed to it being the smash that it was, providing career boosts for both Sinha and Roy, as well as for first time director Subhash Ghai.

Also deserving of mention is Shetty, here once again playing a villain named Shetty. I have to imagine that this provided for some amusement on set given Sinha's frequent, aggrieved bellowing of the character's name. The chrome-domed hyphenate also provides the film's energetic fight choreography, which benefits greatly from the enthusiastic participation of the likes of Sinha and Danny Denzongpa, as well

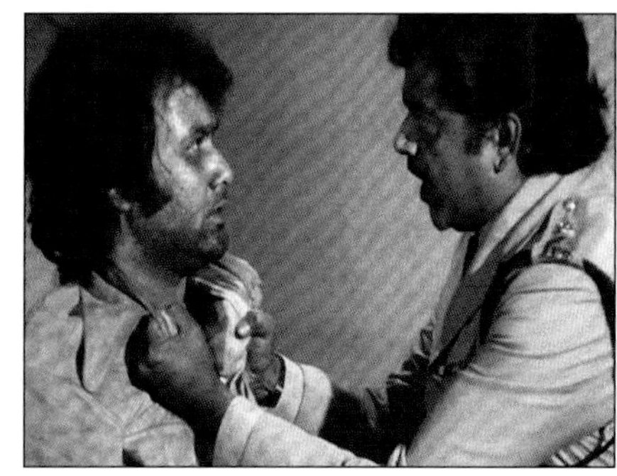

as a large cast of frequently airborne goons. One thing that's struck me in the course of reviewing these films is the daunting scope of Shetty's contribution to them. It's a task to find one in which he didn't appear and, among those, films for which he didn't also stage the fights. Of course, what gets lost in these mathematics is the oft overlooked fact that the man, within the limited scope of his roles, is a fine actor, projecting a chilling sense of menace often without the benefit of dialog.

Also bringing their "A" game to *Kalicharan* are Kalyanji-Anandji, who provide it with a thwacking good score, rich with danger and intrigue. Kalicharan's Bond-like theme, in particular, is a real treat without being too derivative. Among the songs, the standouts include the aforementioned Helen number, the funky "Yeh Pal Chanchal," and "Yeh Log Bhala," in which Sinha, still masquerading as The Lion's shill, sarcastically sings his praises as he and a celebratory crowd nod obliviously along.

While it's not quite as spectacular as its success might suggest, watching *Kalicharan* was beneficial to someone like me who is occasionally dubious about Shatrugan Sinha's appeal as a leading man. It's difficult to watch him here without appreciating why this was a breakthrough. For one thing, while capable of comedy (see *Bombay 405 Miles*), he doesn't swing between comedy and drama as other contemporary stars might. During his most bellicose moments there is instead the subtlest hint of a wink, making him a joy to watch without sacrificing the intensity of the moment. And seeing that intensity, his famed rivalry with Bachchan becomes all the more understandable.

The ever youthful Helen is an ideal spokesperson for Lux Soap.

DIL AUR DEEWAAR
"Heart and Wall"

Released: 1978
Director: K. Bapaiah
Stars: Jeetendra, Moushumi Chatterjee, Rakesh Roshan, Sarika, Ashok Kumar, Prem Chopra, Vijay Arora, Jagdeep, Roopesh Kumar, Madhu Malini, Nirupa Roy, Kamini Kaushal, Rajan Haksar, Pinchoo Kapoor, Jagdish Raj, Komilla Wirk, Tarun Ghosh, Manorama, Tun Tun
Writers: Tarun Ghosh, Charandas Shokh, Yaddanapoodu Sulochana Rani
Music: Laxmikant-Pyarelal (Laxmikant Shantaram Kudalkar & Pyarelal Ramprasad Sharma)
Lyrics: Anand Bakshi
Fights: M.S. Dass, Madhavan Raju

Vijay (Jeetendra) is a crime reporter who likes to get involved, as illustrated when he thwarts a bus hijacking with an exploding soft drink cart. The brains behind that hijacking, another nameless criminal mastermind known only as "Boss" (Prem Chopra), had hoped to leverage the release of his brother, who has been sentenced to death by one Judge Raghunath (Pinchoo Kapoor). Undaunted, he vows to continue his efforts, but also to keep a close eye on Vijay.

Back home, Vijay's life is no less complicated, starting with his death bed promise to his step mother to look after his step-brother Anand (Vijay Arora). Vijay wants Anand to marry Laxmi (Sarika), the sullen and rebellious daughter of his boss Rai Saheb (Ashok Kumar). Anand, however, wants to marry Saroj (Moushumi Chatterjee) a poor girl who lives with her blind, terminally ill mother (Nirupa Roy), shrewish aunt and troubled younger brother Chandu (Rakesh Roshan). Vijay has reason to believe—wrongly—that Saroj is disreputable and opposes the relationship at every turn. When he finds out that Anand and Saroj are planning to wed without his consent, he drugs Anand so that he misses the ceremony. He then drugs Saroj and, while she is unconscious, marries her himself, later threatening to show photos of the ceremony to Anand if she does not stay away from him.

Saroj, a devout girl, later feels duty bound to honor the marital bond between her and Vijay, despite the fact that Vijay holds her in the lowest contempt. This state of affairs slowly and improbably changes, however, as Vijay realizes that he has feelings for Saroj—a state of affairs opposed at all turns by Laxmi, who secretly entertains feelings for Vijay.

Meanwhile, Saroj's brother, Chandu, desperate for cash, takes employment with Boss, accepting as his first assignment the assassination of Judge Raghunath. That done, the gang moves on to stealing two million rupees from an "international smuggler" named Joseph who travels with an "international circus." Vijay and his assistant Kanhaiya (Jagdeep) disguise themselves as clowns and foil the plot, leading a costumed police raid on the circus. Boss, Chandu and Boss's teenage moll Kitty (Komilla Wirk) escape and, in order both to recoup their losses and get revenge against Vijay, decide to kidnap Laxmi's crippled baby sister Rani.

In a modern film, Laxmi would probably be given a trendy diagnosis like Asperger's as an explanation for her deviant behavior.

Eventually, Rai Saheb is introduced to Saroj and her mother, whom he recognizes as the woman who—through a baroque confluence of involuntary circumstances—he abandoned many years before, a fact which makes him Saroj and Chandu's father. Laxmi overhears this and, tasked with delivering Rani's ransom to Chandu, spills the beans about their familial relationship to him. Now realizing that he has kidnapped his own half sister to blackmail his own father, Chandu sets off to Boss's hideout to make things right. Vijay and much of the remaining cast are soon to follow.

***DIL AUR DEEWAAR* IS ANOTHER** masala film that has a hard time successfully integrating its disparate elements of action and drama. The former, especially during the film's opening and closing scenes, are fast paced and colorful, with rollicking fight choreography. But, as the film progresses, it becomes clear that what it wants to be at heart is an obstinately complicated family melodrama. Puzzlement abounds, as, not only does the screenplay evidence considerable confusion as to the actual nature of a crime reporter's work, but also, with all its talk of marriage among half, step, and foster siblings, pretty much creates the certainty of an unhappy draw in the genetic lottery somewhere along the line.

Also straddling the genre divide uneasily is our star, '60s heartthrob Jeetendra, who is required to be a cocky and carefree hero in one section of the movie while elsewhere exhibiting behavior toward its actually sympathetic characters so despicable that it eclipses any good will he might have generated otherwise. Given the misogyny redolent in his treatment of Saroj, the development of a romantic relationship between the two of them is especially preposterous.

Dil aur Deewaar does, however, offer some interesting moments thanks to some of the less well known faces among its cast.

Komilla Wirk's hot pants clad femme fatale, Kitty, adds an extra layer of "ick" to Prem Chopra's Boss by dint of her young age (given as 16 when her character is first introduced). More indelible, however, is the impression left by former child star Sarika's Laxmi. Laxmi is a female character who speaks her mind, and usually in the form of complaint. In the stiflingly conservative world of *Dil aur Deewaar*, this makes her an unconventional girl with strange ideas—and a constant bane to her father, who often wonders aloud what on Earth could have made her this way. The answer to that comes one night when we follow Laxmi to the go-go club, where the reefer smoke is flowing freely and free love slogans adorn the walls. ("All you need is love" reads one. It's 1978.)

B I O:

JEETENDRA

Appears in: *Dil aur Deewaar, Nagin, The Burning Train*

Before he became one of many single-named Bollywood stars, Jeetendra was known as Ravi Kapoor and helped out his parents with their imitation jewelry business. It was in this capacity that he met esteemed director V. Shantaram, who cast the slim teenager as the double for his wife, Sandhya, in the 1959 classic *Navrang*. Shantaram would later cast him as the lead in 1964's *Geet Gaaya Pattharonne*, but it was not until 1967, with his lead role in Ravikant Nagaich's hit spy thriller *Farz*, that he got a taste of true stardom. While groomed as a clean cut hero in the 1960s mold, Jeetendra would continue on as a hero into the 1970s, forging a unique side career as a replacement for Telegu superstar Krishna in Hindi remakes of that actor's South Indian hits. The late 70s, in particular, were a heyday for him, when he became one of the industry's highest paid actors.

In a modern film, Laxmi would probably be given a trendy diagnosis like Asperger's as an explanation for her deviant behavior, rather than pot addiction, regardless of how—in a world where a woman honors a marriage by chloroform out of religious devotion—the fact that she might want to complain seems pretty reasonable.

In Laxmi's nocturnal adventures as elsewhere, *Dil aur Deewaar*'s art direction has a pleasingly psychedelic tint throughout, from the pastel hued, op art interiors of Boss's lair to the modish, two-tiered, heavy-on-the avocado confines of Laxmi and Rani's lavish family home. This, again, stands in contrast to the film's conservatism, which expands its grasp to include a particularly egregious and superfluous gay stereotype among its supporting characters. That there could be such an overlap in flamboyant style between the digs of a debauched crime lord like Boss and those of such overburdened miserables as the Rai family seems like a phenomenon unique to '70s Bollywood.

All of which is definitely to say that an advised application of the fast forward button can magically render *Dil aur Deewaar* watchable. Watch it for the fights and the set design, but proceed with caution once any two characters sit down to talking, especially if opposite sexes are involved. By the time that you get to the climactic free-for-all, during which a young girl in a wheelchair is dangled off a cliff like a cat's chew toy, you'll be glad you did.

PRAN JAYE PAR VACHAN NA JAYE
"A Promise Before Life"

Released: 1973
Director: Ali Raza
Stars: Sunil Dutt, Rekha, Bindu, Ranjeet, Jeevan, Madan Puri, Jayshree T., Iftekhar, Suhail, S.P. Mahendra, Maruti Rao, Jankidas, Keshto Mukherjee, Prem Nath, Rajan Haksar, Birbal, Indira Bansal, Ratnamala, Rajnin Bala, Ramlal, M.B. Shetty, Kirti Kumar, Polson, Sujata Bakshi, Durrani, Fazal Khan, Anjum, Veena, Rajpal, Ramayan Tiwari, Randhir, Daljit, Suresh Chatwal, Harbans Darshan M. Arora
Writer: Ali Raza
Music: O.P. Nayyar
Lyrics: Shi Bihari, Ahmedwasi
Fights: Ravi Khanna

Raja Thakur (Sunil Dutt) is an altruistic bandit with a reputation as a "protector of women." One day, while watching a forced marriage he has arranged between a rape victim and her attacker, he witnesses the dancing of the concubine Janniya (Rekha) and can't help but express his admiration. This, unfortunately, results in the apparently uninterested Janniya thenceforth being considered Raja's property by all in the village—and a person of unwelcome interest for the police, who arrest her in hopes of learning Raja's whereabouts. Janniya tells Inspector Khan that she was not born to her lifestyle, but was instead kidnapped from her wealthy father as a young girl and sold. Khan takes this information to Dhanraj (Iftekhar), a rich man who lost his daughter under similar circumstances, igniting hope in Dhanraj that Janniya might be his long lost Sheetal.

Sadly, also privy to this information is Dhanraj's brother, Jagmohan (Madan Puri), a hood who secretly took part in Sheetal's abduction all those years ago. In this he had help from two other urban gangsters: Dharamdas (Jeevan), who now sells arms to the bandits, and VAT 69 swilling fat cat Mangal Singh (Prem Nath). Meanwhile, Raja hears of Janniya's predicament and decides to break her out of jail, whisking her back to his mountain hideout. Once there, it is decided that Janniya should be married as quickly as possible to quell rumors about her connection to Raja. When no suitable candidate steps forward, Raja marries her himself.

Hearing that Janniya is in Raja's care, Dhanraj goes to Raja's old mother (Veena) and asks her to intervene. She promises that she will have Janniya for him if he returns the next day. She then gets word to Raja, who agrees to the plan. However, in the event, the gangster's thugs raid the meeting place and abduct Janniya anew, mortally wounding Raja's mom in the process. As she dies, Raja's mom extracts a promise from him that he will rescue Janniya and make her good on her promise to Dhanraj. This, of course, will require Raja and his men to leave behind the rural badlands they rule over for the more unfamiliar terrain of the big city.

BASED ON THE ROMANTICIZED exploits of real life bandits in India's Chambal ravine region, the "Dacoit" film is almost as prevalent of a subgenre within Indian action cinema as the urban thriller, cropping up everywhere from the low budget stunt films of the '30s to fact based blockbusters like Shekhar Kapur's 1994 *Bandit Queen*. Of course, for the purposes of this book, we're more interested in those aforementioned urban thrillers, yet *Pran Jaye Par Vachan Na Jaye* is in the unique position of being about a rural dacoit who is forced by honor to enter those films' decadent urban milieu.

This "fish out of water" scenario ends up producing less tension than it otherwise might, however, given *Pran Jaye Par Vachan Na Jaye*'s conflict is less one between country and city than it is that archetypal battle so beloved by Indian audiences of the day: that between the righteous, calloused hands of the working poor and the manicured and corrupt ones of the moneyed classes. Thus Raja's moral authority is all he needs to effectively mop up the well appointed floor with his well heeled opponents. The result is basically one long dick slinging contest, with Raja again and again proving himself the real man (at one point, he taunts Mangal Singh for amassing his illegal fortune through "cowardice," while his stolen riches are the fruits of his "bravery"), whose bandits' code of loyalty and honor is wholly superior to the antagonist's ethos of greed above all.

Given this dichotomy, *Pran Jaye Par Vachan Na Jaye*'s villain's lairs—once the film's action moves to the city—bear a heavy burden in terms of portraying the effeteness of evil. Mangal Singh's digs, in particular, are at once exceptionally gaudy and flimsy looking, like a construction of spit and cheap costume jewelry—or, as Raja puts it, "a palace of glass and wax." (The fact that Mangal Singh wanders their confines playing an autoharp for no apparent reason—a wonderful stroke on somebody's part—does nothing to alleviate their ancient Roman vibe of languid decadence.) When it comes to fortification, the only protection this palace offers Singh is its bar, from behind which he helplessly throws bottles of expensive scotch at Raja, who matches him stroke for stroke with cracks of his whip. To finally drive the message home—in case you are blind to anything but the most minimal application of subtlety—Raja and Mangal Singh's final confrontation takes place along a craggy cliff face, whose rugged contours the porcine Mangal's dainty, pedicured feet are no match for. Cue the unconvincing dummy plummeting into the rapids.

The inevitability of all of this karmic payback makes it no less fun to watch, especially when you have a trembling rogues gallery like Jeevan, Madan Puri and Prem Nath to see it rained down upon. Still, the stifling machismo of the affair overall leaves little for a talented actress like Rekha to do, effectively reducing her to eye candy for most of the film. As "bad" nautch girl and gun moll Lilly, Bindu gets a little bit more heat on the action front, taking part in a lethal knife dance and, thanks to an eleventh hour change of heart, even a bit of climactic heroism. But in a milieu where it's considered chivalrous to force a woman to marry her rapist, it would take a lot more than that to balance the scales. In city as in country, according to *Pran Jaye Par Vachan Na Jaye*, it's a man's world.

HUM KISISE KUM NAHEEN
"We Are the Best"

Released: 1977
Director: Nasir Hussain
Stars: Rishi Kapoor, Tariq, Kaajal Kiran, Amjad Khan, Om Shivpuri, Kamal Kapoor, Ravindra Kapoor, Rinku, Vimal Ahuja, Ashoo, Sushma Shreshta, Murad, Tom Alter, Master Bunty, Baby Rani, S.N. Banerjee, Leena Das, Rani, Shefali, Aarti, Arpana, Ratna, Ranvir Raj, Yashraj, Ahmed Khan, Ashwari Kumar, Rajendra Singh, Bhushan Tiwari, Rana, Amarjeet, Rajesh, Omi, Maqsood, Chandan, Agha, Dolly Jena, Nandita Thakur, Nitin Sethi, Ajit, Zeenat Aman, Yusuf Khan
Writers: Sachin Bhowmick, Nasir Hussain
Music: Rahul Dev Burman (R.D. Burman)
Lyrics: Majrooh Sultanpuri
Fights: Fazal Khan

Rajesh, a nightclub entertainer (Rishi Kapoor), receives a letter from his businessman father informing him that he is fleeing Africa due to the unrest there, and that he has sold his property and business interests in exchange for $250 million in diamonds, which he has stashed in a belt. Sadly, he dies of a heart attack in transit and the belt is unaccounted for. Later, Rajesh is visited by Saudagar Singh and Banjeet Kumar Dana, two businessmen who claim to have seen Rajesh's dying father hand the belt over to Seth Kishorilal (Kamal Kapoor), another businessman whom, despite having a respectable façade is, according to them, a "dangerous smuggler."

Singh and Dana further inform Rajesh that Kishorilal has kidnapped Singh's son and is holding him for ransom. The two have devised a plan to kidnap Kishorilal's daughter Kajal (Kaajal Kiran) in exchange for Singh's son and, if Rajesh will join them in the plot, his father's diamonds as well. Rajesh counters that rather than forcibly taking Kajal and risking the full weight of the law, he can seduce Kajal into falling in love with him, whereupon she will follow them willingly. Everyone thinks that this is a good idea.

Meanwhile, we learn that Seth Kishorilal has a very different version of the story. Upon being handed the belt by Rajesh's father, he was immediately accosted by a gang of thugs who demanded the diamonds. After leading them on a chase through the train station, he stashed the belt in the distinctive looking basket of a parked bicycle, only to see that bicycle ridden off by a guitar slinging youth before he could retrieve it. That guitar slinging youth is Sanjay (Tariq), who works at the run down gas station owned by his father, Ram Kumar (Om Shivpuri).

It is revealed that, in less fortunate times, Kishorilal and Ram Kumar were good friends, and that Kishorilal had asked Ram Kumar to consent to the marriage of Sanjay and Kajal, who were childhood sweethearts. Sanjay is still in love with Kajal, but following her family's ascension into the upper classes has lost touch with her, and has been desperately searching for her for years. When news of Kajal winning a beauty pageant turns up in the local paper, Sanjay and Ram track her down and pay the family a visit. Kishorilal, however, upon seeing the humble state of the two, haughtily reneges on his side of the arrangement, sending the furious father and son back out into the streets.

Not long after, Banjeet Kumar Dana and Rajesh pay a visit to Kishorilal, Rajesh posing as Dana's son Manjeet. During a business discussion, Rajesh lets slip that he has fallen in love with Kajal by way of seeing her picture in the paper. Kishorilal, his mood magnanimous due to the lucrative deal that Dana is proposing, promises to arrange a meeting. Upon learning that Kajal is now living there, Rajesh purchases a house in the Himalayan resort of Nainital in order to be closer to her. Once settled, he interviews for someone to manage the property. Sanjay, unaware of who Rajesh is, applies and gets the job.

When Kajal shows up at Rajesh's house looking for Manjeet, Rajesh is not home, and Sanjay, seeing an opportunity, identifies himself as Manjeet. The two end up spending a romantic day together, despite being tailed by a shadowy figure played by a pompadoured Amjad Khan. Kajal confesses to Sanjay that she is still in love with her childhood sweetheart, whom she hopes to someday marry. A delighted Sanjay tells her that he knows that sweetheart, and will introduce her to him if she comes by the house the next day. Unfortunately, when she arrives, Rajesh is home and, answering the door, introduces himself as Manjeet. He further tells her that Sanjay is merely the house manager. Furious at Sanjay's deception, Kajal freezes him out, denying him any opportunity to tell her the truth.

Rajesh and Kajal embark on a romantic relationship, but Rajesh eventually, feeling the pangs of conscience, starts to entertain the notion of coming clean with her. He foolishly mentions this to Saudagar Singh, prompting him to unmask himself as… Saudagar Singh (Amjad Khan), whom a flurry of headlines reveals is also a fearsome bandit. Now needing more than self interest to keep Rajesh on board with the kidnapping plan, Singh reveals that he has taken Rajesh's sister Mala (Aarti) hostage. Little does Singh know, however, that one of his henchmen has hitched a ride with Ram Kumar and Sanjay, who, having once had a chance meeting with Mala, recognizes the coat the henchman is carrying as hers. Father and son rescue Mala.

This occurs too late for Kajal, however, as Rajesh—embittered over the news that his real fiancé, Sunita (Zeenat Aman!), has married another—has already led her into captivity in Singh's cave lair. Yet, upon returning home to find Mala safe and sound, he is emboldened by Sanjay's heroism to join his former rival in an armed attack on the villains.

HUM KISISE KUM NAHEEN was director Nasir Hussain's long awaited follow up to his 1973 smash *Yaadon Ki Baaraat* and, while it shares many of that earlier film's virtues—outrageously colorful musical numbers, charming stars, shamelessness—looking at the two side by side mainly provides a good way of seeing what, by contrast, *Yaadon Ki Baaraat* got right. For instance, for me it confirmed the feeling that *YKB*'s greatest asset was its tight, Salim-Javed penned script. In comparison, *Hum Kisise Kum Naheen*, while fitfully entertaining, presents us with a sprawling narrative whose sloppiness is only compounded by the sloppiness of its telling.

Yaadon Ki Baaraat's script, after all, performed the mean feat of making that picture's

typically convoluted masala movie plot seem almost organic. *Hum Kisise* performs the equally mean feat of straining the bounds of credulity even within the context of 1970s Indian action cinema's very relaxed standard of verisimilitude. In short, everything that happens in *Hum Kisise Kum Naheen* is a coincidence. No two people can meet without there being some previous connection between them, or one of them taking away some absurdly insignificant detail that will later prove incredibly important. And those few things that aren't coincidences simply make no sense. For instance, why does Rajesh unhesitatingly throw his lot in with Singh and Dana, two complete strangers who are proposing a crazy and dangerously illegal scheme—especially when one of them is so obviously a much younger man in old age makeup?

It performs the mean feat of straining the bounds of credulity even within the context of 1970s Indian action cinema's very relaxed standard of verisimilitude.

Free from blame, I'm happy to say, is *Hum Kisise Kum Naheen*'s cast. And that includes Nasir Hussain discovery Kaajal Kiran, here making her screen debut. As you'll recall, Hussain also "discovered" his own nephew, Tariq, who—here given considerably more to do than in *Yaadon Ki Baaraat*—also acquits himself well. Hussain even seeks to remind us of past glories by recreating one of Tariq's pivotal moments from *Yaadon*, giving us a scene in which Kajal realizes her connection to him when he, during a nightclub performance, sings a song that they sang together as children. To me, Tariq has a geeky vibe that suggests he frequently had his lunch money stolen as a kid, which gives him an unshakable underdog appeal in my book.

As for the normally cuddly Rishi Kapoor (son of Raj, nephew of Shashi), he walks a fine line as Rajesh, a character who, despite many of his actions being detestable, still seems at times to be getting shoehorned into the protagonist slot. True, these films often take an "all's fair in love and war… if you're a dude" approach to their heroes' romantic chicanery, but it seems that Rajesh is only prevented by chance from doing much worse than he already has, making his happy denouement sit a little uncomfortably with anyone who has been paying attention.

Zeenat Aman and Ajit appear in a last minute flashback sequence. Nor does a scene in which Rajesh saves Kajal from an out of control horse bear much fruit. I will say, though, that I appreciated in theory a last minute change up that the film pulls, wherein, instead of the "everybody fights everybody" punch up that I was expecting, we're given a miniature *Dirty Dozen* sequence in which Rajesh, Sanjay and

On a less ambivalent note, a clear highpoint of *Hum Kisise Kum Naheen* is R.D. Burman's eclectic score, which features compositions ranging from qawwalis to random electronic noise. His tunes for Rishi Kapoor's athletic nightclub numbers tend to be on the bubblegummy side, with one being very clearly modeled on ABBA's "Mamma Mia" (another nightclub act is later seen miming to "Honey Honey"—ABBA were very big in 1977). Of these, "Bachna Ae Haseeno" turned out to be the one destined for the hit parade. Hussain makes an interesting choice in picturizing this song, ending it on a shot of Rajesh backstage, heaving for breath and sweating profusely; a rare—and almost anti-Bollywood—instance of the exertions of performance being portrayed in an Indian film.

In addition to making its plot driven action a bit muddled and confusing, *Hum Kisise Kum Naheen* does itself no favors by including a lot of business that does little more than pad its running time (which, at 162 minutes, is pretty healthy). There is no purpose to Rajesh being given a fiancé other than to have an uncredited

Kajal, peeling off automatic weapons fire, try to escape back across the Indian border (from Pakistan, presumably) while being pursued by Saudagar Singh and his men. It's as if, after repeatedly forgetting its "money belt full of diamonds" McGuffin, *Hum Kisise Kum Naheen* has finally forgotten what kind of film it is entirely.

Of course, I may be too far removed both temporally and culturally to cast judgment upon *Hum Kisise Kum Naheen*, because Indian audiences of its day, in defiance of my belated misgivings, made a monster hit out of it. That audience was perhaps delighted by the Zeenat Aman and Ajit cameos, as I well might have been, *had they not appeared for no reason well into the film's third hour.* That audience might also not have been dismayed by the fact that, for its final 15 minutes, it suddenly looked like a Roger Corman produced, shot-in-the-Philippines, low budget war movie. All of this proves to me that no amount of exposure to Bollywood's "anything goes" masala cinema can guarantee immunity to its more extreme examples. Genre, take me away!

VICTORIA NO.203

Released: 1972
Director: Brij
Stars: Ashok Kumar, Pran, Navin Nischol, Saira Banu, Anwar Hussain, Ranjeet, Anoop Kumar, Helen, Jankidas, M.B. Shetty, Mohan Choti, Pratima Devi, Meena Rai, Lolita Chatterjee, Moolchand, Indira Bansal, Baby Gayatri, V. Gopal, Rajan Kapoor, Khurshid, Chaman Puri, Renu, Sabina, Jagdish Raj
Writers: K.A. Narayan, Ehsan Rizvi
Music: Kalyanji-Anandji (Kalyanji Virji Shah & Anandji Virji Shah)
Lyrics: Indeevar, Verma Malik
Fights: Shetty

Fat cat Durgadas (Anwar Hussain) masterminds a museum heist of a priceless collection of diamonds which is carried out by Ranjeet (Jagdish Raj). Sadly for Ranjeet, his double dealing girl Meena (Meena Rai) has informed Durgadas that he and a partner intend to swindle their boss and make off with the diamonds themselves. Thus, when Ranjit emerges with the loot, he is immediately set upon by Shetty (Shetty), Durgadas's strong-arm man, and his gang of equally strong-armed goons. Ranjit flees and manages to hide the diamonds inside a parked Victoria carriage before being stabbed in the back. An old carriage driver (Chaman Puri) comes upon the dying man and tries to help, only to end up being arrested by police on suspicion of the crime. When the man is summarily sentenced to life in prison for the murder, his daughter Rekha (Saira Banu) swears to find the real killer and exonerate him.

Meanwhile, expiring in hospital, Ranjit uses his last breath to make a note of the location of the diamonds, which he hands to an attendant along with a key to a train station locker, instructing him to place the note in the locker and the key in a hiding place prearranged with his partner. That partner eventually finds the key and hides it on his person, but before he can reach the train station, he is captured by Shetty and his men, who torture him for the location of the diamonds but end up, much to Durgadas's displeasure, accidentally killing him. Meena sets off to dispose of the body, which is in the trunk of her car, but is flagged down by Rana (Pran) and Raja (Ashok Kumar), two aging, small-time crooks who have just been released from prison on good behavior. When she stops for gas, the men steal the car, soon finding the body in the trunk and, inadvertently, the key hidden upon it. In a fortuitous coincidence, they later overhear the hospital attendant talking in a bar about his encounter with Ranjit and the key. Based on the timing, they determine that it must have some connection to the highly publicized diamond robbery.

Rekha, meanwhile, has taken to driving her father's Victoria carriage in order to make ends meet, but, because of the restrictions placed on drivers must masquerade as a boy to do so. Her carriage, No.203, is the very one that Ranjit hid the diamonds in. One of her regular customers is a charitably minded playboy named Kumar

(Navin Nischol), who, unknown to her, is the son of Durgadas, the man responsible for her father's death. Smitten by him, she endeavors to meet him in her feminine guise and a romance develops. Meanwhile, having retrieved the note from the locker, Rana and Raja have taken to following Rekha on her rounds and, by following her home, become privy to her gender-bending secret. They introduce themselves to Rekha and her little sister Muni (Baby Gayatri) as long lost uncles who have been away in Africa for almost 20 years. Hearing of the girls' plight, the two soft hearted men pledge to help them find their father's killer.

This hunt eventually leads the men to Shetty who, after a brutal fight, agrees to spill the beans on the real killer in exchange for a payment of 5 lakhs. In order to raise the money, Rana and Raja kidnap Kumar, aware only that he is the son of a wealthy man and not of his relationship with Rekha. Surprisingly, when called about the ransom, Durgadas informs Rana and Raja that Kumar is not, in fact, his son and furthermore says that he will pay them 20 lakhs—double the ransom—to kill him. It turns out that, long ago, when an offspring was required to fulfill the conditions of a will that Durgadas was a beneficiary of, he simply had his man Jaggu snatch a convenient child from a local park. We also learn, in a fleeting aside, that, some years before, Rana had lost his infant son in identical circumstances.

**JUDGING BY FILMS LIKE *BOMBAY 405* ***Miles* and *Chori Mera Kaam*, director Brij had a fondness for lovable small time crooks involved in matters over their heads. And few could be more lovable than the grandfatherly Pran and Ashok Kumar as Rana and Raja in *Victoria No.203*. Once they have taken it upon themselves to be the protectors of the perpetually imperiled Rekha, we are reminded of the unlikelihood of these unlikely heroes' heroism every time they rappel into a scene or crash clamorously through a skylight. All told, it's enough of a source of goodwill to glide us through a film that at times might go a little overboard in piling on the complications.

But, of course, stashed among those complications are many diamonds to be found. For one, we have Shetty—once again playing a character named Shetty—in a fairly substantive role, giving voice to more lines than I think I've ever heard him say in one film. In the role of fight coordinator, he also displays his legendary good sportsmanship in trying to make his tanning by the two relatively brittle protagonists look convincing. Ranjit is also on hand, modeling a very tight shirt with lace up sides accessorized by an apricot ascot. Then there is Meena, a bizarre plot device in femme fatale's clothing who only seems to

And, finally, we have an inexplicable non-musical cameo by Helen, who shows up eating an ice cream cone on the beach.

show up in order to inform one character of his betrayal by another. And, finally, we have an inexplicable non-musical cameo by Helen, who shows up eating an ice cream cone on the beach.

Aside from these familiar faces in its supporting cast, *Victoria No.203* treats us to a starcast refreshingly free of the usual suspects. As the romantic hero, the rakish Navin Nischol comes off like a young Rajesh Khanna while Saira Banu, who has worked my nerves in other contexts, manages to be charming, sexy and antic in judicious measure. Even our villain, Anwar Hussain, while no stranger to heavy roles, is chosen from the less oft-paddled end of the bad guy pool. As in *Chori Mera Kaam*, he again seems to be summoning Madan Puri in his performance, and once again sports a monolithic edifice of hair in the attempt, but earns our ill will and craving for schadenfreude nonetheless.

While being an exemplar of what was apparently Brij's favorite genre, the action comedy, *Victoria No.203* could also qualify as a "Patriotic" film. We are informed early on that the coveted diamonds have been the cause of many conflicts in the history of India so that, later, Kumar can say that they now "belong to India" and thus characterize his father's theft as an act of treason. Low level crooks like Rana and Raja understand this, of course, because they are of the street and, true to Bollywood tradition, derive from that a certain unpolished virtue. It is the wealthy men like Durgadas who, by their very acquisitiveness, are blind to it, as they are to the ties that bind all men.

BIO:

SAIRA BANU

Appears in: *Saazish, International Crook, Hera Pheri, Victoria No.203*

Given the male dominated and nepotistic nature of 1970s Bollywood, it's not too surprising that an actress like Saira Banu might be known as much for being the bride of superstar Dilip Kumar, a man 20 years her senior, as she is for her acting roles. This may in part be due to her admitted weaknesses as a performer, displayed prominently in her shrill turns in films like *Saazish* and *International Crook*. Nonetheless, she did have her career high points, making a smash opposite Shammi Kapoor in 1961's *Junglee* and again as a Westernized vamp in Manoj Kumar's moralizing *Purab aur Paschim*. In between, Banu struggled to sustain a career as a top heroine, though one still gets the sense that she never rose completely above the "B" list. She chose family life over acting in 1976, leaving behind her a fair share of forgettable performances, but also the occasionally charming star turn, such as the cross dressing heroine of *Victoria No.203* or *Hera Pheri*'s charismatic femme fatale Kiran.

ROTI KAPADA AUR MAKAAN
"Food Clothing and Shelter"

Released: 1974
Director: Manoj Kumar
Stars: Manoj Kumar, Shashi Kapoor, Zeenat Aman, Moushumi Chatterjee, Prem Nath, Amitabh Bachchan, Dheeraj Kumar, Kamini Kaushal, Aruna Irani, Madan Puri, Krishan Dhawan, Sulochana Latkar, Manmohan, Raza Murad, Raj Mehra, Kuljit Singh, Agha, Asit Sen, Jani Babu, Meena T., Lalita Kumari, Birbal, Brahm Bhardwaj, C.S. Dubey, Harbans Darshan M. Arora, Sikandar Khanna, Madhup Sharma, Rajan Kapoor, Kamaldeep, Ranvir Raj, Deenanath, Shyam Arora, B.K. Sood, Sol, Panthulu, Chandra, Rajni Bala, Raj Chopra, Gurbachchan Singh
Writer: Manoj Kumar
Music: Laxmikant-Pyarelal (Laxmikant Shantaram Kudalkar & Pyarelal Ramprasad Sharma)
Lyrics: Varma Malik, Santoshanand
Fights: Veeru Devgan

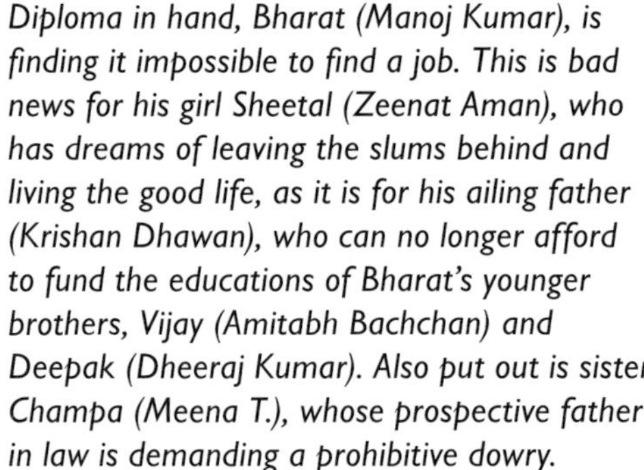

Diploma in hand, Bharat (Manoj Kumar), is finding it impossible to find a job. This is bad news for his girl Sheetal (Zeenat Aman), who has dreams of leaving the slums behind and living the good life, as it is for his ailing father (Krishan Dhawan), who can no longer afford to fund the educations of Bharat's younger brothers, Vijay (Amitabh Bachchan) and Deepak (Dheeraj Kumar). Also put out is sister Champa (Meena T.), whose prospective father in law is demanding a prohibitive dowry.

Bharat takes a job singing on television, but it is not enough to cover his family's numerous obligations. Meanwhile, Vijay is approached by a shadowy figure who offers him 2500 Rs. to stage a strike at his school and hopefully close it down. The figure hints that he is in the employ of a foreign government. Desperate for cash, Vijay accepts the money, only to be upbraided by Deepak, now a policeman, who shames him for his weak morals. Chastened, Vijay vows to leave home and not return until he can look his brother in the eye.

Sheetal, meanwhile, takes a job as a secretary for rich businessman Mohan (Shashi Kapoor). Mohan is attracted to her and she is tempted by the life he has to offer. Nekiram (Madan Puri), another businessman who leads a gang of corrupt fat cats in a commodities hoarding scheme, offers Bharat a job doing his dirty work, but he refuses. He later finds work in construction, but loses the job when the government halts the project. Desperate to buy drugs for his increasingly ill father, he goes to the pharmacy and offers to trade his diploma for medicine. When refused, he attempts to steal the medicine and is jailed. When his father dies, Bharat casts his diploma onto the funeral pyre. Soon after, Sheetal and Mohan return from a business trip to New York to announce that they are getting married, leaving the already devastated Bharat completely shattered.

Elsewhere we see that Vijay has joined the army and—as part of a tiny, decimated unit—is involved in tense combat on the front lines. He later returns home with a missing arm to show for his heroism. The dispirited Bharat, by this time, has decided to take Nekiram up on his offer. However, once he sees the full nature of his scheme, he informs on Nekiram to Deepak, who starts the wheels of justice turning. In the end, all three brothers, along with Mohan and Sheetal, rise up to face the traitors.

ON THE BAD SIDE, *Roti Kapada aur Makaan* is a turgid melodrama leaden with heavy handed symbolism and pretentious, overly didactic dialog. Clearly writer/director/producer/editor/star Manoj Kumar is serious about showing us the losing game faced by India's slum dwellers and passionate about the toll taken by corruption among the upper classes. One just wishes that, barring the insertion of a pratfalling Jagdeep, he showed occasional evidence of having a sense of humor.

On the good side: Look at that cast! Unfortunately, Kumar squanders much potential chemistry by sending all of his characters on separate, divergent paths. Amitabh Bachchan and Shashi Kapoor, later to prove such a winning team, are rarely on screen together. It's almost as if Kumar cast Bachchan in order to flaunt just how much he *isn't* in the movie. Who *is* in the movie, and a lot, is writer/director/producer/editor/star Manoj Kumar, who is rarely off camera. He even ends the film on a freeze frame of his face. His performance here is heavy on his usual taciturn mumbling, which befits a man so bummed out that even Zeenat Aman shimmying around in a wet sari can't cheer him up.

It's difficult to criticize *Roti Kapada aur Makaan* for fear of seeming insensitive to its subject matter. But the truth is that one is aware enough of the gravity of that subject without Kumar's onslaught of flag overlays and on-the-nose monologizing—to the extent that criticizing it almost seems like a form of self defense. Thankfully, Kumar's particular obsessions provide for some odd pockets of enjoyment—such as his frequent employment of "in camera" psychedelia that involves dangling tinsel or garlands in front of the lens. Rather than having what I assume is the desired dream-like effect, this trick instead makes it appear as if the actor's are performing in a department store window. Also in Kumar's auteurist arsenal are spinning camera moves and strobing, hyper fast cuts during moments of high tension and an eerie bit of business where he has Zeenat Aman

The film ultimately manages to wend its way to one of those protracted, all-fists-on-deck, cast inclusive dust-ups that we've become so used to.

and himself soundlessly chattering at one another in fast motion like something out of the video from *The Ring*. Indeed, the only other he-man Bollywood actor/director with a comparable love of gimmickry whom I can think of is Feroz Khan, and even *he* shows more discipline.

I almost reconsidered including *Roti* in this volume, because, for most of its first half, it is relatively action free. However, Kumar seems to view patriotism as a pointedly macho endeavor (while the harsh karmic payback that awaits Zeenat Aman's Sheetal suggests that women are only begrudgingly invited to the party). As such, the film ultimately manages to wend its way to one of those protracted, all-fists-on-deck, cast inclusive dust-ups that we've become so used to. And on the way to that conclusion, we get some pretty rousing "behind enemy lines" business featuring Amitabh and his tiny, outgunned unit. It seems mere talking only suffices until that time when the speakers must put their own blood on the line, and bleed they indeed do.

Roti Kapada aur Makaan's raft of characters makes the stories and relationships within it a little difficult to sort out. This is especially true when those characters serve more of a polemic purpose than a dramatic one—i.e. Moushumi Chatterjee's Tulsi, a young woman whose poverty makes her a victim of repeated rape. What the relationship of Harinam Singh (Prem Nath), her bear like protector, was to her is still unclear to me. (He says he is her brother, but I believe he means that in the more communal sense.) In any case, a repeat viewing of *Roti Kapada aur Makaan* might help me parse all of that, but is nonetheless unlikely to happen. Count me once again on the opposite side of the combined movie going public of India, who made this the highest grossing Bollywood film of 1974.

DHARMA

Released: 1973
Director: Chand
Stars: Pran, Navin Nischol, Rekha, Ajit, Madan Puri, Ramesh Deo, Bindu, Mohan Choti, Asit Sen, Sonia Sahni, Faryal, Jayshree T., Anjali Kadam, Chandrashekhar, Rajan Haksar, Murad, Paro, Jagdish Bhalla, Uma Dutt, Master Mohit, Master Chand, Johnny, Moolchand, Jankidas, Randhir, Harbans Darshan M. Arora, Helen
Writer: Chand
Music: Master Sonik, Om Prakash Sharma (Sonik-Omi)

The fierce bandit Sevak Singh, aka Dharma (Pran), is lured into a trap by Inspector Ajit (Ajit), only to find that the bullets recently requisitioned by his right hand man Bhairon (Rajan Haksar) are blanks. Bhairon, meanwhile, has left his companions to die and, along with his brother and co-conspirator Mangal (Madan Puri), heads back to the band's hideout to rape Dharma's wife, Parvati (Anjali Kadam). Dharma, having escaped the authorities, arrives just in time and strangles Bhairon to death in front of Bhairon's young son Chaman. He then hurries his wife and son, Suraj, into a boat and attempts to flee. Ajit fires upon the boat and hits Parvati. Both she and Suraj fall from the boat and disappear beneath the waves.

Later Dharma, bent on avenging the apparent deaths of his wife and child, shows up at Inspector Ajit's home, only to find his wife Asha (Rekha) and young daughter. Dharma tries to wrest the girl from Asha's grasp and, in the struggle, Asha falls from the balcony and dies. Dharma flees with the child on horseback, but drops her when he is shot by pursuing police. The unconscious girl is later picked up by an unidentified woman who happens by.

Meanwhile, both Ajit Singh and Mangal, who is now the guardian of little Chaman, separately swear an oath of vengeance against Dharma.

Years later, Dharma is leading a double life: on the one hand as the silver haired Chandan, a sophisticated jewel thief with an army of minions and a fabulous underground lair, and, on the other, as the kindly Nawab Sikander Mirza, a man of good works who, in his identity obscuring beardiness, is able to maintain a close friendship with Inspector—now Inspector General—Ajit. When we catch up with him, Dharma/Chandan is repeatedly finding himself the beneficiary of the interventions of a young tough named Raju (Navin Nishchol). He attempts to recruit Raju into his gang, but Raju refuses, while still insisting on a generous cut of the take from the robberies in which he assists. Then, in the course of fleeing police in the aftermath of a heist, Dharma saves Raju's life, causing Raju to pledge that he "belongs" to Dharma for life.

At the same time, Raju has struck up a romance with Radha (Rekha again), a young woman who is mysteriously evasive about her life's particulars. Raju finds out why when, during another mad dash from the authorities, he and Dharma take refuge in a brothel which happens to be owned by Bhairon's grown up son Chaman (Ramesh Deo), who is now a pimp. Radha is a dancer there, and shields them by letting them disguise themselves as members of the band. In return, Raju magnanimously "forgives" her (for, even as a self-described "thief and ruffian," it is his prerogative to reject a lowly nautch girl as being beneath him). Dharma also expresses his gratitude to Radha and promises her anything in return. She tells him that she would like a respectable life. Sharma returns to the brothel the next day in the guise of Nawab Sikander and purchases her freedom. Soon thereafter, I.G. Ajit, upon meeting her at the Nawab's home, is struck by her resemblance to his wife and immediately adopts her.

Meanwhile, Ajit's pursuit of Chandan makes an investigative leap when he obtains a hidden camera photograph of the thief in the act. The picture appears in the newspaper, whereupon Mangal recognizes Chandan as being his sworn enemy Dharma. He and Chaman begin tailing both Chandan and Raju, and when they follow Raju to a temple he regularly visits, Mangal recognizes the old woman who tends the shrine as Parvati, Dharma's wife. He then presents Chaman to Parvati as her long lost son Suraj. Soon Dharma and his family are reunited, although with an imposter in their midst. Only a string of highly unlikely events will ultimately reveal that it is Raju, not Chaman, who is the rightful heir to Chandan's criminal empire. In like fashion, Ajit will learn that Radha's family resemblance is no coincidence.

SOMEONE WITH A BACKGROUND in psychology could write an interesting paper on brain plasticity and the effects of trauma on childhood memory as presented in 1970s Bollywood films. In *Dharma*, little Radha and Suraj, at the time of being separated from their parents, are clearly of schooling age—Suraj is even old enough to have a tattoo. Yet, as adults, neither is able to recognize their parent at close proximity, or recall the rather unusual circumstances under which they were parted from them.

Such are the improbabilities that the lost and found genre thrives upon. Sadly, *Dharam* director Chand doesn't see fit to invest them—or the numerous reunions and dramatic realizations that spring from them—with enough emotional weight to give them much impact. It's enough to make one appreciate anew masters of the form like Manmohan Desai or Nasir Hussain, who, as contrived as their scenarios of atomized families might have been, more often than not assured that they packed an emotional wallop.

Fortunately, its plot mechanics are not *Dharma*'s primary selling point, but instead its status as a showcase for the talents of Pran, one of Indian cinema's greatest character actors. Indeed, Pran could be said to play a double role here, as—despite telling Ajit that he assumed the guise in order to observe his suffering from up close—Nawab Sikander is less like an alter ego of Chandan than he is a separate and better self. As such, we see

the extreme poles of Pran's most oft seen screen personas: In Nawab Sikander, the warm and kindly mentor and, in Chandan, the hard eyed and ruthless ruffian. Pran, as fit and trim as I've ever seen him, also fills the shoes of action hero quite well, wielding a mean whip and carrying off the stunt-filled heist sequences with a serpentine grace. Don't let Navin Nischol's headline billing fool you; this is Pran's film to carry, a fact driven home by his appearance in almost every one of its scenes.

ode to altered states that sees the abrupt appearance of a bunch of stoned looking white people. Also setting hips swiveling is Bindu, who takes part in an especially satisfying sub-narrative number, a qawwali in which she threatens in song to reveal Nawab Sikander's true identity. A host of party guests breezily nod along, none the wiser. Pran, of course, responds in kind, warning her, also in song, and in no uncertain terms, of the consequences of doing so. ("If the secret comes to your lips/I'll punch your face!")

Such are the improbabilities that the lost and found genre thrives upon.

Dharma also provides a nice showcase for lesser known composers Master Sonik and Om Prakash Sharma, collectively known as Sonik-Omi. Of course, it's easy to appreciate any score with the assemblage of item girl talent that *Dharma* sets in motion to it. Our introduction to the staff of Chaman's brothel comes in a succession of energetic dance numbers, one after the other; the first featuring an uncredited Helen, the second—with an Egyptian theme—Faryal, the third Sonia Sahni, and, finally, Jayshree T. with an

Dharma insures that it has its work cut out for it by its inclusion of a small gang of misplaced family members of various origins, as well as all manner of false and mistaken identities on the part of its numerous characters. Yet, in the end, by the means of grudge-bearing informants, timely revealed body art and sheer dumb luck, all is more or less tidily revealed. It comes off a bit like a rote connecting of the dots, but at least we have those item numbers, Chandan's fabulous lair and the majesty of Pran to compensate for it.

SUHAAG
"Husband"

Released: 1979
Director: Manmohan Desai
Stars: Shashi Kapoor, Amitabh Bachchan, Rekha, Parveen Babi, Nirupa Roy, Ranjeet, Kader Khan, Amjad Khan, Jeevan, Hercules, Jagdish Raj, Krishan Dhawan, M. Rajan, Nishan Singh, Daljit Rao, Azad, Komilla Wirk, Ghulam Hussein, Brahm Bhardwaj, Vatsala Deshmukh, Chanda, Raj Rani, Moolchand, Master Tito, Master Ratan
Writers: K.K. Shukla, Prayag Raj, Kader Khan
Music: Laxmikant-Pyarelal (Laxmikant Shantaram Kudalkar & Pyarelal Ramprasad Sharma)
Lyrics: Anand Bakshi
Fights: Ravi Khanna, A. Mansoor, Surinder, Kasam

Durga (Nirupa Roy) goes to criminal kingpin Vikram (Amjad Khan) with her newborn fraternal twins Amit and Kishan. Though he is the father of the boys, Vikram has washed his hands of Durga and wants nothing to do with the children, coldly suggesting that they be taken to an orphanage instead. Bereft, Durga hits the streets, where Jaggi (Kader Khan), posing as a good samaritan, offers to take her to a shelter. That shelter turns out to be a brothel and, when the police raid it, Jaggi grabs little Amit as a hostage and escapes. Soon thereafter, he sells Amit to an indigent and thief named Pascal (Jeevan), who ends up raising him.

Amit (Amitabh Bachchan), under Pascal's tutelage, grows up to be an alcoholic street hustler. Vikram, unaware that he is his son, encounters him one day while the young man is soliciting funds for the construction of a temple to the goddess Durga. Impressed by Amit, he mentally files away his name for future reference. Meanwhile, unaware that he is his brother, Amit befriends police inspector Kishan (Shashi Kapoor), who is still living at home with their mother. Unaware that he is her son, Durga nonetheless treats Amit as one. When Kishan meets a beautiful medical student named Anu (Parveen Babi), Durga recruits Amit to pressure him into marrying her. One thing that is required is for Anu's sister, Basanti (Rekha), to come and give her blessings to the union. However, Basanti is ashamed to see Anu for fear that she will discover that Basanti is working as a dancer in a brothel. Little known to all is the fact that that brothel is the one in which Amit grew up and that Amit has been romancing Basanti for some time.

Meanwhile, Kishan's policeman uncle, Inspector Khan, is murdered by the underworld and, upon learning of this, Kishan vows revenge against those responsible. Kishan's crusade soon comes to the attention of Vikram, who hires Amit to kill him. Amit immediately tells Kishan and the two concoct a scheme to stage a fake assassination during the festival of Navrati. In the event, Vikram sees through the ruse and, in an ensuing fight, permanently blinds Kishan by smashing a chandelier over his head. The sightless Kishan then presses his superiors to let Amit take his place on the police force. After quitting the booze with Basanti's help, Amit takes to this new calling with zeal, staging enthusiastic one man raids on the warehouses of both Vikram and Jaggi, with whom Vikram has forged a tense alliance.

In the course of fleeing one of these raids, Vikram comes upon the lonely Durga and appeals to her sympathies. As a result, their little family is reinstated and Vikram learns that Kishan is his son. Kishan's blindness prevents him from seeing that his father is the one who blinded him, yet he continues to keep tabs on Vikram once he has moved back into the house. By this means he learns of an arrangement between Vikram and Jaggi by which each keeps incriminating evidence against the other—in the case of Vikram, a photograph of him shooting Kishan's uncle—locked in a safe with two keys. When Vikram hires Amit's surrogate "father" Pascal to kidnap Jaggi's son Gopal (Ranjeet), all leads to a warehouse confrontation and a sudden epidemic of everybody realizing everybody's connection to everybody.

***SUHAAG*'S PLOT IS SO DEPENDENT** upon coincidence and hidden family ties that, if you dig deep enough, you could even find that you yourself are related to one or more of its characters. For his last masala film of the '70s, Manmohan Desai dusted off the old "lost and found" formula with predictably fulsome results. So many subplots abound that even poor Rekha gets wrapped up in a wrongful murder accusation that pops up during the final act to be resolved as quickly as it has inexplicably arisen.

Having featured the successful Bachchan/Khanna pairing in his last film, *Parvarish*, Desai here goes with the time tested Bachchan/Kapoor cocktail. And, to be honest, Bachchan's Amit—a street wise con man who is alternately brooding and clownish but overall lovable—is nothing we haven't seen before. However, Kapoor's Kishan, being a bit of a show boat (when we meet him, he's wearing a pimpin' head-to-toe black leather ensemble) has a tad more of an edge than his usual virtuous lawman, which is welcome. We even get what may be a parody of the famous motorcycle duet between Bachchan and Dharmendra in *Sholay*, as the Big B and Kapoor celebrate their friendship in song while the blind Kapoor pilots the motorcycle they're both riding on a perilously haphazard course.

Arrayed against our heroes is a generously spread layer of scum consisting of Amjad Khan—here somewhat absurdly domesticated during the third act (think of the sitcom possibilities!)—a leering Jeevan, a rapey

Ranjeet, and prolific actor and dialogue writer Kader Khan as Jaggi. Their combined performances, alongside the film's unglamorous portrayal of the seamier side of Bombay's underworld, provide the film with a darker than usual cast that contrasts with some of its goofier elements, such as the wire-assisted silliness of some of its fight scenes.

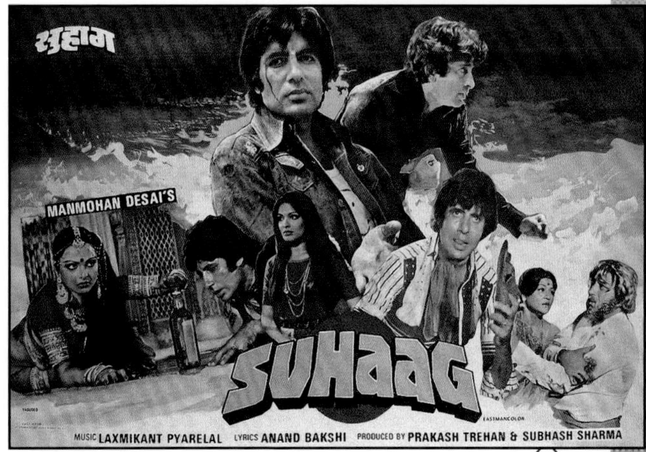

But, of course, between its violent prologue and denouement, what *Suhaag* has on its mind first and foremost is romance. This provides the context for "Main to Beghar Hoon," in my opinion one of the great drunk numbers of all time, which takes place after Kapoor's Kishan ushers Parveen Babi's Anu out of a disco where she has just unwittingly smoked a joint (to the accompaniment of Boney M's "Daddy Cool"). The song's visualization benefits greatly from the miracle of rear projection, as Babi slithers perilously about the exterior of Kishan's moving car while cooing "I'm homeless. Take me to your house." Naturally, it is from this seed that love blossoms.

Suhaag's plot is so dependent upon coincidence and hidden family ties that, if you dig deep enough, you could even find that you yourself are related to one or more of its characters.

During its final act, *Suhaag* takes a pretty hard line on filial loyalty, as Amit, now aware that Vikram is his father, must take pains to save him from a time bomb despite the fact that he has jilted his mother, blinded his brother and repeatedly tried to kill him. In fact, it is at his mother's insistence that he does this. Granted, this manifests itself as Amitabh Bachchan hanging off of an airborne helicopter's skids while wearing a yellow smiley face tee-shirt, so it's hard to be too grim faced about it. Yet it does stress the lost and found film's emphasis on family over all, whereby the family's integrity asserts itself against all obstacles as a natural form of order that cannot remain asunder for too long... even when the center of that family is a craven, murdering bum.

SHAAN
"Valor"

Released: 1980
Director: Ramesh Sippy
Stars: Amitabh Bachchan, Shashi Kapoor, Sunil Dutt, Shatrughan Sinha, Rakhee Gulzar, Parveen Babi, Bindiya Goswami, Johnny Walker, Padmini Kapila, Kulbhushan Kharbanda, Mazhar Khan, Helen, Bindu, Sujit Kumar, Manik Irani, Goga Kapoor, Viju Khote, Katy Mirza, Mac Mohan, Sudhir Pandey, Yunus Parvez, Sharat Saxena, Mohan Sherry, Sudhir, Dalip Tahil
Writers: Salim-Javed (Salim Khan & Javed Akhtar)
Music: Rahul Dev Burman (R.D. Burman)
Lyrics: Anand Bakshi
Fights: Mohammed Ali, Gerry Crampton

Model policeman Shiv Kumar (Sunil Dutt) transfers to Bombay, where he is embarrassed by the antics of his brothers, Vijay (Amitabh Bachchan) and Ravi (Shashi Kapoor), a pair of ne'er-do-wells and full time con artists. He immediately sets to interfering with the operations of the powerful black marketer Shakal, who runs his criminal enterprises from an island base 300 miles off the coast of India. Shakal does not fail to notice Shiv Kumar's efforts and makes eliminating him a top priority.

Soon thereafter, a circus marksman named Rakesh (Shatrughan Sinha), whose wife has been kidnapped by Shakal in order to insure his compliance, makes a couple of attempts to shoot Shiv, but misses both times. Meanwhile, Vijay and Ravi meet their match in Renu (Bindiya Goswami), who manages to bilk them out of 30,000 Rs. for a stolen car that they themselves end up being arrested for stealing. Once Vijay and Ravi have teamed up with Renu and her Uncle Chacha (Johnny Walker), Vijay meets his match in Sunita (Parveen Babi), a nightclub singer who supplements her income with thievery.

Eventually Shakal succeeds in kidnapping Shiv and bringing him back to his island. Shiv manages to escape momentarily, but Shakal hunts him down in his helicopter and fatally shoots him. Somehow his body ends up back in Bombay, where Vijay and Ravi swear vengeance upon his killers. Rakesh then approaches them, confessing to the attempts on Shiv's life while assuring them that he missed on purpose. He also tells them that, because of his failures to kill Shiv, Shakal murdered his wife. The three begin to work together to divine the whereabouts of Shakal's hideout.

A series of attempts are then made on the lives of Vijay, Ravi and Rakesh by Shakal's goons, all of which they narrowly escape. In a particularly brutal scene, the gang even murders Vijay and Ravi's crippled street informant Abdul (Mazhar Khan). Eventually Shakal's gunsel Jagmohan (Mac Mohan), angry over an alleged betrayal by Shakal, steps forward and offers his assistance in getting them to the island. Vijay, Ravi, Rakesh, Renu, Sunita and Chacha infiltrate the island disguised as a musical troupe which also includes Helen. Shakal, however, having laid a trap for them, is not fooled by their ruse, and soon has Vijay wrestling a crocodile in his private tank while Ravi and Rakesh fight a couple of gas mask-wearing goons in a cloud of poisonous smoke.

After a protracted battle within the booby trapped corridors of Shakal's high tech submarine lair, the group finally gets the upper hand on the villain. Some debate over the ethics of shooting him outright takes place. Fortunately, Shakal tries to escape, allowing them to blow him away with impunity.

SHAAN IS A FILM that seems very aware of its status as an "event" picture. It is, after all, Ramesh Sippy's long awaited follow up to his phenomenally popular *Sholay* and, as such, was expected to reap box office rewards nearly as rich as its predecessor (though, in reality, that would take much longer than expected). Its air of moment begins with its opening credits, which closely mimic those of Guy Hamilton's *Goldfinger.* After all, what, in 1980, was more synonymous with spectacle than the James Bond films?

Unlike a James Bond film, however, *Shaan* then takes the customary hour before its plot startles into motion. Not to fear, though, because Sippy spices up that hour with a profusion of flashy business. Indeed, *Shaan* is quite a technically sophisticated piece of work for a Bollywood picture of its time, utilizing numerous helicopter and green screen shots, some wild car chases and not a few bone crunching fights. The special effects were handled by westerner John Gant, whose other credits include *The Spy Who Loved Me*, *Lifeforce*, and *The Neverending Story*, while Englishman Gerry Crampton—who worked on *Raiders of the Lost Ark* and *A View to a Kill*—contributed to the stunt choreography. Then there are the sizeable and expensive looking sets for Shakal's lavish, push button operated underwater lair, complete with crocodile pit and all manner of retractable machine guns and gas hoses, which, in the best Bond tradition—and, by the way: SPOILERS—are dutifully turned to rubble during the last few minutes.

Also something of a special effect is *Shaan's* top heavy cast, fronted by a formidable quartet of heavy hitters in its male leads. Amitabh Bachchan and Shashi Kapoor are brothers in harmony, rather than at odds, this time, capitalizing on an easy chemistry forged over the course of starring in eleven films together. Shatrughan Sinha—who reportedly asked to be paid extra to star opposite Bachchan, whom he disliked—ironically brings a very Bachchan-like mixture of soulfulness and anger to his role, while Sunil Dutt, in the somewhat thankless role of the upright cop who "always puts the law first," manages to ooze charisma notwithstanding. As for Bindiya Goswami, who plays Renu, while she gives a fine performance, her resemblance to Hema Malini can be a bit distracting—especially if one knows that she was hired to replace

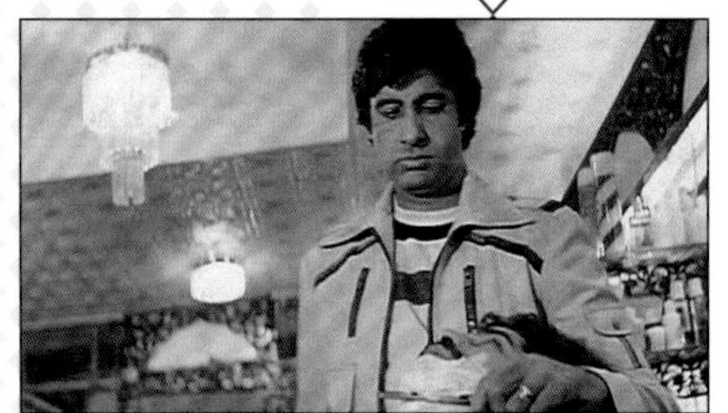

Malini, who, along with Dharmendra, also originally cast in the film, walked off the set after a dispute with the director.

Despite the absence of Dharmendra and Malini, *Shaan* additionally benefits from the work of former *Sholay* alumni in the form of screenwriters Salim-Javed. The pair's script is typically tight and coherent, even while shoehorning in a few non-plot driven sequences that seem to be there only to provide the excuse for another car chase, fistfight, or explosion. (Also, because Bollywood enjoys promoting, alongside the message that romantic love rules over all, the message that men and women fundamentally hate each other, we have to have scenes of Bachchan, Babi, Kapoor and Goswami all subjecting one another to pointless emotional torture.) Unfortunately, while the basic plot for *Shaan* is fairly generic—much as *Sholay*'s could be argued to be—the scribes fail to infuse it with the same level of heart as found in that previous film. Perhaps this is due to their being too many characters to focus on. Nonetheless, *Shaan* is one of the most seamless delivery systems for audacious thrills ever devised by Bollywood, something that its writers, I'm sure, deserve no small amount of credit for.

In many ways, *Shaan* could be seen as a transitional film, an entryway into the more glitzy action pictures of the '80s. Kulbhushan Kharbanda's Shakal, for one, is a clear precursor of Mogambo, Amrish Puri's iconic supervillain from 1988's uproariously successful *Mr. India*. Even though his visual model was obviously Donald Pleasence's portrayal of the bald pated Bond nemesis Blofeld, his throne-like perch, flashy paramilitary outfits—at times reminiscent of a drum majorette's—and frequent, purring, self aggrandizing proclamations cast the mold for Mogambo perfectly. Black Marketers are frequently presented as enemies in Indian cinema, though, if you're like me, you associate that trade with "Prado" bags and bootlegged DVDs. What you don't picture are palatial underwater lairs ridden with shiny sci-fi gadgets. Shakal seems to have somehow worked that back alley trade to the point where he now has a helpless world clasped firmly within his talon-like grasp.

In similar fashion, R.D. Burman, changing with the times as always, gives us a score that's heavy on the disco—with a special debt to Donna Summer's "I Feel Love"—while incorporating lots of squelchy synth blasts to remind us, as so many things in 1980 tried to, that we're in the future now. "Janu Meri Jaan," a traditional sounding song that's juiced up with some percolating electronic interludes, offers up a pleasing example of this approach at its most effective.

I don't want to hammer too much on the fact that *Shaan* is no *Sholay*, because, in the long run, it doesn't matter. Though it didn't manage to measure up to that earlier film's box office success, it has no less managed to attract a loyal cult following in the years since. And if you watch it, you'll see why; it's a wildly entertaining picture. It's also a very slick one by Bollywood standards, though one that still manages to attain camp appeal via the over-the-top performances of Kharbanda and others. Yes, it is kind of dumb, but since when could it be only American pictures that required you to "check your brain at the door"?

SPOTLIGHT ON:

Spies!

IT'S ALMOST IMPOSSIBLE TO OVERSTATE the influence of the James Bond movies upon world popular cinema during the 1960s and '70s. Such was the case that it seemed no nation could feel itself a legitimate player on the world stage without its own answer to 007. Thus we had such globe spanning spymasters as Tony Falcon, the Filipino James Bond; Jeffri Zain, the Singaporean James Bond; Golden Boy, the Turkish James Bond; and, of course, a host of enthusiastic contenders from Italy. In the face of such a cinematic gold rush, certainly no one could expect Bollywood to sit on its hands. Director Ravikant Nagaich was the first to score mainstream spy movie success with his 1967 espionage thriller *Farz*, which paved the way for Ramanand Sagar's well received *Ankhen* the following year. Meanwhile, India's B movie industry went Bond crazy with scrappy titles like *Golden Eyes: Secret Agent 077*, *Spy in Rome* and *Lady James Bond*. Corresponding with this was the sudden prevalence of Bondian trappings—lavish villain lairs, gadgets, exotic femme fatales—in more generalized types of action films and thrillers. 1970s Bollywood's increased emphasis on violence, amoral heroes, and flashy urban style created a cozy environment for the spy film to germinate and thrive on into the next decade, with a few spicy examples to follow.

GUNMASTER G-9: SURAKKSHA

Released: 1979
Director: Ravikant Nagaich
Stars: Mithun Chakraborty, Ranjeeta Kaur, Jeevan, Jagdeep, Iftekhar, Aruna Irani, Prema Narayan, Tej Sapru, K. Balaji, Mala Jaggi, Bhushan Jeevan, Suresh Oberoi
Writers: Ramesh Pant, Ravjansh, Farooq
Music: Bappi Lahiri
Lyrics: Ramesh Pant, Farooq
Fights: Raghavalu

CBI agent Jackson (Tej Sapru) is abducted by a criminal organization called SSO, who believe that he is the key to the whereabouts of a coveted diamond mine. Soon after his disappearance, a crate containing Jackson's corpse is delivered to his family. One of the CBI's top agents, Gopi, codenamed Gunmaster G-9 (Mithun Chakraborty), is assigned to the case.

Jackson's trail soon leads G-9 and his assistant Kabari (Jagdeep) to Goa, where G-9 meets and falls for the beautiful Priya (Ranjeeta Kaur). Also in Goa, G-9 exhumes Jackson's body, only to find that it is that of a surgically altered impostor. He then tracks down the surgeon responsible, Dr. Verma, who is killed before G-9 can meet with him. Verma turns out to be the father of Priya, necessitating some tactful explanation on G-9's part.

Back in Bombay, G-9 is almost killed by a water snake hidden beneath a room service serving dome. He traces the origin of the snake to a company called Serpentile, which is run by two upper level SSO agents, Hiralal (Jeevan) and Neelam (Mala Jaggi). After overpowering several goons, G-9 is directed by Serpentile's receptionist to an address she claims is Jackson's. Arriving there, G-9 is immediately captured by Neelam, only to be rescued by Priya, who subdues the femme fatale after a protracted cat fight (which G-9 watches with manifest enjoyment). Injected with a truth serum, Neelam points them to the "Play Boy Club," where G-9 finds the captive Jackson, paralyzed by means of constant electrocution.

After thwarting several attempts by Hiralal and Neelam to do away with them, G-9 and Jackson resolve to hunt down the diamond mine that is at the center of all the trouble. This path ultimately leads them to the underwater lair of the eye patch wearing Dr. Shiva (K. Balaji), the leader of SSO. Dr. Shiva has created an artificial sun with which he can control the tides and cause devastating tsunamis, a device which he plans to sell to the highest bidding nation. G-9 may be able to put a stop to this evil scheme, but first must have his martial arts skills tested in a series of brutal death matches, as well as face off against an electric zombie called Jango.

DIRECTOR RAVIKANT NAGAICH, as mentioned before, was no stranger to the spy game, having directed one of India's first mainstream spy thrillers, *Farz*, in 1967. It is doubtful, however, that he had ever directed a spy thriller as cheap as *Surakksha*. In fact, one of the most entertaining things about watching *Surakksha* is witnessing all of the methods Nagaich uses to cut budgetary corners. Unfortunately, one of those methods is lots of jagged, rapid fire editing, which, while distracting us from flimsy sets and spectacular stunts that are only vaguely implied, also renders much of the action incomprehensible.

Happily, Nagaich also falls back on his love of crude special effects to keep the purse strings tight. This involves, wherever possible, the use of miniatures that often look as if they came out of a gumball machine. A shark pit is represented using the kind of plastic sharks you get in the Sea World gift shop, which are manipulated with strings to jump hungrily from the water like carnivorous dolphins.

Car crashes are simply a matter of setting a couple of Hot Wheels cars on fire. The resulting placement of *Surakksha*'s action within a sort of cockeyed toyland gives the film overall the feeling of a five and dime version of *Thunderbirds*—although, instead of puppets, we get a very live action version of the young Mithun Chakraborty as a flared and denim clad lady killer.

Chakraborty, a new and somewhat unknown quantity at the time, would gain considerable notoriety with *Surakksha*, setting him on the path to becoming, with 1982's *Disco Dancer*, one of the biggest stars of the '80s. Interestingly, Chakraborty's putative skills as a dancer necessitated that the film contain even more than the usual amount of song and dance, making it truly the first musical James Bond film.

For, indeed, many of Surakksha's key action set pieces are lifted of a piece from the Bond canon, from the poolside opening scene of *Goldfinger* to the funeral from *Live and Let Die*. But, interspersed with these are any number of sequences featuring our super agent hero frolicking on the beach with an assortment of beauties, each trading musical assessments of the other's charms (sample lyric "Gunmaster! I love you! You're mine!"). A minor plot point is even resolved by having Mithun take part in a qawwali competition during the climax.

I generally don't subscribe to that whole "so bad it's good" formulation. If a movie has entertained you, it's done its job. If you then need to call it "bad," that's likely your own shame-based film snobbery talking. Still, I must admit that *Surakksha*'s most entertaining moments tend to be its least well executed ones. In its favor, though, its primary defense against these failings is an almost celebratory disregard for logic, one that can be quite liberating if taken in the right spirit. In any case, such flaws didn't prevent it from becoming a huge hit, paving the way for a 1981 sequel, *Wardaat*, in which our hero faced off against mutant locusts.

CHARAS

Released: 1976
Director: Ramanand Sagar
Stars: Dharmendra, Hema Malini, Ajit, Amjad Khan, Aruna Irani, Asrani, Keshto Mukherjee, Sujit Kumar, P. Jairaj, D.K. Sapru, Sajjan, Sailesh Kumar, Madhumati, Manju, Kuljeet, Birbal, Viju Khote, Subhash, Shahid Bijnori, Amarjeet, Seema, Tom Alter, Hercules, Nasir Hussain, Manmohan Krishna, Agha, Sunder
Writers: Ramanand Sagar, Ved Rahi, Moti Sagar, Akhtar Hussain
Music: Laxmikant-Pyarelal (Laxmikant Shantaram Kudalkar & Pyarelal Ramprasad Sharma)
Lyrics: Anand Bakshi
Fights: Jaswant Singh

The business of Brinddaban (Nasir Hussain) has brought him—along with his son Suraj (Dharmendra) and daughter Munni (Aruna Irani)—to Uganda, but now unrest in that country is forcing his family's return to Mother India. Back in India, this news is received with trepidation by Brinddaban's business associate, Kalicharan (Ajit), largely due to the fact that, in Brinddaban's absence, Kalicharan has sold all of the company's assets for the purpose of investing in his own opium smuggling operation. Not eager to have this treachery come to light, Kalicharan dispatches his enforcer Robert (Amjad Khan) to Uganda to assassinate Brinddaban and his children. This Robert accomplishes by first shooting Brinddaban and then setting the family mansion ablaze with Suraj and Munni inside. Suraj, however, manages to escape, but loses sight of Munni and, as a result, assumes that she has perished.

What Suraj doesn't know is that Munni has survived the blaze, only to be captured by Robert, who has taken her back to his psychedelic, undersea-themed nightclub in Malta. Here the hoodlum keeps the young girl strung out on dope while forcing her to perform drunken item numbers for the club's white hippie patrons. Meanwhile, Suraj has made his way back to India and learned of Kalicharan's skullduggery, leading to much righteous hurling of oaths and pointing of fingers on his part. He is soon thereafter contacted by Interpol, who want Suraj to come on board as an agent in their efforts to smash, not just Kalicharan, but all of the scum-sucking drug runners who are tarnishing India's name.

Also being tarnished is the name of "famous actress" Sudha (Hema Malini), whom Kalicharan is blackmailing with a combination of bogus incriminating photographs and threats against her family. In return, Sudha is reluctantly helping him smuggle opium into Europe by concealing packets of the stuff in her dance troupe's traveling sets. Eventually a combination of investigative effort and pure dumb luck brings Suraj into contact with Sudha, and the two begin a tenuously chaste love affair—each remaining ignorant all the while of the other's connection to Kalicharan.

C*HARAS* IS THE KIND OF MOVIE where everyone has a brightly colored communications console covered with superfluous flashing lights in their office, all the better to speak to a variety of people who are using secret transmitters disguised as everything from shoes to watermelons. It also, in keeping with its obvious Bondian aspirations, boasts some pretty impressive production values—especially in comparison to some of Dharmendra's earlier and more noticeably chintzy action joints from the '70s (perhaps the result of a post-*Sholay* boost in Dharam's popularity?) There are multiple vehicular chases, shot on location in both India and Malta, and, rather than simply stealing the footage of a car being airlifted by a helicopter from *You Only Live Twice*—as 1973's *Jugnu* did so shamelessly—*Charas* actually recreates it, using both a real helicopter and what looks to be a real car.

And then, of course, there are the lairs. And, yes, I am talking in the plural—because, as this movie tells it, life for the Indian opium smuggler circa 1976 is very good indeed. After being forced to flee from his hideout beneath the aforementioned undersea-themed nightclub, Kalicharan simply switches residence to a super-lair housed beneath a castle on a private island off the coast of Malta. Most of what we see of this is a cavernous indoor set of a subterranean dock with room for a number of launches and speedboats—not to mention a catwalk and system of balconies from which Kalicharan's uniformed minions can fire upon the invading forces of the law before picturesquely plummeting to their doom. Given the genre we're discussing here, I don't think it's much of a spoiler to say that it blows up real good.

As for more human scale attractions, *Charas* offers us the chemistry between Dharmendra and Hema Malini, who had become a couple in real life not all that long before. Of course—as films like *Gigli*, *Eyes Wide Shut* and *Shanghai Surprise* have shown us—such real world unions don't necessarily translate into heat on screen. Nonetheless, *Charas*, for an Indian film, gets downright racy in the extent to which it makes palpable just how much these two want to jump each other's bones. Malini's Sudha is determined to behave like a proper Indian woman despite having to share close quarters with Suraj, but she is not above letting us know just how difficult that is. When Suraj asks if she is avoiding being alone with him because she is afraid of him, she replies, "I am afraid of myself."

Charas also gives us a striking example of the Indian "lost and found" film's vision of the familial bond and its inherent, indomitable strength. When the siblings Suraj and Munni are finally reunited, only to be captured soon thereafter by Robert and his men, the two are forced to make their escape while chained at the wrist. Rather than being hindered by their bonds, though, the two find that they are able to use them as weapons against their captors, whipping and garroting the stooges with an almost celebratory zeal as they run. It's at once an enjoyably over-the-top stunt sequence that makes good use of stars Dharmendra and Aruna Irani's particular talents in that regard, and a stern warning to any goon who would be so foolhardy as to try to drive a wedge between any two members of such a staunch Indian family.

Slick, loud, and colorful, *Charas* is perhaps not as soulful as other masala pictures of its day, but it is nonetheless generous in spirit. Perhaps most emblematic of this spirit is its inclusion of both Ajit and Amjad Khan in what amounts to a thrilling double dip of virtuosic villainy. Khan in particular shines, thanks in part to an amplification of grotesquery that's accomplished via an oatmeal-y facial appliance and a seeming vat load of pomade. He's also granted the film's best line, when, in response to Dharmendra's warnings of karmic retribution, he says, "I have never seen a man die because he committed crime." Then, sticking his rifle in Dharam's face, "I have seen him die after being shot!"

Charas may not be everyone's drug of choice, but those with a taste for old fashioned thrills and bold stroke comic book trappings should find that it delivers a powerful buzz.

AGENT VINOD

Released: 1977
Director: Deepak Bahry
Stars: Mahendra Sandhu, Asha Sachdev, Iftekhar, Jagdeep, Pinchoo Kapoor, Nasir Hussain, Ravindra Kapoor, K.N. Singh, V. Gopal, Viju Khote, Sunder, Master Bhagwan, Jayshree T., Birbal, Vishwa Mehra, Rajan Kapoor, Sharat Saxena, Shail Chaturvedi, Kamaldeep, Brajendra Mohan, Darshan, Ranvir Raj, Master Romi, Helen, Sheetal, Leena Das, Julie, Asha Potdar, Mona, Shobhna Shah, Geeta Khanna, Rehana Sultan
Writers: Girish, Khalid Narvi
Music: Vijay Patil, Raam (Raam Laxman)
Lyrics: Ravindra Rawal
"Thrills & Car Chase": Veeru Devgan

Agent Zarina (Rehana Sultan) is caught photographing a gang who are responsible for a series of bombings. The gang gives chase, but Zarina manages to hide the film within a hotel phone before they capture her. Later, the same gang, each of whom has a distinctive scorpion brand on his or her thumb, kidnaps the noted professor Ashok Saxena (Nasir Hussain) in hopes of wresting from him a much coveted "formula." Swinging secret agent Vinod (Mahendra Sandhu) is put on the case.

One of Vinod's first orders of business is a rendezvous with Zarina, who has been replaced with an impostor who informs the gang of Vinod's involvement in the case. The first order of the gang, per their ruthless leader Madanlal (Iftekhar), then becomes to eliminate Vinod by whatever means necessary. While evading these near constant murder attempts, Vinod encounters Chandu (Jagdeep), a hapless wannabe who tells everyone that he's James Bond. Chandu soon gets mistaken for Vinod and gets enmeshed in the web of dancer and gang moll Lovelina (Helen). Ultimately he escapes by climbing out on a ledge and hitching a ride on a passing bouquet of helium balloons. After a long flight, he ends up in a gypsy camp, where the gypsies take him in as one of their own.

Vinod also finds himself stalked by a mysterious woman who turns out to be Prof. Saxena's daughter Anju (Asha Sachdev). After ironing out all confusions of identity between them, the two fall in love. One day, while out driving, they are chased by Madanlal's goons and crash. The two eventually make their way to the gypsy camp where Chandu touched down. The gypsies shield them until the goons arrive at the camp and start threatening children, at which point Anju gives herself up. The gang takes her back to their island lair to use her as leverage against her father. To insure maximum trauma, she is stripped in front of him.

At the same time, the Scorpions decide to get rid of the captive Zarina by flooding her cell with water. Instead, she swims up the drainpipe and sneaks back into the compound, where she attempts to flee with Prof. Saxena on a motorcycle. Madanlal catches up to her and fatally shoots her. Soon thereafter, Vinod, Chandu, and some of Chandu's gypsy friends arrive on the island by boat. After stumbling upon Zarina's body, Vinod has a confrontation with Madanlal and shoots him dead. The group then sneaks into the compound disguised as goons, where Vinod comes face to face with the true leader of the gang, his own uncle John (Pinchoo Kapoor).

WHILE IT'S ARGUABLY TRUE that one must master a form before they can successfully satirize it, *Agent Vinod* suffers from a slightly different problem: it wants to be at once a spoof and the thing itself. Agent Vinod, the character, is a guy in a white suit who casually breaks the fourth wall, kills with a snide bon mot, and not only calls all women "baby," but also slaps them around when it suits him. *Agent Vinod*, the movie, is one that features Jagdeep wearing a funny hat and hitching rides on party balloons accompanied by whacky sound effects and people's glasses spontaneously riding up on their heads (weeooop!). Do you get what I'm saying?

Without all the slapstick shenanigans, *Agent Vinod* would be just an average Indian Bond-alike, though an entertaining one overall. Director Deepak Bahry keeps the film's action at a constant peak, sparing no number of hapless fruit carts in the several automobile chases that transpire and giving our hero no shortage of exotic weapons to

kill people with while making jokes. In terms of production value, it's no *Cleopatra*, but it's also nowhere near as impoverished as the later *Gunmaster G-9* films.

Like Gunmaster G-9, Vinod (played by *Khoon Khoon* star Mahendra Sandhu) receives an all singing introduction in which he is surrounded by a gaggle of adoring babes. But no matter how swoon-worthy he may be, Sandhu lacks the teen idol appeal of the young Mithun Chakraborty. Agent Vinod himself, in fact, lacks much to admire in general, especially when contrasted against Rehana Sultan's Agent Zarina. Zarina is both courageous and admirable and, as such, is afforded a very honorable death, complete with a tear stained soliloquy at death's threshold. (Indeed, if K.S.R. Doss had directed the film, she might have been the main character.) Vinod, meanwhile, does not seem to be making much progress on the case that's not dependent on coincidence and instead seems to view his job as being solely about throwing attitude. In this way, *Agent Vinod* makes the same mistake that any number of Italian Eurospy films did during the '60s: thinking that their heroes could simply appropriate all of James Bond's smirk and swagger without the ineffable gravitas of a Sean Connery to back it up.

While vacillating between violence and tomfoolery, *Agent Vinod* takes pains to provide all of the reckless stunts, death traps, and exploding lairs that one expects from the genre. Chacha John's submarine island digs are no slouch in the art design department, featuring among its accoutrements a giant toy robot with which Zarina pummels a minion at one point. All of these elements, of course, corny and thrilling alike, were part of a stew that Indian audiences of the time were well accustomed to and should, to some extent, be judged from that perspective. In any case, they didn't prevent *Agent Vinod* from becoming a respectable hit—one that is today remembered to the extent that an update of it, starring Saif Ali Khan, was produced in 2012.

KEEMAT "The Price"

Released: 1973
Director: Ravikant Nagaich (as Ravi Nagaich)
Stars: Dharmendra, Rekha, Ranjeet, Prem Chopra, Rajendra Nath, Agha, Satyendra Kapoor, Murad, Murad Puranik, V.D. Puranik, J.N. Anand, Prem Kumar, Kirti Kumar, Subhash, Arjun Kumar, Suhail, Shabnam, Indira Bansal, Halam, Kamal, Munni, Rani, Jayshree T., Padma Khanna, K.N. Singh, Jayadev, Maruti Rao
Writers: Vishwamitter Adil, Ram
Music: Laxmikant-Pyarelal (Laxmikant Shantaram Kudalkar & Pyarelal Ramprasad Sharma)
Lyrics: Anand Bakshi
Stunts: Raghavulu (in Madras), Azeem (in Bombay)

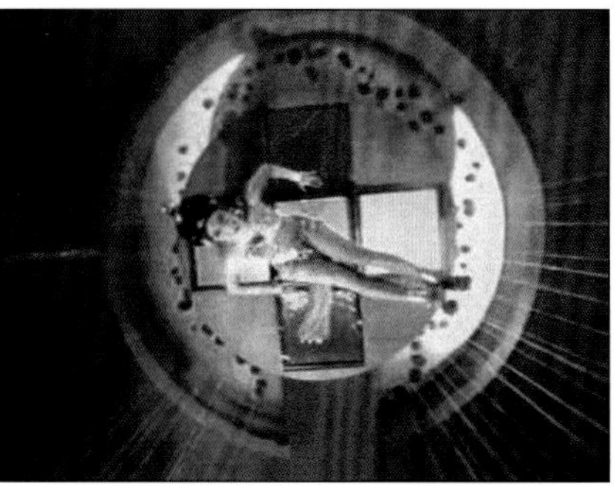

Young women are disappearing from India's villages and disadvantaged urban areas, lured from their meager circumstances by promises of fame and fortune, never to be seen again. In one instance, we see a sharply dressed slickster named Pedro (Ranjeet) pick a girl up and take her to a hippie bar, where he feeds her a sugar cube presumably laced with acid. Soon the inhibited lass is on stage singing lustily with the band of dirty hippies and dancing lasciviously. Pedro snaps pictures of the performance, which he later uses to pressure the mortified girl into going along with his demands. Later she is seen despondently being shuttled with a dozen or so other girls to a dock, where they all board a ferry to destinations unknown.

This situation having reached epidemic proportions, the head of the Secret Service (K.N. Singh) interrupts one of his top agents, Gopal, Agent 116 (Dharmendra), in the middle of a hot date to report for duty. Meanwhile, CBI Inspector Deshpande (Satyendra Kapoor) and his men are making inroads of their own into the investigation, and manage to intercept the aforementioned ferry in transit, only to find it empty once they board. Gopal makes a diving expedition at the site of the discovery, whereupon he finds the weighted bodies of the girls who had been onboard floating on the ocean floor, an eerie forest of corpses.

The investigation next reveals that a bar girl going by the name of Maria very closely matches the description of one of the missing girls, whose real name is Nanda (Padma Khanna). Gopal arranges a meeting with her at a restaurant and, as they dine, notices a lone woman at a nearby table spying on them. When he steps away momentarily, the woman comes over to the table and angrily confronts Nanda about her masquerade. This is Sudha (Rekha), Nanda's sister. When he later takes Nanda back to her place, Gopal confronts her about her real identity. But just as she is launching into a teary confession, Pedro's men arrive and violently cart her away, leaving Gopal to fight for his life against two chain wielding goons.

In the wake of Nanda's abduction, Sudha makes herself a fixture in Gopal's life and, after a series of attempts on the part of Pedro and his hideously scarred gunsels to rub Gopal out, determines that the only way to get to the bottom of things is to pose as a mark for the gang and let herself be captured. This leads to her eventually being herded onto that fateful ferry, which Gopal follows to a mysterious island far offshore where, this being a Ravikant Nagaich film, things start to get really twisted. Rekha and the other captives initially find themselves in a militarized prison camp staffed by butch female guards, but are later shuttled, via a long submarine tunnel, to a lavish lair deep beneath the island.

At that lair, we meet the real boss of the organization, a sadistic madman by the name of Shaktimaan (Prem Chopra), who amuses himself by trying to goad girls into attempting escape so that he can set his vicious dogs upon them. We also see that an auction is about to get under way, at which visiting decadents from a variety of non-South-Asian countries—Saudi Arabia, Hong Kong, Africa, Europe, "Mr. Johnny from America"—are going to bid for the pleasure of owning one or more of the captured girls.

The auction ultimately involves the women being forced to display themselves in a musical pageant that is part Las Vegas and part Miss Universe, and concludes dramatically with Shaktimaan outing Gopal, who is in attendance disguised as an Arab Sheikh. Gopal is forced into a fight to the death with a frothing, Island of Doctor Moreau style beast-man wheeled out in a cage. Then Shakti-maan lets Gopal and Sudha loose in the island's jungle interior, giving them a sixty second head start before following with his dogs and armed soldiers. But with only Gopal's superhuman wits and agility to depend upon, will our hero and heroine survive?

IN 1967, RAVIKANT NAGAICH, the director of *Keemat*, directed *Farz*. One year later, its star, Dharmendra, headlined *Ankhen*. Both were among the first A list Bollywood films to capitalize on the James Bond craze, and audiences of the time were appropriately wowed by their combination of (relatively) fast paced action, pan-Asian locales, and sophisticated gadgetry.

By the time of *Keemat*'s release in 1973, the novelty of such films had probably worn off somewhat, but *Keemat* takes advantage of the era's looser standards with racier content. Gone are the foreign terrorists of those previous films, replaced by the threat of sex trafficking, which is handled with as much good old exploitation movie verve as propriety would allow. The final "island of captive women" portion of the film includes every classic Women in Prison trope but the shower scene. There's the butch warden who gets inappropriately handsy with her charges (the sequence where she angrily tears at Rekha's blouse must have been particularly shocking) and, when Rekha's Sudha attempts to stage a breakout, she does so with a Dolls Squad of lady prisoners dressed in tiny pink negligees.

Interestingly, Nagaich intended *Keemat* as a sequel to *Farz*, despite the fact that, when it came to casting, he ended up with Dharmendra, *Ankhen*'s Agent Sunil, playing the role—that of Gopal, Agent 116—played in the original by Jeetendra. Of course, *Ankhen* was a career making turn for Dharmendra, the break of a wave that he was still riding high at the time of *Keemat*'s production, while Jeetendra was a lesser yet nonetheless still viable star. The switch could also be due to Jeetendra being more of a leading man in the 1960s mold, more suited to romances and musicals, while Dharmendra more fit the mold of the two-fisted man of action increasingly required by the 1970s more violent fare, of which *Keemat* is a fairly blunt exemplar.

None of this is to suggest, of course, that the characters of either Agent Sunil or Agent Gopal were so well developed that Dharmendra might be inappropriate for the part. Still, it must be said that *Keemat* suffers from the portrayal of the then-thirty-eight-year-old Dharmendra as an overgrown boy that filmmakers of the time seemed so inextricably enamored of. Gopal is churlish with his superiors and, at times, unaccountably tongue tied with the stock spy movie vixens that he encounters. In addition, every new witness or informant he interviews is a new opportunity for the film to introduce a different comedic bumpkin or stooge, all of whom Gopal feels very comfortable telling to shut up or otherwise berating. I guess this is what was perceived as needed to make such an unpolished character seem suave and Connery-esque by comparison.

Other elements of *Keemat*'s casting are spot on. We get a rare opportunity to see the flamboyant Ranjeet explicitly cast as a pimp, which allows him, for a change, to blend in with the film's milieu, rather than appear like someone who has dropped down from another sartorial planet. Prem Chopra's Shaktimaan is a ravening maniac and, if you're familiar with that actor's work at all, I don't need to tell you just how pleasurable it is to watch him cut loose. Rekha, for her part, plays a character that moves through a lot of personas in the course of the film, yet manages to not surrender to either stock women-in-peril hysterics or preposterous kung fu girl voguing. Lastly, if *Keemat* needs a comic relief supporting character—and it seems sorely inevitable that it does—it's a lucky thing that it's Rajendra Nath, who has a warmth that many such players from the era were lacking, as well as little of their desperation and shrillness.

Aside from some somewhat jarring violence and grotesquerie, *Keemat* boasts that rote, generic quality that makes all Indian spy films at once so entertaining and unremarkable. We know that it is going to hit all the right beats, from the exotic henchman to the exploding lair. In between, director Nagaich spices things up with his familiar brand of thrifty movie magic; smallish or incomplete sets are rendered lavish through the use of glass mattes and models, we get some nifty animated gun sight wipes, and there is an ambitious miniature sequence in which a jeep tries to outrace a raging flood in a subterranean tunnel.

Composers Laxmikant-Pyarelal keep things lively, including toe tapping item numbers for both Jayshree T. and Padma Khanna, as well as an adorable "drunk" song for Rekha—"Bol Bol Darwaaza"—whose character we're meant to believe is so innocent that she could drink an entire tumbler of gin mistaking it for water. (My take away from this is that, when visiting India, the motto should be "DO drink the water.") In short, the film is an enjoyable time waster, but probably won't serve well those aspiring secret agents who are looking for practical tips.

The final, "island of captive women" portion of the film includes every classic Women in Prison trope but the shower scene.

JAMES BOND 777

Released: 1971
Director: K.S.R. Doss
Stars: Ghattamaneni Krishna (Superstar Krishna), Jyothi Laxmi, Vijaya Lalitha
Music: Sathyam

***James Bond 777*'s Superstar Krishna, in all his monumentally quaffed 1970s glory.**

A prowler breaks into Commander Rao's house in order to steal a briefcase, stabbing the Commander's wife to death when she tries to intervene. Rao himself then comes home and is also murdered. These shocking events are witnessed by Rao's young son Kishore, who tries to stop the prowler but fails. Years later, Kishore has grown up to be the quick shooting CBI agent known as James Bond 777 (that's Superstar Krishna to you).

Meanwhile, policewoman Sopa (Vijaya Lalitha) comes home to find her own father murdered by the forces of world evil. This event aligns Sopa and Kishore in a battle against an international criminal mastermind known as "Boss," who has a high tech hideout aboard an ocean bound cruise ship. Boss has many resources at hand to aid his plot for world destabilization and domination, among them a retinue of robotic goons in referee shirts and Panama hats and a trio of friendly looking dogs he has trained to act as bank robbers and hit men.

Boss also has a pair of formidable femme fatales at his disposal. One of these is Cindy, who seems to spend a great deal of her time berating her minions, calling them "bloody fools" and the like. The other is Jamilla (Jyothi Laxmi), who operates from a secret lair hidden beneath a "beauty paralour." Jamilla also has a twin sister (Laxmi again) who is less evil than she is. Yes, they will fight.

LEAVE IT TO K.S.R. DOSS to turn a simple James Bond knockoff into not only a family revenge drama in the traditional Telegu vein, but also a cowboy picture. When we first meet Superstar Krishna's Kishore, he is dressed in classic Tollywood cowpoke attire—much like his character in Doss's *Mosagallaku Mosagaadu*—happily gunning down banditos on the range. Then a coterie of army brass in a jeep shows up and hips him to his next assignment. Along with his trademark, disconcertingly kabuki-like make-up, Krishna is sporting his usual towering pompadour. But there is a new and bigger pompadour in town, and that belongs to "Boss." Needless to say, the presence of two hairstyles of such equally monolithic proportions necessitates a battle to the death.

As I've mentioned before, discussing Doss's films tends to tax the vocabulary. I choose to see this less as a matter of sameness than one of reliability—in that you can pretty much rely on them to be the same. *James Bond 777*, for instance, features the usual onslaught of cartoonish, under-cranked action, big hair, twangy guitar music, and voyeuristic dance numbers. Yet the requirements of genre also add the bonus of lots of ultra-low-budget approximations of Bondian gadgetry and high tech accoutrements. For a pulp film fan like myself, this is an unadulterated win.

James Bond 777 also offers such Dossian strokes of genius as the happy looking dogs that it's suggested are tearing innocents limb from limb off screen and the idea of hot and cold running Jyothi Laxmis. The catfight that the typically ferocious Laxmi has with herself during the final act is a career highpoint for both director and star. Doss also provides another welcome showcase for his *Rani Mera Naam* star, the birdlike berserker Vijaya Lalitha, who here demonstrates Hong Kong action cinema's influence upon Telegu filmmaking with a pole fight right out of one of Ti Lung's Shaw Brothers movies.

It is one of the great tragedies of home entertainment that Doss's films are not more widely available. Those that have seen commercial release are on VCDs in atrocious transfers that lack subtitles of any kind. The rest, like *James Bond 777*, when they can be found at all, are fragmented and in horrible disrepair (and also lack subtitles). Clearly, Doss is an artist ripe for cult appreciation. All that's missing is the access.

BREAKDOWN:
K9 Assassins Strike!

CLOSE-UP ON:

Curry Westerns!

DURING THE 1960S AND '70S, Mumbai's movie theaters were a crossroads for world popular cinema. One could see not only the latest hits from Bollywood, but also everything from Hong Kong martial arts sagas to the various products of the prolific Italian film industry. Among these latter were the Spaghetti Westerns, those uniquely Italian riffs on the territory of Ford and Hawks that revitalized the cowboy film in the eyes of a new young audience. International hits like Sergio Leone's *A Fistful of Dollars, The Good, the Bad and the Ugly* and Sergio Corbucci's *Django* had a worldwide cultural impact, so it's perhaps not that surprising that they made their way into the stew of influences drawn upon by Indian filmmakers at the time. In fact, their cynical and hard bitten tone made them especially in tune with the "angry" Bollywood of the 1970s, leading to the production of what have come to be known as the "curry westerns" (or, in some cases, "basmati westerns"). Often borrowing liberally from the films that inspired them, these movies nonetheless could never be characterized as mere copies; their inescapable Indian-ness makes them unique. Some examples follow.

KHOTTE SIKKAY "Fake Coins"

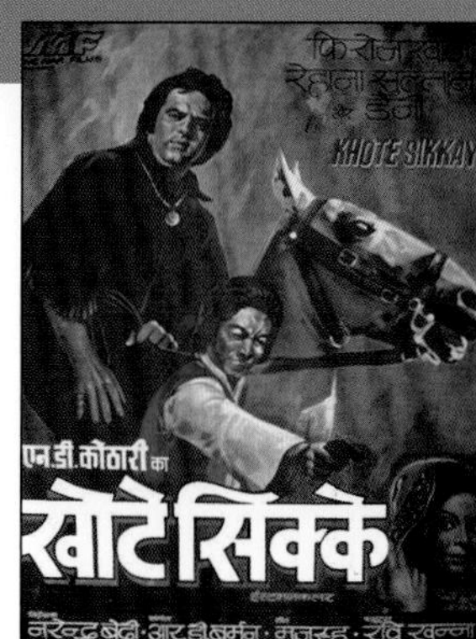

Released: 1974
Director: Narendra Bedi
Stars: Feroz Khan, Danny Denzongpa, Ajit, Alka, Madhu Chanda, Alankar Joshi, Kamal Kapoor, Satyendra Kapoor, Leela Mishra, Narendra Nath, Ranjeet, Paintal, Sudhir, Bhushan Tiwari, Murad, Rehana Sultan, Johnny Whisky, Kanwar Ajit Singh, Ajit Singh Deol
Writers: Narendra Bedi, Satish Bhatnagar
Music: Rahul Dev Burman (R.D. Burman)
Lyrics: Majrooh Sultanpuri
Action Director: Ravi Khanna

The timid yet essentially decent population of a small village is terrorized by the bandit Jhanga (Ajit), an especially nasty example of his kind whose preferred method of cancelling his victims is by disemboweling them hara-kiri style with a sickle-like blade. When his father is killed by the bandit, young Ramu (Paintal) flees to the city to ask the help of his uncle Jaggu (Narenda Nath), a small-time gang leader. Jaggu agrees to help, and asks five of his friends from the local underworld to join him. Among these are Danny (Danny Denzongpa); Salim, a liquor smuggler (played by Ranjeet, who throughout the movie wears a distinctive muscle shirt with a heart-shaped window cut in the chest); and Bhaghu, a scheming womanizer (Sudhir). The task of defending the humble village and teaching its residents how to defend themselves

awakens in these hard cases a sense of purpose and belonging heretofore unknown to them, and they ultimately decide to make the village their home. Of course, before they can really settle down, there's the small matter of settling Jhanga's hash, which, of course, means a series of increasingly violent confrontations with the bandit and his bloodthirsty, heavily armed gang. Eventually joining this magnificent five is a mysterious, black clad rider (Feroz Khan), who has a score of his own to settle against Jhanga, who many years before murdered his father.

KHOTTE SIKKAY, like its follow-up *Kaala Sona* (which also starred Feroz Khan and Danny Denzongpa), is a classic example of the Curry Western, one that, in this case, combines the story of the *Magnificent Seven* with plot elements, scenes and actual music from Sergio Leone's *For a Few Dollars More* to create its own distinctly Indian take on the Spaghetti Western. Though I imagine that some might dismiss such a film for being a slavish imitation of a superior Western product, those people really wouldn't have been paying attention, because the adoption of such familiar genre elements only highlights the markedly different approach that a film like *Khotte Sikkay* takes to the themes typically addressed by its Italian forebears.

Unlike the Spaghetti Western, which raised the archetype of the rootless, self-sufficient loner to the level of fetish object, the Indian take on the genre has a far more sociable agenda. Because, while the Italian oaters typically sought to depict a frontier that was as barren of decency and brotherly human feeling as it was of modern comforts, the Curry Western presents the raw land and the community that grows around its cultivation as a source of virtue, redemption and spiritual sustenance. This is not too surprising, given that, while the Spaghetti Western was a retooling of the Western geared toward the more cynical sensibilities of a late sixties/early seventies urban audience, Bollywood at the time of *Khotte Sikkay* still depended to a great extent on India's vast rural population for its viewership. To illustrate the difference, compare a film like *Sholay* or *Khotte Sikkay* to, say, *Django, Kill!*, one of a number of Spaghetti Westerns that depicts a community driven to depravity by its isolation from civilization—no doubt the manifestation of an urbanite's worst nightmare.

Despite being imbued with such communal spirit, however, *Khotte Sikkay* is far from cuddly in its presentation, and true to its inclusion of the perpetually two-fisted Feroz Khan in its lead role, falls squarely on the more exploitative end of 1970s Bollywood action cinema. In fact, the film has more rough edges even than the decidedly pulpy *Kaala Sona*. This is exemplified by the gritty, obviously on-the-fly (notice the watching crowds on the periphery) location shot scenes in the streets and back alleys of the city that make up the first part of the film. As in *Sholay* and *Kaala Sona*, *Khotte Sikkay*'s heroes are modern day urban ne'er-do-wells, making a hardscrabble living by whatever illicit means is at hand, who find themselves changed by their experience of protecting a tight-knit rural community from a malevolent outside force.

Khan here plays a role that is essentially an amalgamation of the Clint Eastwood and Lee Van Cleef characters from *For a Few Dollars More*: a black-clad Man With No Name looking to settle a score with the villain for a murder committed many years before (in *Dollars* the victim was Van Cleef's sister; here it's Khan's father). The very significant musical pocket watch from *Dollars* also makes an appearance in this context, as does the climactic duel in which it plays such an integral part. Original to Khan's character, however, is the self-appointed guardian angel role he takes in relation to the nautch girl Rani (Rehana Sultan), who was orphaned as a result of Jhanga's murderousness. Of course, since the Sergio Leone *Dollar* films weren't too big on either romance or female characters—both things that no Bollywood masala could stay afloat without—it's expected that *Khotte Sikkay* would make corrections in this regard.

Though the heroes' spiritual regeneration through honest labor and communal participation is the central arc of *Khotte Sikkay*, the beneficial exchange of values doesn't just go in one direction. The relatively progressive values of the city boys are a definite boon to the widowed Madhu (Madhu Chanda), who, in keeping with some especially conservative aspects of Hindu tradition, is cruelly ostracized by the village community until Jaggu and his friends plead on her behalf. Of course, the fact that Jaggu has fallen in love with Madhu probably has more to do with this than any nascent feminist leanings on the guys' parts, since they don't exhibit any such liberal attitudes when it comes to Rani's de facto second class status. Denzongpa's Danny, in particular, is all for keeping things status quo as far as the ladies are concerned, a stance exemplified in a cringe inducing "he hit me and it felt like a kiss" exchange between him and his girlfriend Reeta (Alka) that takes place early in the film.

Watching *Khotte Sikkay*, I couldn't help being struck by its similarities to *Sholay*, which was released just one year later. Of course, most of those similarities are the result of what each film borrowed from a commonly available source—namely, the Sergio Leone Spaghetti Westerns, but not all of them. For instance, the tentative courtship between Jaggu and the widow Madhu bears a distinct resemblance to that between Amitabh Bachchan's Jai and Jaya Bhaduri's widowed character Radha in the latter film. Still, the unusually long and much publicized time that *Sholay* spent in production suggests that, if there was any borrowing between the two, it was probably on the part of *Khotte Sikkay*. Just as likely is the possibility that these were just ideas that were in the air at the time. In any case, while *Khotte Sikkay* is a strong entertainer, it lacks the epic scope or iconic characters that would make it any kind of threat to *Sholay*'s awesome legacy.

The version of *Khotte Sikkay* that I saw was abnormally compact for a Bollywood film of its era, clocking in at just over two hours. The score by R.D. Burman was equally abbreviated, consisting of only two songs—though one of them was repeated *three times* over the course of the movie. Whether this was an edited version or not, the brevity served the film well. Like the other Feroz Khan actioners I've seen, it's the type of movie that's best served up fast and funky, and would risk overstaying its welcome otherwise. While I didn't enjoy it quite as much as its follow-up *Kaala Sona*—mainly because that later film contained some phantasmagorical elements that gave it an added WTF appeal—I would highly recommend *Khotte Sikkay* as an entertaining example of a fascinating Bollywood sub-genre.

MOSAGALLAKU MOSAGAADU "Cheat of Cheats"

Released: 1971
Director: K.S.R. Doss
Stars: Ghattamaneni Krishna (Superstar Krishna), Vijaya Nirmala, Jyothi Laxmi, Gummadi Venkateswara Rao, Mukkamala, Dhulipala, Nagabhushanam, Kaikala Satyanarayana, M. Prabhakar Reddy, Rao Gopal Rao, Nagesh
Writer: Arudra
Music: P. Adinarayana Rao
Lyrics: Arudra-Appalacharya

The mythical kingdom of Amaravedu is invaded and taken over by the British. Before this can take place, however, two of the kingdom's loyal sons, Daanaala and Pagadaala, spirit its vast treasure away and secure it in a cave hiding place that can only be accessed with five special keys. Another loyal son of Amaravedu is Prasad (Superstar Krishna), whose disgust with the corruption that thrives under British rule spurs him to leave the kingdom and style himself as a Robin Hood-like defender of the poor and oppressed. Prasad has a racket going with the wanted criminal Nakkajittula Naagana (Naga Bhushanam), whom he repeatedly turns in for reward money and then saves at the moment of execution.

Ultimately, Prasad becomes one of a number of people aware of the existence of the treasure and sets out to find it. Arrayed against him in this endeavor is an assortment of villains that includes Bijili (Jyothi Laxmi), a mean cowgirl who takes an unwelcome shine to Prasad. Prasad's romantic interests instead lie with Radha (recent Mrs. Superstar Krishna, Vijaya Nirmala), the vengeful daughter of Daanala, who has since been killed by Sathyam (Kaikala Satyanarayana), one of the treasure seekers. Bijili repeatedly tries to get Radha out of the way and finally, with the help of Nakkajittula—with whom Prasad has had a falling out—tries to do away with Prasad himself.

Finally Prasad learns from Radha that the much coveted keys were last left in the hands of one Constable Komarayya, Prasad's own father. Prasad rushes home, only to find his mother and father dying as a result of an attack by a quintet of treasure hunters who have since made off with the keys. Prasad must then take a break from his treasure seeking to exact bloody vengeance against each of the killers. Meanwhile, Bijili has learned of the location of the stash and, along with the other miscreants, is closing in on it. All leads to a wild confrontation between all parties in the cave where the treasure is hidden.

IN A 2007 INTERVIEW with the website telegucinema.com, Telegu director K.S.R. Doss made the claim that his *Mosagallaku Mosagaadu* (dubbed into Hindi as *Gun Fighter Johnny*) was India's first cowboy film. And who am I to disagree? It certainly predates the country's most well known example of the genre, 1975's *Sholay*, as well as earlier Bollywood oaters like the Feroz Khan starrers *Khotte Sikkay* and *Kaala Sona*. Though I think it has to be said that there are some older films in the less well respected and documented stunt genre that could arguably be described at least in part as being cowboy films—even though my saying so is more of an act of compulsive nerdery than anything else.

In that same interview, Doss emphatically denied that *Mosagallaku Mosagaadu* was a remake of *The Good, the Bad and the Ugly*. And while that denial is true in spirit, it's nonetheless impossible to miss the signs of *Ugly*'s influence on *Mosagallaku*—especially given that the latter takes great pains to recreate several of the key scenes from the former. These include, memorably, Clint Eastwood's forced march through the desert at the hands of Eli Wallach—although here Doss uses that scenario as an opportunity to have Jyothi Laxmi and Nagabhushanam perform a jaunty musical number, during which they dance around and mock Krishna, the film's hero, as he dies of heat exposure. The vertigo-inducing overlap of sensibilities that this particular bit embodies makes for a surreal cinematic moment unique even in Doss's singular oeuvre.

Those familiar with Indian cinema's often freewheeling approach to period won't be surprised to learn that *Mosagallaku Mosagaadu*'s is a bit hard to nail down. Its opening narration places its plastic-Stetson-wearing, gun-slinging, Wild West action somewhat preposterously around the time of the Battle of Bobbili—in other words, sometime near the middle of the 1700s. Chances are that the writers were simply trying to capture some of the aura of heroism projected by that pivotal event in the history of the state of Andhra Pradesh—as well as find an excuse to use all of the stock footage we see of the French storming the fortress walls that obviously came from another, much better funded movie.

For the most part, *Mosagallaku* chronicles the assorted double-crosses and skullduggery—not to mention the many, many fistfights—which the race between all parties to find the treasure entails. Yet, at a later point, when one of the subsets of mustache and pompadour sporting no-goods manages to murder both of Prasad's parents, the film is temporarily transformed, for a good portion of its final third, into a bloody revenge thriller *a la*… well *a la* pretty much every other one of K.S.R. Doss's films. Though this episodes ends with Prasad retrieving all five of the needed keys, it's still digressive enough to feel like another movie nested within the larger one. Perhaps this was due to the filmmakers feeling that a South Indian action film featuring Tollywood's Amitabh, Superstar Krishna (hence the name), absent those revenge elements would be too outside the norm for their audience to relate to. But, whatever the case, it affords us the opportunity to see the righteous and true hearted Prasad gorily chopping people with axes, beating them to death with branches, and totally going postal on a bunch of angry tribals who are this film's stand-ins for "renegade" native Americans.

While *Mosagallaku Mosagaadu* delivers in spades on all of the trashy thrills that I've come to expect from K.S.R. Doss's films, I have to say that its primary visual attraction is its wardrobe. Krishna's ever-changing assortment of monochromatic cowboy outfits—ranging from powder blue to deep purple to olive green—are really something to behold. I imagine that the free-spirited female retiree from Florida for whom they were obviously designed would describe them as "fun" and wear them on her holidays (while her husband wore the white pants with pictures of classic cars printed all over them). Clearly, being a thief with a conscience such as Prasad requires a lot of things, but the element of surprise isn't one of them.

PISTOLWALI

Released: 1972
Director: K.S.R. Doss
Stars: Jyothi Laxmi, Ramakrishna, Satyanarayana Kaikala, Prabhakar Reddy, Ramdas, Tyagraj, Balakrishna, Vijayashri, Dhanasri, Surya Prabha, Helen, Jayshree T.
Writers: Mohan Kaul, Raj Joshi
Music: Sathyam
Lyrics: Mohan Kaul
Fights: K.S. Madhavan

Pistolwali *is the Hindi dubbed version of K.S.R. Doss's Telegu film* Pilla Pidugu. *I'm going to skip the usual synopsis here because, to be honest, I have yet to find a subtitled version of it. Still, the film deserves inclusion for being a distillation of so much that is noteworthy about Doss's work as a director, especially in regards to that work he did with his muse, kung fu cowgirl Jyothi Laxmi. In other words, Pistolwali is two solid hours of rapid fire chasing, leaping, hitting, falling and shooting.*

Here Laxmi plays Neelu, a devoted and pious daughter on one hand and, on the other, a staunch defender of her town against the many, many bloodthirsty bandits who have made it their home. This means that we get to see Laxmi switch on a dime from being a coy village belle in one moment to throwing down like a luchadore in another. Neelu seems to find a kindred spirit in vigilante cowboy Amar (Ramakrishna), but their courtship, true to formula, is a prickly one, as there is much work to be done in the area of bandit thrashing.

This is especially true once one of the gangs steals a golden crown from an idol of Vishnu that stands in a local shrine. Neelu, using her individual brand of Wild West martial arts, cuts a bloody swath through the gang until the crown is finally retrieved. The bandits then up the ante considerably by killing Neelu's old Mom, at which point she is on the vengeance trail. Not even wild tigers can stop her, as seen when she is thrown into a pit with one and handily wrestles it to its death. Eventually she shoots, chops, punches and high kicks her way through every level of the gang, finally confronting the dreaded Raaka (Satyanarayana Kaikala). And it is at the moment of her final victory that a shocking revelation about her true parentage is made (cue lightning strike).

***PISTOLWALI* MANAGES** to be extraordinarily bloody and rough edged without really being what you would call gritty. This is largely due to the hyper realist, comic book backdrop which Doss creates for it all to play out against. No amount of under-cranked camera work, apparently, could be over-used toward the end of speeding up the numerous fights and chase scenes, nor the use of fisheye lenses to accent the grotesquerie of a villain's face or send bodies hurling toward the audience. And then there are the outfits. This last is best exemplified by Laxmi, who, throughout the film, is kitted out like a psychedelic Annie Oakley—perhaps her most striking adornment being a purple fringed vest made out of shiny plastic. The action in the film is often correspondingly wacky. At one point the villains, rather than simply stealing a woman from her bed, instead hitch her bed up to their horses and drag it and her out of her home and across the prairie, her screaming in protest throughout while still tucked snugly into her bedclothes. The actors contribute to this general state of over-ness by mugging and gesticulating to a degree seldom seen since the silent era.

Although she is given last billing in the Hindi version—as "South Bomb Shell Jyothi Laxmi"—Laxmi is clearly the star of *Pistolwali.* As such, the film provides her with an impressive showcase. Far from what Hollywood has trained us to think of as a classic beauty, Laxmi nonetheless has an undeniable sexual presence. Our introduction to her, in which she does a hip-thrusting hoochie coochie while splashing around in a revealing—by Indian cinema standards—swimsuit, is not one to soon be discarded from memory. This is an actress who is an ultra-curvy example of 100% pure womanhood—generous proportions that not only make her a welcome sight, but also lend a considerable amount of credibility to those scenes in which she is seen lustily hurling her male opponents about like so many pompadoured ragdolls.

In many ways, Laxmi's Pistolwali is a descendant of the whip wielding lady avenger Hunterwali, a character made popular onscreen by Fearless Nadia in 1935. Born Mary Anne Evans, the Australian born Nadia was a circus performer who rose to considerable fame during the '30s and '40s as the star of a long series of Indian "stunt pictures," *Hunterwali* being the one that's since become most embedded in South Asian pop culture. A female performer who partook in such roughneck acts of daredevilry as Nadia did had not previously been seen in Indian cinema, and it can certainly be said that she paved the way for other woman action stars that followed after her. No one in the modern era, however, seemed to pick up that gauntlet with quite the enthusiasm of Telegu actresses like Laxmi and *Rani Mera Naam*'s Vijaya Lalitha. Laxmi would even star in a Telegu version of *Hunterwali* in 1972.

Of course, Doss and Laxmi are not the only ones who make *Pistolwali* the crackling entertainment that it is. The film also gains added spark from the work of music director Sathyam, who composed a wistful, Spaghetti Western style theme for Laxmi that's all the more stirring when it acts as a prelude to her stomping someone into a quivering pulp. Sathyam also provides the backing for three upbeat item numbers: one for Helen, who wears transfixing clear blue contact lenses; one for Jayshree T.; and one tribal themed number for Laxmi herself. Doss films these dance sequences in his typical style, sending his camera into places that Bollywood cameramen might as a rule shy away from, often nestling it in the crotches of the actors as if it was mounted on the head of an over-friendly dog.

Overall, *Pistolwali* is Doss at his most Doss-ian: an injection of pure cinema that gives us bodies in constant, violent motion against a backdrop exploding with color and excess. True, watching it without translation makes it difficult to parse the finer details of its plot, but it is far from a wasted effort. However he may be dubbed, Doss speaks a language that any fan of extreme pulp cinema can understand.

KAALA SONA "Black Gold"

Released: 1975
Director: Ravikant Nagaich
Stars: Feroz Khan, Parveen Babi, Prem Chopra, Danny Denzongpa, Farida Jalal, Imtiaz Khan, Helen, Durga Khote, Keshto Mukherjee, Bipin Gupta, Polson, Abhijeet, Shyam, Gurinder, Mamaji, Agha, Master Raju, Sabina, Habib, Raj Pal, K.N. Singh, P. Jairaj, Satyendra Kapoor, Krishnakant, Karan Dewan, Master Bhagwan, Maruti, Birbal, Seema Kapoor, Narendra Nath
Writers: Harish Khatri, Ramesh Pant, V.D. Puranik
Music: Rahul Dev Burman (R.D. Burman)
Lyrics: Majrooh Sultanpuri
Fights: Ravi Khanna

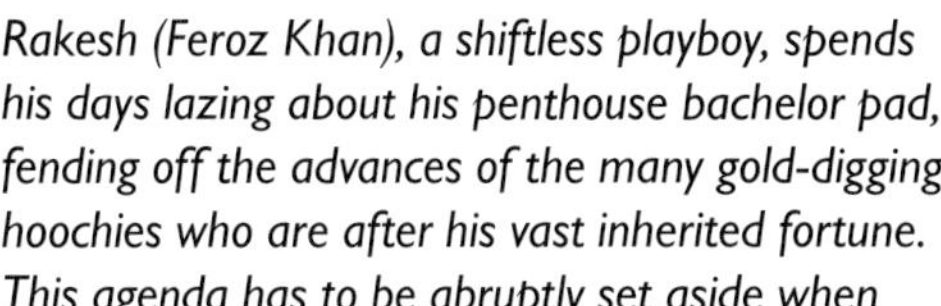

Rakesh (Feroz Khan), a shiftless playboy, spends his days lazing about his penthouse bachelor pad, fending off the advances of the many gold-digging hoochies who are after his vast inherited fortune. This agenda has to be abruptly set aside when a telegram arrives from an old family servant, summoning Rakesh to his death bed. Rakesh makes haste to the servant's side, at which point the servant breaks the news that Rakesh's father, a land developer long thought to have died in an

accident, was actually murdered by the notorious bandit Poppy Singh. Furthermore, Poppy Singh, long thought to have died himself, is actually alive and well and hiding out in the mountainous northern region of Himachal Pradesh.

Without time for so much as a training montage, Rakesh, now displaying formidable skills at both gunplay and horseback riding, storms his way into the lush Kangra Valley, which he soon finds is completely in the stranglehold of Poppy Singh. Only the estate of the kindly Thakur Ratansingh (Bipin Gupta) appears to offer any kind of oasis of relative calm—until Rakesh discovers that the Thakur and his family, too, have reluctantly come under the bandit's sway. Poppy's gang has kidnapped the Thakur's young son (Master Raju) and, in order to ensure his safety, the Thakur's eldest daughter, Durga (Parveen Babi), has been forced to assist in smuggling the opium produced by the gang out of the region. That opium is harvested and refined—using the local residents as slave labor—within Poppy Singh's virtually impenetrable compound, located high in the mountains across a yawning, un-bridged ravine.

Rakesh soon meets up with a vigilante band dedicated to defeating Poppy Singh, their leader a strapping young buck named Shera (Danny Denzongpa). Shera and Rakesh become fast friends and, after pairing off with the Thakur's daughters—Rakesh with Durga and Shera with her younger sister Bela (Farida Jalal)—decide to take on the treacherous task of raiding Poppy Singh's compound. When they do, they find a surreal world ruled over by Poppy (Prem Chopra), a freaky monomaniac with a goatee, skullcap, one disconcerting milky eye, and a personal strongman in studded bondage gear. Naturally, Singh will make a much harder time for our heroes getting out of his lair than they had getting in.

I'VE WRITTEN BEFORE about how Bollywood films often have a tendency to turn into entirely different movies somewhere around their second half. *Kaala Sona* is a shining example of this—though in this case more due to director Ravikant Nagaich's fanciful approach to art direction than any specific plot development. With Rakesh's entry into Poppy Singh's compound, *Kaala Sona* abruptly goes from being a hardboiled Western to something more akin to one of those surreal old Russian fantasy films. The largely location-shot natural exteriors of the first half give way to a candy-hued sound stage artificiality, including a limitless expanse of poppy fields that appear to have been imagined by someone whose only experience of poppy fields was from watching *The Wizard of Oz*. This "we've got some crude matte paintings and we're going to use them" visual approach carries through until the film's final action set piece, which takes place on an extraordinarily phony looking ice shelf with flappy cloth icicles hanging from it. Of course, far from hurting *Kaala Sona*, this trippy turn of events simply serves to make it overall a far more memorable —and awesome—viewing experience than it probably would have been otherwise.

Equally vertigo inducing is the character arc that our hero, Rakesh, traces within only the first ten minutes of the film. Within an edit he goes from being a foppish ne'er-do-well to a formidable gunslinger, ready to provide a lead inner lining to any scoundrel who crosses his path. Of course, that Rakesh is more convincing as a rugged man of action than as an effete member of the leisure class is not all that surprising, given that he is played by Feroz Khan. Khan, in addition to being its star, was also the director of the sublimely over-the-top *Qurbani* and, while *Kaala Sona* doesn't go quite as far, it has a similar feeling of raw pulp vitality and absurdly over-heated machismo. It doesn't stray too far from the normal Bollywood conventions—and all of the exuberant trappings that they entail—but it clearly has a violent B movie heart beating within it, which makes for a pretty entertaining—and, at times hallucinatory—combination.

Like *Sholay*, which came out within just two weeks of it, *Kaala Sona* is a Western in feel rather than period, setting its action in the present day while taking advantage of some of the still relatively untamed regions lying within India's borders. Such an approach allows both films to highlight a favorite Bollywood theme: the urbanized ne'er-do-well who, in being called upon to defend a rural community from a destructive outside force, has his soul awakened to the simple and essential virtues embodied by that community. (In more recent films, that urbanized ne'er-do-well tends to be, more specifically, a Westernized product of the Diaspora, but same idea.) Representing the "close to the land" locals is Danny Denzongpa, whose exotic features the filmmakers take advantage of in casting him as the Tonto to Khan's Lone Ranger. This provides for much scenes of bare chested male bonding between the two, as well as double the normal amount of courting ballads once they couple off with the Thakur's comely daughters.

Kaala Sona features music by R.D. Burman, which makes for a lot of catchy and propulsive tunes, as well as some very enjoyable production numbers. Probably the best of these is the one set to the psychedelic-tinged "Ek Bar Jaane Jaana," in which Parveen Babi appears before a bunch of drunken louts—Keshto Mukherjee among them, of course—as a gyrating apparition and splits, thanks to some simple yet effective opticals, into multiples to form a hazy chorus line of one. But the climactic number, which pairs Babi with the always welcome Helen for some frenzied hoofing, is also a visual treat. In addition to its songs, the film boasts an instrumental score complete with some amusing Bollywood flavored stabs at Morricone-style western themes, trilling, non-verbal vocalizations and all.

Add in Prem Chopra's whacked-out turn as Poppy Singh—who appears intended to be some kind of mad Chinese warlord—and *Kaala Sona* ends up being a cheerily intoxicating ride. There's just something about the combination of the Western genre's Spartan, rough-hewn aesthetic with Bollywood's tendency toward the exuberant and phantasmagorical that's hard to resist. If you want to travel down the curry western rabbit hole, *Kaala Sona*—pulpy and compact, yet unburdened by *Sholay*'s accumulated baggage of expectations—is as good a place as any to start.

SHOLAY "Embers"

Released: 1975
Director: Ramesh Sippy
Stars: Dharmendra, Sanjeev Kumar, Hema Malini, Amitabh Bachchan, Jaya Bhaduri, Amjad Khan, A.K. Hangal, Satyendra Kapoor, Iftekhar, Leela Mishra, Vikas Anand, Mac Mohan, Keshto Mukherjee, Sachin, Alankar Joshi, Viju Khote, Major Anand, Bihari, Bhagwan Sinha, Arvind Joshi, Baby Bhanumati, Mushtaq Merchant, Mansaram, Mamaji, Jerry, Birbal, Raj Kishore, Habib, Rajan Kapoor, Darshan, Maula, Kedar, Saigal, D. Jyothi, Rajeshwari, Krishna, Vinni, Girija, Surendra, Rajesh, Asrani, Gita Siddharth, Helen, P. Jairaj, Jagdeep, Jalal Agha, Om Shivpuri, Sharad Kumar
Writers: Salim-Javed (Salim Khan & Javed Akhtar)
Music: Rahul Dev Burman (R.D. Burman)
Lyrics: Anand Bakshi
Stunts: Mohammed Ali, Gerry Crampton

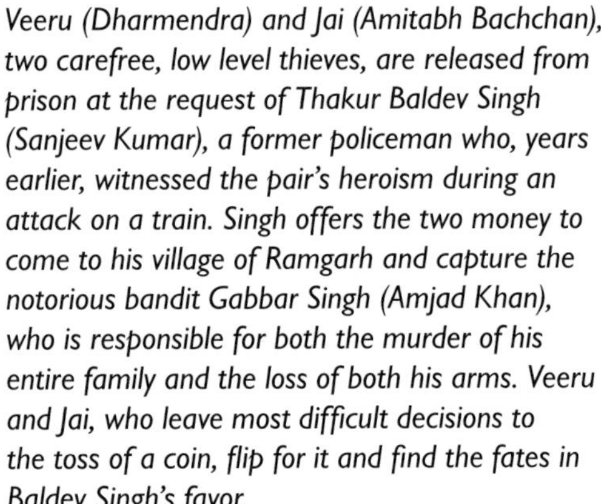

Veeru (Dharmendra) and Jai (Amitabh Bachchan), two carefree, low level thieves, are released from prison at the request of Thakur Baldev Singh (Sanjeev Kumar), a former policeman who, years earlier, witnessed the pair's heroism during an attack on a train. Singh offers the two money to come to his village of Ramgarh and capture the notorious bandit Gabbar Singh (Amjad Khan), who is responsible for both the murder of his entire family and the loss of both his arms. Veeru and Jai, who leave most difficult decisions to the toss of a coin, flip for it and find the fates in Baldev Singh's favor.

Upon Veeru and Jai's arrival in Ramgarh, the Thakur is emboldened to refuse Gabbar Singh's men the provisions which they've become accustomed to extorting from his farms. Gabbar Singh responds by having his men attack the village during festival season, but Veeru and Jai manage to drive them off. The bandit then continues to terrorize the timid villagers in a campaign of murder and intimidation, demanding that they turn Veeru and Jai over to him. As a result, tensions begin to erupt between Baldev Singh and the pacifist farmers, who feel that his insistence on maintaining dignity and honor is endangering their lives. Veeru and Jai, meanwhile, find themselves enchanted by certain of the village's women folk: in Veeru's case, Basanti (Hema Malini), a chatty carriage driver, and, in Jai's, the Thakur's widowed daughter-in-law Radha (Jaya Badhuri). All the while, they find their urbanized hearts warming to life in the small rural town, as do the villagers to their presence.

During a proposed rendezvous with Veeru, Basanti is chased down and captured by Gabbar Singh's men. Veeru gives pursuit, but is himself captured. Gabbar Singh then forces Basanti to dance for his men under threat of Veeru's execution. Jai arrives just in time to rescue them and a gun battle ensues. Soon they run out of bullets and, after a coin toss, Veeru is selected to head back to the village with Basanti for more. Veeru returns to find Jai mortally wounded, in his pocket a trick coin which he used to fool Veeru into going in his stead. Jai watches his friend die in his arms, then heads off after Gabbar Singh, almost forgetting his promise to deliver the bandit to Baldev Singh alive.

***SHOLAY* SPENT TWO AND A HALF** years in production, an unheard of amount of time in the breakneck world of Bollywood. The thing is, that extra time spent really makes a difference on screen. Whatever else you may have heard about it, *Sholay*, which was the first Indian film shot in widescreen, is gorgeous to look at, cinematographer Dwarka Divecha's fluid camera constantly craning and swerving to enfold us within its picturesque wide open spaces. That prolonged period of gestation also gives *Sholay* a sense of overall refinement that sets it apart from most other Indian action films of its day.

Sholay's story is not a particularly complex one, nor is it all that original. But what is refreshing in director Ramesh Sippy's approach to it is how he uses Bollywood's expansive mode of storytelling—in a film that clocks over three hours—not to pile on narrative details, but to let that story breathe, to give it space and the odd contemplative moment amid all of the gunfights, chases and tomfoolery. For example, a pair of bookend scenes set at twilight, in which the hauntingly silent Radha snuffs out the lanterns on her balcony one by one as, in the courtyard below, Jai plays a mournful melody on his harmonica, are among the most subtly romantic in Bollywood cinema, incorporating a hush and stillness that seldom would have room for air in a typical masala film.

Sholay's performances, as well, show the results of being honed and refined and, as such, offer a blueprint for a decade of typecasting to come. As the taciturn Jai, Amitabh Bachchan turns what could have been a simple sidekick role into a star turn, cementing his superstar status in the wake of *Deewaar*'s conquering the box office. Dharmendra, on the other hand, plays the clown to Amitabh's long suffering straight man, turning his courtship of the motor-mouthed Basanti into a series of—mostly charming—comic vignettes. It is in Jai's tentative courtship of the withdrawn Radha, however, that we see, by contrast, a dawning soulfulness and maturity. (Meanwhile, the fact that both actors ended up romancing—and, in fact, marrying—their leading ladies off screen gives us added reason to pay close attention.)

Silence and space also benefit the performance of Amjad Khan, as it is during those spaces that we tensely await his transition from a tone of sneering mock solicitude to one of sudden, violent rage. This is the one that set the tone for all future Amjad Khan performances henceforth, with the problem being that future filmmakers would try to match the size of that performance with that of Khan's villainous accoutrements. His Gabbar Singh, by contrast, has no high tech lair to lord over, but merely a dusty campground and a ragged band of grimy hoods to call his own. That grounding of his monstrous portrayal within a relatively more believable context increases his menace all the more.

Gabbar Singh gets quick energy from Glucose D!

But, all in all, it is the epic friendship of Veeru and Jai that lends *Sholay* its epic status. Theirs is truly one of the premier bromances in Indian film. Not only is there lots of tender hand holding and mutual serenading between them, but we also learn, during a scene in which the two envision married life, that Veeru sees Jai as part of his household even after he and Basanti have gotten hitched. The way that both actors breezily move between affection and good natured antagonism adds gravity to this bond, showing their mutual admiration to be almost a begrudging one while at the same time communicating its depth. Needless to say, their tragic separation at film's end is as ruthless in its tear jerking as it is well earned.

Of course, for all its celebrated majesty, it can't be said that *Sholay* is a flawless gem. A prison episode in which Asrani portrays a warden as a Chaplinesque Hitler is superfluous and mostly unfunny, as is a tacked on feeling bit of early business featuring Jagdeep. The movie does a good job of setting up the story without them and, since it doesn't really reveal its soul until we arrive in Ramgarh, delaying that seems cruelly unnecessary. It could also be said that it wears its influences too pronouncedly on its sleeve. Should the scene depicting the murder of the Thakur's family—which feels like a near carbon copy of the slaughter of the McBain clan in Sergio Leone's *Once Upon a Time in the West*—simply be considered an homage?

Whatever the answer, there's no question that *Sholay* was beloved by Indian cinema audiences of its day, breaking records both in terms of its take at the box office and the length of its theatrical run. In its aftermath it was assured not only that Amjad Khan would always be bad, but that Hema Malini would always be garrulous and charming and that smalltime thieves and con men would, more often than not, be lovable and hold a deep seated sense of honor. Like a lot of Indian popular films of its day, it combined violence, romance and humor, but thanks to the extra time and care with which director Sippy stirred the pot, it was one masala that apparently got the mixture just right.

EPILOGUE

ACTION REMAINS AN IMPORTANT ELEMENT in Bollywood films in the twenty-first century. But while it was expressed, in the '70s, through antic Bruce Lee impersonations set to deafening sound effects, at the dawn of the new millennium it became the impetus for an over-reliance on *Matrix* style "bullet time" effects and Hong Kong style wire work. An example of this approach actually working can be seen in Farah Khan's 2004 hit *Main Hoon Na*, an endearing hybrid of *Grease* and *Die Hard* in which fortyish superstar Shah Rukh Khan poses as a carefree college student in order to catch a gang of anti-India terrorists. Khan, a choreographer as well as a director, stages her fight scenes as absurdist antigravity ballets, during which an actor could conceivably text a message home in the course of executing a back flip.

This trend toward effects driven action has in turn led to the science fiction film—effectively off limits to Bollywood in previous eras—making a belated claim on India's theater screens, though, as in modern Hollywood, having been almost completely co-opted by the action genre. Recent examples include the *Tron* inspired superhero epic *Ra.one* (2011) and the completely bonkers Rajnikanth vehicle *Enthiran*, aka *Robot* (2010). A notoriously less successful venture into this territory, albeit an early adopting one, was Rajkumar Kohli's *Jaani Dushman: Ek Anokhi Kahani*, in which a reincarnated snake spirit (Arman Kohli) inexplicably takes on the attributes of Robocop, the T-1000 from *Terminator 2*, and the titular creature from Stephen Sommers's *The Mummy* by way of embarrassing, ColecoVision level CG effects.

At the same time, Bollywood movies of the current era have been prone to looking back upon the '70s as a golden age, often by way of musical pastiche and gentle parody. Another Farah Khan blockbuster, 2007's *Om Shanti Om*, tells the story of an extra in 1970s Bollywood (again the inescapable Shah Rukh Khan) who dies and is reincarnated as a superstar in the Bollywood of today. By this means, the contrasts between these two very different incarnations of India's dream factory are starkly laid out.

The sensuous curves of the starlets of yesteryear melt into the hard, unforgiving angles and ripped abs of today's robo divas, while the bouncy tabla rhythms of yesterday's item numbers morph into the hard, four-on-the-floor thump of House. Despite the film being an affectionate, if occasionally barbed, celebration of the industry as a whole, one gets the sense of something soft and welcoming in that older version of Indian cinema being lost.

And for those who grew up with that cinema, there likely is some sense of loss, which puts those of us who are new to the game at something of an advantage. Because, for us, the Bollywood of the '70s is not gone, but freshly found, and plentiful enough to offer a whole lifetime's worth of catching up. As someone who's developed an unhappy fixation upon the popular films of countries whose cinematic histories have largely been lost to the ages—Thailand, Turkey, the Philippines—it's hard for me to express my joy at just how much of India's vast filmic output, old and new, is easily accessible to the common consumer. As I write this, dozens of companies continue to produce low cost—and, admittedly, sometimes technically dodgy—DVDs of Indian films past and present, all of which can be purchased from numerous online retailers, your local Indian grocer, or even rented from Netflix. Meanwhile, new for-pay streaming sites featuring Bollywood content seem to pop up on a regular basis, some offering long out of circulation titles that many of us thought we had little hope of seeing. (See also: YouTube.) Combined, this accounts for thousands of titles on offer, among which, I'm delighted to report, are most of the films listed in this book. That means that those films needn't be just memories, nor something merely described and dimly imagined. They can be your NOW.

Happy hunting.

Alphabetical Index of Films

Chronological Index of Films

Chronological Index of Films

Chronological Index of Films

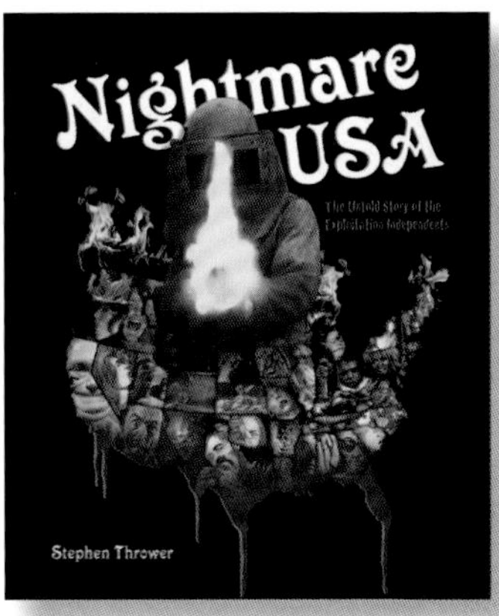

BEYOND TERROR
The Films of Lucio Fulci

Master of the Macabre Lucio Fulci is celebrated in this lavishly illustrated in-depth study of his extraordinary films. From horror masterpieces like The Beyond and Zombie Flesh-Eaters to his notoriety as the man behind the banned slasher epic The New York Ripper, every detail of his varied career is explored. Re-issued at last in 2015.

NIGHTMARE USA
The Untold Story of the Exploitation Independents

Pages: 528 / Price: UK £39.99, US $69.95

A Kaleidoscopic Journey Through the Heyday of Horror and Exploitation Cinema in America! Many of the movies in this book are discussed for the first time ever, spotlighting the output of an era unchecked by notions of 'good taste'.

BLAXPLOITATION CINEMA
The Essential Reference Guide

Pages: 240 / Price: UK £14.99, US $24.95

A Super-Bad Blast from the Past! Everything you need to know about the most colorful film movement of the 1970s, including a complete filmography featuring more than 270 movie listings, reviews, interviews and commentaries.

HOUSE OF PSYCHOTIC WOMEN
An Autobiographical Topography of Female Neurosis in Horror and Exploitation Films

Pages: 360 / Price: UK £19.99, US $29.95

NEW COVER, 2ND PRESSING: Anecdotes interweave with film history and cult film imagery to create a reflective celebration of female madness, both onscreen and off.

FAB PRESS
PUBLISHING QUALITY BOOKS ABOUT GREAT CULT MOVIES FROM ACROSS THE GLOBE
www.fabpress.com

EXCLUSIVE AUTOGRAPHED & NUMBERED EDITIONS DIRECT FROM THE FAB PRESS WEBSITE
www.fabpress.com
Twitter updates: @FAB_Press

NO BORDERS NO LIMITS
Nikkatsu Action Cinema

Pages: 192 / Price: UK £7.99, US $15.95

Drawing inspiration from Hollywood and the French New Wave, Nikkatsu Action pictures blended East and West along with the gritty realities of life in postwar Japan to define the meaning of cool for a whole generation.

ANY GUN CAN PLAY
The Essential Guide to Euro-Westerns

Pages: 480 / Price: UK £24.99, US $39.95

Complete with a foreword by Euro-Western legend Franco Nero, this stunningly illustrated reference guide takes aim at the lingering notion that the genre has little to offer beyond the 'Dollars' films and a fistful of others.

IRON MAN
The Cinema of Shinya Tsukamoto

Pages: 240 / Price: UK £14.99, US $24.95

Illustrated with rare stills, behind-the-scenes pictures and personal photographs from Shinya Tsukamoto's private collection, Iron Man reveals the mind, the methods and the madness of Japan's most influential and unique filmmaker.

RE-AGITATOR
A Decade of Writing on Takashi Miike

Pages: 160 / Price: UK £19.99, US $34.95

From dusty film sets in Japan to festival intrigue on the Riviera, and from the straight-to-video ghetto to the stage, Tom Mes covers the full scope of Takashi Miike's life and work with the intimacy that only an insider can provide.